LUMINOUS LIVES

T0325314

'Brog mi Lo tsā ba

STUDIES IN INDIAN AND TIBETAN BUDDHISM

Luminous Lives

The Story of the Early Masters of the Lam 'bras Tradition in Tibet

by

Cyrus Stearns

WISDOM PUBLICATIONS • BOSTON

Wisdom Publications, Inc.
199 Elm Street
Somerville MA 02144 USA
www.wisdompubs.org

© 2001 Cyrus Stearns
All rights reserved.
No part of this book may be reproduced in any form or by any means, electronic or mechanical, including photocopying, recording, or by any information storage and retrieval system or technologies now known or later developed, without permission in writing from the publisher.

Library of Congress Cataloging-in-Publication Data
Stearns, Cyrus
Luminous lives : the story of the early masters of the Lam 'bras tradition in Tibet / Cyrus Stearns
p. cm.
Includes bibliographical references and index.
ISBN 0-86171-307-9
1. Sa-skya-pa lamas—China—Tibet—Biography.
2. Lam-'bras (Sa-skya-pa)—History. I. Title.
BQ7672.9.A2 S74 2001 2001045572

ISBN 0-86171-307-9

06 05 04 03 02
6 5 4 3 2

Cover Ilustration: Vajradhara, Nairātmyā, Virūpa, and Kahna. The first four figures in the Lam 'bras lineage. Thang ka painting, fifteenth century. (Tibet Collection: Barbara and Walter Frey, Zurich, F753)

Designed by Gopa & Ted2

Wisdom Publications' books are printed on acid-free paper and meet the guidelines for permanence and durability set by the Committee on Production Guidelines for Book Longevity of the Council on Library Resources.

Printed in the United States

Contents

Illustrations

Preface

It was a summer day in 1989, and the dusty reading room of the National Archives in Kathmandu felt like a sauna. Trying to decipher the script on the glaring screen of the microfilm reader brought a splitting headache within minutes. But there it was, in a tiny scribbled annotation on the last page of the handwritten Tibetan text, "Dmar from the central region," clarifying the name of Chos kyi rgyal po, the author of the *Zhib mo rdo rje (The Incisive Vajra)*. Written almost eight hundred years ago, this ancient manuscript told the story of the early masters of the tantric tradition known in Tibet as the Lam 'bras, the "Path with the Result." I had learned that this work was a fundamental historical source, but none of my elder Tibetan teachers had ever seen it, and it was presumed lost long ago. I was ecstatic. With the kind help of Franz-Karl Ehrhard, then director of the Nepal-German Manuscript Preservation Project, I acquired a copy of the film.

My teacher, Bco brgyad Khri chen Rin po che (Chogye Trichen Rinpoche), had often emphasized the importance of another work by the same author, Dmar ston Chos kyi rgyal po (c. 1198–c. 1259), for the study and practice of the Lam 'bras. Mkhan po Bstan 'dzin kindly presented me with the gift of an ancient manuscript of the very text my teacher had been telling me about. A few years later, on yet another microfilm made by the Nepal-German Manuscript Preservation Project, I located a short biography of Dmar ston. I decided to find out as much as I could about this little-known teacher whose works were so important to the early tradition, and to prepare a translation and study of the *Zhib mo rdo rje*.

After my return to the United States in 1991, Jeffrey Schoening generously gave me a copy of the *Zhib mo rdo rje* that he had located in Beijing. A few years later Leonard van der Kuijp also visited Beijing, and upon his return kindly allowed me to copy another manuscipt of the same text that he had found in the library there. The manuscript I located in Nepal contains a number of small handwritten annotations not found in the first text from Beijing. The second work from Beijing contains many of the same small annotations as the Nepal manuscript, with quite a few additional ones. For this reason I have chosen to use the second manuscript from Beijing as the basis for the present study. In the notes, the Nepal manuscript will be referred to as "manuscript N," and the first Beijing text as "manuscript B1." The small annotations found in the Tibetan manuscript have been translated in a smaller grey typeface. Most of these original Tibetan annotations were added to the *Zhib mo rdo rje* in a way that allows them to blend grammatically with the body of the Tibetan text. In the English translation this has not always been possible. All the titles and section headings within the translation have been added for the sake of clarity. Tibetan words in this book are transliterated according to the Wylie system, but with capitalization of the initial letter. Sanskrit words are given with diacritics.

The original Tibetan manuscript of the *Zhib mo rdo rje* is written in a cursive *dbu med* script, with numerous tiny annotations scattered between the lines and in the margins. The spellings in the original manuscript are very inconsistent, with the same words being found in various forms at different points. In the translation of the *Zhib mo rdo rje* the unusual spellings of names, places, and so forth have usually been retained, but in other parts of the book the most commonly recognized forms have been used. In the Tibetan text reproduced in this book the spellings from the original manuscript have been retained, with the following exceptions. All of the condensed words and compounds *(bsdus yig)* have been unpacked and spelled out in full form. In the manuscript, a retroflex letter *ṇa* was used as a shorthand sign for the word *med,* but the word itself has been reintroduced here. The numeral 1 was used indiscriminately throughout the manuscript in place of the words *gcig, cig, zhig,* and *shig.* In the reproduced text the numeral 1 has been replaced by the full words. Other numerals used as a form of shorthand have also been replaced with words. Archaic spellings have been retained. The paragraphing of the reproduced Tibetan text corresponds to the paragraphing of my translation. I am grateful to Jeffrey Schoening, Dennis Oliver, Lee Harris, and David Kalil for carefully checking my initial transliteration of the Tibetan text. The *Zhib mo rdo rje* was never published in Tibet, and has circulated in manuscript form for almost eight hundred years. With this publication, the Tibetan text will finally be accessible to all interested readers.

The *Zhib mo rdo rje* tells the story of the masters of the Lam 'bras in Tibet during the tenth through the thirteenth centuries, strictly from the viewpoint of the Sa skya tradition. In this work Dmar ston records the words of his teacher, the great Sa skya Paṇḍita Kun dga' rgyal mtshan (1182–1251). In later Tibetan works these stories were expanded with information from other early sources, particularly from the Zha ma tradition. In the translation of the *Zhib mo rdo rje* I have followed the example of later Tibetan authors, and supplemented the brief stories in Dmar ston's work with extensive notes drawn from other sources. The reader will find a great deal of essential information in these storytelling notes, much drawn from rare unpublished works.

The modern reading audience for this book could hardly be further removed from the audience for whom the *Zhib mo rdo rje* was originally written. With the hope of conveying at least some of the flavor and depth of the oral tradition in these stories, I have decided to present them "on stilts," as George Steiner has said, with voluminous notes supporting the small original work. Despite the clumsiness of such an approach, it seems more than justified, because the background knowledge assumed by Dmar ston is absent in those who will read this book.

For years I have been inspired by the unforgettable stories from the Lam 'bras tradition, told with peerless eloquence and humor by the late Sde gzhung Sprul sku Rin po che (Dezhung Tulku Rinpoche, 1906–87) and by Bco brgyad Khri chen Rin po che. I am very grateful to Mkhan po A pad Rin po che (Khenpo Apey Rinpoche) for his kind help with several difficult passages in the Tibetan text. David Jackson, Jeffrey Schoening, Dan Martin, and E. Gene Smith all read earlier versions of this book, and provided very helpful criticism and corrections, as well as copies of rare manuscripts. Hubert Decleer also offered very useful suggestions. Mkhan po A pad Rin po che, Guru Lama, Leonard van der Kuijp, and Jan-Ulrich Sobisch graciously provided copies of rare texts. Ulrich von Schroeder generously made photographs of rare art from the Lam 'bras tradition available for reproduction. In particular, my thanks go to Tim McNeill and E. Gene Smith for enduring the difficulties of bringing this book to print, and for including it in Wisdom Publications's series "Studies in Indian and Tibetan Buddhism." I am also grateful to David Kittelstrom for his fine editorial work.

As the first study of the historical tradition of the Lam 'bras in a language other than Tibetan, I hope that this modest contribution will encourage further investigations in the future. Although Dmar ston's work was brief, it inspired all the later Sa skya histories of the tradition. Now that it will be widely available in both Tibetan and English, perhaps it will again form a basis for research into the early history of the Lam 'bras in Tibet.

PART ONE

The Early History of the Lam 'bras

Mahāsiddha Virūpa

Introduction

A story bypasses rhetoric and pierces the heart.
Terry Tempest Williams

THE TEACHINGS of Śākyamuni Buddha were first introduced in Tibet during a period of dynastic rule that lasted from the beginning of the seventh century to the middle of the ninth century. From the middle of the ninth century until the late tenth century there was degeneration and chaos following the disintegration of the centralized dynastic power structure. At the end of this period of stagnation there was a cultural renaissance inspired by the revival of Buddhism through a huge influx of new teachings from India and Nepal. In this way the Tibetan culture began to again absorb Buddhist knowledge in the late tenth century, a process that continued through the middle of the thirteenth century, and to a much lesser degree even into the seventeenth century.

The renaissance of Buddhism in Tibet is said to have begun in the west with the translation work of Lo chen Rin chen bzang po (958–1055). A massive amount of Buddhist knowledge began to flow into Tibet from this time. Specifically, many tantric scriptures were now translated into Tibetan for the first time, and the doctrines and practices of these systems spread rapidly. For example, during the eleventh century hundreds of translations were made of the tantric scriptures, commentaries, and ritual texts connected with the cycles of the *Hevajra tantra*, the *Kālacakra tantra*, the *Vajrabhairava tantra*, the *Guhyasamāja tantra*, the *Cakrasaṃvara tantra*, and so forth. A dazzling array of tantric meditation practices flooded Tibet during these years, although many faded away with the passage of time.

In the sixteenth century the Rnying ma master Prajñāraśmi (1517–84), also known as 'Phreng bo gter ston Shes rab 'od zer, referred to eight early Indian and Tibetan teachers, and eight surviving systems of esoteric instruction:

> Ba gor Bai ro, the consummate translator; the layman 'Brom ston, the heir of the Victors; Khyung po rnal 'byor pa, the great realized scholar; the great master 'Brog mi, who spoke two languages; the venerable lord Mar pa, the lord of yogins; Dam pa Rgya gar, who dwelled on the spiritual level of attainment; the translator Gyi jo; and the realized scholar O rgyan pa were the eight great pillars supporting the practice lineages in the northern regions.
>
> Here in the glacial mountain ranges those eight great pillars [supported] the practice lineages that came from glorious Vajradhara and are the legacy of former adepts. Those who wish liberation should also follow those paths.[1]

By the middle of the nineteenth century the lineages from several of these teachers had almost died out, and they were revived only through the extraordinary efforts of 'Jam dbyangs mkhyen brtse'i dbang po (1820–92) and 'Jam mgon Kong sprul (1813–99).[2] These eight groups of practices are usually referred to now as the "eight great chariots" *(shing rta chen po brgyad).*

Only the first of the eight great systems of meditation was introduced into Tibet before the eleventh century. After that time these earlier teachings from the dynastic period came to be known as the Rnying ma tradition, the "Old Ones," in contrast to the various lineages introduced in the eleventh century that were then known as the Gsar ma, the "New Ones." The teachings and lineages of the Rnying ma tradition are numerous and complicated. In particular, the Rdzogs chen, the "Great Perfection," was first brought to Tibet, translated, and spread in the eighth century by the Tibetan Ba gor Bai ro tsa na. This "consummate translator" had received the profound instructions in India from the master Śrīsiṃha. Bai ro tsa na was responsible for translating and spreading two distinct traditions of the Great Perfection that were known as the Sems sde, "Mind Series," and the Klong sde, "Space Series." A third tradition of the Great Perfection, known as the Man ngag sde, "Series of Esoteric Instructions," was brought to Tibet by the master Vimalamitra. It is essentially this lineage, blended with teachings from the master Padmasambhava, that became known as the Snying thig, "Heartdrop," and has been practiced to the present day, especially on the basis of the writings of Klong chen Rab 'byams pa (1308–63) and 'Jigs med gling pa (1730–98).[3]

Only the last of the eight lineages mentioned above by Prajñāraśmi came into Tibet after the eleventh century. The teachings of the Rdo rje gsum gyi bsnyen sgrub, "Propitiation and Attainment of the Three Adamantine States," often known as the O rgyan bsnyen sgrub, "Propitiation and Attainment from Uḍḍiyana," was brought back to Tibet by the "realized scholar" O rgyan pa Rin chen dpal (1230–1309). This Tibetan master had received the transmission of special meditation practices related to the Six-branch Yoga of the Kālacakra system from the tantric goddess Vajrayoginī during a trip to Uḍḍiyana. Although the practice of these teachings flourished for at least two hundred years, the transmission lineages were extremely scarce by the end of the nineteenth century.[4] All that seems to remain now is the reading transmission of several fundamental texts.

The remaining six practice lineages were all introduced in Tibet during the eleventh century, a fact that underscores the crucial importance of this period in Tibetan history. The layman 'Brom ston Rgyal ba'i 'byung gnas (1004–63), referred to above as "the heir of the Victors," was probably the most important disciple and spiritual heir of the Indian master Atiśa (982–1055), who came to Tibet in 1042 and was instrumental in the Buddhist renaissance. The lineages passed down through Atiśa in Tibet came to be known as the Bka' gdams pa, the tradition of "Precepts and Instructions." This tradition survived for some time as an independent entity, but later fell into decline. Some of its special transmissions, such as the teachings of the Blo sbyong, "Mind Training," were absorbed into the other independent traditions. Many more were inherited by the great Tsong kha pa Blo bzang grags pa (1357–1419), and came to be emphasized in the Dge ldan pa or Dge lugs pa tradition established by his followers.

Khyung po rnal 'byor (b. 990?), "the great realized scholar," traveled three times to India and Nepal, where he is said to have studied with 150 teachers. He founded a number of monasteries in Tibet, especially in the Shangs Valley, and so his tradition came to be known as the Shangs pa bka' brgyud, the "Shangs Tradition of Transmitted Precepts." At the heart of this tradition are the practices of the Chos drug, the "Six Doctrines," and the Mahāmudrā or Phyag chen, the "Great Seal," that Khyung po rnal 'byor received from the Indian women teachers Niguma and Sukhasiddhi. Emphasized by masters such as the great adept Thang stong rgyal po (1361–1485), and the Jo nang masters Kun dga' grol mchog (1507–66) and Tāranātha (1575–1635), these teachings spread throughout the other Tibetan traditions. By the middle of the nineteenth century the Shangs pa transmissions had become very scarce, but were revitalized through the efforts of 'Jam dbyangs mkhyen brtse'i dbang po and 'Jam mgon Kong sprul.

The master 'Brog mi Lo tsā ba Shākya ye shes (993–1077?), who "spoke two languages," traveled to Nepal and India in search of Buddhist instructions, and studied with prominent teachers for thirteen years. After his return to Tibet he received the transmission of the Lam 'bras, the "Path with the Result," and a number of other important tantric teachings from the Indian master Gayadhara (d. 1103). 'Brog mi translated a large number of tantric scriptures and commentaries, the most significant of which are the *Hevajra tantra* and its two explanatory tantras, as well as the *Rdo rje tshig rkang (The Vajra Verses)* of the Indian adept Virūpa, which is the basic text of the Lam 'bras. A number of different lineages existed for many centuries, but all eventually died out or were absorbed into the Sa skya lineage, which is now the only tradition of the Lam 'bras. Through the efforts of masters such as Sa chen Kun dga' snying po (1092–1158), Ngor chen Kun dga' bzang po (1382–1456), and Tshar chen Blo gsal rgya mtsho (1502–66), this tradition spread very widely in Tibet.

The venerable lord Mar pa Chos kyi blo gros (1000–1081), the "lord of yogins," was another great translator who spent years in India and Nepal, where he received many tantric transmissions, especially from the masters Nāropa and Maitrīpa. The teachings of the Chos drug, the "Six Doctrines," and the Mahāmudrā or Phyag chen, the "Great Seal," that Mar pa obtained from these and other teachers became the fundamental practices of the lineage known as the Mar pa bka' brgyud, the tradition of the "Transmitted Precepts of Mar pa." Inspired by the example of Mar pa's famous disciple, Rje btsun Mi la ras pa (1028–1111), this practice lineage was initially spread by masters such as Sgam po pa (1079–1153), was disseminated later through the activities of the Karma pa heirarchs, and has remained strong to the present day.[5]

The Indian master known as Dam pa Rgya gar, the "Holy Indian," or as Pha dam pa Sangs rgyas (d. 1105), who "dwelled on the spiritual level of attainment," traveled to Tibet a number of times, and established the tradition known as Zhi byed, "Pacification." His famous woman disciple Ma gcig Lab sgron (1055–1153) formulated the related tradition known as Gcod, "Severance." The Zhi byed tradition was extremely rare by the middle of the nineteenth century, when 'Jam dbyangs mkhyen brtse'i dbang po and 'Jam mgon Kong sprul sought out the surviving teachings.[6] Although the transmission of a few texts has survived, there does not seem to be any practice of this tradition today. On the other hand, the lineage of Gcod spread widely in the Rnying ma, Bka' brgyud, and Dge lugs traditions, and there are still many practitioners.

The "translator" Gyi jo Zla ba'i od zer is generally thought to have been the first to translate the *Kālacakra tantra* and its major commentary into Tibetan. The special teachings of the perfection stage of the Kālacakra, usually known as the Rdo rje rnal 'byor, the "Vajrayoga," or in full form, as the Rdo rje rnal 'byor yan lag drug pa, the "Six-branch Vajrayoga," were transmitted in many Tibetan lineages and were incredibly influential. The Kālacakra and the Six-branch Yoga became the specialty of the Jo nang tradition, as exemplified by the teachings of Dol po pa Shes rab rgyal mtshan (1292–1361), and the Zhwa lu tradition, as spread in particular by Bu ston Rin chen grub (1290–1364). The Jo nang tradition later suffered from governmental suppression, but the lineage of their teachings of the Six-branch Yoga has survived into modern times through the efforts of Rig 'dzin Tshe dbang nor bu (1698–1755), Si tu Paṇ chen (1700–1774), 'Jam mgon Kong sprul, and others.[7] The Zhwa lu lineage has been passed down to the present in the Dge lugs tradition, as well as in others schools.

During the eleventh century, when most of these great systems of meditation arrived in Tibet, there was no strong concept of "sects" or "schools." During this period, and for at least another two centuries, numerous currents of Buddhist teachings *(bka' babs)* flowed through the land, and these groups of practices were sought out indiscriminately by masters and students. This sort of eclectic approach seems to have been much more commonplace from the eleventh through the thirteenth centuries than in later times. A good example is found in the *Zhib mo rdo rje (The Incisive Vajra),* the early thirteenth-century text translated in part two of this book. The master Zur po che Shākya 'byung gnas (1002–1062) was one of the great teachers of the Rnying ma tradition, and is particularly important for the Sems sde rdzogs chen, the "Mind Series of the Great Perfection." The story of Zur po che's study of newly translated tantric instructions with 'Brog mi Lo tsā ba is described in detail in the *Zhib mo rdo rje.*

On the other hand, from the beginning of the renaissance there was also a certain tension between the followers of the old Buddhist traditions of Tibet and those who practiced the newly translated materials introduced during the eleventh century. After all, the new influx of teachings had begun because of a widespread impression that the old practices had become hopelessly corrupt during the previous period of cultural stagnation. There is also evidence of this tension in the *Zhib mo rdo rje*, where the yogin Zhang ston Chos 'bar (1053–1135), who taught the Rdzogs chen during the day and practiced the Lam 'bras in secret at night, initially rejected his future disciple Sa chen Kun dga' snying po with the words, "Are you not mistaken? I don't even know the Dharma you want. You so-called practitioners of the new secret mantra are very opinionated. I teach the Rdzogs chen."[8]

In contrast to the voluminous exegetical literature surrounding the tantric scriptures themselves, the major systems of esoteric practice entered Tibet primarily by means of secret oral transmissions *(snyan brgyud)*. Although these systems were essentially oral in nature, in most cases there were also at least a few written texts from India, the most fundamental of which were often referred to by the term *rdo rje tshig rkang*, "vajra verses." Only two of the eight great systems arrived in Tibet without any written records. The *Rdo rje tshig rkang* of the Rdo rje gsum gyi bsnyen sgrub was placed in writing by O rgyan pa Rin chen dpal only after his return to Tibet.[9] The tradition of the Lam 'bras was unique among the systems that had been passed down through a series of Indian teachers in that there seem to have been no written texts whatsoever in India. The *Rdo rje tshig rkang* of Virūpa, the fundamental text of the Lam 'bras, is said to have been memorized and passed down orally in Tibet for a hundred years before finally being written.

Chapter One
The Literary Tradition

The practice of Buddhist meditation in Tibet has almost always meant the practice of tantra. Deity yoga, a distinctive technique of the Vajrayāna, has been the defining feature of religious life in Tibet for more than a thousand years. Many different tantric traditions developed in Tibet, and a vast indigenous literature grew along with the expansion of the teachings. One important aspect of this literature is the historical and biographical works that are used to authenticate the origins of each tradition and to document the qualities of the masters through whom they have passed. While the historical development of several of these Tibetan traditions has received some attention, that of the Lam 'bras, the "Path with the Result," has been generally neglected.

The teachings of the Lam 'bras were originally transmitted to the Indian master Virūpa by the tantric goddess Vajra Nairātmyā, the consort of Hevajra. Inspired by her direct transmission, Virūpa is said to have quickly reached the sixth spiritual level *(bhūmi)* of the path.[10] When Nairātmyā's succinct instructions were formulated by Virūpa, these teachings became known as the *Lam 'bras bu dang bcas pa'i gdams ngag dang man ngag tu bcas pa, (The Oral Instructions, Together with the Esoteric Instructions, of the Path with the Result),* which is always simply referred to in the tradition as the *Rdo rje tshig rkang (The Vajra Verses).*[11] According to most accounts, Virūpa formulated the *Rdo rje tshig rkang* for his disciple Kahna, who is considered to be the prime example of a recipient suited to the gradual approach. Kahna had recently renounced the life of a wandering Hindu yogin, and Virūpa gave him the *Rdo rje tshig rkang* as a summation of the entire path to enlightenment in the tradition of Buddhist tantra.[12] Everything from the most basic instructions for someone who has recently entered the Buddhist path—such as

Kahna—up through the sublime experiences of buddhahood are found in this brief text, which is therefore often compared by the tradition to a "wish-fulfilling gem."

Virūpa's Lam 'bras became one of the major systems of tantric practice in Tibet, and according to some authors had also been well known in India. This is mentioned by Mus chen Dkon mchog rgyal mtshan (1388–1469), recording the opinion of his teacher Ngor chen Kun dga' bzang po (1382–1456):

> This [system] also became famous and authoritative in India. When explaining the condensed style of the perfection stage path of realized masters, Ācārya Śraddhākaravarman finely stated the way to traverse the path of the four initiations according to the intentions of the Lord of Yogins [Virūpa].[13] Ācārya Munidatta also quoted several basic phrases *(gzhung tshig)* of the *Rdo rje tshig rkang* of this [system] as sources in the commentary on the spiritual songs of the eighty great adepts.[14] And Darpaṇa Ācārya also quoted basic phrases of the *Rdo rje tshig rkang* as sources in the *Kriyāsamuccaya.*[15]

This information points to at least some possible knowledge of the Lam 'bras by Indian masters other than the known members of the lineage. Mang thos klu sgrub rgya mtsho (1523–96) also agreed with the statements of those who ascribed a partial knowledge of the Lam 'bras to Śraddhākaravarman and Munidatta.[16] 'Jam dbyangs mkhyen brtse'i dbang phyug (1524–68) stated that the Lam 'bras was passed in a unique transmission *(chig brgyud)* in India, to only one individual in each generation. Although it was known in India, it was kept very secret and most great scholars and realized saints never heard about it. According to Mkhyen brtse'i dbang phyug, the authors of the *Kriyāsamuccaya* and the commentary to *Vīraprabhāsvara's collection of the spiritual songs of the great tantric adepts may have cited Virūpa as an authentic source, but they had not actually received his esoteric instructions.[17]

In the Sa skya tradition, the *Rdo rje tshig rkang* and all the instructions encoded within it are said to have been transmitted orally without any written material whatsoever for at least eight generations. The *Rdo rje tshig rkang* was spoken by Virūpa to Kahna, by him to Ḍamarupa, by him to Avadhūti, and by him to Gayadhara (d. 1103). Gayadhara came to Tibet in 1041, and spoke the verses to the great Tibetan translator

'Brog mi Shākya ye shes (993–1077?).[18] As specifically pointed out by Mkhyen brtse'i dbang phyug, the fact that there is no Indian language title at the beginning of 'Brog mi's Tibetan translation of the *Rdo rje tshig rkang*, and the fact that there is no colophon, are essential indications that he did not write a translation.[19] 'Brog mi memorized the verses in the original Indian dialect and then spoke them in Tibetan to the disciples who later received the Lam 'bras from him. The *Rdo rje tshig rkang*, now in Tibetan, continued to be memorized and passed down in an oral transmission until the time of Sa chen Kun dga' snying po (1092–1158). It was Sa chen who finally wrote them down, when he first taught the Lam 'bras, probably in 1141, exactly 100 years after the arrival of the tradition in Tibet.[20]

Nevertheless, it is curious that the first verse of the *Rdo rje tshig rkang* specifically states that it "will be written" *(bri bar bya)*.[21] Perhaps because of this the Zha ma tradition of the Lam 'bras maintained that the *Rdo rje tshig rkang* was originally written by Virūpa himself. In 1304 Cha rgan Dbang phyug rgyal mtshan wrote, "[Virūpa] placed the *Rdo rje tshig rkang* in writing [for Kahna] as a mnemonic tool."[22] Five hundred years later 'Jam mgon Kong sprul, perhaps the last to comment on this issue, clearly thought the text had been originally written in India:

> 'Brog mi, Gyi jo, and 'Brom all translated the *Rdo rje tshig rkang* according to the Indian text *(rgya dpe)*. Cha rgan and Jo nang Kun spangs pa made revisions in which they disrupted the sequences without reference to the Indian text. Gzungs kyi dpal ba stated in his manual that there was also a translation by Paṇḍita Rāhula. Thus there were six versions.[23]

Kong sprul's statement was certainly based in part on the writings of earlier masters. In the fifteenth century Ngor chen referred to the existence of a translation of the *Rdo rje tshig rkang* by the famous translator Gyi jo Zla ba'i od zer, who had once invited Gayadhara to Tibet. Ngor chen also referred to the fact that 'Brog mi's disciple 'Brom De pa ston chung had taught the *Rdo rje tshig rkang* in great detail without translating it from the Indian language, thus implying that he knew Sanskrit.[24] Ngor chen also mentions Cha rgan's revision, and the extensive revision and editing done by Jo nang Kun spangs pa (1243–1313) on the basis of the different versions of the *Rdo rje tshig rkang* found in the Zha ma, 'Brom, and Sa skya traditions.[25] However, in none of these cases does Ngor chen refer to the existence of an original Indian text. The work by the Rdzong master Gzungs kyi dpal ba (1306–89) that mentions a translation by the Indian teacher Paṇḍita Rāhula is otherwise unknown, as is the translation.

According to the Zha ma tradition there was also originally a cycle of five scriptures *(Lung skor lnga)* said to have been brought from the "Dharma palace of Uḍḍiyana" by Virūpa's disciple Kahna to serve as supports for the teachings of the *Rdo rje tshig rkang*. These mysterious texts are said to have been extracts from the five hundred thousand-line *Hevajra tantra* preserved in Uḍḍiyana.[26] Following the Zha ma lineage, Cha rgan also repeatedly mentions these works, and says that at 'Brog mi's request Gayadhara even wrote down brief texts as mnemonic tools *(rjed tho'i yig chung)* to insure that the *Rdo rje tshig rkang* and the cycle of five scriptures would not be forgotten if 'Brog mi later encountered severe difficulties.[27] Even the identity of the cycle of five scriptures was unknown in the Sa skya tradition, and the texts themselves, assuming that they were indeed written texts, long ago vanished with the demise of the Zha ma tradition.

The Lam 'bras is a system of tantric theory and practice based generally on all the anuttarayoga tantras, specifically on the three scriptures known as the *Kye rdor rgyud gsum (The Tantra Trilogy of Hevajra)*, and especially on the *Hevajra tantra* itself.[28] The *Rdo rje tshig rkang* represents an oral revelation of the distilled essence of these tantras. Among the earliest written materials in this tradition are three texts, apparently by Sa chen Kun dga' snying po and his son Bsod nams rtse mo (1142–82), devoted to validating the relationship of the *Rdo rje tshig rkang* to these tantric scriptures. The largest of the three works, almost certainly by Sa chen, closely follows the structure of the *Rdo rje tshig rkang*, applying quotations from the tantric scriptures to each section in turn.[29]

According to Sa chen's son Rje btsun Grags pa rgyal mtshan (1147–1216), this system is referred to as "The Oral Instructions of the Path with the Result" (Lam 'bras bu dang bcas pa'i gdams ngag) because the result itself is utilized as the path (*'bras bu lam du byed pa*).[30] Mkhyen brtse'i dbang phyug also stated, "The obtainable result exists during the time of the path, because if this were not so it would be meaningless to meditate." He then goes on to mention one of the key themes of this lineage, that is, the indivisible nature of the spiritual ground, path, and result. The unrecognized enlightened state present in all living beings as the spiritual ground is veiled by temporary obscurations. When these obscurations are removed through the practice of the path, the naturally present enlightened state is recognized. This is given the name "result" *('bras bu)*.[31]

The "path" (*lam*), or technique used to remove the obscurations and enhance realization of the naturally present enlightened state, is basically twofold. The practitioner meditates on the creation stage *(utpattikrama, bskyed rim),* in which the animate and inanimate worlds are transformed into the deity and the deity's maṇḍala; and the perfection stage *(sampannakrama, rdzogs rim),* which is generally composed of the yogas of the vital winds *(prāṇāyāma, srog rtsol),* the fierce fire *(cāṇḍālī, gtum mo),* and the seminal drops *(bindu, thig le).* In the *Rdo rje tshig rkang* these techniques are implied but not actually presented. The specific practices are performed in conjunction with the four tantric initiations and were first explained in writing by Sa chen in his commentaries to the *Rdo rje tshig rkang,* and by Grags pa rgyal mtshan in the *Pod ser (The Yellow Volume).*

The Lam 'bras is thus a tradition fundamentally concerned with the practice of meditation and not with the scholastic exegesis of the tantric scriptures. In the *Zhib mo rdo rje* of Dmar ston translated below, as well as in the various texts of other tantric traditions, the primary role of meditation is stressed, and the necessity for secrecy emphasized. This custom of secrecy is now being gradually relaxed by leading Tibetan masters. While scholars today may choose to respect or ignore this traditional concern, it is indisputable that it has been of vital importance within the tradition itself. In his catalogue to the *Pod ser,* Rje btsun Grags pa rgyal mtshan stated, "This is not a Dharma understood through texts, and so one should be very diligent in reflection."[32]

According to the tradition of the Lam 'bras, the actual meaning of the *Rdo rje tshig rkang* is only revealed through meditation practice. Kahna had already received all the oral instructions and practiced them for some time before Virūpa finally gave him the *Rdo rje tshig rkang* as a mnemonic tool.[33] A text of this type is traditionally intended only for people who are already intimately familiar with the meditations of the system. This is very different from the scholastic approach to epistemology, abhidharma, or other common topics of the Buddhist tradition. There are many statements to this effect in the literature, such as the final advice given by Zhang ston Chos 'bar (1053–1135) to his disciple Sa chen Kun dga' snying po:

> "For eighteen years my brother [Gzi brjid 'bar] made great efforts, but he had to return three times to eliminate conceptual elaborations. He was energetic in regard to the technical terminology, while I was energetic in meditation. In the short term, the master [Se ston] was also pleased with him in regard to the Lam 'bras. Later, our understanding on the basis of the *Rdo rje tshig rkang* was not equal, and he also took me as his master.
>
> "If doubts in regard to this Dharma are not severed from within by means of experience in meditation it will be impossible to unravel the knots of the technical terminology from without. It is imperative to listen intently and be energetic in meditation....
>
> "In order to eliminate conceptual elaborations, for eighteen years you must be energetic in practice without mentioning even the name of the oral instructions. Then you will be the owner of the Dharma and may even write texts. This profound Dharma had almost died out, but having passed it to you, its owner, my aspiration is fulfilled.
>
> "Secret mantra is realized in secret. For experience and realization it is necessary to practice a hidden yoga."[34]

As Zhang ston's comments illustrate, a student must receive the personal transmission of specific keys to a text such as the *Rdo rje tshig rkang*, which may be seen as a description of the experienced meaning of the tantras. The crucial point made within the tradition itself is that the essential teachings of the Lam 'bras have always been transmitted orally. This is the case even though many texts have been written down over the centuries and a form of the teaching has been given to large groups of people. Sa skya Paṇḍita Kun dga' rgyal mtshan (1182–1251) reiterated this when he said, "Followers of the Lam 'bras who rely just on the *[Pod ser]* volume will not understand this."[35]

Another important point made by Zhang ston in the previous quotation is the traditional insistence on the secrecy of the oral instructions. All tantric traditions stress the need for secrecy. This is considered to be an essential ingredient of correct practice, without which the actual attainment of the result is not possible.[36] It has always been felt within the tradition that a certain spiritual energy is accumulated through keeping the nature of one's meditation practice private. In the previous quotation, Zhang ston told Sa chen that it was necessary to practice a "hidden yoga" *(sbas pa'i rnal 'byor)* in order to destroy conceptual elaborations about the teachings before venturing to explain them to others.

This traditional emphasis on tantric secrecy will sometimes be obvious in the *Zhib mo rdo rje,* translated in part two. 'Brog mi Lo tsā ba's comments about not explaining the oral instructions to more than one person at a time, and his admonition to Sa chen's father Dkon mchog rgyal po (1034–1102), are good examples:

> ['Brog mi] would not teach the Lam 'bras to as many as two persons, saying, "I don't explain oral instructions to four ears and there is no mantra for six ears."
>
> At that time, when the spiritual friend Dkon mchog rgyal po was explaining the *Brtag pa gnyis pa* to seventeen persons in Sa skya, master ['Brog mi] sent a message scolding him, "Explaining the perilous root tantra to seventeen persons; do you have an indestructible life-force?"[37]

The tantric teachings were also kept secret in India and Tibet because they were traditionally felt to be actually dangerous, and not just in the sense of being misunderstood. In the previous episode 'Brog mi is alluding to the danger of attracting the wrath of the ḍākinīs, protectors of the tantric tradition, by revealing the secrets to many persons. On another occasion 'Brog mi was very displeased when his disciple Gsal ba'i snying po wrote a clear commentary on the *Kye rdor rgyud gsum (The Tantra Trilogy of Hevajra),* exclaiming that he had essentially "torn out the living hearts of the ḍākinīs" to give to others.[38] A similar example from another tradition is found in the story of the translator Mar pa Do pa and his disciple Cog ro Chos rgyal ba. Mar pa Do pa had a special instruction on the four stage *(rim bzhi)* Cakrasaṃvara practice, which was later considered especially dangerous. Cog ro only learned about it from Mar pa Do pa's son, and when he requested the instruction, Mar pa Do pa was furious with his son and shouted, "Is your spinal cord made from diamond *(srog pa rtsa rdo rje pha lam las byas pa yin nam)*?" Mar pa Do pa did finally agree to give the teaching, but died immediately afterward. When his son was preparing for the funeral rites, he was stabbed and killed by robbers.[39] These examples have been mentioned here to illustrate the awe, respect, and trepidation with which Tibetans have traditionally viewed tantric teachings. While few seem to share this viewpoint today, an awareness of it will contribute to a deeper understanding of texts such as the *Zhib mo rdo rje.*

This study of the lives of the early masters of the Lam 'bras in Tibet is a work of historical research and does not attempt to explain the doctrine or practices of this system. In striking contrast to the oral origins of the tradition, in later centuries a dauntingly vast number of historical and practical works were composed. The twentieth-century published collection of the Sa skya tradition of the Lam 'bras fills thirty large volumes.[40] This collection does not even include many works scattered in other locations, or rare texts that still exist only in manuscipt form. Although there were once many different systems of the Lam 'bras in Tibet, only those of the Sa skya and Zha ma lineages survived for an extended period, and the Sa skya tradition alone is intact today. Almost all the texts now available are from the Sa skya tradition. From among the numerous Sa skya works composed during the previous 850 years, the following survey will focus on Sa chen Kun dga' snying po's eleven commentaries on the *Rdo rje tshig rkang* and on the most important collections compiled through the sixteenth century. Virtually all of these texts are concerned with explaining the meaning of the *Rdo rje tshig rkang* and the meditation techniques of the Lam 'bras, or with discussing the lives of previous teachers.

Sa chen's Eleven Commentaries on the Rdo rje tshig rkang

Sa chen Kun dga' snying po received the Lam 'bras from Zhang ston Chos 'bar during a period of four years beginning in 1120.[41] He then spent the next eighteen years in intense meditation, forbidden by Zhang ston from teaching or even mentioning the name of the instructions. In 1138, when he was forty-six years old, Sa chen experienced an extraordinary visitation from the Indian adept Virūpa, who bestowed on him the direct transmission of the Lam 'bras. When the eighteen-year restriction expired in 1141, Sa chen first taught the Lam 'bras to A seng Rdo rje brtan pa and, for his benefit, recorded in writing the *Rdo rje tshig rkang* as well as a brief verse commentary.[42] Over the remaining years of his life he taught the Lam 'bras to his sons, Slob dpon Bsod nams rtse mo and Rje btsun Grags pa rgyal mtshan, and numerous other disciples.

From 1141 until his death in 1158 Sa chen is said to have written "about eleven commentaries" explaining the cryptic meaning of the *Rdo rje tshig rkang.*[43] Two different terms are used to describe these texts. The first is simply "commentary" *(rnam 'grel),* whereas the second, which has become more common, means "explication of the treatise" *(gzhung bshad).* Gung ru ba Shes rab bzang po (1411–75) notes that the term "explication of the treatise" *(gzhung bshad)* must be understood to mean "a commentary on the *Rdo rje tshig rkang*" and mentions that each of Sa chen's works is somewhat different in its style of explanation and method of presenting the meaning.[44]

Although Sa chen's eleven commentaries *(rnam 'grel bcu gcig)* are the basic sources for the study of the *Rdo rje tshig rkang* and the practice of the Lam 'bras, there has been considerable confusion from a very early time about their actual identification. As Mus srad pa Rdo rje rgyal mtshan (1424–98) carefully pointed out, Rje btsun Grags pa rgyal mtshan's statement that his father had written "about eleven" commentaries left room for doubt as to the actual number.[45] Further difficulties certainly arose because of the secret nature of the material and the fact that these commentaries only circulated in manuscript form for about eight hundred years, until they were finally gathered together by 'Jam dbyangs rgyal mtshan (1870–1940) and published at Sde dge in a xylograph edition in the early twentieth century. It also seems that they were never transmitted as a group of eleven, which probably also contributed to problems of identification.[46] Almost all the surviving examples also lack original colophons or clear statements of authorship.

In their discussions of Sa chen's eleven works, Sa skya masters over the centuries have basically expressed three opinions and have usually disagreed about the identity of only one or two of the commentaries. These differences will be noted below. Only one of the three opinions corresponds exactly to the eleven surviving texts. Against all expectations, these eleven commentaries have apparently been preserved according to the tradition of the Rdzong lineage of the Lam 'bras, which was absorbed into the mainstream Sa skya tradition centuries ago. Only one text devoted solely to solving problems of identification concerning the eleven commentaries has survived. This unsigned work, bearing the title *Man ngag gsal byed (Clarification of the Esoteric Instructions),* can now be identified as a composition of Mus srad pa Rdo rje rgyal mtshan, who was one of the most outstanding masters of the Rdzong tradition.[47] Mus srad pa seems to have been working from texts at hand, and his list corresponds exactly to the surviving works.[48] Not only that, three of the actual manuscripts owned by Mus srad pa have survived.[49]

Perhaps due to the scarcity and the similar content of the eleven commentaries, by the seventeenth century at the latest, the reading transmissions *(lung)* for all but three had been lost. The three for which the lineal transmission has continued to the present day are the *A seng ma (The Explication for A seng),* the *Sras don ma (The Explication for the Benefit of the Sons),* and the *Gnyags ma (The Explication for Gnyags).*[50] However, in the twentieth century the great master Rdzong gsar Mkhyen brtse 'Jam dbyangs chos kyi blo gros (1893–1959) received the transmission of the commentaries in a visionary dream from Sa chen himself. Rdzong gsar Mkhyen brtse then passed the revived transmission to a master by the name of Bla ma Blo dga', who has in turn imparted the reading transmissions of the eleven commentaries to many disciples in Tibet. This revived transmission of the eleven commentaries has not yet been received by Sa skya teachers living outside Tibet.[51]

(1) The *A seng ma (The Explication for A seng)*

Also known as the *Don bsdus ma (The Condensed Meaning),* this short verse text was the first of Sa chen's eleven commentaries on the *Rdo rje tshig rkang.* Sa chen gave it to the Khams pa master A seng Rdo rje brtan pa in 1141. According to Gung ru ba, some members of the tradition later made the mistake of identifying the *A seng ma* and the *Don bsdus ma* as two different commentaries.[52] A seng was the nephew of Sa chen's teacher Sgyu ra A skyabs. According to Mkhyen brtse'i dbang phyug, the *A seng ma* was actually composed by Sa chen, whereas the remaining ten commentaries were written down by the requestors and then proofread and corrected by Sa chen.[53] Apparently there were both short and long versions of this commentary, although only the short one has survived. According to the Rdzong master Nam mkha' dpal bzang, this short verse text formed the basis of a longer commentary which explained its meaning.[54] Mus srad pa also mentions the existence of two works: a short text of twenty verses and a commentary on it that was also said to be a fine work. He further notes with some reservation that this longer text was sometimes identified with another commentary known as the *Mang dkar ma (The Explication for Mang dkar).*[55] Commentaries to the *A seng ma* itself were later written by Spru lung pa Kun smon, who was a disciple of Chos rgyal 'Phag pa (1235–80), and by Go rams Bsod nams seng ge (1429–89).[56] The *A seng ma* was later included in the *Pod ser* compiled by Sa chen's son Rje btsun Grags pa rgyal mtshan.

In addition to studying the Lam 'bras with Sa chen, A seng Rdo rje brtan pa also received many teachings from Rgwa Lo tsā ba Rnam rgyal rdo rje, especially the transmissions of the Six-branch Yoga of the Kālacakra (Dus 'khor sbyor drug) and special teachings of Mahākāla.[57] A seng later became a teacher of Phag mo gru pa Rdo rje rgyal po (1110–70), to whom he transmitted the teachings of Rgwa Lo tsā ba, especially the Six-branch Yoga. A seng is frequently mentioned in biographies of the time.

(2) The *Sga theng ma (The Explication for Sga theng)*

According to 'Jam mgon A mes zhabs (1597–1659), the *Sga theng ma* was the second commentary composed by Sa chen. If this is correct, it was the first of the ten major works, preceded only by the brief *A seng ma*. The man known as Sga theng was from the region of Ldan ma in Khams, and was partially lame.[58] The earliest mention of the circumstances of the composition of the *Sga theng ma* is found in the original annotations of the *Zhib mo rdo rje* translated below in part two:

> Rga theng studied under the great master for a long time. When [Sa chen] came to Ru 'tshams he saw Rga theng's summarizing notes. He thought, "He has received it many times; will it be reliable?" It was nothing but errors. He thought, "Well, after I have died this Dharma will be gone," and for the benefit of Rga theng he composed the *Rga theng ma*. So it has been stated.[59]

Much later, 'Jam mgon A mes zhabs also gave a similar account of these circumstances, but mentioned that Sa chen was invited by Sga theng to a Dharma Council at Ru mtshams, and that "several key points were mistaken" in Sga theng's original composition.[60] This text is a very important work, and perhaps served as the model for the following commentaries. However, there are some serious doubts about the actual identity of the surviving version of the *Sga theng ma*. This topic will be treated in detail below when discussing the works of Phag mo gru pa.

(3) The *Bande ma (The Explication for Bande)*

As stated by Mus srad pa, this work was written for the tantric layman Bande Gshin rje, who was from Ngam shod in Dbus. Some authors also identified him with a master known as Grub thob 'Dar phyar.[61] Jo nang Tāranātha (1575–1635) provides the most information about Grub thob 'Dar phyar Rin chen bzang po, who lived in two different caves at Jo nang, where he had a vision of Padmasambhava and received the transmission of the entire Dharma cycle known as the *Rta mgrin yang gsang (The Supersecret Hayagīva).* He also had visions of the fifteen goddesses of Nairātmyā and of a form of Cakrasaṃvara.[62] The *Bande ma* is not included among the eleven commentaries listed by other Sa skya masters, and is instead sometimes listed among the commentaries on the *Rdo rje tshig rkang* written by Sa chen's disciples.[63] Bande Gshin rje is also known as Bande Gshin rje grags, one of Rje btsun Grags pa rgyal mtshan's four disciples with "grags" at the end of their names.

(4) The *Zla rgyal ma (The Explication for Zla rgyal)*

This commentary was written for the master Byang sems Zla ba rgyal mtshan, who is best known for his special tradition of practical meditation instructions *(dmar khrid)* focusing on the deity Mahākaruṇika. He was also an important teacher of Phag mo gru pa Rdo rje rgyal po.[64] Zla ba rgyal mtshan gave the vows of a celibate Buddhist layman to Rje btsun Grags pa rgyal mtshan at Sa skya in 1149, which establishes his presence there during the early years when Sa chen's commentaries are known to have been written.[65]

(5) The *Ldan bu ma (The Explication for Ldan bu)*

According to Mus srad pa, this commentary was written for Jo gdan Ldan bu. He also notes that it contains some Sanskrit terms, and says that when Sa chen taught the oral instructions to a śrāvaka monk paṇḍita from Sindhu in India, Jo gdan Ldan bu also received them. At that time Sa chen is said to have taught in Sanskrit, which was later translated into Tibetan.[66] The surviving examples of the *Ldan bu ma* do indeed contain an unusual number of Sanskrit terms. The story of Sa chen's Ceylonese mendicant disciple, whom Sa skya Paṇḍita also says was from Sindhu in India,[67] and the teachings given to him by Sa chen at Gung thang, is provided by Dmar ston in the *Zhib mo rdo rje* translated in part two. The *Ldan bu ma* is only included in the lists of the two Rdzong writers, Mus srad pa and Nam mkha' dpal bzang, and is not mentioned by other Sa skya authors.[68]

(6) The *Yum don ma (The Explication for the Wife)*

Mkhyen brtse'i dbang phyug states that the *Yum don ma* was written for Ma gcig Btsad tsha, who was the first of Sa chen's two wives and the mother of his eldest son Kun dga' 'bar.[69] She was also known as Jo lcam Phur mo.[70] After Kun dga' 'bar died in India at the age of twenty-one, his mother turned to serious Dharma practice, and Sa chen wrote this commentary for her.[71] The *Yum don ma* is unique in that Cakrasaṃvara is utilized for the creation stage meditations, while the techniques from the Lam 'bras are emphasized for the perfection stage.[72] Mkhyen brtse'i dbang phyug notes that the original text was said to have been somewhat different from the one of his time without being more specific.[73] It is odd that some early masters thought the *Yum don ma* had been written for Byang sems Zla ba rgyal mtshan, an opinion rejected by both Mus srad pa and Gung ru ba.[74] Curiously, the edition of the *Yum don ma* published in Sde dge states in the title that it was written for the benefit of Ma gcig Zhang mo, Sa chen's mother, while an earlier manuscript copy is not specific.[75] The honorific term *yum* can mean either "wife" or "mother."

(7) The *Klog skya ma (The Explication for Klog skya)*

This commentary was written for Klog skya Jo sras Chos grags.[76] According to Mus srad pa, Klog skya was from Gtsang, and Mkhyen brtse'i dbang phyug further specifies that he was from Sgyer bu.[77] The *Klog skya ma* contains a large number of detailed annotations perhaps composed by a Grags pa (or Grags dpal) bzang po who is mentioned in a final versified annotation.[78] This may refer to Klog skya himself.

(8) The *Zhu byas ma (The Explication for Zhu byas)*

This work was composed for the master known as Zhu byas Dngos grub. Mang thos klu sgrub mentions that Zhu byas was from Lho, whereas Mkhyen brtse'i dbang phyug says that he was the nephew of

Zhu ston Rog po in La stod and gives several amusing stories about his miraculous abilities. Zhu byas apparently spent much time in India.[79] Mus srad pa mentions that Zhu byas was the teacher of the Tshal Gung thang master Bla ma Zhang G.yu brag pa (1123–93). He also says that this commentary received the name *Zhu byas ma* because Sa chen's sons Bsod nams rtse mo and Grags pa rgyal mtshan were performing an offering ritual one evening in Sa skya when Zhu byas arrived from Bodhgayā. The brothers requested this explanation of the *Rdo rje tshig rkang* from him orally and wrote it down themselves.[80] A verse at the end of the surviving examples of the *Zhu byas ma*, written by Bsod nams rtse mo, verifies that he recorded it in writing.[81] This information all seems to conflict with the more common statement that Sa chen wrote the commentary for Zhu byas.

(9) The *Sras don ma (The Explication for the Benefit of the Sons)*

The *Sras don ma* is the most extensive and important of Sa chen's eleven commentaries. As the title of the work states, it was written "for the benefit of [my] son[s]." The fifteenth-century authors Mus srad pa and Gung ru ba both record two different traditions about this text.[82] The first tradition is that the work was written for Gnyan Phul byung ba, whom Gung ru ba refers to as "spiritual son" *(thugs sras)*. This tradition was later followed by Mang thos klu sgrub, who simply says this commentary was written for the "spiritual son" *(thugs sras)* Gnyan Phul byung ba Gtsug tor rgyal po, whose actual name was Bsod nams rdo rje.[83] The second tradition mentioned by Gung ru ba is that Gnyan Phul byung ba edited together the scrolls *(shog dril)* that Sa chen had written for the benefit of his sons Bsod nams rtse mo and Grags pa rgyal mtshan.[84] When referring to this second tradition, Mus srad pa quotes a statement he says is found at the end of some manuscripts of the *Sras don ma*: "This text was composed for the benefit of the sons. It was in fragments, and was edited by Lord Phul byung ba."[85] These words are actually found at the end of surviving copies of the *Sras don ma*.[86] This second tradition was later followed by Mkhyen brtse'i dbang phyug, who also notes that most of the miscellaneous material edited by Gnyan Phul byung ba was specifically concerned with difficult points in the *Rdo rje tshig rkang*.[87] Finally, 'Jam mgon A mes zhabs, the last to write about the topic, brings together both traditions by stating that the *Sras don ma* represents instructions by Sa chen given for the benefit of all three sons *(sras)*. In saying this he refers to the scrolls written for Sa chen's actual sons *(sras)* Bsod nams rtse mo and Grags pa rgyal mtshan, which were edited together by his spiritual son *(thugs sras)* Gnyan Phul byung ba.[88]

(10) The *'A 'u ma (The Explication for Lady 'A 'u ma)*

Mus srad pa also refers to this commentary as the *Jo 'bum ma*, and says that it was written for Jo mo 'A 'u ma, "The Howling Lady," who was from G.ya' lung. The work became known as the *'A 'u ma* because this woman had the experience of being a dog, and howled, "Ah Ooo! Ah Ooo!" *('a 'u 'a 'u)*.[89] While Gung ru ba also refers to Lady 'A 'u ma's howling experience, it is only Mkhyen brtse'i dbang phyug who later reveals the real cause, when he says that she howled when "the purification of birth as a dog dawned" *(khyi'i gnas sbyong shar)*.[90] The use of this phrase points to a deep meditative experience in which the vital winds and essential constituents are drawn into specific locations in the network of subtle channels within the body. In the case of Lady 'A 'u ma, the vital winds and essential constituents had gathered in a certain channel-syllable *(rtsa yig)* related to rebirth in the animal realm. Experiences such as this are explained in considerable detail in the various commentaries to the *Rdo rje tshig rkang*. When such an experience occurs, it is said that the causes for future rebirth in the corresponding realm are thereby purified.[91] Mus srad pa also notes the opinion by some that this commentary is the same as the work known as the *Mang chung ma (The Explication for Mang chung)*.[92]

(11) The *Gnyags ma (The Explication for Gnyags)*

All sources agree that the *Gnyags ma* was the last commentary on the *Rdo rje tshig rkang* written by Sa chen Kun dga' snying po, and that it was written for the teacher Gnyags Gzhi ra ba Dbang phyug rgyal mtshan.[93] The *Gnyags ma* was the only one of Sa chen's extensive commentaries on the *Rdo rje tshig rkang* included in the *Pod ser* later compiled by his son Grags pa rgyal mtshan. When choosing to include the *Gnyags ma*, Grags pa rgyal mtshan stated, "This was composed very late and is a short treatise with detailed meaning."[94] To further enhance the text, Grags pa rgyal mtshan then composed very informative and extensive annotations, which are found in the surviving example.[95] Moreover, Grags pa rgyal mtshan referred to the existence of nine places in the *Gnyags ma* where Sa chen had omitted details of practice and had only written, "This is to be learned from the mouth [of the master]." Grags pa rgyal mtshan thus included in the *Pod ser* twenty-three texts to clarify the *Gnyags ma*, some written by his father and some by himself.[96] In later times there were also several works written to further clarify the meaning of the *Gnyags ma*. There are references to a text by Chos rgyal 'Phag pa's student Spru lung pa to assist in understanding the *Gnyags ma*, a clarification of Sa chen's work by the fourteenth-century master Bar ston Rdo rje rgyal mtshan, and an elucidation of its intention by Paṇ chen Ngag dbang chos grags (1572–1641), only one of which seems to have survived.[97]

In the *Zhib mo rdo rje*, Dmar ston gives some further important information about the *Gnyags ma*:

> Moreover, last of all, the *Gnyag ma*, composed in response to the request by the spiritual friend Gnyag, is succinct in words but extensive in meaning and well formulated. Considered suitable [by later masters], it has been used as the teaching manual up until the present.[98]

Dmar ston's statement indicates that Grags pa rgyal mtshan and Sa skya Paṇḍita had chosen to use the *Gnyags ma* when explaining the *Rdo rje tshig rkang* and teaching the Lam 'bras.[99] In the seventeenth century, 'Jam mgon A mes zhabs singled out the *Gnyags ma* from among the eleven commentaries, and said that the explanation *(bshad bka')* of this text was still unbroken in his time.[100] The *Gnyags ma* is still the text most often used to explain the *Rdo rje tshig rkang*.

Different Opinions about Sa chen's Eleven Commentaries

The previous discussion of the identification of Sa chen's eleven commentaries has been based on the eleven texts that have survived, and which surprisingly match the list given by the Rdzong master Mus srad pa Rdo rje rgyal mtshan, who was one of the earliest to write about the subject. His contemporary, Gung ru ba Shes rab bzang po, a master of the Ngor and Na lendra traditions, followed the same list with only one exception. Instead of the *Bande ma* in Mus srad pa's list, Gung ru ba includes a commentary written for Stod sgom Byang chub shes rab.[101]

About a hundred years after Gung ru ba, in 1566, the Tshar pa master Mang thos klu sgrub recorded a slightly different list, which was also given by his contemporary in the Tshar pa tradition, Mkhyen brtse'i dbang phyug.[102] These two authors both based their lists on an ancient eulogy to Sa chen written by his disciple Zhu byas Dngos grub, for whom Sa chen had written one of his eleven commentaries. This eulogy, which contained old annotations, had come into the hands of Bdag chen Rdo rje 'chang Blo gros rgyal mtshan (1444–95), who had felt it to contain the solution to the questions of identification.[103] The eulogy mentions that Sa chen wrote commentaries for eight men and three women, who are identified in the annotations and by Bdag chen Rdo rje 'chang. This information led these authors to include two commentaries known as the *Bzang ri ma (The Explication for Bzang ri),* written for the teacher Bzang ri phug pa, and the *Mang mkhar ma (The Explication for Mang mkhar),* written for Lady Mang mkhar, and to not include the *Bande ma* and the *Ldan bu ma.*[104] In this way, their lists include commentaries for eight men and three women, whereas the surviving texts were written for nine men and two women.[105] It is not known whether Klu sgrub and Mkhyen brtse had actually seen all the texts they list, whereas it is clear that Mus srad pa was in possession of the texts he wrote about.

Commentaries on the Rdo rje tshig rkang *by Sa chen's Disciples*

While the eleven works of Sa chen are certainly the most significant explanations of the *Rdo rje tshig rkang,* according to Mkhyen brtse'i dbang phyug the total number of commentaries by both Sa chen and his disciples was about twenty.[106] Disagreement in the lists of Sa chen's eleven works was often due to differences in opinion about whether Sa chen or one of his disciples had composed a certain commentary. It is customary in all Tibetan traditions for records of a teacher's explanations made by a student to be regarded as the work of the teacher. For example, Mus srad pa says that the *Dpe mdzod ma (The Library Explication)* written down by Sa chen's disciple Phag mo gru pa Rdo rje rgyal po was sometimes counted as one of the eleven by Sa chen.[107] As mentioned above, another disagreement was about the *Bande ma.* This work was included in the list of eleven according to the Rdzong tradition, but was considered by Mang thos klu sgrub to be the work of a disciple.[108]

The earliest list of commentaries by Sa chen's disciples is by Gung ru ba, who says that many explications of the *Rdo rje tshig rkang* were written by disciples such as Bzang ri phug pa, Zhu brag Mar pa, Zhang se Mar pa, Dbu ma pa chen po of 'U yug, the Mi nyag master Prajñājvala, and Phag mo gru pa.[109] Mang thos klu sgrub does not list Bzang ri phug pa among the students who wrote texts. He places the work for him among Sa chen's eleven commentaries, but adds Na ro Bandhe and Stod sgom Byang chub shes rab to Gung ru ba's list.[110] 'Jam mgon A mes zhabs follows Mang thos klu sgrub, and also notes that if the larger of the two commentaries known as the *A seng ma* were added to the general list there would be a total of twenty-one works.[111] Only one of these commentaries on the *Rdo rje tshig rkang* by Sa chen's disciples may have survived.

The Works of Phag mo gru pa

The preceding discussion has focused on the traditional Sa skya accounts of the first commentaries on the *Rdo rje tshig rkang* of Virūpa. But there is mounting evidence of another untold story barely touched upon in Sa skya writings about the Lam 'bras. This concerns the unacknowledged role of Phag mo gru pa Rdo rje rgyal po (1110–70) in the very earliest recording and compilation of the teachings of his master Sa chen Kun dga' snying po. According to the Sa skya tradition, the first collection of texts on the Lam 'bras was the *Pod ser (The Yellow Volume)* compiled by Grags pa rgyal mtshan, which contains the earliest writings of Sa chen and his sons. This collection will be examined in detail below. However, it is now clear that at least some of the texts contained in the *Pod ser* were actually authored by Phag mo gru pa, who also wrote down other anonymous works attributed to Sa chen. Grags pa rgyal mtshan later included these texts in the *Pod ser.*[112] Grags pa rgyal mtshan rewrote or revised some of these works. He may have added annotations to others, and kept some in their original form.

This discovery opens up many extremely interesting lines of research that cannot be fully explored here. Strangely enough, it seems that no lineage holders of the Lam 'bras ever actually compared Phag mo gru pa's writings to those in the *Pod ser*. His crucial role in the formation of the early literature has certainly been ignored in the Sa skya tradition.

According to Bka' brgyud and Sa skya sources, Phag mo gru pa first came to Sa skya in about 1138 to receive instructions from Sa chen, and continued to study and meditate there for the next twelve years.[113] If this is correct, he arrived in Sa skya three years before Sa chen first taught the Lam 'bras, wrote down the *Rdo rje tshig rkang*, and composed the first of the eleven commentaries for A seng Rdo rje brtan pa in 1141. Sa chen's son Slob dpon Bsod nams rtse mo was born the next year, 1142, and Grags pa rgyal mtshan five years later in 1147. During the period of Phag mo gru pa's stay, from approximately 1138 to 1150, before Sa chen's sons had been born or while they were still very young, he was one of Sa chen's closest disciples and a foremost practitioner of the Lam 'bras. This is clear from many accounts. For example, the Sa skya master Ngor chen Kun dga' bzang po stated:

> That great being endowed with the three names of Bde gshegs Phag mo gru pa, Rje Khams pa Rdor rgyal, and Dpal Mtha' rtsa ba, requested [the Lam 'bras] from the great Lord Sa skya pa, and lived at Sa skya for twelve years. Having pleased the master by [enduring] infinite hardships, he placed in writing the esoteric instructions he had obtained, thereby composing *(mdzad)* the great treatise known as the *Lam 'bras bshad mdzod ma*. Some call it the *Dpe mdzod ma*, which appears to be a corruption.[114]

Other sources provide further details. 'Brug chen Padma dkar po (1527–92) notes that Phag mo gru pa was Sa chen's most learned disciple. After Phag mo gru pa's experience of the spiritual warmths and signs from meditation on the subtle channels and vital winds, Sa chen recognized in him the high realization of the Path of Seeing *(mthong lam)*.[115]

The most detailed and interesting account of Phag mo gru pa's activities at Sa skya, and his relationship with Sa chen, is found in an unfinished work by the 'Khon master Bsod nams dbang po (1559–1621), later edited by his nephew, 'Jam mgon A mes zhabs. This text would seem to record the accounts of Sa skya history passed down in the 'Khon family itself. Bsod nams dbang po mentions that Phag mo gru pa received the entire Lam 'bras from Sa chen, and that Sa chen also dictated an instruction manual for his benefit, which became widely known as the *Gzhung bshad phag gru (The Explication of the Treatise for Phag gru)*.[116]

Bsod nams dbang po also relates a fascinating apocryphal episode in which the great yogin Rje btsun Mi la ras pa and his disciple Ras chung Rdo rje grags pa (1083–1161) come to the door of Phag mo gru pa's cave at Sa skya. When Mi la ras pa rattled his hand-drum at the sealed door, Phag mo gru pa's previous connections with him were awakened, and he rushed to the door. But then he realized that he could not break the retreat without his teacher's permission, and remained in the cave.[117] While it is possible that Ras chung pa visited Sa skya during this period, Mi la ras pa had certainly passed away some years earlier.

In 1692 the Sa skya master Sangs rgyas phun tshogs, the twenty-fifth abbot of Ngor monastery, also recorded much of the same information that is found in Bsod nams dbang po's work, including the aborted meeting with Mi la ras pa, but with a number of important changes and details. Sangs rgyas phun tshogs says Phag mo gru pa arrived in Sa skya at about the time of Sa chen's famous visionary encounter with Virūpa in 1138, and requested the Lam 'bras. He meditated in a cave there, and when Sa chen's teachings were finished Phag mo gru pa composed an explication of the treatise *(gzhung gi bshad pa mdzad).*[118] According to the chronology in Sangs rgyas phun tshogs's discussion these events happened some time before the expiration of the eighteen-year restriction placed on Sa chen by his teacher Zhang ston, and the arrival of A seng in 1141. All other sources are unanimous in stating that Sa chen first taught the Lam 'bras to A seng, and only then placed the *Rdo rje tshig rkang* in writing.

Phag mo gru pa's commentary recording Sa chen's instructions on the *Rdo rje tshig rkang* is usually referred to as the *Dpe mdzod ma.* A very interesting statement by Sa chen's great-grandson Chos rgyal 'Phag pa is found in the history of the Stag lung branch of the Bka' brgyud tradition. According to a conversation between Chos rgyal 'Phag pa and Sangs rgyas dbon (1251–96), Phag mo gru pa had written his summarizing notes *(zin bris)* of the Lam 'bras and offered them to Sa chen for his approval, but Sa chen felt that the work would put words in the mouth of his son (*jo sras*=Bsod nams rtse mo?). Phag mo gru pa then asked Sa chen to keep the work secret, which he did. Sa chen placed it in the library *(dpe mdzod),* and the text became known as the *Dpe mdzod ma (The Library Explication).* The text was also not to be shown to anyone at Sa skya during the lifetime of Slob dpon Jo sras (=Slob dpon Bsod nams rtse mo?).[119] This information supports the view that Phag mo gru pa did not record the commentary until after the birth of Bsod nams rtse mo in 1142. One of the biographies of Phag mo gru pa gives a similar account, with yet another name for the text:

> [Phag mo gru pa] met the honorable Sa chen Kun dga' snying po. Since [Phag mo gru pa] knew many volumes [of scripture, Sa chen] was pleased and agreed to whatever Dharma he requested. He bestowed the *Hevajra*, the *Pañjara*, the *Sampuṭa*, the Lam 'bras, as well as the Lam skor, and countless profound Cakrasaṃvara initiations.
>
> When [Phag mo gru pa] made summarizing notes *(zin bris)* for the Lam 'bras, and so forth, [Sa chen] exclaimed, "Spiritual friend from Khams, your knowledge is great, but this won't do—the profound oral instructions are too clear!"
>
> It was hidden in a cave *(skye tshang)*, and thus became known as the *Lam 'bras skye tshang ma*. Furthermore, he was told not to show it to many [persons]. A fine understanding was also born. And he gained a great reputation for being learned and venerable.[120]

These stories lead to the conclusion that the *Dpe mdzod ma* must have been the earliest major commentary on the *Rdo rje tshig rkang*, otherwise Sa chen would not have felt that it was too clear. These accounts also show that the text was originally kept very secret.

The *Dpe mdzod ma* and Phag mo gru pa's other writings on the Lam 'bras were transmitted for centuries in the Bka' brgyud and Jo nang traditions. For example, the master Karma Phrin las pa (1456–1539), who taught both Sa skya and Bka' brgyud instructions, is known to have once explained the *Dpe mdzod ma* when teaching the Lam 'bras to many Sa skya scholars at the monastery of Na lendra.[121] Only in the last few years have several unpublished manuscripts of Phag mo gru pa's writings on the Lam 'bras become available. It is of great interest that they match very closely the list given in the sixteenth century by Padma dkar po, who had received them all. Jo nang Tāranātha also received the full transmission of Phag mo gru pa's Lam 'bras.[122]

There are about twenty texts concerning the Lam 'bras in the surviving Phag mo gru pa collections. With the exception of the *Dpe mdzod ma*, a short biography of Virūpa that is perhaps by one of Phag mo gru pa's disciples, and one other brief text, all these works are also found in the *Pod ser* later compiled by Grags pa rgyal mtshan. But, as noted above, many of the texts have gone through considerable editing and rewriting. In particular, the manuscript copies of the *Dpe mdzod ma* create a very difficult problem. Unfortunately, there is only limited space here to investigate this topic.

The problem is that the surviving manuscripts of the *Dpe mdzod ma* in the collected works of Phag mo gru pa are absolutely identical to the surviving copies of the *Sga theng ma*, which is thought to have been the first of Sa chen's extensive commentaries on the *Rdo rje tshig rkang*. The only differences are the titles given to the works, and a third-person colophon in the *Dpe mdzod ma* that simply says, "The *Lam 'bras Dpe mdzod ma* composed by glorious Phag mo gru pa."[123] Obviously, at some point during the last eight hundred years the two texts were confused, and one has been lost. But which has survived: the *Dpe mdzod ma* or the *Sga theng ma*? This question is impossible to answer with certainty at the present time, but a few points should be considered.

When Grags pa rgyal mtshan was only three years old, Phag mo gru pa left Sa skya. All sources agree that Phag mo gru pa composed his works on the Lam 'bras at Sa skya, and so it seems certain that his writings were codified as a group long before Grags pa rgyal mtshan's compilation of the *Pod ser*. Phag mo gru pa's works on the Lam 'bras were passed down in an active lineage in the Bka' brgyud tradition for centuries, whereas Sa chen's eleven commentaries were never collected together and transmitted as a group. Taking all of this into consideration it seems that the odds were better for the survival of the *Dpe mdzod ma*, which is at least known to have been taught over a long period, than for the *Sga theng ma*, for which there is not a single record of transmission. In any case, the manuscripts of the *Sga theng ma* and the *Dpe mdzod ma* probably represent the first major commentary on the *Rdo rje tshig rkang*, which then became the model for the remaining nine attributed to Sa chen, all of which have the same basic structure. These problems will require further research.

When it comes to the smaller works in Phag mo gru pa's volume, some more definite conclusions can be reached. Two of the clearest examples will be discussed briefly. One example is related to a work attributed to Sa chen in the *Pod ser*, and the other is related to a work by Grags pa rgyal mtshan.

Among the works of Phag mo gru pa is a text entitled *Lam 'bras bu dang bcas pa'i zhal gyi gdams pa (Personal Instructions on the Path with the Result)*. In the *Pod ser* there is an untitled text attributed to Sa chen that is referred to by Grags pa rgyal mtshan as *Byung rgyal du mi gtong ba'i gnad rnam pa bzhi (Four Key Points Not to Be Allowed Natural Expression),* in reference to its content.[124] The two texts are very closely related, and yet quite different. There is no colophon in the *Pod ser* text, but Phag mo gru pa's work has a significant first-person statement at the end: "The profound personal instructions of the Lord Sa skya pa, written by the monk Rdo rje rgyal po."[125] Phag mo gru pa's work contains no annotations, whereas the text in the *Pod ser* has a large number of detailed annotations. A comparison of the two works shows that the text in the *Pod ser* is definitely a reworking of the text in Phag mo gru pa's writings. The annotations were added later, most likely by Grags pa rgyal mtshan, who is known to have written many other annotations to texts in the *Pod ser,* such as the *Gnyags ma.* Moreover, the final statement of authorship by Phag mo gru pa has been omitted in the revised text found in the *Pod ser.*

One further example will suffice to show the extent of Grags pa rgyal mtshan's revisions of Phag mo gru pa's works when later compiling the *Pod ser.* In the collected writings of Phag mo gru pa there are two separate texts, both written in prose, entitled *Lam 'bras kyi 'phrin las sum bcu (The Thirty Actions of the Path with the Result)* and *Lam 'bras kyi yan lag lnga sbyong (Excercising the Five Limbs in the Path with the Result).* Both of these works lack colophons.[126] In the *Pod ser* there is a single text, written in verse, entitled *Phrin las sum cu rtsa gnyis kyi 'khrul 'khor (The Yogic Exercises of the Thirty-two Actions),* which contains a clear first-person statement at the end saying that it was composed *(sbyar ba)* by Grags pa rgyal mtshan. Furthermore, one of the final verses of the text states that it was written to clarify confusing points in "the small text[s] of a former venerable lord" *(rje btsun gong ma'i dpe'u chung yi ge).*[127] A comparison of the three texts leaves no room for doubt that Grags pa rgyal mtshan rewrote Phag mo gru pa's two small prose works into a single versified text.

What does this really mean? All the works in both Phag mo gru pa's volume and the *Pod ser* certainly originate from the oral instructions of Sa chen Kun dga' snying po. Many of these teachings were originally written down by Phag mo gru pa in Sa skya, between the years 1141 and 1150. This was before Sa chen's sons were born, or while they were very young. After leaving Sa skya, and later meeting Lord Sgam po pa, Phag mo gru pa became a great lineage holder of the Bka' brgyud tradition, and thereafter taught according to that lineage. Thus later Sa skya followers may have found it awkward to acknowledge the importance of his contribution to the preservation of the Lam 'bras while at Sa skya. Grags pa rgyal mtshan definitely received from his father or elder brother the transmission of all the original materials that he later edited together in the *Pod ser*. It now seems certain that a number of Sa chen's most important instructions that were originally written down by his disciple Phag mo gru pa were among the texts later transmitted by Sa chen to his sons.

The Pod ser

When compiling his definitive volume of early texts concerning the Lam 'bras, Rje btsun Grags pa rgyal mtshan specifically stated that the oral instructions had been passed down to him in an oral transmission without any texts.[128] In light of what has been discussed above, this should be understood to mean that Grags pa rgyal mtshan first received an oral transmission of the Lam 'bras, although there were texts in existence at that time. Moreover, Sa chen's reported reaction to Phag mo gru pa's work should be seen in light of the importance of keeping the tradition oral. He may have felt that placing the oral instructions in writing would be harmful to the education of his sons, who might then rely upon texts instead of memory. The written records of Sa chen's teachings were certainly guarded very closely during his life and for some time thereafter. The fact that the teachings remained essentially oral even during the lifetime of Grags pa rgyal mtshan is clear from the story of his disciple Dpyil ston Rgyal ba bzang po, who received the Lam 'bras eighteen times, but during all of those years never saw a single written text.[129] According to Grags pa rgyal mtshan, the instructions were memorized by every master in the lineage up until his time, as well as by himself and several of his own disciples. It had finally become necessary to record them in writing only to prevent corruption of the teachings and to benefit others.[130]

The *Rdo rje tshig rkang*, together with a number of Sa chen's early texts concerning the Lam 'bras, were kept locked in a leather box *(sag sgam* or *gseg sgam)* during Sa chen's lifetime. These teachings were referred to as the *Sag shubs ma* or *Gseg shubs ma (The Leather Case)*.[131] As mentioned above, it now seems certain that a number of these works were originally written down by Phag mo gru pa. During the first part of Grags pa rgyal mtshan's life the texts were wrapped in a yellow cloth and were known as the *Pod ser ma (The Yellow Volume).*[132] Grags pa rgyal mtshan later supplemented the original collection with a number of small texts, such as those meant to clarify the nine points not elaborated on by Sa chen in the *Gnyags ma,* and he wrote a catalogue to permanently establish the contents of the volume *(glegs bam).*[133] He also wrote a number of works himself to explain other points, after about half of the original collection was lost.[134] Mkhyen brtse'i dbang phyug provides some fascinating details about this:

> [The texts] were later arranged in a volume by the great venerable lord [Grags pa rgyal mtshan]. To symbolize that this Dharma is difficult to understand, but that if it is understood all needs and wishes are fulfilled, he drew a vajra on the face of the front cover-board and a jewel on the back one. To symbolize that those [teachings] are understood from the oral instructions of a master endowed with the transmission, he drew the figures of the transmission line of the Oral Instructions on the inside of the cover-board. Since it had a yellow cloth on it, it was known as the *Pod ser ma.*[135]

Mang thos klu sgrub notes that in its earliest form this collection did not contain the text on dependently arisen connections *(rten 'brel),* the *Don bsdus,* or the basic text and commentary on the view.[136] The first two of these works are Sa chen's *A seng ma,* also known as the *Don bsdus ma,* and a short text on the five dependently arisen connections according to the Lam 'bras teachings.[137] The last two works are by Grags pa rgyal mtshan. These are the versified *Rin chen snang ba (Illuminating the Jewel)* and its autocommentary, which are the definitive texts on the view of the indivisibility of saṃsāra and nirvāṇa *(lta ba 'khor 'das dbyer med)* that is the special view of the Lam 'bras.[138] These two texts are the basis for all the works that were later written to explain the "three continuums" *(rgyud gsum),* which is a fundamental topic of the Lam 'bras. The mention of the two works in Grags pa rgyal mtshan's catalogue to the collection, and their inclusion in the volume, make it possible to fix a definite time period for the final compilation of the collection and the composition of the catalogue. The versified *Rin chen snang ba* was written in 1206, and the autocommentary in 1212.[139] Grags pa rgyal mtshan passed away in 1216. Thus the collection was finalized, and the catalogue written, between 1212 and 1216.

The *Pod ser* contains most of the essential writings on the Lam 'bras composed by Sa chen and his sons Bsod nams rtse mo and Grags pa rgyal mtshan. Although there has been some discussion in the tradition about which texts belong in the collection, sixty is the usually accepted number. In his catalogue to the collection Grags pa rgyal mtshan says seven of these works may either be included or kept separate.[140] These seven works have not been included in the single published edition of the *Pod ser*. Generally speaking, the remaining fifty-three texts are grouped in the following way. The basic text is the *Rdo rje tshig rkang*, accompanied by a short outline and the *Gnyags ma*, both by Sa chen. Following this commentary are twenty-three small works, thirteen of which are attributed to Sa chen; the remaining ten were written by Grags pa rgyal mtshan. These texts together constitute a complete explanation of the *Rdo rje tshig rkang*.[141]

Then there is a group of six texts by Grags pa rgyal mtshan, the most significant of which are the versified *Rin chen snang ba*, written in 1206, and its autocommentary, written in 1212. These are the only dated texts in the entire collection.[142] Next is a group of four small works referred to as "the four small texts for removal of impediments" *(gegs sel yig chung bzhi)*, three of which are attributed to Sa chen, and one of which was composed by Grags pa rgyal mtshan.[143] Both Phag mo gru pa texts discussed above are in this group. These ten texts also relate to the *Rdo rje tshig rkang*. All of the works mentioned so far are referred to as explaining the "extensive path" *(lam rgyas pa)*.[144]

Then the "medium path," or the "path without the basic text," and the "condensed path" are each presented in small works.[145] Next is a group of nine texts, divided into what are known as the "four great fundamental works" *(gzhung shing chen po bzhi)* and the "five Dharmas to produce realization" *(rtogs pa bskyed pa'i chos lnga)*. Two of these are by Grags pa rgyal mtshan; seven are attributed to his father Sa chen.[146] At the end of this group is one small work on guruyoga, probably written by Grags pa rgyal mtshan.[147]

In the published edition of the *Pod ser* there follows a large group of texts on what is known as the Lam skor phyi ma brgyad, the "Eight Later Cycles of the Path." These texts are not traditionally included in the *Pod ser*, and are not mentioned by Grags pa rgyal mtshan in his definitive catalogue to the collection. They will not be discussed here.[148] Following this group are several more texts that do belong to the collection. First is a group of three works concerned with supporting the esoteric instructions with quotations from scripture *(lung sbyor)*. There has been some uncertainty as to the authorship of these works, with the consensus being that the first two were composed by Bsod nams rtse mo and the last by Sa chen.[149]

The *Pod ser* concludes with two small but important texts by Grags pa rgyal mtshan, which are the only histories of the Sa skya tradition of the Lam 'bras that predate the *Zhib mo rdo rje* of Dmar ston. Sa chen wrote the first works on the practice of the Lam 'bras, but no historical texts. One of Grags pa rgyal mtshan's works is an account of the tradition in India and the other is an account of the first few generations of the tradition in Tibet. It may be assumed that these writings embody the stories of the early masters as told to him by his father Sa chen and his older brother Slob dpon Bsod nams rtse mo. The first text, entitled *Bla ma brgyud pa rgya gar ba'i lo rgyus (The Indian Story of the Lineal Masters)*, is essentially an account of the life of the great adept Virūpa that is incorporated into all later Sa skya histories of the Lam 'bras with only minor additions or deletions.[150] This is the fundamental source for any study of Virūpa's life. Only one page in this work is devoted to the next three Indian masters of the tradition. Appended to this text are some of the famous vajra songs of Virūpa, given both in a transcription of the Prakrit original and with Tibetan translation and annotations.[151] Grags pa rgyal mtshan's second text, entitled *Bla ma brgyud pa bod kyi lo rgyus (The Tibetan Story of the Lineal Masters),* is basically a sketch of the life of 'Brog mi Lo tsā ba, the first Tibetan master of the Lam 'bras.[152] Only the last two pages of this work provide mention of the generations between 'Brog mi and Grags pa rgyal mtshan.

The Writings of Sa skya Paṇḍita and His Disciples

According to Mang thos klu sgrub, there were also several other volumes *(glegs bam)* of instructions that did not correspond to Grags pa rgyal mtshan's catalogue to the *Pod ser*. For example, Dkar Shākya grags, a major disciple of Grags pa rgyal mtshan, composed a commentary to the *Rdo rje tshig rkang* that he supplemented with other small works and compiled into a volume on the Lam 'bras *(lam 'bras glegs bam)*. Sa chen's disciple Zhang ze Dmar pa, who was mentioned above, also compiled a similar volume using the *Gnyags ma* as the basic text and supplementing it with other brief works.[153] But the primary transmission of the

Lam 'bras was given by Grags pa rgyal mtshan to his nephew, Sa skya Paṇḍita Kun dga' rgyal mtshan. Before and during Sa skya Paṇḍita's lifetime the instructions were mainly taught on the basis of the *Pod ser.*[154] Sa skya Paṇḍita himself then wrote a number of small but important texts on specific topics within the Lam 'bras.[155] Some of these writings were included in his collected works, but others were kept more secret until they were included in the fifteenth-century collection known as the *Pusti dmar chung (The Little Red Volume),* which will be discussed below. Some of the works on the Lam 'bras by Sa skya Paṇḍita's nephew Chos rgyal 'Phag pa were also later included in this collection. The reading transmission of all of Sa skya Paṇḍita and Chos rgyal 'Phag pa's works has been preserved to the present day.

Sa skya Paṇḍita's disciple Dmar ston Chos kyi rgyal po (c. 1198–c. 1259) recorded his teacher's explanation of the *Rdo rje tshig rkang* and his stories of the lives of the Tibetan teachers of the Lam 'bras, as well as a number of other works. Dmar ston's works, which were never gathered into a separate volume *(glegs bam),*[156] will be discussed in detail below. Another of Sa skya Paṇḍita's main disciples, Tshogs sgom Kun dga' dpal (1210–1307), composed an instruction manual *('khrid yig)* for teaching the Lam 'bras, and Tshogs sgom's disciples Nyan chen Bsod nams brtan pa and Gnyag Snying po rgyal mtshan also composed similar texts.[157] But none seem to have survived.

The Pod nag

The fifteenth patriarch of Sa skya, Bla ma dam pa Bsod nams rgyal mtshan (1312–75), was the most important Sa skya teacher after the period of the Five Supreme Masters *(gong ma lnga).*[158] Bla ma dam pa composed a monumental collection of esoteric instructions on the Lam 'bras between the years 1342 and 1347.[159] Bla ma dam pa's work became known as the *Pod nag ma (The Black Volume)* because of the color of the cloth in which these texts were wrapped.[160] Unlike the *Pod ser,* which contained works by several authors, the *Pod nag* was composed entirely by Bla ma dam pa, who carefully utilized the writings of his predecessors.

With the *Pod nag,* Bla ma dam pa created a cohesive group of texts that cover virtually all the major topics of the Lam 'bras. His *Man ngag gter mdzod (Treasury of Esoteric Instructions),* written in 1342, is a masterful commentary on the *Rdo rje tshig rkang.* In this work Bla ma dam pa largely drew material from Sa chen's *Sras don ma* and *Gnyags ma*, and Dmar ston's commentary on the *Rdo rje tshig rkang*, entitled *Gsung sgros ma (The Oral Account)*. He also incorporated several small works by Grags pa rgyal mtshan and Sa skya Paṇḍita.[161] Bla ma dam pa's text was the last full-length commentary on the *Rdo rje tshig rkang* written in Tibet.[162] Together with Sa chen's *Sras don ma* and *Gnyags ma*, and Dmar ston's commentary, the *Man ngag gter mdzod* has since remained one of the essential texts for the study of the *Rdo rje tshig rkang*.

In 1347 Bla ma dam pa also wrote an important instruction manual *('khrid yig)* entitled *Sbas don kun gsal (A Full Clarification of the Hidden Meaning)* that explains both the "three appearances" *(snang gsum)* and the "three continuums" *(rgyud gsum)*, which are the preliminary and main subjects of the Lam 'bras teachings.[163] This text was based on the writings in the *Pod ser* and the earlier manuals by Tshogs sgom, Nyan chen pa, and Gnyag Snying po rgyal mtshan mentioned above, as well as oral teachings.[164] In addition, the *Pod nag* includes several important writings for daily meditations on Hevajra and a history of the Lam 'bras.

For the present study the most significant text in the collection is Bla ma dam pa's 1344 history, the *Ngo mtshar snang ba (Illuminating the Marvels)*, which was written at the ancient retreat center of Kha'u Skyed lhas near Sa skya.[165] This work marks a major turning point in the historical literature of the Lam 'bras. The text begins with a brief account of Buddhism in India and its transmission into Tibet with royal patronage. A unique feature of the *Ngo mtshar snang ba* is that Bla ma dam pa chose to first describe the tradition in Tibet; only at the end of his work does he discuss the life of Virūpa, the Indian source for the lineage.[166] This text is also the earliest surviving history to include brief information on the transmission and sources of the other systems of the Lam skor dgu, the "Nine Cycles of the Path," among which the Lam 'bras is foremost. The last biographical summary in the work is of Chos rgyal 'Phag pa, together with a list of his disciples. Bla ma dam pa completely incorporated Dmar ston's *Zhib mo rdo rje* into his new work. In addition he added much new information, some of which must have been from oral sources, and some no doubt from written records now unavailable. On several occasions where the *Zhib mo rdo rje* only alludes to an event or topic, Bla ma dam pa gives detailed information. These points will be discussed below in the annotations to the translation of Dmar ston's work. More than a hundred years after the death of Bla ma dam pa, a work to clarify his *Ngo mtshar snang ba* was written by Mus srad pa Rdo rje rgyal mtshan. While 'Jam mgon A mes zhabs had access to Mus srad pa's text in 1621, it now seems to have been lost.[167] The reading transmission of the *Pod nag* is still current.

The Pusti dmar chung

Between 1212 and 1216 Grags pa rgyal mtshan finalized the contents of the *Pod ser* and at the same time alluded to the existence of other minor esoteric instructions *(man ngag phra mo)* not included in the collection.[168] From the time of Sa chen and his sons up to the time of Ngor chen Kun dga' bzang po (1382–1456) many different masters had written brief texts that were not included in collections such as the *Pod ser* or the *Pod nag*. These minor texts *(yi ge phra mo)* were finally gathered together into a collection that became known as the *Pusti dmar chung (The Little Red Volume)*.[169] According to Gung ru ba, his teacher Ngor chen searched for all the many minor esoteric instructions originally alluded to by Grags pa rgyal mtshan—as well as those by later teachers—collected them and, so that they would not become scattered again, compiled them into a small volume with a catalogue.[170] The catalogue for the volume was written by Ngor chen's nephew, Rgyal tshab Kun dga' dbang phyug (1424–78), the fourth abbot of Ngor monastery.[171] As was the case with the *Pod ser* and the *Pod nag*, this collection also received its name from the color of the cloth in which the texts were originally wrapped.[172]

The *Pusti dmar chung* contains a large number of texts, almost all concerned with esoteric aspects of the practice of the Lam 'bras. It begins with sixty texts written by authors before the time of Ngor chen.[173] Included in this group are many important writings by Sa chen and his sons that were not included in the *Pod ser*, as well as later works by Sa skya Paṇḍita, Chos rgyal 'Phag pa, Dmar ston, and other masters of the thirteenth and fourteenth centuries. Following these texts are ten supplementary writings by Ngor chen himself.[174] The published edition contains another text by Ngor chen and one by his disciple Mus chen Dkon mchog rgyal mtshan, but these works are not mentioned in the original catalogue.[175] The reading transmission of this entire collection is still unbroken.

The Glegs bam phra mo

After the time of Bla ma dam pa, several different subsects began to appear in the Sa skya tradition. One interesting lineage that later died out was known as the Rdzong tradition, which received its name from the Rdzong chung palace in Sa skya. The palace was the residence of the tradition's founder, Sngags 'chang Gzungs kyi dpal ba (1306–89), who was a disciple of Bla ma dam pa. The Rdzong tradition was later represented by great masters such as Mus srad pa Rdo rje rgyal mtshan.

As mentioned above, when Grags pa rgyal mtshan compiled the *Pod ser* he noted the existence of other minor esoteric instructions (*man ngag phra mo*) not included in the collection.[176] A number of important texts on the Lam 'bras originally composed by the Five Supreme Masters of Sa skya, as well as further works for clarifying some of these according to the Sa skya and the Rdzong traditions, were later gathered into a collection known as the *Glegs bam phra mo (The Volume of Minor Esoteric Instructions).* Though it did not include the earliest writings from the *Pod ser*, or Sa chen's eleven commentaries to the *Rdo rje tshig rkang*, this collection contained many other crucial works on the Lam 'bras. In 1474 Mus srad pa Rdo rje rgyal mtshan composed a very detailed catalogue to this collection.[177]

Although no account of its compilation has been located, the collection may also have been made by Mus srad pa. Unfortunately, it seems to have been lost. From Mus srad pa's catalogue it can be seen that many interesting works by authors such as Gnyag Snying po rgyal mtshan and his disciple Bar ston Rdo rje rgyal mtshan were preserved in this collection, and nowhere else. However, all the writings by the Five Supreme Masters of Sa skya contained in the *Glegs bam phra mo* are also found in the *Pusti dmar chung* that was compiled at approximately the same time. It is to be hoped that the *Glegs bam phra mo* may yet be located in Tibet or China.

Unveiling the Slob bshad

By the middle of the fifteenth century, the monastery established by Kun dga' bzang po in 1429 at Ngor had become a great Sa skya center of tantric study and practice, especially of the Lam 'bras. Ngor chen's main successor, Mus chen Dkon mchog rgyal mtshan, was so highly regarded that the Sa skya throne-holder Bdag chen Blo gros rgyal mtshan traveled in secret to Ngor in 1464 to receive the vows of complete monastic ordination and extensive Dharma teachings from him.[178] Foremost among the teachings he received was a very special transmission of the Lam 'bras:

> To begin with, up through the instructions of the "three appearances" *(snang gsum)* he received [the teachings] together with a huge assembly of numerous spiritual friends and so forth. After the tantric path began, [Mus chen] bestowed [the teachings] in the tradition of the instructions of the profound Tshogs bshad for six months to a few masters and disciples in common. Over either afternoon tea or evening tea he bestowed in a unique transmission (*chig brgyud*), to only this lord, [the instructions] that existed as an oral transmission of the uncommon Slob bshad.[179]

The unique transmission referred to in this passage as the Slob bshad, the "Explication for Disciples," had always existed in the tradition of the Lam 'bras, but had been kept extremely secret. Although Blo gros rgyal mtshan received the uncommon *(thun mong ma yin pa)* transmission from Mus chen at Ngor, he had already received a transmission even more uncommon that the uncommon *(thun mong ma yin pa'i yang thun mong ma yin pa)* from his father 'Jam dbyangs nam mkha' rgyal mtshan (1398–1472) at Sa skya.[180] What is significant now is the terminological distinction of Tshogs bshad, "Explication for the Assembly," and Slob bshad, "Explication for Disciples." These terms had not been used before the time of Bdag chen Blo gros rgyal mtshan, and many would later object to such a classification.[181] For several more generations the Slob bshad instructions remained essentially oral and were completely unknown outside of a very small circle of great teachers and their students. Only a few significant texts were composed by Blo gros rgyal mtshan and his disciple Kun spangs Rdo ring pa (1449–1524).[182]

Although the terminology was new, evidence of a special transmission of unwritten key instructions could be found in the writings of several earlier masters, such as Grags pa rgyal mtshan and Sa skya Paṇḍita. For example, in his catalogue to the *Pod ser*, Grags pa rgyal mtshan said, "I have heard many unwritten esoteric instructions of the oral transmission,

Ruins of Kha'u Brag rdzong

and there are many that have been taught and not taught to others."[183] Sa skya Paṇḍita also stated, "Followers of the Lam 'bras who rely on just the *[Pod ser]* volume will not understand this."[184] Both of these statements are often quoted within the tradition to demonstrate the existence of an oral transmission of the Slob bshad from the earliest period of the Lam 'bras in Sa skya.[185]

Bdag chen Blo gros rgyal mtshan's disciple, Kun spangs Rdo ring pa, passed the esoteric instructions of the Slob bshad to the greatest figure of this tradition, Tshar chen Blo gsal rgya mtsho (1502–66). From 1518 to 1524 Tshar chen received the transmission of the lineage at the isolated retreat site of Kha'u Brag rdzong.[186] The key esoteric instructions were whispered privately by Rdo ring pa to Tshar chen alone, in a small tea room, and other secluded places. And sometimes while they were walking outside alone, or circumambulating a stūpa, Rdo ring pa would squat down and instruct him.[187]

While Tshar chen himself did begin to write some of these special instructions down, most notably in the *Nyi ma'i 'od zer (The Sunbeams),* his definitive explication of the Hevajra practice according to the Slob bshad tradition,[188] it was left to his main students—'Jam dbyangs mkhyen brtse'i dbang phyug and Mang thos klu sgrub rgya mtsho—to record their teacher's uncommon explanations of the full Lam 'bras.

In the winter of 1551 Mang thos klu sgrub first received the entire transmission of the Lam 'bras from Jo nang Kun dga' grol mchog (1507–66), who was a disciple of Kun spangs Rdo ring pa. The next year, when he was twenty-eight years old, he traveled to the hermitage of Chos 'khor yang rtse in the 'Dar valley, where he met Tshar chen and again received the Lam 'bras.[189] More than forty years later, in 1594, Mang thos klu sgrub wrote what has continued to haunt all later critics of the instruction manuals in which he recorded Tshar chen's esoteric transmission of the Slob bshad:

> When I offered before [Tshar chen's] eyes the texts that I had made as summarizing notes, he was delighted and exclaimed, "You are one with fine residual karma from training in secret mantra in previous lifetimes. Otherwise this kind of understanding without great training earlier in this lifetime would never happen."
>
> Once when I went again to offer some summarizing notes, he was delighted and said, "No one else except you understands exactly my Lam 'bras Slob bshad. The one who has collected the quintessence, the practitioner of the Lam 'bras who is like the fat—that's you."[190]

With this statement Mang thos klu sgrub claimed that Tshar chen had approved of his record of the instructions of the Slob bshad. Nevertheless, while Tshar chen himself was beyond criticism in the tradition, Mang thos klu sgrub's interpretations of his teachings have been the subject of considerable debate ever since. Although it is clear from this passage that Mang thos klu sgrub first made summarizing notes of Tshar chen's instructions of the Slob bshad in 1522, the first-person colophons to his finished works provide unambiguous dates of 1587, 1588, and 1589.[191] Mang thos klu sgrub, apparently, maintained the oral tradition of teaching the Slob bshad while using his summarizing notes, and then finalized these texts only in the last decade of his life.

In 1555 Tshar chen became abbot of the ancient monastery of Zhwa lu, and ascended the teaching throne of the great Bu ston Rin chen grub.[192] In 1559, after Mkhyen brtse'i dbang phyug had taken over as Zhwa lu abbot, Tshar chen bestowed the entire transmission of the Lam 'bras Slob bshad. These teachings were given to only eighteen fortunate disciples, led by Mkhyen brtse'i dbang phyug, who also recorded Tshar chen's explanations in summarizing notes.[193]

Mkhyen brtse'i dbang phyug passed away in 1568, at the age of forty-four. Mang thos klu sgrub did not pass away until 1596, at the age of seventy-three, and was certainly the dominant teacher of the Slob bshad tradition for the thirty years following the death of Tshar chen in 1566. The transmission of Mang thos klu sgrub's interpretation of the teachings was upheld by great disciples such as Paṇ chen Ngag dbang chos grags, and spread widely. The transmission of the lineage based on Mkhyen brtse'i dbang phyug's works remained particularly strong at Zhwa lu monastery, where later members of his 'A zha clan, such as Dbang phyug rab brtan (1558–1636) and Bka' 'gyur ba Bsod nams mchog ldan (1603–59), also occupied the abbot's throne.

The detailed works of Mang thos klu sgrub form a complete compendium of information for the meditation practices of this tradition, but they later became rather controversial, largely because of some statements he made concerning the identification of the cause continuum of the universal ground *(kun gzhi rgyu rgyud).*[194] On the other hand, the instruction manuals of Mkhyen brtse'i dbang phyug were left slightly unfinished, perhaps because of his early death.

From among Mkhyen brtse'i dbang phyug's writings, his complete account of the lives of the Indian and Tibetan teachers of the Lam 'bras is a unique work, drawing on many different written sources as well as special oral information.[195] Mkhyen brtse included in his composition basic biographical material culled from earlier Sa skya sources, most notably Bla ma dam pa's *Ngo mtshar snang ba*—and thus ultimately Dmar ston's *Zhib mo rdo rje*—as well as from the history of the Zha ma tradition by Cha rgan. Mkhyen brtse was the first to synthesize material from both these lineages. There are also many details in his work that are not found in earlier extant texts, especially in the lives of 'Brog mi, Se ston, and Zhang ston. These extra touches perhaps represent the private oral information Mkhyen brtse received from Tshar chen. Mkhyen brtse's work is chronological in structure, and often focuses upon what is specifically of esoteric significance in order to understand the import of the external events. The rich extra detail in the stories of the earlier masters, and the informal and lively style of presentation, makes Mkhyen brtse's work an indispensable mine of information about the tradition. Even after a more ambitious history was written in 1621 by the Sa skya throne-holder 'Jam mgon A mes zhabs,[196] Mkhyen brtse'i dbang phyug's text remained the definitive work referred to most in the tradition itself.

For about a hundred years after the death of Mkhyen brtse'i dbang phyug, his incomplete instruction manuals were supplemented by the use of other works by Bla ma dam pa and Mang thos klu sgrub.[197] By the middle of the seventeenth century the use of Mkhyen brtse'i dbang phyug's writings seems to have gained prominence over those of Mang thos klu sgrub, perhaps due to their emphasis by the Zhwa lu masters mentioned above. This trend was furthered by the efforts of the Fifth Tā la'i bla ma, Ngag dbang blo bzang rgya mtsho (1617–82), who wrote a supplement to complete Mkhyen brtse'i dbang phyug's work after receiving the complete transmission of the Slob bshad instructions in 1649 from the Zhwa lu abbot Bka' 'gyur ba Bsod nams mchog ldan.[198]

The main controversy that arose when the Slob bshad first became widely known concerned certain special yoga practices. The practice of the Slob bshad in the Tshar pa tradition is largely the same as the traditional practices according to the mainstream Sa skya and Ngor pa, which became known as the Tshogs bshad, but with some crucial differences of both technique and content. The main difference in technique is that during the teaching of the Slob bshad an experiential instruction *(nyams khrid)* on certain key points is given, and these points are meditated upon. In contrast, during the Tshogs bshad these same points are merely explained by means of a reading transmission *(lung).* In regard to content, the instruction manual of Mang thos klu sgrub contains specific teachings about the intermediate state between lives *(bar do),* dream yoga, and the illusory body that were not found in earlier writings on the Lam 'bras. The supplement to the work of Mkhyen brtse'i dbang phyug later written by the Fifth Tā la'i bla ma also records similar instructions passed orally to him by his teacher Bka' 'gyur ba.[199] The validity of these practices was hotly contested by Sa skya followers who were not involved in the practice of the Slob bshad.

Mang thos klu sgrub and his disciples seem to have become the main defenders of the oral tradition of the Slob bshad.[200] And Tshar chen himself had also written of Kun spangs Rdo ring pa's earlier refutations of those who attacked the oral tradition.[201] Specifically, it was the practice of the dream yoga that attracted criticism. Opponents of the Slob bshad within the Sa skya tradition charged that such techniques had been taken from the Bka' brgyud traditions of the "Six Doctrines" *(chos drug)* of Nāropa or Niguma, and were not part of the 'Lam 'bras. Mang thos klu sgrub disdainfully refuted such objections, and pointedly drew attention to references about dream yoga in the writings of Sa skya Paṇḍita.[202] As for the teachings of illusory body *(sgyu lus)* presented in his instruction manual, he confidently stated, "I have not seen these instructions of illusory body in the writings of former masters, but whether my former teacher clearly saw them or received the meaning, they are certain."[203]

More than 150 years after the death of Mang thos klu sgrub these issues were still such a problem that Ngag dbang blo bzang rgya mtsho, the fifth Tā la'i bla ma, felt it was necessary to strongly defend the Slob bshad teachings, and to refute criticism of the special practices of the tradition.[204] But as the years passed the controversies gradually subsided, and the Slob bshad became accepted throughout the Sa skya tradition as the definitive version of the Lam 'bras. After all, even the greatest masters of the Tshogs bshad, such as Ngor chen Dkon mchog lhun grub (1497–1557), had referred in their writings to the existence of an uncommon oral tradition that they were not recording in their instruction manuals of the Tshogs bshad.[205]

Lord Gayadhara

Chapter Two
The Early Masters in Tibet

1. *The Mystery of Lord Gayadhara*

THE STORY of the early masters of the Lam 'bras that is translated in part two of this book does not delve into the Indian origins of the tradition. Nevertheless, it is an important source of information about the life of the Indian master Gayadhara, who brought the teachings to Tibet in 1041. The Lam 'bras is said to have originated with the tantric goddess Nairātmyā, who bestowed it on the Indian master Virūpa. Virūpa formulated the *Rdo rje tshig rkang* for his disciple Kahna, who then bestowed the teachings on Ḍamarupa, who transmitted them to Avadhūti, who granted them to Gayadhara. Gayadhara is a major figure in Dmar ston's story of the advent of the teachings in Tibet, but there are a number of problems concerning his trips to Tibet and the different names he used during those visits. It will be helpful to first investigate Gayadhara's Indian background and then discuss the problem of his visits and names in some detail.

The Lam 'bras was passed down in a unique transmission *(chig brgyud)* for five generations in India, and Gayadhara was the sole recipient.[206] Although he was an extremely important participant in the influx of the tantras into Tibet in the eleventh century, Gayadhara has remained mysterious and controversial, and is completely unknown to Indian sources.[207] Gayadhara was not only the source of the Lam 'bras in Tibet, but also the Indian master with whom at least five Tibetan translators worked to translate a number of major tantras, such as the *Hevajra*, *Guhyasamāja*, *Kālacakra*, and *Caturpiṭha*, as well as numerous commentaries, making him an even more intriguing figure.[208] Yet there are controversies about Gayadhara's actual identity, the number of trips he made to Tibet, and the validity of some of the tantric traditions he is said to have taught.[209]

Very little is known about Gayadhara's origins. What meager information there is about his life before he first came to Tibet is chiefly found in the different historical studies of the Lam 'bras. Only Mang thos klu sgrub attempted to give dates to Gayadhara, saying that he was born in 753 and died in 1103 at the age of 350![210] The earliest source, written in the late twelfth or early thirteenth century by Rje btsun Grags pa rgyal mtshan, contains only this brief note about Gayadhara before his arrival in Tibet:

> [Avadhūti gave the teachings] to one with the name *kāyastapa* Gayadhara, who was of the caste of scribes, or *kāyastapa*, for a line of kings in the eastern direction. He had some stability in the creation stage, beheld several emanated buddha-bodies, could place a vajra and bell in midair, and actualized the unimpeded ability of corpse-animation and transference.[211]

The *kāyastha* (*kā ya sta pa* in the Tibetan text) were a scribal caste much disliked in India as obstinate bureaucrats, and were described as such in many literary works. Other tantric masters are also known to have come from this caste.[212] In his use of the expression "some stability in the creation stage" *(bskyed rim la cung zad brtan pa),* Grags pa rgyal mtshan is actually conveying specific information about Gayadhara. This expression is technically used to refer to a state of realization where meditative concentration is balanced and all appearances dawn as the deity, due to a total integration of appearances and emptiness. All sounds actually dawn as mantra, and the meditator feels that the stream of blissful primordial awareness has stabilized.[213] Gayadhara was also known to be an expert in the practices of corpse-animation *(grong 'jug),* in which the consciousness is transferred to a fresh and undamaged corpse, and transference *('pho ba),* in which the consciousness is transferred to a higher realm at the moment of death. This may have something to do with why he was said to have lived to the fantastic age of 350. There are also fascinating similarities between the lives of Gayadhara and his contemporary, Pha dam pa Sangs rgyas. Both are said to have been experts in corpse-animation, to have brought important systems of tantric practice to Tibet at about the same time, to have used a number of different names, to have visited Tibet multiple times, and to have lived for hundreds of years before finally passing away in Tibet.[214]

The first Tibetan work to provide a fuller picture of Gayadhara's activities in Tibet is the *Zhib mo rdo rje* of Dmar ston, written in the early thirteenth century not long after Grags pa rgyal mtshan's sketch. But Dmar ston has nothing at all to say about Gayadhara's Indian background. Both the works of Grags pa rgyal mtshan and Dmar ston follow only the Sa skya tradition of the Lam 'bras, recording respectively the stories related by Sa chen Kun dga' snying po and Sa skya Paṇḍita. Only the chronicle of Cha rgan Dbang phyug rgyal mtshan, written in 1304, provides more details about Gayadhara in India. Cha rgan's history includes information from the Zha ma tradition of the Lam 'bras.[215] Later eclectic histories of the Lam 'bras by Mkhyen brtse'i dbang phyug and 'Jam mgon A mes zhabs would draw heavily from Cha rgan's study. Cha rgan states:

> Dhamapa, the Lord of Yogins, told [Avadhūti], "You must bless the continuum of that lord of all mantra and dialectics, the great paṇḍita who knows the five sciences, and is called Gayadhara, the great scribe of *Rupacaṇḍakṣa, the king of Bengal in the east."[216]
>
> [Avadhūti] dispatched a messenger bearing a letter that said, "If the time has come for you to request mantra and put it into practice, come to me."
>
> This coincided with [Gayadhara's] own good omens, and he went into the presence of Avadhūti. When they met, he first offered prostrations and honors, and then placed [Avadhūti's] feet on his head and asked to be graced. Permission was granted, and [Avadhūti] bestowed initiation and the explanatory guidance of the esoteric instructions, as well as giving the prediction of practice.
>
> Practicing as a hidden yogin, [Gayadhara] realized saṃsāra and nirvāṇa to be [like] dream and illusion. Beholding the entire maṇḍala in the hearth of the burnt offering, he was unimpeded in the four styles of enlightened activity. This great paṇḍita-yogin Gayadhara could place his vajra and bell in midair, and sit with crossed legs in midair. He perfected the practices of transference and corpse-animation.[217]

This is the most extensive account of Gayadhara's earlier life, although other isolated references do add some details. Writing about a hundred years after Cha rgan, Ngor chen Kun dga' bzang po repeats some information he says came from the 'Brom tradition of the Lam 'bras. Ngor chen says that after receiving the Hevajra initiation from Avadhūti, Gayadhara sustained for three nights the primordial awareness that had dawned during the initiation, and the meditative concentration of the great stage of Sublime Dharma on the Path of Application *(sbyor lam chos mchog)* arose. Then he was able to leave his hand-drum in midair, where it would rattle by itself, and his parasol would float in midair on its own without being held by a handle, and so forth.[218]

Gayadhara was a tantric lay practitioner, not a monk. The late Sde gzhung Rin po che, Kun dga' bstan pa'i nyi ma, used to humorously tell me how some Tibetan critics had said Gayadhara just came to Tibet to get gold with which to feed his many children back in India. The historian Dpa' bo Gtsug lag phreng ba (1504–66) also specifically noted that Gayadhara was a layman, and in several surviving paintings he is depicted wearing the white robe of a lay Indian master.[219] Furthermore, several sources state that Gayadhara was the father of the Indian master known as Ti pu Gsang sngags sdong po, a disciple of both Nāropa and Maitrīpa who later became one of the teachers of Ras chung Rdo rje grags pa.[220]

The most important of Gayadhara's teachers was Avadhūti, from whom he received the complete transmission of the Lam 'bras. Only the Bka' brgyud master Dpa' bo Gtsug lag phreng ba mentions that Gayadhara was also the disciple of many other adepts, such as Nāropa and Maitrīpa.[221] From the Indian brahmin Śrīdhara, Gayadhara received the *Mar me'i rtse mo lta bu'i gdams ngag (The Oral Instruction Like the Tip of a Lamp Flame),* composed by the great tantric adept Padmavajra, which he translated into Tibetan with 'Brog mi Lo tsā ba. He also received from Śrīdhara the teachings of Kṛṣṇacaryā's *Gtum mo lam rdzogs (The Complete Path of Fierce Fire)* and Kṛṣṇa U tsi ṭa 'chi ba med pa's *Yon po bsrang ba (Straightening the Crooked).* These instructions, which are three of the Lam skor dgu, the "Nine Cycles of the Path," he passed on to 'Brog mi Lo tsā ba.[222] Gayadhara also received the trilogy of *Arali* tantras from a Ceylonese yoginī,[223] who is perhaps to be identified with the Ceylonese yoginī Candramālā, with whom 'Brog mi later translated some works.

This portrait of Gayadhara becomes even more confusing once he appears in Tibet. There is a good deal of disagreement in Tibetan sources about how many times Gayadhara actually came to Tibet. This is compounded by the fact that everyone agrees that he used a number of different names during the various trips. Gayadhara traveled to Tibet three or four times, and was known by at least four or five different names at various points during these trips. Moreover, at least one name he used was also used by another famous (or notorious) Indian master who came to Tibet at approximately the same time. Much of this garbled information can be clarified after sifting through the available sources.

Only the Bka' brgyud author Dpa' bo Gtsug lag phreng ba simply says that Gayadhara came to Tibet many times and used a different name each trip.[224] Histories of the Lam 'bras are quite specific. According to both Grags pa rgyal mtshan and Dmar ston, Gayadhara came to Tibet three times. The first trip occurred after Gayadhara sent a message to 'Brog mi Lo tsā ba to come welcome him at the border of Tibet and Nepal. The second was at the invitation of 'Gos Lo tsā ba Khug pa lhas rtse. The third was at the invitation of Lo tsā ba Gyi jo Zla ba'i 'od zer.[225] The accounts of both Grags pa rgyal mtshan and Dmar ston represent the Sa skya tradition of the Lam 'bras, and neither author makes any mention of the use of names other than Gayadhara.

Cha rgan's chronicle relates a different story, according to which Gayadhara traveled to Tibet on four occasions. During his first trip Gayadhara appeared one day at the door of 'Brog mi Lo tsā ba's retreat. No announcement had been sent. Speaking in Sanskrit, Gayadhara identified himself as a paṇḍita, and begged for food and money. 'Brog mi replied, "I will give you food, but I have no money." After being invited inside, Gayadhara scolded 'Brog mi for saying such an awful thing to a paṇḍita who had appeared at the door of a translator. When 'Brog mi replied that he had said nothing bad, Gayadhara stood in a dancing posture and repeated 'Brog mi's words in Sanskrit. 'Brog mi also repeated what he had said, and even wrote it down. Then they performed a grammatical analysis of what the words meant, and it turned out that he had said, "Cover your ass with your right hand and get out!" 'Brog mi was mortified, bemoaned his ignorance after so many years of study in India, and wept. Gayadhara consoled him, remarking that Sanskrit grammar was like a vast sea that even he did not perfectly understand. After some further discussion, 'Brog mi quickly realized that Gayadhara was an incredibly learned and accomplished master.[226]

Gayadhara had previously been in west Tibet, where he had met the translator Gzhon nu shes rab, also known as Pu rang Lo chung.[227] At his insistence, Gayadhara had promised to return to Pu rang at a later time. Gayadhara now told 'Brog mi that after returning to Pu rang and spending some time there, he had to go back to India. He would return to Tibet in two or three years. They agreed on what Gayadhara would teach and how much 'Brog mi would offer for the instructions. Gayadhara said he would send a message for 'Brog mi to come escort him from Skyid grong near the Tibetan border with Nepal. After six months had passed Pu rang Lo chung arrived at 'Brog mi's place and escorted Gayadhara back to Pu rang, where he spent a year before returning to India. During this trip Gayadhara was known by the name Paṇḍita Dmar po zhabs, "The Red Paṇḍita."[228]

Here is the first mention of a pseudonym for Gayadhara. This alias is found in a number of forms in addition to Paṇḍita Dmar po zhabs, such as Ā tsa ra Dmar po, Lwa ba dmar po, La ba'i na bza' can, and Paṇḍita Lwa ba dmar po can.[229] These names all refer to him as "The "Red Master," or "The One with a Red Robe." These nicknames have caused a great deal of trouble in the historical sources. The reason for the confusion is that a great tantric master from Uḍḍiyana by the name of Prajñāgupta was also active in Tibet during this same period. Prajñāgupta was widely known by many of the same names as Gayadhara, such as Paṇḍita Dmar po zhabs, Ā tsa ra Dmar po, Jo bo Dmar po, and so forth.[230] To complicate matters even more, this "Red Master" Prajñāgupta was a teacher of both 'Brog mi Lo tsā ba and 'Khon Dkon mchog rgyal po, to whom he taught the *karmamudrā* practices of Indrabhūti's *Phyag rgya'i lam skor (The Cycle of the Path of the Mudrā),* which is one of the Lam skor dgu.[231] In Tibetan polemical and historical literature Prajñāgupta was widely accused of spreading evil and perverted tantric sexual practices in Tibet and causing the ruin of many monks and nuns. Due to their identical pseudonyms, Gayadhara was often confused with Prajñāgupta and thus severely condemned by some Tibetan authors. This problem was recognized by 'Jam dbyangs mkhyen brtse'i dbang phyug, who specifically noted that Gayadhara should not be confused with another Ā tsa ra Dmar po found in the lineage of teachings such as those of the tantric guardian goddess Dmag sor ma.[232] Nevertheless, some later authors persisted in identifying them as the same teacher.

Perhaps the most interesting example of this type of polemic confusion is found in the *Ri chos (The Mountain Dharma)* of the Rnying ma and Bka' brgyud master Karma chags med (c. 1605–70).[233] First of all,

Karma chags med identified the Indian paṇḍita Śraddhākaravarman, who was the teacher of Lo chen Rin chen bzang po (958–1055), as the father of the Indian master Ti pu pa. As noted above, this is also said of Gayadhara. In addition, Karma chags med stated that when Śraddhākaravarman came to Tibet a second time he was known as Ā tsa ra Dmar po and spread many perverted teachings.[234] When he returned a third time he was known as Gayadhara and was the teacher of 'Brog mi Lo tsā ba.[235] It would lead us too far astray to prove that Śraddhākaravarman, Gayadhara, and the Ā tsa ra Dmar po (i.e. Prajñāgupta) were in fact three different people. Karma chags med does not seem to have been fully familiar with the historical sources of the Lam 'bras.

According to Cha rgan's account, based on the Zha ma tradition, two years after he had first met 'Brog mi in Tibet, Gayadhara sent a message telling him to come to Skyid grong and welcome him to Tibet again.[236] During this visit he taught the full instructions of the Lam 'bras to 'Brog mi, and they translated many important works, such as the *Kye rdor rgyud gsum (The Tantra Trilogy of Hevajra).* In the Zha ma tradition it is said that he was known as Gayadhara during this second trip.[237] Cha rgan's description of this second trip basically matches what Grags pa rgyal mtshan and Dmar ston refer to as the first trip. Attempting to bring these two versions of Gayadhara's travels into agreement, Mkhyen brtse'i dbang phyug later remarked that Gayadhara apparently came to Tibet four times, but that it was customary by the mid-sixteenth century to consider the first two trips together as one.[238] Nevertheless, opinions still varied in regard to what names Gayadhara used. For example, Mang thos klu sgrub says he was known as Gayadhara during this period, but 'Jam mgon A mes zhabs states that he was known as Lwa ba'i na bza' can or Ā tsa ra Dmar po during the years he spent with 'Brog mi teaching the Lam 'bras.[239]

During his next trip Gayadhara was invited to Tibet by 'Gos Lo tsā ba Khug pa lhas btsas, who had met him in Nepal. In order to compete with his former teacher 'Brog mi, 'Gos Lo tsā ba had left the country to invite the famous master Maitrīpa to Tibet.[240] When 'Gos Lo tsā ba met Gayadhara in Nepal, Gayadhara said, "I am Maitrīpa." 'Gos Lo tsā ba was delighted and invited him to Tibet. Not only did Gayadhara begin this trip by impersonating Maitrīpa, he was apparently known during this visit by yet another name—Sprin gyi shugs can (*Megavegin). This new name is not mentioned in any of the early histories of the Lam 'bras, such as those of Grags pa rgyal mtshan, Dmar ston, Cha rgan, or Bla ma dam pa. But the Zha ma tradition of the Lam 'bras did maintain that Gayadhara was known as Paṇḍita Sprin gyi shugs can during this trip.[241]

According to Ngor chen, the identification of Gayadhara with Sprin gyi shugs can originally came from 'Gos Lo tsā ba's tradition of the *Guhyasamāja tantra*. Ngor chen also points out that if Gayadhara was indeed the master known as Sprin gyi shugs can, he must be included among the eighty-four great adepts of India. One of the great adepts is addressed by this name in a collection of eulogies composed by the Indian teacher Vajrāsanapāda. But in his eulogy Vajrāsanapāda states that the master known as Sprin gyi shugs can was born in the *kṣatriya* caste *(rgyal rigs)*, which conflicts with what is known about Gayadhara.[242] The *Guhyasamāja tantra* was among the many works that Gayadhara and 'Gos Lo tsā ba translated together. In 'Jam mgon A mes zhabs's study of the Guhyasamāja tradition, written in 1634, it is clear that 'Gos Lo tsā ba received the *Guhyasamāja tantra* from Paṇḍita Sprin gyi shugs can, and reference is also made to the comments by Ngor chen mentioned above.[243] In yet another text, A mes zhabs simply states that Gayadhara was known as Sprin gyi shugs can during this visit.[244] During this trip to Tibet, Gayadhara gave 'Gos Lo tsā ba many tantric instructions, but not the Lam 'bras.

All the available sources agree that when Gayadhara was invited to Tibet for the last time, by the translator Gyi jo Zla ba'i 'od zer, he was simply known as Gayadhara.[245] According to Ngor chen, during this visit Gayadhara and Gyi jo completed many important translations of tantric commentaries, and Gayadhara transmitted the complete Lam 'bras to Gyi jo. Gyi jo translated Virūpa's *Rdo rje tshig rkang*, and his successors wrote commentaries, lineage histories, and so forth. However, by Ngor chen's time there were no remaining upholders of Gyi jo's tradition of the Lam 'bras.[246] Gyi jo's tradition was the only lineage of the Lam 'bras in Tibet that did not pass through 'Brog mi Lo tsā ba.

In 1103, while staying with some disciples of Gyi jo in Tibet, Gayadhara became aware of his impending death.[247] As noted above, the earliest sources of the tradition mention his expertise in the transference of consciousness at the moment of death. The *Zhib mo rdo rje* records this in detail:

> The lord said to the two great meditators Se and Rog, "All my sons, you must not lack diligence in practice! Even though I only went back and forth between Tibet and India, and I have

not practiced much, when a mantra practitioner dies, he dies like this."

He sat with body in the crossed-legged position. He took the vajra and bell in both hands and performed the globe of light transference.[248] A light about the size of a pellet ejected from the crown of his head, went as far as everyone could see into the sky, and he passed away.[249]

Lord Gayadhara's legacy remains strong today. While the Lam 'bras is certainly the most important tantric system he introduced in Tibet, Gayadhara's lineage of the *Kye rdor rgyud gsum*, which was transmitted through 'Brog mi Lo tsā ba, and his lineage of the *Guhyasamaja tantra*, which was transmitted through 'Gos Lo tsā ba, have also survived to the present.

2. *The Tibetan Masters*

In addition to Gayadhara, the *Zhib mo rdo rje* of Dmar ston discusses the lives of 'Brog mi Lo tsā ba and his disciples, Se ston Kun rig (1025–1122) and his disciples,[250] Sa chen Kun dga' snying po and his disciples, and the first part of the life of Sa skya Paṇḍita. Dmar ston's stories of these masters formed the basis for all later treatments of this subject in the Sa skya tradition of the Lam 'bras. However, as in the case of Gayadhara's trips to Tibet, important supplementary, and sometimes contradictory, information was recorded in other Lam 'bras lineages, most notably that of the Zha ma tradition as represented by Cha rgan's chronicle. The most significant variations will be discussed in the notes to the translation of Dmar ston's text in part two.

Gayadhara first taught the Lam 'bras to 'Brog mi Lo tsā ba and later to Gyi jo Zla ba'i 'od zer. As mentioned above, the tradition of Gyi jo never spread widely, although it did survive for several hundred years. On the other hand, from 'Brog mi and his spiritual descendents a large number of lineages developed and spread throughout Tibet. Although their lists differed somewhat, Tibetan historians generally agreed that there were eighteen lineages of the Lam 'bras in Tibet, and sometimes condensed this number to twelve or expanded it to twenty-four. This identification of eighteen lineages of the Lam 'bras seems to have been made first by the early Sa skya master Byang chub dpal, also known as

Khams chen Rgan lhas pa.[251] With the sole exception of Gyi jo's tradition, the pivotal figure in all these lineages was 'Brog mi Lo tsā ba, whose story is also the main focus of the *Zhib mo rdo rje*.

'Brog mi was born in 993, early in the second spread of Buddhism in Tibet, which is usually reckoned to have begun with the translation work of Lo chen Rin chen bzang po (958–1055). He grew to become one of the most important Tibetan interpreters of Indian tantric lore, especially the traditions of the anuttarayoga class. 'Brog mi first learned the Indian vernacular from some Indian beggar-yogis in Tibet, and then as a young man traveled to Nepal, where he studied for a short period before continuing to India. He received many teachings from great Newar and Indian masters, much of which will be described in Dmar ston's history. 'Brog mi spent thirteen years studying in Nepal and India. During these years, and later in Tibet, he translated nearly seventy tantric texts with Gayadhara, Prajñendraruci, also known as Vīravajra, the Ceylonese yoginī Candramālā,[252] Ratnavajra, Ratnaśrīmitra,[253] and perhaps also the "Red Paṇḍita" Prajñāgupta.[254] He also received important esoteric transmissions from the Indian master Amoghavajra.[255]

After his return to Tibet, 'Brog mi made his residence in a complex of thirteen caves at Mu gu lung, where he lived with his consort and disciples.[256] There he received the transmission of the Lam 'bras from Gayadhara, and in the "Translation Cave" *(sgra sgyur lo tsā phug)* he and Gayadhara translated the *Hevajra tantra* and its explanatory tantras, the *Vajrapañjara* and *Sampuṭa*, all in 1043.[257]

'Brog mi's two most important teachers were Gayadhara, from whom he received the Lam 'bras and other esoteric transmissions, and Prajñendraruci, more often known as Vīravajra, from whom he also received the transmission of the *Kye rdor rgyud gsum* and various esoteric instructions. As his Indian teachers had advised him to do, 'Brog mi later demanded much gold from his own disciples in order to test their sincerity and emphasize the value of the oral instructions. Vīravajra had told 'Brog mi in India, "Material wealth is necessary to bring into alignment the dependently arisen connections of secret mantra." And Gayadhara also emphasized to 'Brog mi the importance of testing his students with demands for food and wealth.[258]

Obviously, 'Brog mi was charismatic and eccentric. His enigmatic actions that sometimes defy easy explanation should be understood in the context of his role as a tantric master. Eccentric behavior in Buddhist tantric traditions is as old as the traditions themselves, as exemplified by the eighty-four great Indian adepts, such as Virūpa. The actions of Gayadhara and 'Brog mi are perfect examples of "deliberate behavior" *(brtul zhugs spyod pa),* which is actually prescribed in the tantras and used for specific purposes by those who have progressed to the highest levels of the tantric path.[259] One need look no further than the life of 'Brog mi's student and younger contemporary Mar pa Chos kyi blo gros to find clear evidence of a similar but better known eccentric master.[260]

'Brog mi was apparently the most influential and prolific translator of the anuttarayoga tantras in Tibet. But as the story of his life will show, he was first of all a great tantric master who devoted himself to translation and teaching until the age of sixty-two, and then spent the remaining twenty or more years of his life chiefly in solitary meditation.[261] Before his departure from Tibet after teaching 'Brog mi the Lam 'bras, Gayadhara made some prophecies that are important for understanding certain events at the end of 'Brog mi's life. Gayadhara told 'Brog mi that there would be serious problems with his sons, and that his family line would end with them. He urged 'Brog mi himself to practice the techniques for the transference of consciousness at death *('pho ba),* and said that he would then be able to proceed directly to the pure land of Khecara without experiencing the intermediate state *(bar do)* between lives.[262] The *Zhib mo rdo rje* is the earliest source to mention the strange events surrounding 'Brog mi's death:

> At the point of passing away ['Brog mi] said, "Leave this body of mine for seven days without burning! In seven days this same intrinsic awareness will enter into this same body, and I will achieve the sublime attainment of Mahāmudrā."
>
> But without inspection the people quickly moved [his body] from the place while the warmth had not faded. So it has been stated.[263]

A detailed description of the circumstances surrounding 'Brog mi's death first appears in the chronicle of Cha rgan. After warning those closest to him that there would be trouble, and that they must abide by his orders, 'Brog mi sat in the meditation posture and passed away without any signs of illness. After three days had passed, an astrological calculation indicated that if the master's body were not cremated by noon two days later there would be evil consequences for 'Brog mi's sons. Several of the elder disciples decided that nothing was now more important than the welfare of the sons Indra and Rdo rje, and that they must act according to the astrological calculation. On the fifth day, three disciples and the astrologer started to move the body and discovered that the warmth had not faded. The astrologer assured the disciples that this was not unusual, and they cremated 'Brog mi's remains. One of the three disciples died on each of the next three days. On the fifth day the astrologer died. The rumor began to circulate that 'Brog mi had been cremated alive, and his family and the disciples began to fight among themselves. The disciples scattered to different places, and Indra and Rdo rje were at odds. Then Indra burned to death in a bizarre accident and Rdo rje died after hearing the news. By means of the practice of the transference of consciousness, 'Brog mi Lo tsā ba is said to have passed straight to the pure land of Khecara without experiencing the intermediate state between lives.[264]

Although a number of 'Brog mi's disciples are mentioned in the *Zhib mo rdo rje*, very few received the entire Lam 'bras. The first of those who did was Lha btsun Ka li, the brother of 'Brog mi's wife. But he died young and never taught. Most histories of the Lam 'bras list a transmission of the teachings to 'Brog mi's sons Indra and Rdo rje as one of the eighteen lineages, but they also died before spreading the tradition widely.[265]

The powerful sorcerer 'Brom De pa ston chung received the entire Lam 'bras from 'Brog mi, and a transmission from him is listed as one of the eighteen lineages, although there is some disagreement about this in the historical accounts. According to the *Zhib mo rdo rje*, 'Brom did not transmit the lineage to anyone. But Ngor chen later traced two different lineages of the Lam 'bras transmitted from 'Brom, one of which continued for eight generations and the other for five. Therefore, Ngor chen says, the statement in the *Zhib mo rdo rje* is totally false.[266]

The tale of 'Brom is told in detail in the *Zhib mo rdo rje* and all subsequent histories of the Lam 'bras. Early in life 'Brom had cruelly destroyed seven of his enemies through his expertise in sorcery. Afterward, he felt great remorse for his actions, and went to 'Brog mi seeking oral instructions with which to purify his sins and attain enlightenment. In this respect there are striking similarities between the early lives of 'Brom and Rje btsun Mi la ras pa. According to Cha rgan's explanation, for six years 'Brom made great offerings to 'Brog mi each day during the teaching of the Lam 'bras. Then, just as the teachings were almost complete, he ran out of gold and could not find any to purchase. He asked 'Brog mi if he could use something of equal value for an offering. 'Brog mi replied, "If you're out of gold, I'm out of Dharma." But 'Brog mi's wife, Mdzes ldan 'od chags, gave 'Brom the necessary gold in exchange for a fine necklace of *gzi* beads that belonged to his consort. Using this gold for offerings, 'Brom received the few remaining teachings of the Lam 'bras. Cha rgan also tells the eerie tale of how 'Brom's consort died after having a vision of many women beckoning her and telling her that 'Brom was coming the next year and that they had come to take her away in advance.[267] 'Brom's tragic death and 'Brog mi's emotional reaction will also perhaps remind the reader of the story of Mar pa Lo tsā ba and the death of his son Dar ma mdo sde.

Se ston Kun rig, also known as Se mkhar chung ba, was the final recipient of the Lam 'bras from 'Brog mi, and it is through this simple shepherd that the Sa skya and Zha ma lineages are traced.[268] Se ston's story is told in detail in the *Zhib mo rdo rje*, and further information from the Zha ma tradition is provided by Cha rgan. For example, when some people hoeing their fields first told Se ston about 'Brog mi, he fainted for a moment. When he was revived he decided to go to Mu gu lung. Se ston discussed his idea with a young relative who knew where his mother had hidden some gold. They secretly took the gold to provide them with funds for food during their trip, and joined together with about twenty young tantric practitioners they met who were also going to see the face of the famous 'Brog mi Lo tsā ba. When Se ston first saw 'Brog mi, tears cascaded down his face, a great warmth spread through his body, all manifest phenomena seemed to shimmer and swirl about him, and he cried out and began to shake. Everyone looked around to see what had happened, and 'Brog mi asked him what was wrong. Se ston replied that something had happened that he couldn't explain. 'Brog mi was pleased and said that his blessings had entered into Se ston, and made some further auspicious comments. After a while the other young travelers left, but 'Brog mi's consort, Mdzes ldan 'od chags, advised Se ston to stay and request initiation because of the auspicious things the master had said.[269] Thereafter Se ston endured severe trials under 'Brog mi, but eventually pleased him with his devotion and persistence, and by his great desire for the esoteric instructions. He stayed with 'Brog mi and his wife for seventeen years and mastered the entire Lam 'bras and related systems of tantric practice.

The most important of Se ston's disciples were Zhang ston Chos 'bar and his brother Gzi brjid 'bar, and Lady Ma gcig Zha ma (1062–1149) and her brother Lord Khum bu ba Chos rgyal (1069–1144).[270] The "female lineage" *(mo brgyud)* of the Zha ma tradition passed from Ma gcig, while the "male lineage *(pho brgyud)* passed from her brother Lord Khum bu ba. These are usually counted as two of the eighteen lineages of the Lam 'bras.[271] While little is known about her brother, Ma gcig Zha ma's life was recorded in detail for the first time in the *Zhib mo rdo rje.* Ma gcig was a great tantric adept who had been the consort of the translator Rma Chos 'bar (1044–89) and had also studied with the Indian master Pha dam pa Sangs rgyas at Ding ri. But she was plagued by strange illnesses for many years. After hearing that Se ston was a great expert in techniques for the removal of impediments, Ma gcig, who was also known as Zha chung ma, came to him with her problems. The earliest record of their meeting is found in the *Zhib mo rdo rje*:

> While she told the story of how she had become ill, he was tapping a cane on one of his boots, and commenting, "That is also a meditative concentration, that is also a meditative concentration."
>
> When the master asked, "Well, didn't it happen like this to you?" it matched Zha chung ma's experiences, and she struck her forehead on the ground and prostrated, exclaiming, "Lord, are you the one known as the Buddha?"[272]

Se ston taught Ma gcig the Lam 'bras, and she was cured by the practice of the esoteric instructions. Ma gcig achieved the highest results in meditation, but according to the histories of the Sa skya tradition she and her brother did not receive a few final minor instructions from Se ston, and left him prematurely.

The Sa skya transmission of the Lam 'bras is traced through Zhang ston Chos 'bar, the elder of the two brothers who received the instructions from Se ston. These brothers first worked as finishers of scriptural texts. According to Cha rgan, when Se ston later agreed to teach them the Lam 'bras he said that for expertise it was necessary to learn the technical terms and jargon, and for realization it was necessary to meditate. The elder brother Chos 'bar said, "I will meditate," and so Se ston told Gzi brjid 'bar to focus on the technical meaning of the words. They did as they were told and the master was extremely pleased with both of them. They received the entire teachings of the Lam 'bras over a period of seven years. Five years later the younger brother Gzi brjid 'bar died of a stroke *(grib)*. Zhang ston Chos 'bar led the life of a hidden yogin *(sbas pa'i rnal 'byor)*, practicing the Lam 'bras with great energy at night, but farming and teaching the Rdzogs chen during the day. After eight years of living like this he gained magical abilities and clairvoyance, and began to carefully give teachings to individual worthy disciples.[273]

Zhang ston's greatest student, Sa chen Kun dga' snying po, was born in 1092. Stag tshang Lo tsā ba Shes rab rin chen (b. 1405) briefly mentions the circumstances of Sa chen's birth in his genealogy of the 'Khon family,[274] but the full story is found only in the account by Sa chen's descendent 'Jam mgon A mes zhabs. According to the account of A mes zhabs, 'Khon Dkon mchog rgyal po's teacher Gnam Kha'u pa became concerned that Dkon mchog rgyal po's wife Rdo rje dbang phyug ma had not borne an heir. Gnam Kha'u pa had a vision of Avalokiteśvara Khasarpaṇa in the sky above the nearby Dkar gong Valley and knew this was an omen that an emanation of Avalokiteśvara was to be born. In order to establish the necessary auspicious circumstances for this to occur, Gnam Kha'u pa repeatedly called for Dkon mchog rgyal po to come up the valley from Sa skya to his residence in Kha'u Skyed lhas for teachings. Dkon mchog rgyal po would usually ride home again before evening. One afternoon they talked later than usual and then the master gave him the price of a bowl of beer and told him to be sure and spend the night in Dkar gong Valley. Dkon mchog rgyal po was very disappointed that the master kept him late in conversation and then didn't even invite him to spend the night. But he knew to carry out whatever his teacher told him, and rode down to Dkar gong Valley before sunset. At the same time, by auspicious coincidence, the woman Ma gcig Zhang mo had walked down to the stream to draw water and was returning home. The two of them met. Dkon mchog rgyal po asked her for a place to spend the night, and Ma gcig invited him to her home. He asked her to sell him some beer, and when she brought a delicious drink in a fine uncracked bowl he realized what an auspicious situation it was and spent the evening there as his teacher had advised. Some months passed, and when it became known that Ma gcig Zhang mo was pregnant, the master Gnam Kha'u pa invited her up the valley to a place near his retreat center in order to care for her. After Sa chen was born, he took the infant on his lap and made many predictions of the child's future greatness.[275]

Sa chen Kun dga' snying po first met Se ston Kun rig when the latter was a very old man, and briefly heard about the Lam 'bras from

Top: Ruins of Ma gcig Zhang mo's home

Bottom: Ruins of stūpa and temple at Phru ma

him. However, Sa chen did not receive the teachings in full form until Zhang ston Chos 'bar, also known as Lord Dgon pa ba, instructed him for a period of four years beginning in 1120.[276] The *Zhib mo rdo rje* of Dmar ston is the first text to describe the circumstances:

> Then the master [Sa chen] took a full leather bag of tea, a bolt of yellow silk, and a coat of armor, arrived in front of Lord Dgon pa ba at Sag thang in Dings, and requested a meeting. Lord Dgon pa ba was a hidden yogin, and although he was ordained, he was spinning thread and making a lot of random talk in the midst of some vagrants, and came over wearing a goatskin. When [Sa chen] made a gift of the coat of armor and requested the Oral Instructions [of the Lam 'bras], Lord Zhang replied, "Are you not mistaken? I don't even know the Dharma you want. You so-called practitioners of the new mantra are very opinionated. I teach the *Rdzogs chen rtsa mun ti*, the *Bram ze'i skor*, and so forth," and didn't agree.[277]
>
> [Sa chen] asked again and again, but he said, "I don't know it," and didn't agree. Then the great master thought, "Well, does he really not know it?" turned around, and left.[278]

Through a further series of interesting events, Zhang ston came to realize that Sa chen was the son of Dkon mchog rgyal po, who had been one of the teachers of his own master, Se ston, and agreed to teach him the Lam 'bras. After receiving the complete transmission, Sa chen then spent the next eighteen years in intense meditation, forbidden by Zhang ston from teaching or even mentioning the name of the instructions.

The histories of the Lam 'bras list among the eighteen lineages both a sequential transmission *(ring brgyud)* and a direct transmission *(nye brgyud)* of the teachings to Sa chen. The sequential transmission was received from Zhang ston. In 1138, when Sa chen was forty-six years old, he experienced an extraordinary visit from the great adept Virūpa, who bestowed on him the direct transmission of the Lam 'bras.

When Zhang ston's eighteen-year restriction expired, Sa chen first taught the Lam 'bras to A seng Rdo rje brtan pa in 1141. At the same time he recorded the *Rdo rje tshig rkang* in writing, and composed a brief verse commentary, the *A seng ma*.[279] During the following years Sa chen taught the Lam 'bras to his sons, Slob dpon Bsod nams rtse mo and Rje btsun Grags pa rgyal mtshan, as well as many other disciples. As described in chapter one, Grags pa rgyal mtshan was especially important for the codification of the Lam 'bras, both by means of editing his father's writings and composing new treatises himself. Nevertheless, there is scant biographical information about him in Dmar ston's chronicle or in other histories of the Lam 'bras.[280]

The tradition of Sa chen's early disciple Phag mo gru pa Rdo rje rgyal po is also considered to be one of the eighteen lineages of the Lam 'bras.[281] Phag mo gru pa and his writings on the Lam 'bras have been discussed above in chapter one. Phag mo gru pa's lineage of these teachings is considered to be Sa skya, even though his writings were later passed down in the Bka' brgyud tradition.

The final section in Dmar ston's story of the masters of this tradition is a biography of his own teacher, Sa skya Paṇḍita Kun dga' rgyal mtshan. The treatment of Sa skya Paṇḍita's life is incomplete because it was written while he was still at Sa skya, decades before his debate with the Hindu teacher Harinanda (c. 1240) and his later departure for Mongolia in 1244. Internal evidence shows that Dmar ston's text was written after the death of Grags pa rgyal mtshan in 1216, which is the only date in the text, but before the composition of Sa skya Paṇḍita's major works. It may be significant that Dmar ston refers the reader of the *Zhib mo rdo rje* to Sa skya Paṇḍita's biography of Grags pa rgyal mtshan, but mentions no biographies of Sa skya Paṇḍita himself. The *Zhib mo rdo rje* may be the earliest record of the events in the first part of Sa skya Paṇḍita's life. In chapter three, it will be shown that the annotations found in the manuscript of the *Zhib mo rdo rje* also represent very early material about Sa skya Paṇḍita's life. This section in the *Zhib mo rdo rje* can now be identified as Dmar ston's lost biography of Sa skya Paṇḍita listed in the colophon of the *Gsung sgros ma* biography attributed to Ngor chen Kun dga' bzang po.[282]

The importance of Sa skya Paṇḍita's teachings for the tradition of the Lam 'bras cannot be overestimated. Sa skya Paṇḍita is famous for being a consummate scholar, and even in the *Zhib mo rdo rje* this is how he is portrayed by Dmar ston, although his perfection of meditative concentration is also mentioned. Most previous research has focused solely on the scholarly aspect of his life and legacy.[283] Nevertheless, Sa skya Paṇḍita was also a supreme master of tantric meditation. He played a crucial role in the transmission of the practice lineage of the Lam 'bras in particular and all other tantric teachings of the Sa skya tradition in general. Everything passed through him. Although it is not emphasized in

Tibetan biographies and histories, Sa skya Paṇḍita obviously performed many years of meditation retreat and practice, without which he would never have been able to transmit the tantric teachings. And his practice of tantric meditation was not limited to the traditional Sa skya practices. For example, he had a special interest in the Kālacakra, and received all the textual and practice transmissions from the great master of Kashmir, Śākyaśrībhadra (1140s–1225?). Sa skya Paṇḍita then practiced the Six-branch Yoga of the Kālacakra in a dark room *(mun khang)* beneath the library of the ancient Sgo rum temple in Sa skya. He is said to have had special success in the practice of certain prāṇāyāma techniques included in the third of the six branches.[284]

Sa skya Paṇḍita's emphasis on the removal of doubts through rigorous intellectual discipline and reflection was specifically intended to prepare his students for serious meditation practice. The following quote from his disciple Tshogs sgom Kun dga' dpal (1210–1307) illustrates this point well:

> As for the necessity of removing doubts through study and reflection, the Dharma Lord [Sa skya Paṇḍita] said, "This is extremely important. Some now say, 'I'm going to stay in the mountains for all the years of my life.' They will have no [genuine] experiences whatsoever. If you listen to me, and if you study for ten years and then meditate, the genuine [experiences] will arise."[285]

There are many other instances in the earliest texts of the Lam 'bras that make it clear how concerned Sa skya Paṇḍita was with the actual practice of meditation, and not merely with study and teaching. Some of his most influential works, such as the monumental *Sdom gsum rab dbye (Distinguishing the Three Vows),* were also written as a result of visionary inspiration. Sa skya Paṇḍita's disciple Grub chen Yon tan dpal (1237–1323), who was one of the main upholders of his tradition of meditation practice, made the following comments about the composition of this famous text:

> In general the practice of the Doctrine is the practice of study, reflection, and meditation, but today some types of serious meditators say, "If you understand one word, that is one too many. If you understand two words, that is two too many."

> Because they refute explication and study, the Doctrine has nearly died out.
>
> When the Dharma Lord [Sa skya Paṇḍita] prayed to Mañjuśrī he was told in a dream, "Emphasize explication and study, compose a treatise distinguishing the three vows, and serve the Doctrine."
>
> Because he acted in that way there is a continuity of the Doctrine today.[286]

While Sa skya Paṇḍita was both a serious practitioner and a teacher of tantra, it would seem that he did not have many disciples who strenuously practiced meditation.[287] From among those who did, Grub chen Yon tan dpal, Tshogs sgom Kun dga' dpal, and Sa skya Paṇḍita's nephew Chos rgyal 'Phags pa (1235–80) continued his teachings of the practice lineage. The Bka' brgyud master Rgyal ba Yang dgon pa (1213–58) was also a disciple who dedicated his life to meditation practice, including that of the Lam 'bras.[288] But it was Dmar ston Chos kyi rgyal po who had the most important role in recording his master's tantric teachings in writing.

Both during and soon after Sa skya Paṇḍita's lifetime several further lineages of the Lam 'bras developed in Tibet. Some of these transmissions were partially connected to the Sa skya tradition, while others were offshoots of the Zha ma line, and still others were combinations of several lineages. All are listed among the eighteen lineages of the Lam 'bras. For example, the master Ko brag pa Bsod nams rgyal mtshan (1170–1249) combined the teachings of both the "male" and "female" lines of the Zha ma tradition, as well as the Six-branch Yoga of Kālacakra, and his lineage was later passed down mostly in the Bka' brgyud tradition.[289] Cha rgan Dbang phyug rgyal mtshan, whose history has been frequently mentioned in the pages of this book, combined the teachings of both Zha ma lineages with that of the Sa skya tradition.[290]

Jo nang Kun spangs pa, the founder of Jo nang monastery, made extensive rearrangements in the structure of the *Rdo rje tshig rkang* and combined instructions from the Sa skya, Zha ma, and 'Brom lineages. His disciple La stod Dbang rgyal then combined the teachings of the Lam 'bras, the Six-branch Yoga of Kālacakra, and the Rdzogs chen into an unprecedented system. Both these Jo nang lineages were considered corrupt by later writers, and were soon not even followed in the Jo nang tradition itself.[291] Several other systems are also listed among the eighteen lineages. Mang lam Zhig po seems to have combined instructions from 'Brog mi's sons and the two Zhang ston brothers. The adept Lce sgom pa received the Sa skya tradition from Sa chen's disciple Rgyal tsha Tal phug pa (1118–95), the founder of the Khro phu branch of the Bka' brgyud tradition, and combined the Lam 'bras and the teachings of the Mahāmudrā or Phyag chen (Great Seal).[292] All of these traditions died out or were absorbed into the main Sa skya lineage centuries ago.

Outer reliquary of Sa chen

Sa skya Paṇḍita

Chapter Three
Dmar ston and the *Zhib mo rdo rje*

1. *The Author*

DMAR STON CHOS KYI RGYAL PO (c. 1198–c. 1259) was an important figure in the transmission of several systems of tantric practice in the Sa skya tradition. His primary legacy is the invaluable record he left of the history and meditation practices of the Lam 'bras. Dmar ston was one of the chief disciples of Sa skya Paṇḍita, and his works were composed with the specific intention of recording Sa skya Paṇḍita's own teachings of the Lam 'bras.[293] Dmar ston's writings are especially significant because Sa skya Paṇḍita himself wrote no major works on the Lam 'bras and only a handful of brief texts concerning its practice.

The primary source of information on Dmar ston's life is a short biography written by Glo bo mkhan chen Bsod nams lhun grub (1456–1531). This work was apparently based on a history of the Vajrapāṇi Mahācakra teachings, of which Dmar ston was the foremost master in Tibet.[294] Dmar ston's father died when the boy was still young, but at an early age he received from his uncle, Dmar Brtson 'grus seng ge, the transmissions of a number of tantric lineages, and is said to have mastered them all. At the age of sixteen his uncle sent him to Sa skya to study with the peerless master of the Vajrayāna, Rje btsun Grags pa rgyal mtshan.[295] For three years Dmar ston studied the *Cakrasaṃvara mūla tantra* and became skilled enough to give some initial teachings to others. From Grags pa rgyal mtshan and Zur chos pa Rig 'dzin grags pa he also received the *Kye rdor rgyud gsum* and various oral instructions related to these tantric scriptures.[296]

After Rje btsun Grags pa rgyal mtshan passed away in 1216, Dmar ston began to study with his teacher's nephew, Sa skya Paṇḍita. He received ordination from Sa skya Paṇḍita, who gave him the name Chos kyi rgyal mtshan. Dmar ston was an extremely bright youth. Under Sa skya Paṇḍita's direction he is said to have mastered in one year a number of texts, including Dharmakīrti's *Pramāṇavārttika*, the *Sa sde lnga (The Five Divisions of the Yogacaryābhūmi)*,[297] and Sa skya Paṇḍita's own *Tshad ma rigs gter (Treasury of the Science of Epistemology)*.[298] In one more year of serious study Dmar ston is said to have mastered the major scriptures of the tantric tradition together with their commentaries, such as the *Hevajra tantra*, the *Vajrapañjara tantra*, the *Kālacakra tantra*, the *Kṛṣṇa Yamāri*, the *Tattvasaṃgraha*, and the *Caturpiṭha*.

According to his biographer, when Dmar ston received the Lam 'bras from Sa skya Paṇḍita he experienced immediate results.[299] He then composed a number of texts recording Sa skya Paṇḍita's teachings. The most important of these are the *Gzhung bshad dmar ma (Dmar's Explication of the Treatise)*, also known as the *Gsung sgros ma (The Oral Account)*, which is a commentary on the *Rdo rje tshig rkang* of Virūpa; and the *Zhib mo rdo rje*, which is a collection of stories about the early Tibetan masters of the Lam 'bras. Both of these texts will be discussed below. When the *Gsung sgros ma* was offered to Sa skya Paṇḍita for his inspection he was delighted and exclaimed:

> You have gained an understanding of the words in my explanation, without leaving out a single word. You will become a great expert who achieves mastery of everything knowable.[300]

At this time Sa skya Paṇḍita gave him the name Chos kyi rgyal po ("King of Dharma"), by which he is most often known. Dmar ston himself recorded Sa skya Paṇḍita's pleasure on seeing the *Zhib mo rdo rje*:

> When this text of stories was offered into the hands of the great Master Translator [Sa skya Paṇḍita], he was pleased and praised it highly, so it should be respectfully accepted without doubts.[301]

Dmar ston probably studied with Sa skya Paṇḍita for eight years.[302] During this time he received various tantric initiations and oral instructions, as well as many reading transmissions, such as those for the works of the earlier founders of Sa skya and of Sa skya Paṇḍita's own writings. It is certain that Dmar ston was in Sa skya at least through the water-horse year of 1222, when he requested from Sa skya Paṇḍita a short text on the removal of impediments.[303]

At the end of these years of study, Dmar ston was ordered by Sa skya Paṇḍita to begin teaching the *Kālacakra*, the *Hevajra*, and the *Pramāṇa-vārttika*. He held classes for six months at Sa skya on these subjects, gathering many disciples. His reputation as a great expert is said to have rivaled even that of Sa skya Paṇḍita himself.[304] Dmar ston later traveled to Dbus and established a large Dharma institute where he gave many initiations and teachings. After some time, Sgang ston Shes rab bla ma, who had been a disciple of Dmar ston in Sa skya, invited him from Dbus back to Gtsang.[305] Sgang ston offered Dmar ston the monastery of Lhas phug in the upper valley of Spun gsum. Dmar ston lived there and gathered many disciples while giving explanations of the tantras such as the *Kālacakra* and the *Vajrapañjara*, and teaching their systems of meditation.

When Dmar ston was forty-nine years old (c. 1247), he gave his seventeen year old son, Dmar Shākya dbang phyug, many initiations, reading transmissions, and esoteric instructions.[306] According to his biography, when Dmar ston was sixty-one years old (c. 1259) he gave instructions for a vast offering to be arranged on the fifteenth day of the middle month of summer. He performed the practice of Vajrapāṇi Mahācakra and then engaged in the perfection stage prāṇāyāma practices. While holding a vajra and bell, he rang the bell, and at that moment a vapor is said to have risen from the crown of his head as he passed away. Witnesses observed many rainbows touch his remains and saw the room fill with light. When he was cremated there were also said to have been many relics, and images of Vajrapāṇi Mahācakra and Mañjuśrī are reported to have appeared on his skull.[307] The monastery of Lhas phug was taken over by Dmar ston's son, Dmar Shākya dbang phyug, who fulfilled his father's wishes by maintaining the lineages such as that of Vajrapāṇi Mahācakra.[308]

Dmar ston had many disciples, but according to his biography there were six outstanding ones. Sgang ston Shes rab bla ma and Tshogs sgom Zhig po from Khro phu were expert in the yogas of the subtle channels and vital winds *(rtsa rlung)* described in Dmar ston's commentary on the Lam 'bras. Sgang ston was the most important of Dmar ston's disciples, and the teacher who later passed on the transmission of his works on the Lam 'bras. Snyi ba Rin chen from 'Bring 'tshams was an expert who reached attainment through the practices of Cakrasaṃvara according to the system of the great Indian adept Lūhipa.[309] Shes rab grub Mi bskyod rdo rje was expert in the inner practice of Vajrapāṇi. Gan phyag rdzi chung ba Dbang phyug rgyal was expert in the inner and secret practices of Vajrapāṇi Mahācakra.[310] Rin chen 'bar of Shug phug in 'Jad was expert in the yogas of the kriyātantra.[311]

2. *The Work*

Dmar ston wrote a number of works recording the teachings of Sa skya Paṇḍita, most of which deal with the meditation practices of the Lam 'bras.[312] From among Dmar ston's compositions, two form a pair that is of special importance: his commentary on the *Rdo rje tshig rkang* of Virūpa and his study of the lives of the Tibetan masters of the Lam 'bras. The first of these works is usually known as the *Gzhung bshad dmar ma (Dmar's Explication of the Treatise)* or the *Gsung sgros ma (The Oral Account)*.[313] This text is the most important of Dmar ston's works, recording Sa skya Paṇḍita's own explanations of the *Rdo rje tshig rkang*. It was very rare in Tibet and circulated only in manuscript form until it was recently published in India. As noted in the previous sketch of Dmar ston's life, the *Gsung sgros ma* was proofread and praised by Sa skya Paṇḍita himself. Sa skya Paṇḍita's other chief disciples, such as Tshogs sgom Kun dga' dpal, Lho pa kun mkhyen Rin chen dpal, and Grub chen Yon tan dpal, also recognized this text as precisely matching the explanation of the Lam 'bras that they had heard from Sa skya Paṇḍita. As a result, they used it as the basis for their own explanations when they taught, even though they had never received the reading transmission of the text from Dmar ston.[314]

Although there is no separate reading transmission for the *Gsung sgros ma* today, the transmission of most of its contents has survived by virtue of inclusion in Bla ma dam pa's *Man ngag gter mdzod*, for which there is a transmission.[315] Study of the *Gsung sgros ma* itself has continued, and it is held in highest regard by masters of the Lam 'bras today. Bco brgyad Khri chen Rin po che, the present head of the Tshar pa subsect of the Sa skya tradition and the senior master of the Slob bshad, has often emphasized to me the importance of the *Gsung sgros ma* for the practice of the Lam 'bras. Bco brgyad Rin po che also says that his own teacher, Dam pa Rin po che, Ngag dbang blo gros gzhan phan snying po (1876–1953), the sixty-fourth abbot of Ngor, always kept his copy of the *Gsung sgros ma* next to his pillow. The *Gsung sgros ma* may have always been particularly valued at Ngor monastery. Glo bo mkhan chen states that his teacher Kun dga' dbang phyug, Ngor chen's nephew who was the fourth abbot of Ngor, followed the instructions for the perfection stage practices *(rdzogs rim)* precisely as explained in the *Gsung sgros ma* when he taught the Lam 'bras.[316]

Dmar ston's second text is translated in part two of this book. This work is known in the tradition as the *Zhib mo rdo rje (The Incisive Vajra)*, a title found only in the colophons of the surviving manuscripts. The *Zhib mo rdo rje* is the companion historical piece to the *Gsung sgros ma*. Dmar ston wrote the work at the temple of Na la tse gnas po che in Gung thang, and the composition was also praised by Sa skya Paṇḍita himself. From the known chronology of Dmar ston's life and studies it is certain that the text was not composed before 1217, and probably not after 1224.[317] Dmar ston's work was later entirely incorporated into the *Ngo mtshar snang ba* of Bla ma dam pa Bsod nams rgyal mtshan, which accounts for the fact that there is no separate reading transmission for it today. The *Zhib mo rdo rje* was also never published in Tibet.

Rje btsun Grags pa rgyal mtshan was the first to record stories about the early masters of the Lam 'bras, in the late twelfth or early thirteenth century. His extremely brief *Bla ma brgyud pa bod kyi lo rgyus (The Tibetan Story of the Lineal Masters)* devotes just three pages to the stories of 'Brog mi and Gayadhara, and only a single page to the remaining members of the lineage through Sa chen.[318] Grags pa rgyal mtshan clearly made no effort in his work to write down everything he knew about the oral history of these teachers, which he would have heard from his father Sa chen, his elder brother Bsod nams rtse mo, and Sa chen's elder disciples. His text is just the basic thread of the narrative, which he would have greatly expanded upon orally when he actually taught the Lam 'bras to small groups of disciples.

Grags pa rgyal mtshan's main disciple was his nephew Sa skya Paṇḍita. Since it is known that Grags pa rgyal mtshan taught the Lam 'bras many times, Sa skya Paṇḍita certainly heard the teachings from him on more than one occasion, and learned from his uncle stories about his grandfather and the earlier masters of the lineage. Sa skya Paṇḍita became a repository of the lore that had been passed down in his family and which he drew on when he later taught the Lam 'bras himself. There can be no doubt about where the detailed information in Dmar ston's record of Sa skya Paṇḍita's teachings came from—it came from Grags pa rgyal mtshan, who had received it from his father and brother, and later from Sa chen's elder disciples. Sa chen had received it from Zhang ston and Se ston, the latter having spent seventeen years with 'Brog mi Lo tsā ba himself. The absence of prior *written* evidence for the information in Dmar ston's chronicle is not evidence of an absence of the information itself. The stories, like the Lam 'bras, were essentially oral until the time of Grags pa rgyal mtshan. And the stories were considered very special both by those who told them and by their disciples. These teachers were not facing a critical audience. The sole purpose of the stories was to engender faith in the lineage and certainty in the esoteric instructions that both teachers and students were practicing as the most important endeavor in their lives. Dmar ston's history was thus written for a very select group, and would have been read only by those engaged in the study and practice of the Lam 'bras. It was not even meant for a general audience in Tibet, let alone for foreign readers almost eight hundred years later.

Dmar ston had first studied with Grags pa rgyal mtshan for three years, and then became a disciple of Sa skya Paṇḍita. The opening verses of the *Zhib mo rdo rje* mention an earlier account of "the Tibetan masters such as 'Brog mi." This is clearly a reference to Grags pa rgyal mtshan's little text, but Dmar ston also emphasizes that his own work deserves a respectful reception because it is a precise record of Sa skya Paṇḍita's explanations.[319] A comparison of the two works by Grags pa rgyal mtshan and Dmar ston shows for the first time just how important Sa skya Paṇḍita's version of the life stories of the early masters was for the tradition after him. It is now obvious that Dmar ston's record of Sa skya Paṇḍita's stories, and not the sketch by Grags pa rgyal mtshan, provided the essential material for all succeeding histories of the Lam 'bras in the Sa skya tradition.[320] Nearly every word from Dmar ston's chronicle was incorporated into the *Ngo mtshar snang ba* by Bla ma dam pa Bsod nams rgyal mtshan in 1344. Bla ma dam pa's work then became the definitive historical source until the *Gsang chen bstan pa rgyas byed (The Expansion of the Doctrine of Great Secrets),* written by Mkhyen brtse'i dbang phyug in 1559. An examination of Mkhyen brtse'i dbang phyug's text shows that he used all the sources that were then available to him. He supplemented the versions from Bla ma dam pa, and thus ultimately Dmar ston, with the Zha ma accounts recorded by Cha rgan, and oral information he received from his teacher Tshar chen Blo gsal rgya mtsho. This type of eclectic approach had not been followed by Bla ma dam pa, who had used sources from only the Sa skya tradition. In 1621 'Jam mgon A mes zhabs also utilized all available sources to create a compendium of information from the different lineages.[321] Today, Mkhyen brtse'i dbang phyug's work is always referred to by the masters of the Lam 'bras as the definitive historical account.

Sa skya Paṇḍita's stories that are recorded in the *Zhib mo rdo rje* are succinct, simple, and realistic. The teachers have not been overly idealized and events have not been sanitized for consumption by a more general and critical audience, as was done in some other traditions to caste a master in the best possible light.[322] There are, of course, some miraculous events described, but nothing that any Tibetan of the time would have questioned. From the contemporary Tibetan point of view this was an authoritative historical record. The world-view of the original audience and that of the readers of this book today are quite different. Very human stories will be found here, full of character and personality, and triumph and tragedy. They still retain an oral flavor both in content and language, and are clearly not based on any textual tradition. And in the few instances where there is evidence that Dmar ston used the writings of Grags pa rgyal mtshan and Sa skya Paṇḍita the oral feeling is retained, because those stories were recording oral material as well.

The *Zhib mo rdo rje* became very rare in Tibet. Even the elder masters of the Lam 'bras in recent years had never seen copies of it. For example, the late Sde gzhung Rin po che was not familiar with Dmar ston's commentary on the *Rdo rje tshig rkang* or with the *Zhib mo rdo rje*, other than by references in later literature. Bco brgyad Khri chen Rin po che had also never seen the *Zhib mo rdo rje* until I offered him a copy in 1989.

The annotations found in two of the surviving manuscripts of the *Zhib mo rdo rje* greatly supplement the information in the text and are of considerable historical interest. Their importance becomes even more apparent when it is noticed that not only Dmar ston's text, but these annotations as well, have been almost entirely copied by Bla ma dam pa in the *Ngo mtshar snang ba*. In later histories the information originally found in the annotations to the *Zhib mo rdo rje*, but now incorporated without comment into the main text of Bla ma dam pa's work, is taken as authoritative. Why would Bla ma dam pa have included the information from the annotations to the *Zhib mo rdo rje* as though it were as reliable as the main text, and without identifying it as coming from another source? I believe this question can be answered, but only after some detective work in various sources.

The first clue about the source of the additional information in the annotations is that the statements of a Chos rje, "Dharma Lord," are frequently quoted throughout. In the *Zhib mo rdo rje* itself, and the Sa skya tradition in general, this is the respectful term used to refer to Sa skya Paṇḍita.[323] At one point in the annotations this is made explicit by referring to Dpal chen 'od po (1150–1203), who was the father of Sa skya Paṇḍita, as "the Dharma Lord's father."[324] And it is clear that the annotations were recorded sometime after the death of Sa skya Paṇḍita in 1251.[325]

The second clue is that the annotations represent the additional comments of their author's teacher, merely referred to as Rin po che ("Precious One"), the most common of all Tibetan terms of respect for a spiritual teacher:

> In regard to the Dharma Lord's life story, Rin po che commented, "Ācārya Mātṛceṭa stated, 'Not being omniscient [myself], while you are omniscient, how can I understand you, Omniscient One?' Likewise, the expression of his [i.e. Sa skya Paṇḍita's] qualities must be spoken by one equal to him. Others are not able to express them. Nevertheless, since blessings will come, I will express a little. This Dharma Lord,…"[326]

What is of special interest is that "Rin po che" speaks here and at other points in the annotations in a way that shows he was a personal disciple of Sa skya Paṇḍita.[327] The author of the annotations is therefore recording the words of his teacher who had actually studied with Sa skya Paṇḍita. Among Sa skya Paṇḍita's main disciples the only one constantly referred to as Rin po che was Tshogs sgom Rin po che Kun dga' dpal.[328] The next clue in making the connection between Tshogs sgom Rin po che and the annotations is found in the fragment of an untitled biography that begins on the same page that the original manuscript of the *Zhib mo rdo rje* ends.[329] This incomplete biography opens with the following comment:

> Like [he] stated above [in regard to Sa skya Paṇḍita's life], it is fitting that the life story of Bla ma Rin po che, the spiritual son of the Dharma Lord himself, should also be expressed by

> one who is equal to him. Nevertheless, since there will be some increase of merit, I will express a little.[330]

Now it becomes certain that this incomplete biography is of the same Rin po che who was quoted in the previous annotations in the *Zhib mo rdo rje*. It is also clear that this Rin po che was indeed a disciple of Sa skya Paṇḍita, and that the author of the annotations and the author of the biography of "Bla ma Rin po che" are the same person.

The next step is to identify the subject of this biographical fragment. Here we are on firmer ground. The opening passages of the text are a close match with the beginning of the published biography of Tshogs sgom Rin po che.[331] Although there are some short phrases in the published edition not found in the manuscript fragment, there can be no doubt that both works concern the same subject. Unfortunately, the published biography of Tshogs sgom is anonymous. And yet perhaps the author can in fact be identified. In the preface to his *Mdo smad chos 'byung (History of Dharma in Mdo smad),* the nineteenth-century author Dkon mchog bstan pa rab rgyas (b. 1801) provides an exhaustive list of historical sources for his work. In listing the biographies of early Sa skya masters of the Lam 'bras he largely follows the order of the biographies in the published edition of the Lam 'bras. In the list he says that the author of the biography of Tshogs sgom Rin po che was named Gnyag Snying po rgyal mtshan.[332] Here we have it. Gnyag Snying po rgyal mtshan was one of the main disciples of Tshogs sgom Rin po che, especially for the transmission of the Lam 'bras in the Rdzong tradition.[333] Little else is know about him.

The annotations in the *Zhib mo rdo rje* thus record Tshogs sgom Rin po che's further oral expansions of Sa skya Paṇḍita's stories when using Dmar ston's text during his own teachings of the Lam 'bras. Glo bo mkhan chen specifically mentions that his own teacher, Rgyal tshab Kun dga' dbang phyug, had said that Sa skya Paṇḍita's great disciples other than Dmar ston, such as Tshogs sgom Rin po che, Lho pa kun mkhyen, and Grub chen Yon tan dpal, all used Dmar ston's *Gsung sgros ma* when they taught the Lam 'bras.[334] The *Zhib mo rdo rje* is the companion volume to the *Gsung sgros ma*, used to establish the authentic lineage and the spiritual qualities of previous masters. The *Zhib mo rdo rje* would have been used by Tshogs sgom Rin po che and the others when they taught the *Gsung sgros ma.*

The information in the annotations to the *Zhib mo rdo rje* was accepted as authoritative by later authors, in particular Bla ma dam pa Bsod nams rgyal mtshan. This was because these annotations represented a further record of Sa skya Paṇḍita's own teachings about the lives of the early masters of the Lam 'bras. Moreover, they represented a purely Sa skya lineage of explanation without any mixing with other versions, such as that of the Zha ma tradition.[335] The *Zhib mo rdo rje*, also known as the *Bla ma dam pa bod kyi lo rgyus (The Tibetan Story of the Excellent Masters)*, is the work of Sa skya Paṇḍita's disciple Dmar ston Chos kyi rgyal po. But the text reproduced in part two also contains information from another of Sa skya Paṇḍita's disciples, Tshogs sgom Rin po che Kun dga' dpal. This additional material was added to the text by one of Tshogs sgom's disciples, most likely Gnyag Snying po rgyal mtshan.

PART TWO

Translation

THE TIBETAN STORY OF THE EXCELLENT MASTERS

བླ་མ་དམ་པ་བོད་ཀྱི་ལོ་རྒྱུས་བཞུགས་པ་ལགས་སོ་དབང་།།

[༄༅ ། །དཔེ་རྒྱུན་དཀོན་པ་གང་ཞིག་ལ་དཔྱ་མེད་ཕོག་ཕྱག་བསྐྱར་གནང་བའི་ཕྱག་དཔེ་འདི་བཞིན་ཏ་ལམ་མི་ལོ་བརྒྱད་བརྒྱ་ཙམ་གྱི་རིང་ལ་ཁྱབ་འཕེལ་བྱུང་ཡང་བོད་ནང་དཔར་བསྐྲུན་རྩ་བ་ནས་བྱུང་མེད། ཕྱག་དཔེ་འདིའི་ནང་བརྗ་སྙིང་བའི་ཐ་སྙད་དང་། དག་ཆ་ནོར་བ་དུ་མ་ཞིག་མཆིས་ཀྱང་འདི་གར་དག་བཅོས་ཞུས་མེད། འདི་གར་དཔྱ་མེད་ནས་དཔྱ་ཅན་གྱི་ཕོག་ཏུ་སྒྱུར་བསྐྲུན་ཞུས་པ་དང་། མ་ཕྱིའི་ནང་གི་བསྡུས་ཡིག་དག་ཀྱང་དཀྲུས་ཡིག་ཏུ་གཟུགས་སྒྱུར་ཞུས་པ་ཙམ་ལས་དག་ཆ་ཧེ་ཡོད་རང་སོར་བཞག་ཡོད་པས་མ་ཕྱིའི་འདྲ་བཤུས་ངོ་མ་ཞིག་ཡིན། མ་དཔེའི་ནང་དུ་གསལ་བའི་མཆན་བུ་རྣམས་འདི་གར་ཐལ་མདོག་ཅན་གྱི་དཔར་རྩ་ཆུང་དུའི་ལམ་ནས་སྒྱུར་བསྐྲུན་ཞུས་ཡོད།]

བླ་མ་དམ་པའི་ཞབས་ལ་སྤྱི་བོས་གུས་པར་ཕྱག་འཚལ་ལོ།།

གང་ཞིག་ཕྱི་ནང་གསང་བ་མཐར་ཐུག་རྟེན་འབྲེལ་དེ་ཁོ་ན།།
སོར་འཕྲེད་ཅན་དང་འཇམ་དབྱངས་མཐུ་སྟོབས་དབང་ཕྱུག་རྡོ་རྗེ་འཆང་།།
དཔལ་ལྡན་བླ་མ་མཚུངས་མེད་རང་གི་སེམས་ཉིད་ལྷན་ཅིག་སྐྱེས།།
དབྱེར་མེད་རྟེན་ཅིང་འབྲེལ་འབྱུང་སྟོན་མཛད་དམ་པའི་ཞབས་པད་འདུད།།

འགྲོག་མི་ལ་སོགས་དཔལ་ལྡན་བླ་མའི།།
བོད་ཀྱི་ལོ་རྒྱུས་གསལ་བར་མཛད་ཟིན་མོད།།
འོན་ཀྱང་ཆོས་རྗེའི་གསུང་ལ་རབ་དད་ནས།།
ཇི་བཞིན་བྲིས་པ་འདི་ཡང་གུས་པས་ལོང་།།

འདིར་བླ་མ་བོད་ཀྱི་ལོ་རྒྱུས་ས་སྐྱ་པཎ་ཊི་ཏའི་གསུང་ཇི་ལྟ་བ་བཞིན་བརྗོད་ན།

Prologue

I respectfully prostrate with the crown of my head at the feet of the excellent master.

> I bow at the lotus feet of the excellent master who reveals the dependently arisen connections of the outer, the inner, the secret, the ultimate, and thatness,[1]
> The dependently arisen connections in which Aṅgulimāla, Mañjughoṣa, the Powerful Lord, Vajradhara, and the splendid and peerless master are indivisible from the coemergent nature of one's own mind.[2]

> While the Tibetan story of the splendid masters such as 'Brog mi has already been clearly composed,
> Nevertheless, this has been precisely written out of supreme faith in the words of the Dharma Lord, and should also be respectfully received.[3]

The Tibetan story of the masters will be stated here precisely according to the words of Sa skya Paṇḍita.

དེའང་ཆོས་འཁོར་གྲོམ་པ་རྒྱང་ཞེས་བྱ་བ་འདི་པད་འབྱུང་གིས་རབ་གནས་རྒྱང་ནས་མཛད་པ་ཡིན་གྱི་རྣལ་མ་ནི་རྣམ་དག་སྒྲིབ་སེལ་གྱི་རྩུག་ལག་ཁང་ཅེས་སོ་སྔོན་གྱི་རྒྱལ་བློན་གྱིས་ལྷ་ས་རྩིག་པའི་དུས་སུ། རུ་ནོན་དུ་བརྩིགས་པའི་རྩུག་ལག་ཁང་བཞི་ལས་གཡས་རུ་ན་ཙང་འཕྲང་། རུ་ལྷག་ན་རྒྱང་། གཡོའ་རུ་ན་ཁྲམ་འབྲུག། སྦྲུ་རུ་ན་ཀ་ཚལ་དང་བཞི་ལས་རྒྱང་གི་བདག་པོ། ལྷ་རྩེའི་ལྷ་བཙུན་མཆེད་གསུམ་ཟེར་ཀྱང་གསུང་ལ་གཉིས་བཀའ་བགྲོས་ཏེ། འོ་ཅག་ལ་བླའི་མཆོད་གནས་ཤིག་དགོས་པར་འདུག་པས་སུ་དྲག་ཟེར་ཏེ། དེ་དུས་ན་རྒྱན་གོང་ན་ལོ་སྟོན་རྡོ་རྗེ་དབང་ཕྱུག་བཞུགས་པས་ཁོང་གི་མཁན་བུ་རྒྱ་ཤཱཀྱ་གཞོན་ནུ་ཞེས་བྱ་བ་དང་། སེ་ཡེ་ཤེས་བརྩོན་འགྲུས་ཞེས་བྱ་བ་གཉིས་བཏང་སྟེ་སྤྱན་དྲངས་ནས། སེ་ཡིས་མཁན་པོ་མཛད་རྒྱ་ཡིས་སློབ་དཔོན་མཛད་ནས་ཡོད་པའི་དུས་སུ། སྟག་ལོ་གཞོན་ནུ་བརྩོན་འགྲུས་དང་འབྲོག་མི་ཤཱཀྱ་ཡེ་ཤེས་གཉིས་རབ་ཏུ་བྱུང་ནས། དེ་ཡང་བླ་ཆེན་འབྲོག་མི་འདི་ཡུལ་དྲིལ་ཆེན་ཀུ་སྡེའི་གདུང་འབྲོག་མི་སྐྱུ་ཚེ་དང་བན་ཚེ་གཉིས་ལས་བན་ཚེ་ཡིན། མཚན་ཡང་མཁན་སློབ་ཀྱི་མཚན་ལས་གྲུས་ནས་བཏགས་སོ།།

མཁན་སློབ་དེ་གཉིས་ལ་སྤྱིར་མཁན་བུ་མང་པོ་ཡོད་ཀྱང་། སྟག་འབྲོག་གཉིས་ཁོ་ན་བཅད་པ་དང་སྤྱུག་སྤྲན་ཆེ་བར་དགོངས་ཤིང་། ཁྱད་པར་དུ་སློབ་དཔོན་གྱིས་བསྟན་པ་ལ་དགོངས་ཏེ་ཐུགས་གཉེར་ཆེར་མཛད་ནས་གསེར་ཕྱེ་མང་པོ་བཏྲངས་ཏེ། རྒྱ་གར་དུ་སློབ་གཉེར་ལ་འགྲོ་དགོས་གསུང་ནས་ཞལ་སློས་གསུམ་མཛད་དེ། སངས་རྒྱས་ཀྱི་བསྟན་པའི་རྩ་བ་དང་འདྲ་བ་ཡིན་པས་དམ་པའི་ཆོས་འདུལ་བ་དང་། བསྟན་པའི་སྙིང་པོ་དང་འདྲ་བ་ཡིན་པས་ཤེས་རབ་ཀྱི་

ONE
The Life of 'Brog mi Lo tsā ba

'Brog mi Lo tsā ba

THE TEMPLE of Chos 'khor Grom pa Rgyang, consecrated from afar by Padmasambhava and actually known as the temple of Rnam dag sgrib sel,[4] was built to suppress the "horns" during the period of the construction of Lha sa by the early kings and ministers. There were the four of Tsang 'phrang in G.yas ru, Rgyang in Ru lhag, Khram 'brug in G.yo' ru, and Ka tshal in Sbu ru.[5] From among these, Rgyang's rulers were called the Three Divine Venerable Brothers of Lha rtse.[6] So it has been stated. Two of them had a discussion, and said, "We need a court chaplain. Who would be best?." At that time Lo ston Rdo rje dbang phyug was living in Rgyan gong, and his two disciples known as Rgya Shākya gzhon nu and Se Ye shes brtson 'grus were sent.[7] They were invited, and during the period when Se was serving as abbot and Rgya was serving as teacher, both Stag Lo Gzhon nu brtson 'grus and 'Brog mi Shākya ye shes were ordained. Furthermore, this great master 'Brog mi was from the region of Dril chen chu sde, and of the 'Brog mi clan. From among the two, the Skye subclan and the Ban subclan, he was of the Ban subclan.[8] His name was derived from the names of the abbot and the teacher.

Travels in Nepal and India

In general, although both the abbot and the teacher had many students, they realized that only the pair of Stag and 'Brog had great discernment

པ་རོལ་དུ་ཕྱིན་པ་དང་། བསྟན་པའི་ཉིང་ཁུ་དང་འདྲ་བ་ཡིན་པས་གསང་སྔགས་དང་དེ་དག་མཁས་པའི་ཡན་ལག་དུ་སྒྲ་ཚད་ལ་སོགས་པ་མང་དུ་སློབས་ལ་ཞོག་གསུང་སྐད་ཆོས་རྗེའི་ཞལ་ནས་ཆོས་ཀྱི་བབས་པོ་བའི་ཞལ་སློབ་སུ་འདུག་གསུང་། དེ་ནས་བླ་ཆེན་གྱིས་པིག་པ་ཧ་བསླབས་པས་ཆོས་ཉན་དུ་འདོད་པ་ཙམ་མཁྱེན་ཟེར་ཀྱང་འཕྲུལ་སྐད་ཙམ་ཤེས་བོད་ཆོས་ཀྱང་ཅི་རིགས་པ་མཁྱེན་སྐད།

ལམ་ཡང་མང་ཡུལ་ཚོངས་པའི་སྒོ་བྱ་བ་ཕར་བྱོན་པ་བར་ཆད་རྐྱེན་ཞིང་རྩུར་འཐོན་པ་བསྟན་པ་ལ་ཕན་པ་བཀྲ་ཤིས་པར་བྱུང་བ་ཡིན་པས་དེ་ནས་སོང་གསུང་དེ་ནས་གཉིས་ཀྱིས་མང་ཡུལ་ནས་བལ་ཡུལ་དུ་བྱོན་ནས་རྒྱང་སྦྱོང་བའི་ཕྱིར་བལ་ཡུལ་ན་བླ་རོ་རྡོ་ཕུང་ཅེས་ཀྱང་ཟེར་ཙ་ཏ་ཏུ་ཡང་ཟེར་བལ་པོ་སྐྱི་ཐེར་ཡང་ཟེར་མཚན་དངོས་ནི་ཤན་ཏ་བྷ་དྲ། བོད་སྐད་དུ་ཞི་བ་བཟང་པོ་ཅེས་བྱ་བའི་བལ་པོའི་པཎྜི་ཏ་ཞིག་ལ་དབང་བསྐུར་བ་ཞུས་ནས། གསང་སྔགས་ལོ་གཅིག་དུ་གསན་སྒྲ་ཡང་ཅུང་ཟད་གསན།

དེ་ནས་བདག་ཅག་རྒྱ་གར་དུ་འགྲོ་བས་རྒྱ་གར་ན་མཁས་པ་ཌི་ལྷ་བུ་བདོག་ཌི་ལྷར་བྱུས་ན་ལེགས་ཞུས་པས།

པཎྜི་ཏའི་ཞལ་ནས་བསྟན་པ་རྣལ་མ་རྒྱ་གར་ན་ཡོད་པས་ཤིན་དུ་ལེགས་སོ་ཁྱེད་རྒྱ་གར་དུ་འགྲོ་ན་ངའི་སློབ་དཔོན། བརྗོད་པའི་དུས་ཀྱི་ཐམས་ཅད་མཁྱེན་པ་གཉིས་པར་གྲགས་པ་མཁས་པ་ཤན་ཏི་བ་ཅེས་པ། དེ་ཡང་རྒྱ་གར་ན་ཨོ་ཏན་ཏ་པུ་གྲི་ན་ལེན་འདྲ་སོ་མ་སྦུ་གྲི་སོགས་ཡོད་ཀྱང་མ་ག་ཏའི་གནས་བྷི་ཀ་མ་ལ་ཤི་ལའི་རྩུག་ལག་ཁང་ན་ཉན་ཤད་དར་མཁས་པ་སྒོ་དྲུག་གི་ཡ་ཅིག་ཡིན་པས་དེའི་དྲུང་དུ་སོང་གསུང་ནས

དེར་ཕྱིན་སྔོན་རྒྱ་གར་ན་སྲོལ་བཟང་པོ་ཡོད་པས་རང་རེའི་ཆ་རྐྱེན་ཐམས་ཅད་བླ་བྲང་དེར་བཏད་ནས་བླ་བྲང་ནས་འཕྲུལ་གྱི་རྒྱུགས་དཔེ་ཆ་འབྲི་བའི་ཆ་རྐྱེན་རྩུན་ཅོད་སྦྱར་ནས་རང་རེ་སློབ་གཉེར་འབའ་ཞིག་བྱས་པས་ཆོག་ཏེ་ཁོང་གིས་ཀྱང་དེ་བཞིན་བྱས་སོ་ཆོས་རྗེ་པ་ད་ལྷ་སྐྱེ་པ་ཀུན་ཆོས་གཞི་འདེགས་པ་འདང་དེའི་སྲོལ་ཡིན་གསུང་།

དེའི་དུས་ན་བྷི་ཀ་མ་ལ་ཤི་ལའི་མཁས་པ་སྒོ་དྲུག་ནི་ཤར་ཕྱོགས་ཀྱི་སྒོ་བསྲུངས་པ་རད་ན་ཨ་ཀ་ར་ཤན་ཏི་བ་རིན་ཆེན་འབྱུང་གནས་ཞི་བ་ཅེས་སོ་བཞུགས་པ་ལ་སྒྲ་དང་ཚད་མ་ལ་གཙོ་བོར་འདྲི། དེ་བཞིན་དུ་ལྷོ་ཕྱོགས་ན་ངག་གི་དབང་ཕྱུག་གྲགས་པ་ཅེས་པ་རྗེ་བཙུན་མ་སྒྲོལ་མ་ལ་ཆོས་

and endurance. In particular, the teacher made great efforts in consideration of the Doctrine, and sent them off with much gold dust, saying, "You must go study in India."[9] He is said to have given three orders: "Since it is like the root of the Buddha's Doctrine, study the monastic code of the excellent Dharma. Since it is like the heart of the Doctrine, study the *Prajñāpāramitā*. And since it is like the quintessence of the Doctrine, study secret mantra and also much grammar, epistemology, and so forth, as the limbs for expertise in those [subjects], and then return!" The Dharma Lord stated, "This is the order of one who understands the crux of the Dharma."[10] It is said that the great master ['Brog mi] then studied the *vivarta* [script] and knew enough to be able to listen to Dharma. So it is said, but he understood just the vernacular, and also knew various Tibetan Dharmas.[11]

By the route known as "The Door of Brahmā"[12] in Mang yul, there would be few obstacles on the outward journey and benefit to the Doctrine on their return, which would be auspicious, so they went by that route. So it has been stated.[13] Then the two arrived in Nepal from Mang yul. In order to adjust to the water,[14] they studied secret mantra for a year in Nepal after requesting the bestowal of initiation from the Newar paṇḍita called Bha ro Haṃ thung, also called Tsa ha ngu and Bal po Spyi ther, whose real name was Śāntabhadra, which is Zhi ba bzang po in Tibetan.[15] They also studied some grammar.

Then they said, "We are going to India. What kind of experts are in India, and what would be best for us to do?"[16]

The paṇḍita replied, "Very good, because the genuine Doctrine is in India. If you go to India, my teacher is famed as a second Omniscient One in the age of strife, and is known as the expert Śāntipa. Furthermore, Odantapuri, Nālandā, Somapuri, and so forth are in India, but he is one of the six experts at the gates of the temple of Vikramaśīla in the region of Magadha where study and explication have spread. Go to him."[17]

['Brog mi] went there.[18] Previously in India there was a fine custom. We gave all our supplies to the master's residence there, and then the immediate needs, down to supplies for writing out texts, were provided from the master's residence, and we could just study. He also did like that. The Dharma Lord stated that the support of all the establishments now by means of monastic estates is also in that custom.

At that time, there were experts at the six gates of the temple of Vikramaśīla. From Ratnākaraśānti Rin chen 'byung gnas zhi ba, who resided as the gate guardian of the eastern direction, ['Brog mi] primarily inquired about grammar and epistemology. Likewise, from Vāgīśvarakīrti in the southern direction, a great expert teacher who had actually heard [Dharma] from holy Tārā, he especially inquired about everything such

དངོས་སུ་གསན་པའི་སློབ་དཔོན་མཁས་པ་ཆེན་པོ་དེ་ལ་ཁྱད་པར་དུ་སྨྲ་ཚད་སྙན་ངག་དང་ལུང་ལ་སོགས་པ་ཐམས་ཅད་ལ་འདྲི་བ་འོང་།། ནུབ་ཕྱོགས་ན་ཤེས་རབ་འབྱུང་གནས་བློ་གྲོས་ལ་ཁྱད་པར་དུ་མུ་སྟེགས་ཀྱི་གྲུབ་མཐའ་ལ་འདྲི་བ་མང་། བྱང་ཕྱོགས་ན་ཇོ་བོ་ན་རོ་ཏ་པ་ལ་ཐེག་པ་ཆེན་པོ་ལ་འདྲི་བ་དང་ལུང་ནོད་པ་མང་གསུང་ངོ་།།

དབུས་ཀྱི་ཀ་ཆེན་གཉིས་ནི་རིན་ཆེན་རྡོ་རྗེ་དང་གཉ་ན་ཤྲི་མི་ཏྲ་བོད་སྐད་ཡེ་ཤེས་དཔལ་བཤེས་གཉེན་སྟེ། དེ་གཉིས་ལ་ཀ་ཆེན་ཟེར་ཀྱང་གཞན་པས་ཡོན་ཏན་ཆེ་རྒྱུ་ནི་མེད་གསུང་།

བླ་ཆེན་འབྲོག་མིས་སློབ་དཔོན་ཤན་ཏི་པ་ལ་དམ་པའི་ཆོས་འདུལ་བ་དང་། ཕ་རོལ་དུ་ཕྱིན་པ་ཡང་གསན་སློབ་དཔོན་ཉིད་ཀྱིས་མཛད་པ་ཕར་ཕྱིན་གྱི་འགྲེལ་པ་ཉི་ཁྲི་དག་ལྡན་སྙིང་པོ་མཆོག་ལ་སོགས་ཀུན་ཡང་གསན། དེ་ནས་སྔགས་ཀྱི་ཆོས་སྐོར་ཀྱེའི་རྡོ་རྗེའི་རྒྱུད་གསུམ་བདེ་མཆོག་ལ་སོགས་པ་མང་དུ་གསན་ཞིང་ལོ་བརྒྱད་བཞུགས་སོ།། གཞན་རྣམས་དང་ཡང་ཆོས་འབྲེལ་བག་རེ་ཡོད་གསུང་དེ་དུས་ན་མཁས་པ་གྲྭ་འདོགས་པས་ཚིག་གི་ཟུར་ཚོལ་བས་ཤན་ཏི་པ་ལྟ་བ་ལ་འཁྲུལ་སེམས་ཙམ་ཡིན་ཟེར། ངག་གི་དབང་ཕྱུག་སྤྱོད་པ་ལ་འཁྲུལ་ལས་དང་པོ་པ་རང་ནས་གཉིས་སྣང་གི་སྤྱོད་པ་བྱེད། ན་རོ་པ་དབང་ལ་འཁྲུལ་དབང་གི་དུས་སུ་མཐོང་ལམ་སྐྱེ་ཟེར་ཀྱང་མཁས་པ་ཆེན་པོ་དེ་རྣམས་ལ་འཁྲུལ་པ་ཆེན་པོ་མི་མངའ་གསུང་།

དེ་ནས་ཡུལ་དུ་བྱོན་དགོངས་ཙམ་ན། རྒྱ་གར་ཤར་ཕྱོགས་རཱ་ཌ་ན་འཕགས་པ་སྤྱན་རས་གཟིགས་དབང་ཕྱུག་འཁར་ས་པ་ནི་བཞུགས་པ་དེ་གྲགས་པ་ཆེ་བས་དེ་ལ་ཕྱག་དང་བསྙེན་བཀུར་བྱ་བའི་ཕྱིར་བྱོན་པའི་ལམ་ན། ཀུ་བ་ཚལ་བྱ་བའི་ནགས་སྟུག་པོ་ཞིག་གི་ནང་ན་དགེ་སློང་ཆོས་གོས་གསུམ་ལྷུང་ཟེད་དང་བཅས་པ་ཞིག། ཤིང་གི་ལྡུམ་ལ་བསོད་སྙོམས་སློང་ཞིང་འདུག་པའི་དུས་སུ་ལྗོན་ཤིང་གི་སྡོང་པོའི་ནང་ནས། ལུས་མི་སྟོན་པར་ལག་པ་རིན་པོ་ཆེ་སྣ་ཚོགས་ཀྱིས་བརྒྱན་པ་ཞིག་གིས་བསོད་སྙོམས་འདྲེན་པ་མཐོང་བས། དེ་ལ་དད་པ་དང་ངོ་མཚར་ཆེར་སྐྱེས་ནས་འདི་དངོས་གྲུབ་ཐོབ་པ་ཞིག་འདུག་སྙམ་ཏེ།། དགེ་སློང་དེ་ལ་ཕྱག་དང་བསྐོར་བ་དང་བསྙེན་བཀུར་མཛད་ནས། བདག་རྗེས་སུ་གཟུང་བར་ཞུ་བྱས་པས་ཅི་དོན་དུ་གཉེར་ཟེར་ཆོས་གཉེར་དེ་ནས་ཀྱང་གསང་སྔགས་གཉེར་བྱས་པས་དབང་བསྐུར་དགོས་ཟེར་སྔར་བལ་པོ་དང་ཤན་ཏི་བ་ལ་ཐོབ་བྱས་པས་དེས་མི་ཕན་ང་རང་གི་དགོས་ཟེར་དེ་ཆོས་རྗེ་པ་ན་རེ་འཐད་དེ་ད་ལྟ་དེ་སྐད་བྱས་ན་མི་ཉན་འདུག

as grammar, epistemology, poetics, and reading transmissions. From Prajñākaramati in the western direction he especially made many inquiries about the philosophical tenets of the tīrthika. From Lord Nārotapa in the northern direction he inquired about the Mahāyāna, and also received many reading transmissions. So it has been stated.[19]

The two great central pillars were Ratnavajra and Jñānaśrīmitra, Ye shes dpal bshes gnyen in Tibetan. These two were called "pillars," but they did not have greater qualities than the others. So it has been stated.[20]

From the teacher Śāntipa, the great master 'Brog mi also received the monastic code of the excellent Dharma, and the *Prajñāpāramitā.* He also received all the commentaries composed by the teacher himself on the *Prajñāpāramitā,* such as the *Nyi khri dag ldan* and the *Snying po mchog*. Then he received many Dharma cycles of mantra, such as the *Kye'i rdo rje'i rgyud gsum,* and Saṃvara.[21] He stayed for eight years. He also had a slight Dharma link with each of the others.[22] So it has been stated. At that time, critical[23] experts seeking the implications of words claimed that Śāntipa was mistaken in regard to the view, and was a Cittamātrin; Vāgīśvarakīrti was mistaken in regard to conduct, and advocated the conduct of the renunciation of duality even for beginners;[24] and Nāropa was mistaken in regard to initiation, because he stated that the Path of Seeing arose at the time of initiation. But those great experts made no great mistakes. So it has been stated.

Then he decided to return home. At that point, since the noble Avalokiteśvara Khasarpaṇa residing at Raḍa in eastern India was very famous, he set off to offer it prostrations and honors.[25] On a path inside a dense forest known as Ku ba tshal there was a monk with the three Dharma robes and an alms-bowl begging alms from a tree deity. At that moment the alms were being provided from within the trunk of a tree by an arm adorned with various jewels, without revealing a body. When he saw this he felt great faith and awe toward him, and thought, "This one has reached attainment." He offered prostrations, circumambulations, and honors to that monk. Then he said, "Please accept me." [The monk] asked, "What do you seek?" He replied, "I seek the Dharma, and moreover, I seek secret mantra." "You need the bestowal of initiation," he said. "I have received it before from the Newar and from Śāntipa," he replied. "That doesn't help. You need mine," he said. In regard to that, the Dharma Lord commented, "That is correct, but if it is said now, [people] don't listen."[26] He agreed, and performed the bestowal of initiation. That teacher's name was Prajñendraruci, which if translated into Tibetan is Shes rab dbang po mdzes pa. His secret name was Vīravajra. He came to Mu gu lung, composed the *Ratnajvāla,* and saying, "I'm going to see the

གསུང་དེས་གནང་ནས་དབང་བསྐུར་བ་མཛད། སློབ་དཔོན་དེའི་མཚན་པྲ་ཛྙཱ་ཤྲཱི་ཛྙཱ་རུ་ཌཱི་ཅེས་པ་བོད་སྐད་དུ་བསྒྱུར་ན། ཤེས་རབ་དབང་པོ་མཛེས་པ། གསང་མཚན་དཔའ་བོ་རྡོ་རྗེ་ཞེས་པ་ཏེ་མུ་གུ་ལུང་དུ་བྱོན་རིན་ཆེན་འབར་བ་མཛད་གདངས་མགྲོན་འགྲོ་གསུང་ནས་ཉི་ཟེར་ལ་ཆིབས་ནས་གཤེགས། དེས་ན་དགེ་སློང་དཔའ་བོ་རྡོ་རྗེ་ཞེས་ཡོངས་སུ་གྲགས་སོ།།

དེ་ལྟ་བུ་དེ་ལ་ཀྱེའི་རྡོ་རྗེ་རྒྱུད་གསུམ་སློབ་དཔོན་ཊོམ་བྷི་བའི་རྗེས་གནང་དང་བཅས་པའི་སྒྲུབ་ཐབས་དང་འགྲེལ་པའི་སྐོར་ཐམས་ཅད་ཀྱང་གསན། ལམ་འབྲས་རྩ་བ་མེད་པ་ཞིག་ཀྱང་གསན། བསམ་མི་ཁྱབ་ལ་སོགས་པའི་ལམ་སྐོར་འགའ་ཞིག་ཀྱང་གསན་ཞིང་ལོ་བཞི་བཞུགས་སྐད་སྤྱན་རས་གཟིགས་ལ་ཡང་འབྲུལ་ལོ། སློབ་དཔོན་ཤན་ཏི་བས་དགེ་སློང་དཔའ་བོ་རྡོ་རྗེའི་གསང་སྔགས་ཀྱི་ཆ་ཤད་སྤྲོལ་ལེགས་ཤིང་གདམ་ངག་ཀྱང་ཆེ་བར་དགོངས་གསུང་ཏེ་ཤན་ཏི་བའི་སྡེ་སྣོད་སྤྱི་དང་བསྟུན་པའི་རྒྱུ་ཆེ་བར་བྱུང་། དཔའ་བོ་རྡོ་རྗེའི་ཉམས་སུ་བླང་བདེ་བ་མན་ངག་དུ་དྲིལ་ནས་བྱུང་། དེ་གཉིས་ཀྱིས་ཕྱི་ནང་གི་སྒྲོ་འདོགས་ཀུན་ཆོད་པས་ཐུགས་ཤིན་དུ་བདེ། སྤྱིར་བལ་པོ་དང་རྒྱ་གར་གཉིས་སུ་ལོ་བཅུ་གསུམ་བཞུགས་གསུང་།

དེ་ནས་སྟག་འབྲོག་གཉིས་ཀྱིས་ཚུར་བོད་དུ་བྱོན་རྒྱ་གར་ནས་བལ་ཡུལ་མན་ཆད་ལོ་པན་བྱོན་ན་འདིར་བྱོན་བྱ་བའི་སྲོལ་ཡོད་གསུང་། མཁན་སློབ་གཉིས་ཀྱིས་བསུ་བ་མཛད་ནས་ཆོས་ཀྱི་ལོ་རྒྱུས་མཛད་པས། བླ་ཆེན་འབྲོག་མི་ཤིན་དུ་མཁས་པ་ཆེན་པོར་གྱུར་ནས་ཤིན་དུ་མཉེས་སྐད། སྟག་ལོ་ལ་ཅི་ཤེས་དྲིས་པས་ཤེས་རབ་སྙིང་པོ་རྒྱ་ཀློག་དུ་ཀློག་པ་ཙམ་ལས་མི་འདུག་སྐད།

མཁན་སློབ་གཉིས་ཀྱི་ཞལ་ནས་འབྲོག་མི་འདི་མཁས་པ་ཆེན་པོར་གྱུར་འདུག་པ་ལ། ཁྱོད་ཀྱིས་ཅི་ཡང་མི་ཤེས་པ་ཇི་ལྟར་ཡིན་གསུང་བ་ལ།

སྟག་ལོ་ན་རེ་ཁོ་ཀ་བ་ལི་རེ་ཁྱེར་ནས་དེ་ཤེད་དུ་འགྲོ་ཡིན་འདུག ཁོ་བོ་རྡོ་རྗེ་གདན་གྱི་བྱང་ཆུབ་ཆེན་པོ་ལ་དད་པར་བྱུང་ནས་བསྐོར་བ་འདྲ་བྱས་ཟེར་སྐད།

འོན་ཀྱང་ཁོང་ཤིན་དུ་བརྩོན་པས་སྟག་ཚོའི་སྡེ་པ་ཆེན་པོ་ཚུགས་སོ།

Himālaya," he mounted a sunbeam and left.[27] Therefore, he is widely famed as Bhikṣu Vīravajra.

From such a one as him, ['Brog mi] also received the *Kye'i rdo rje rgyud gsum,* the teacher Ḍombi's method for realization, with the ritual permission and all his cycles of commentary. He also received a Lam 'bras without the basic text.[29] He also received several of the Lam skor,[30] such as the *Bsam mi khyab.*[31] It is said that he stayed for four years. He had also visited the Avalokiteśvara.[32] The teacher Śāntipa thought that Bhikṣu Vīravajra's system for the explication of secret mantra was excellent, and that the oral instructions were also great. So it has been stated. Śāntipa's vast [teachings] corresponded to the piṭakas in general. Vīravajra's were encapsulated in esoteric instructions to facilitate practice. Since all outer and inner doubts had been eliminated by means of those two, ['Brog mi] was extremely happy. In general, he stayed for thirteen years in both Nepal and India. So it has been stated.[33]

Return to Tibet

Then both Stag and 'Brog returned to Tibet. If translators and paṇḍitas came from India as far as Nepal, it was customary for them to come here [to Tibet]. So it has been stated. Both the abbot and the teacher welcomed them.[34] When an account of the Dharma was made, it is said that they were extremely pleased because the great master 'Brog mi had become a very great expert. When they asked what Stag Lo knew, it is said that he could do nothing except read the *Prajñāpāramitāhṛdaya* in the Indian [language].[35]

Both the abbot and the teacher asked, "How is it that 'Brog mi here became a great expert, but you don't know anything?"

It is said that Stag Lo replied, "He took a skull cup and went elsewhere.[36] I had faith in the Mahābodhi of the Vajrāsana [at Bodhgayā] and performed some circumambulations."

Nevertheless, he was very venerable, and founded the great establishment of the Stag.[37]

བླ་ཆེན་གྱིས་སྐྱུ་ཆེའི་སྟོད་ལ་ཆཤད་པ་རྒྱ་ཆེན་པོ་མཛད་སྐྱིད་ལ་སྨུ་གུ་ལུང་དང་ལྷ་རྩེ་བྲག་དང་། གསམ་པའི་རྫོང་བྲོ་བ་བྲག་ཆེན་པོ་ཞིག་ཡོད་དེར་བཞུགས་ནས་བསྒོམས་པས་ལྷ་ལྷམ་གཅིག་ལ་སྤྲུས་ཨེ་ཀྲུ་དང་རྡོ་རྗེ་འདང་དེར་བལྷམས་གསུང་སྐབས་སུ་སྤྱ་དྲོའི་རྩུར་ཉེ་བ་གནམ་ཐང་དཀར་པོའི་འགྲོག་པས་སྤྱན་དྲངས་ནས། ཆོས་ཀྱི་ཉན་ཤད་མང་པོ་མཛད་ཅིང་བཞུགས་པའི་དུས་སུ། ཇོ་བོ་ཀླུ་ཡ་ཧྲ་རས་པཎྜི་ཏ་ཡོང་གིན་ཡོད་པས་སུར་ཤོག་ཅེས་པའི་འཕྲིན་བཏང་ནས་བྱུང་བ་ལ། ཆོས་ཅི་ཤེས་དྲིས་པས་ཕྱིར་མང་འ་རིག་པའི་པཎྜི་ཏ་ཡིན་བྱེ་བྲག་དུ་སྔགས་དེ་ནས་ཀུང་མ་རྒྱུད་ཁྱད་པར་དུ་རྣལ་འབྱོར་དབང་ཕྱུག་གི་གདམ་ངག་ལ་མཁས་ཟེར་བས་སྒོམ་པ་ལ་རྩ་དང་ཐུད་པ་བཞིན་དགྱེས་ཏེ་རྡོ་རྗེ་ཐེག་པ་ལ་མཁས་པར་རྟོགས་ནས་དགྱེས་པས་སྐྱེ་གྲོང་ནས་བསུ་ཏེ་གྲོམ་པ་ལྷ་རྩེའི་བྲག་ལ་ཟླ་བ་གཅིག་ཏུ་ཆོས་ཀྱི་ལོ་རྒྱུས་དང་། བླ་མ་ལྔ་བཅུ་པའི་སྒོ་ནས་དཔོན་སློབ་ཀྱི་འབྲེལ་རྟོག་ཅིང་བཞུགས་སྐད་པཎྜི་ཏས་ལོ་ཚ་བའི་སྐད་མ་གོ་བར་དུས་པའི་ཏམ་ཡོད་དེ་མ་དག།

དེར་དཔོན་སློབ་གཉིས་སློབ་དཔོན་མཚན་ཉིད་དང་སློབ་མ་སྟོད་ལྷན་པར་ཤེས་ནས་གཅིག་ལ་གཅིག་ཕན་རྩུན་མཉེས་ནས། པཎྜི་ཏ་མང་འགར་སྨུ་གུ་ལུང་དུ་སྤྱན་དྲངས་ནས་ལོ་ལྷུར་བཞུགས་པ་དང་། གསུང་ངག་མ་ལུས་པར་གནང་བར་ཞལ་གྱིས་བཞེས། ལོ་ཚ་བས་ལོ་རེ་ལ་གསེར་སྲང་བརྒྱ་བརྒྱ་སྟེ་ལྔ་བརྒྱ་འབུལ་བར་ཁས་བླངས་ནས་ཆོས་ཀྱི་ཉན་ཤད་བྱེད་ཅིང་ལོ་གསུམ་སོང་བ་དང་། པཎྜི་ཏའི་ཞལ་ནས་ང་རྒྱ་གར་དུ་འགྲོ་གསུང་བ་ལ།

བླ་ཆེན་གྱིས་དང་པོ་ལོ་ལྔ་བཞུགས་པར་ཞལ་གྱིས་བཞེས་པ་ལགས་མོད། ད་རྩུང་བཞུགས་པར་ཞུ་བྱས་པས

ཇོ་བོའི་ཞལ་ནས་ཁྱོད་ཀྱི་ཆོས་མ་ཚར་ན་སྡོད་པ་ལ། ཆོས་ཐམས་ཅད་ནི་ལེགས་པར་ཚར་བས་ང་འགྲོ་ཁྱོད་རང་གི་གསེར་ཕྱི་གསུང་བ་ལ།

ལོ་ཚ་བས་གསེར་རྫོགས་པར་དབུལ་དགོངས་ནས་གསེར་སྲང་བཞི་བརྒྱ་ཙམ་རྙེད་ནས་བརྒྱ་མ་རྙེད་པ་ལ་ཟུར་པོ་ཆེ་ཤཱཀྱ་འབྱུང་གནས་སྲུམ་པ་ལྷ་གདོང་བ་ཡིན་གཡས་རུ་ཐག་གི་བྲག་རྒྱ་བོ་ལ་ཡང་དག་གི་སྒྲུབ་པ་མཛད་ཅིང་བཞུགས་པའི་དུས་སུ། སྔར་ཡང་ཆོས་འབྲེལ་ཙམ་ཡོད་བླ་ཆེན་གྱིས་མི་བཏང་ནས་གདམ་ངག་སྤྱིན་གྱིས་ཡར་ཤོག་བྱས་པས།

Lord Gayadhara's First Trip to Tibet

The great master ['Brog mi] gave extensive explications during the earlier part of his life, and during the latter [lived] at Mu gu lung and the cliffs of Lha rtse.[38] There was a great cliff known as Gam pa'i rdzong. He stayed there in meditation. The sons Indra and Rdo rje were also born to Lha Lcam gcig there. So it has been stated.[39] Once he received an invitation from the nomads of Gnam thang dkar po near Spa dro.[40] While he was staying there giving many explanations of Dharma, he received a message sent by Lord Gayadhara that said, "A paṇḍita is arriving; come welcome him!" When he asked what Dharma he knew, he was told that [Gayadhara] was a paṇḍita who knew everything in general, and in particular mantra. From within that, he knew the mother tantras, and was especially expert in the oral instructions of the Lord of Yogins. ['Brog mi] was joyful like a thirsty man coming upon water. Delighted to know that he was an expert in the Vajrayāna, he welcomed him by way of Skyid grong.[41] It is said that they stayed at the Brom pa Lha rtse cliffs for one month evaluating the link between teacher and disciple by means of Dharma accounts, and the *Gurupañcāśikā*.[42] The tale of the paṇḍita not understanding the speech of the translator, who wept, is corrupt.[43]

At that point, after it was understood that the paṇḍita was qualified and the disciple was worthy, both teacher and disciple were pleased with each other. The paṇḍita was invited to Mu gu lung in Mang 'gar, and agreed to stay for five years and to give absolutely all the Oral Instructions [of the Lam 'bras].[44] The translator agreed to offer five hundred ounces of gold, one hundred ounces for each year. Three years had passed with the teaching and learning of Dharma when the paṇḍita said, "I am going to India."

The great master replied, "Surely you agreed at first to stay for five years. Please continue to stay."

The lord said, "If your Dharma were not completed, I would stay, but since all the Dharma has been carefully completed, I am going. Reduce your gold."

But the translator decided to offer the gold in full. Just four hundred ounces of gold had been obtained; one hundred had not been obtained. Zur po che Shākya 'byung gnas, who was from Sram pa wa gdong, was performing the practice of Yang dag at the vast cliffs of Thag in G.yas ru. They also had a slight Dharma link before.[45] The great master sent a man to tell him, "Come up and I will give you oral instructions!"

Some disciples said, "It is an obstacle. Please don't go."

སློབ་མ་ལ་ལ་ན་རེ་བར་ཆད་ཡིན་པས་མི་བཞུད་པར་ཞུ་ཟེར་བ་ལ།

ཟུར་ན་རེ་སྒྲུབ་པ་བྱས་ཀྱང་ཆོས་དོན་དུ་གཉེར་བ་ལས་མེད་འབྲོག་མི་ལོ་ཙཱ་བ་ཆེན་པོ་ཡིན་པས་ངེས་པར་གདམ་ངག་ཟབ་མོ་མངའ་བས་འགྲོ་ཟེར་ནས

མུ་གུ་ལུང་དུ་བྱོན་གསེར་སྔ་ཕྱིར་ཆོས་ཞུས་པ་ཅོ་ལ་སྲང་བརྒྱ་ཙམ་ཕུལ། བླ་ཆེན་གྱིས་བསམ་མི་ཁྱབ་ཀྱི་གདམས་པ་དང་། རྒྱུད་ཀྱི་མངོན་རྟོགས་ཀྱི་ཆ་ཤད་པ་ཡམ་མེ་བ་ཞིག་གནང་བས་ཁོང་དགེས་ནས།། བླ་མ་ཆེན་པོའི་བཀའ་དྲིན་གྱིས།། ཨ་པོའི་མདོ་རྒྱུ་འཕྲུལ་སེམས་ཕྱོགས་ནོར་དུ་བཏང་།། ཟེར་ལོ།

དེའི་དུས་སུ་བེར་གྱི་ཐོག་དུ་ཚར་མ་ཁུར་བས་གཞན་ན་རེ་བེར་ཆུད་འཛེ་བྱས་པས

ཟུར་པོ་ཆེ་ཆུད་མ་ཟོས་ན་བེར་ཆུད་ཟོས་པས་མི་སྡོ་ཟེར་སྐད།

དེ་ལྟར་ཐམས་ཅད་སྡོམ་པས་གསེར་སྲང་ལྔ་བརྒྱ་འཁར་གཞོང་གི་ནང་དུ་བླུགས་ཏེ། བླ་ཆེན་འབྲོག་གིས་ཇོ་བོ་ལ་ཕུལ་བས། གསེར་མངས་པའི་སྟོབས་ཀྱིས་སྒྱུ་མ་ཡིན་ནམ་ཅི་ཡིན་སྙམ་ནས་ཇོ་བོ་ཡིད་མ་ཆེས་ནས། མང་གར་དྲིལ་ཆེན་གྱི་མི་གང་མང་སར་གསེར་ཁྲེར་སྡེ་བསྟན་ནས། འདི་ཅིར་འདུག་དྲིས་པས

མི་རྣམས་ཀྱིས་གསེར་དུ་གདའ་བྱས་པས། བཟོད་ཡིད་ཆེས་ཏེ་སློབ་མ་གཅིག་གིས་བླ་མ་གཅིག་ལ་འབུལ་བ་བྱས་པ་དེ་བས་ཆེ་བ་བྱུང་བ་མེད་གསུང་དེས་མཉེས་ནས

ད་ཁྱོད་ཅི་འདོད་གསུང་བ་ལ།

གསུང་ངག་རིན་པོ་ཆེ་ལ་ལྷག་མ་བདོག་ན་ཞུ་བྱས་པས

ལྷག་མ་མ་ལུས་པར་བྱིན་པ་དེ་ཡིན་ད་ཅིག་ཀྱང་མེད། གཞན་ཅི་འདོད་གསུང་བ་ལ

འོ་ན་ཇོ་བོའི་དགོངས་པ་འདི་ཡིན་ནམ་སྙམ་ནས། གསུང་ངག་རིན་པོ་ཆེ་འདི་བོད་གཞན་ལ་མི་གནང་བར་ཞུས་པས

འདི་བརྫུན་མེད་པའི་རྟགས་ཡིན་ཞལ་གྱིས་བཞེས། པཎ་ཊི་ཏ་གསེར་བསྡོམས་ནས་རྒྱ་གར་དུ་གཤེགས་སོ་ལན་གསུམ་བྱོན་པའི་དང་པོ།། མར་ལོས་དང་སེང་ལྡེང་གི་རྟ་ཞིག་ཧ་ནག་པོ་ཕུལ་ནས་ཆོས་ཞུས་པས་མ་བྱུང

But Zur replied, "I am practicing, but I seek nothing except the Dharma. 'Brog mi is a great translator, so he certainly has profound oral instructions. I am going."

He traveled to Mu gu lung and offered about one hundred ounces of gold for the Dharma he requested earlier and later. When the great master bestowed the oral instructions of the *Bsam mi khyab*, and a rough explanation of the [method] for direct realization of the tantra, he was pleased, and claimed, "By the kindness of the great master, this old guy's *Māyājāla sūtra* and Sems phyogs are enriched."[46]

When he carried briarwood [for 'Brog mi] on his cloak during that time, others exclaimed, "The cloak will be spoiled!"

It is said that he replied, "If Zur po che is not spoiled, it doesn't matter if the cloak is spoiled."

In that way, adding it all together, the great master 'Brog poured the five hundred ounces of gold inside a copper basin and offered it to the lord. Because there was so much gold the lord thought, "Is this an illusion? What is this?" and couldn't believe it. He took the gold to a place where there were many people of Mang gar Dril chen, showed it, and asked, "What is this?"

When the people replied, "It is gold," he was able to believe it, said, "A disciple has never presented a master with an offering greater than this," and was pleased.

Then he asked ['Brog mi], "What do you now want?"

He replied, "If you have any more of the Precious Oral Instructions, I request them."

"I gave absolutely everything. That's it." he said, "Now there is nothing left. What else do you want?"[47]

Thinking, "Well, is this also the intention of the lord?" he replied, "Please do not give these Precious Oral Instructions to another Tibetan."

The paṇḍita agreed, took the gold, this was a sign that he had not lied, and traveled to India. This was the first of three trips.[48] Mar Lo also offered ['Brog mi] a sandalwood saddle and a black horse, and requested Dharma, but it didn't happen.[49]

Lord Gayadhara's Return to Tibet with 'Gos Lo tsā ba

Then, at a later time, 'Gos Khu pa lha btsan, from the region of Rta nag, also requested [Dharma from 'Brog mi], but it didn't happen. At that time, ['Gos,] due to the great reputation of the Son of the Victors, Maitrīpa, came to invite him

དེ་ནས་དུས་ཕྱིས་ཡུལ་རྟ་ནག་པ་འགོས་ཁུ་པ་ལྷ་བཙན་གྱིས་ཀྱང་ཞུས་པས་མ་བྱུང་དེ་དུས་ན་རྒྱལ་སྲས་མི་ཏྲི་པ་བླ་ཆེན་འབྲོག་རྒྱ་གར་ན་ཡོད་ཅེ་ན་ལྷོ་དཔལ་གྱི་རི་ལ་ཕྱིན་ཟེར་ཡི་འདུག་གཞན་ཀུན་ཟེ་ཆོམ་ཟ་ཡིན་འདུག་ཤ་བ་རི་པ་ལ་སྙིང་པོ་སྐོར་གསན་རྟོགས་པ་ཁྱད་པར་ཅན་བྱུང་དོ་ཧཱ་བདུན་ན་མདའ་བག་ཙམ་ཡོད་པས་མདའ་བདག་རྩོད་པ་ལས་རྒྱལ་བས་རྒྱལ་བ་བྱ་བ་ཡིན། ན་རོ་ཏ་པའི་ཉེ་འབྲེལ་བྲམ་ཟེ་སྐུ་སྡིགས་པ་ཡིན། ན་རོ་ཏ་པས་རིགས་ཕབ་ནས་ཆོས་ལ་བཙུགས་པ་ཡིན་རིགས་སོར་ཆུད་པ་ལ་རིགས་དབྱུང་གི་ཚོ་ག་དགོས་གསུང་སྐན་པའི་གྲགས་པ་ཆེ་བས། དོ་མོ་ན་ཆུར་སྤྱན་འདྲེན་དུ་འོངས་པ་ལ་ལམ་དུ་འཛིགས་པ་ཆེ་བས། གསེར་ཟོ་ཐོད་པ་བམ་རིལ་གྱི་ལྷག་ཁུང་དུ་བླུགས་ཏེ་ལ་ཆས་ཁ་བཅད་ནས་བཙག་དང་རམས་ཀྱི་རི་མོ་བྱས་ཏེ་འོངས་པ་ལ། མོན་ཀུན་ན་རེ་བོད་ཀྱི་ལྷ་འདྲེ་ཐམས་ཅད་ལྷོ་བལ་དུ་སོང་ཟེར་རོ།།

དེ་ཙམ་ན་གྲོ་མོ་ན་ཇོ་བོ་སླ་ཡ་ཧྣ་ར་བཞུགས་པ་དང་རྒྱ་འགྲམ་ཞིག་དུ་འབྲལ་ནས་ལོ་རྒྱུས་གྱིས་པས། ང་རྒྱལ་བ་མི་ཏྲི་བ་ཡིན་གསུངས་བ་དང་།

ཆོས་ཀྱང་མཁས་གདམ་ངག་ཀྱང་ཆེ་བར་འདུག་པས་མགུ་ནས་སྤྱན་དྲངས་སྟེ་བོད་དུ་བྱོན་པའི་ལམ་གར་སྔར་ཀྱི་མོན་ཀུན་ན་རེ་ཁ་ཞེང་སོང་བའི་འདྲེ་ཡིན་ཟེར་བ་དེ་ཀུན་བོད་ཀྱི་ལོ་ཙ་བ་གསེར་མང་པོ་ཁྱེར་ནས་པཎ་ཌི་ཏ་སྤྱན་དྲངས་ནས་ཡོང་གིན་ཡོད་པར་འདུག་ཟེར་ནས། ལམ་ཐམས་ཅད་ན་སྒྲུགས་ནས་ཡོད་པའི་གཏམ་ལོ་ཙ་བས་ཐོས་ནས།

ལོ་ཙ་བ་དཔོན་གཡོག་གིས་གྲོས་བྱས་པས་མགོས་ཀྱི་སློབ་མ་ཤེས་རབ་སྒྲོན་ལམ་ན་རེ། བླ་མ་ལོ་པཎ་མི་བཞུགས་ན་བོད་ཐམས་ཅད་ཀྱི་མིག་དུས་གཅིག་ལ་ལོང་བ་དང་འདྲ་བ་ཡིན་པས། ངས་བླ་མར་རྫུས་ལ་འགྲོ་ཟེར་ནས་

ལོ་ཙ་བ་དང་སེ་གཉིས་ཆ་ལུགས་རྗེས་ཏེ། ལོ་ཙ་བས་མུ་ལྡོ་བར་རྫུས་པས་ཐར། སེ་བླ་མ་ལ་གུས་པ་དང་སེམས་བསྐྱེད་བཟང་པོའི་སྟོབས་ཀྱིས་མ་སོད་པར་ཐར་སྐད།

སྤྱིར་བོད་དུ་བླ་མའི་དོན་དུ་སྲོག་གཏོང་ནུས་པ་སེ་ཤེས་རབ་སྒྲོན་ལས་མ་བྱུང་གསུང་།

དེར་ལོ་པཎ་གྱིས་བོད་དུ་བྱོན་པས་འགོ་ཡུལ་དུ། ཇོ་བོ་སླ་ཡ་ཧྣ་རའི་སྔར་གྱི་སློབ་མ་ཀུན་དང་ཕྲད་པས། རྒྱལ་སྲས་མི་ཏྲི་བ་མིན་པར་འདུག་པས། མགོས་ཀྱིས་བླ་མས་ང་ལ་བརྫུན་བྱས་ཅེས་སྨྲས་པས།

up from Dro mo.[50] While the great master 'Brog had been in India, [Maitrīpa] was claiming to have gone to Śrīparvata in the south, although everyone else doubted it, and to have heard the *Snying po skor* from Śabaripa, which caused an exceptional realization to arise. Because he had some influence at the Vajrāsana he was "the Sovereign," and because he was victorious in debate he was called "the Victor."[51] He was a brahmin tīrthika who was a relative of Nārotapa. Nārotapa stated that having descended from caste and entered the Dharma, a rite of restoration would be necessary to reestablish caste. Because he was very frightened on the path, ['Gos Lo tsā ba] poured the gold into the hole in the back of a complete skull, sealed it with wax, and painted it with designs of red ochre and indigo. When he came, all the Mon people exclaimed, "All the gods and ghosts of Tibet[52] are going south to Nepal!"

At that point, Lord Gayadhara was staying in Gro mo. They met on the banks of a river and ['Gos Lo tsā ba] asked about his story.[53] [Gayadhara] replied, "I am the Victor Maitrīpa."

Since he was expert in Dharma and also had great oral instructions, ['Gos Lo tsā ba] was pleased, and invited him. On the path as they traveled to Tibet, the translator heard the news that all the Mon people from before were waiting along all the paths, saying, "All those we said were ghosts passing by last year were a Tibetan translator carrying much gold. He invited a paṇḍita, and is returning."[54]

When the translator and his attendant discussed it, [Se] Shes rab smon lam, who was a disciple of Mgos, said, "If the masters, the translator and the paṇḍita, do not live it would be like the eyes of all Tibetans being blinded at the same moment. I will go impersonating the master."

The translator and Se both exchanged clothes. It is said that the translator escaped by impersonating a beggar, and that Se escaped without being killed due to the force of his devotion to the master and his fine awakening of the enlightenment mind.

In general, there has been no one in Tibet except Se Shes rab smon able to sacrifice his life for the sake of the master. So it has been stated.

When the translator and the paṇḍita reached Tibet, they met all the previous disciples of Lord Gayadhara in 'Go yul, and [it was revealed] that he was not the Son of the Victors, Maitrīpa.[55] Mgos said, "The master has lied to me."

The lord replied, "Don't you want the Dharma? I am more expert in the Dharma than Maitrīpa."[56] And Mgos was also extremely pleased with the Dharma.

ཇོ་བོའི་ཞལ་ནས་ཁྱོད་ཆོས་འདོད་པ་མ་ཡིན་ནམ་ཆོས་ནི་མི་ཧྲི་བས་ང་མཁས་གསུང་བ་ལ། ཆོས་ལ་མགོས་ཀྱང་ཤིན་དུ་མགུ

དེ་ནས་ལྷ་ཆེན་འབྲོག་དང་འབྲལ་ནས། ལྷ་ཆེན་གྱིས་ཇོ་ཐུགས་དམ་དང་འགལ་བར་མཆིའོ་ཞུས་པས།

ཇོ་བོའི་ཞལ་ནས་ཁྱོད་རང་ལ་དམ་ཚིག་གི་ཉེས་པ་བྱུང་བར་མཆིའོ། ཁོང་གཞུང་གི་བཤད་པས་ཚིམ་ནས་གདམ་ངག་ཁུངས་དང་མི་གཅོད་པར་འདུག་གསུང་ནས

ཕྱིས་ཀྱང་གསུང་ངག་མ་གནང་བགྱི་བར་གདའ། རྒྱུད་གསུམ་ལ་སོགས་ལ་འགོས་ཀྱིས་པ་ཚབ་ཏུ་འགྱུར་ཡང་བྱས། ཉན་བཤད་ཀྱང་མང་དུ་མཛད་ནས། གསེར་མང་པོ་ཕུལ་ཏེ་རྒྱ་གར་དུ་གཤེགས་ཏེ་ལན་གཉིས་པ།

ཡང་དུས་ཕྱིས་ཡུལ་ལོ་ཁ་བ་ཀྱི་ཇོ་ཟླ་བའི་འོད་ཟེར་གྱིས་སྤྱོད་ཕུ་རངས་ན་རྩུར་སྤྱན་དྲངས་ནས། དེ་ཙམ་ན་ལྷ་ཆེན་འབྲོག་ནི་སྐུ་གཤེགས། དེ་ནས་པཎ་ཌི་ཏས་བླ་མ་འབྲོག་མི་ལ་གསེར་བཙོལ་བ་བླངས་པ་ལ་སོགས་པའི་བརྫུན་གྱི་གཏམ་དེ་དག་བོར་བར་བྱའོ།།

དེའི་དུས་སུ་གྱི་ཇོའི་སློབ་མ་གཉོས་འབྱུང་པོ་ལ་སོགས་པས་ཁ་རག་ཏུ་སྤྱན་དྲངས་ནས་བཞུགས་པའི་དུས་སུ། ཇོ་བོ་ལ་འཆི་ལྟས་བྱུང་ནས་ངའི་བུ་ཚའོ་བོད་ཕུ་ན་ཡོད་པས་དེར་སྐྱོལ་གསུང་།

གཉོས་ལ་སོགས་པ་ན་རེ་བླ་མའི་ཚེ་འདིའི་འབྲེལ་པ་ནི་རྒྱ་གར་ན་བདོག་ཆོས་ཀྱི་ཕྱོགས་ཀྱི་བུ་བདག་ཅག་ཀ་ལགས་མོད་བོད་ཕུ་ན་འབྲོག་མིའི་སློབ་མ་སེ་རོག་གཉིས་བྱ་བ་ཡོད་པ་ཡིན། དེད་ཅག་བླ་མ་དངོས་ཀྱི་སློབ་མ་ལགས་ན་འདིར་བཞུགས་པར་ཞུ་བྱས་པས

དེས་མི་ཕན་ཡར་སྐྱོལ་གསུང་ནས

བོད་ཕུར་བྱོན་ཏེ། སྒོམ་ཆེན་སེ་རོག་གཉིས་ལ་ཇོ་བོའི་ཞལ་ནས་བུ་ཀུན་བསྒྲུབ་པ་ལ་བརྩོན་འགྲུས་མ་ཆུད་ཅིག། ངས་བོད་དང་རྒྱ་གར་ལ་ཕར་འགྲོ་ཚུར་འགྲོ་འབའ་ཞིག་བྱས་བསྒྲུབ་པ་ཙམ་མ་བྱས་ཀྱང་སྤུགས་པ་འཆི་ན་འདི་ལྟར་འཆི་བ་ཡིན་གསུང་ནས།

ལུས་དཀྱིལ་དཀྲུངས་མཛད་རྡོ་རྗེ་དྲིལ་བུ་ཕྱག་གཉིས་སུ་བཞེས་སྟེ་འོད་ཀྱི་གོང་བུའི་འཕོ་བ་མཛད་པས། སྤྱི་ཙུག་ནས་འོད་རིལ་བ་ཙམ་ཞིག་འཕྲོན་ནས་ནམ་མཁའ་ལ་ཐམས་ཅད་ཀྱིས

Then they met the great master 'Brog. The great master said, "The lord has broken his promise."[57]

The lord replied, "It is you to whom a transgression of sacred commitment will occur.[58] Satisfied with the explanation of the scripture, he has not found out about the oral instructions."

Even later he did not give the Oral Instructions [of the Lam 'bras]. Translations of the *Rgyud gsum* and so forth were also made by 'Gos at Pa tshab. After much studying and teaching, he offered a large amount of gold, and [Gayadhara] traveled to India.[59] This was the second trip.

Lord Gayadhara's Third Trip to Tibet, and His Death

Again, at a later time, [Lord Gayadhara] was invited up to Pu rangs in Stod by Gyi jo Zla ba'i 'od zer, who was from the region of Lo kha.[60] At that time the great master 'Brog had passed away. Those false stories of the paṇḍita then picking up gold that had been entrusted to master 'Brog mi, and so forth, should be rejected.[61]

During that time, disciples of Gyi jo, such as Gnyos 'Byung po, invited [Gayadhara] to Kha rag.[62] While he was staying there the signs of death appeared to the lord, and he said, "My [spiritual] grandsons are in Thod phu. Take me there."

Gnyos and the others said, "The master's relatives in this life are in India, but we are certainly your Dharma sons. Two disciples of 'Brog mi called Se and Rog are in Thod phu.[63] If we are true disciples of the master, please stay here."

"That won't help," he replied, "Take me up there!"

They went to Thod phu, and the lord said to the two great meditators Se and Rog, "All my sons, you must not lack diligence in practice! Even though I only went back and forth between Tibet and India, and I have not practiced much, when a mantra practitioner dies, he dies like this."

He sat with body in the crossed-legged position. He took the vajra and bell in both hands and performed the globe of light transference. A light about the size of a pellet ejected from the crown of his head, went as far as everyone could see into the sky, and he passed away.[64]

Later, the lord's personal painted image of Śrī Hevajra and his manuscript of the *Brtag gnyis* were given as representations of the deity to 'Phags pa Chos snang, who was the close attendant disciple of both the spiritual friends Se and Rog.[65] Chos snang and Nag ston were master and disciple. He offered them to Nags ston Lo tsā ba. Nags ston and the great

མཐོང་གི་བར་དུ་སོང་ནས་སྐུ་འདས།

ཕྱིས་ཇོ་བོའི་ཐུགས་དམ་དཔལ་ཀྱེའི་རྡོ་རྗེའི་བྲིས་སྐུ་དང་བརྟག་གཉིས་ཀྱི་དཔེའ་རྣམས་དགེ་བཤེས་སེ་རོག་གཉིས་ཀྱི་སློབ་མ་ཉེ་གནས་འཕགས་པ་ཆོས་སྣང་ལ་ལྷ་རྗེན་དུ་གནང་། ཆོས་སྣང་དང་ནག་སྟོན་དཔོན་སློབ་ཡིན་པ་དེས་ནགས་སྟོན་ལོ་ཙ་ལ་ཕུལ་ནགས་སྟོན་དང་བླ་ཆེན་ཕར་སློབ་ཚུར་སློབ་ཡིན་པ་ཆོས་འཁོར་ལ་སློབ་དཔོན་རིན་པོ་ཆེ་བྱོན་ཙ་དཔེའ་དེ་རེས་མ་ཕུལ་འབུམ་བཅུ་བཞི་དུས་ཞིག་ཕུལ་གྲིལ་བུའི་ཡུ་བ་ཆག་འདུག་གསུང་། རྡོ་རྗེ་རྗེ་པ་ཏུ་མཚམས་སུ་བྱོན་ཙམ་ན་གཡུང་སྟོན་བྱ་བ་ཞིག་གི་ལག་ན་འདུག་གར་ཚར་གཅིག་ཞུ་འདི་འབུལ་ཟེར་བ་ལ་ས་སྐྱ་མིན་པར་རྒྱུད་གཉན་པོ་ཤད་མི་ནུས་གསུང་འཉན་པས་དང་པོ་རྒྱུད་ཤད་འཕྲོ་ལ་དགེ་བཤེས་གྲོངས་པ་མང་པོ་བྱུང་། ཕྱིས་ཡིག་རྒྱའི་ཐུན་བྲུས་ནས་ཤད་ནས་རྡོ་རྗེ་དེ་ལེན་པ་ཡིན་པ་ལ་གསུང་། བྲིས་སྐུ་དང་བརྟག་གཉིས་ནག་སྟོན་ལོ་ཙ་བ་ལས་བརྒྱུད་ཏེ་ས་སྐྱར་བྱོན་ནས་ད་ལྟ་ཡང་ས་སྐྱ་ན་བཞུགས། དྲིལ་བུ་ཡིན་ཟེར་བ་ཞིག་ཀྱང་རྗེ་ཏུ་མཚམས་སུ་བྱོན་ཙམ་ན་ཕྱུག་དུ་བྱོན་ནས་ད་ལྟ་འང་ས་སྐྱ་ན་ཡོད་དོ།

དེ་རྣམས་ཀྱིས་ཇོ་བོ་ཀླུ་ཡ་ཧྲ་ར་ལས་འཕྲོས་པ་བར་སྐབས་ཀྱི་ལོ་རྒྱུས་ཡིན་གསུང་།།

དེ་ལྟ་བུའི་བླ་མ་ལ་གསུང་ངག་རིན་པོ་ཆེའི་མཛོད་རྙེད་པའི་རྗེ་མུ་ལུང་པ་དེ་ལ་ཡོན་ཏན་གྱི་ཁྱད་པར་ཅི་མངའ་ཞེ་ན་མཁས་པ་མངའ་རིག་པ། བསྐྱེད་པའི་རིམ་པ་ལ་བརྟན་པ་ཐོབ་ལུས་གཅིག་ནས་གཉིས་སུ་སྤྲུལ་བ་དང་སྦྱིན་སྲེག་གི་ཐབ་ནས་ཡོ་བྱད་ལེན་ནུས་རླུང་གི་ནུས་པས་ནམ་མཁའ་ལ་དཀྱིལ་ཀྲུང་འཆའ་ནུས་པ་བསམས་ན་ཤེས་པའི་མངོན་པར་ཤེས་པ་ཅི་རིགས་པ་ཡོད། འཕོ་བ་བྱེད་པར་ནུས་སྐད་དེ་ལ་སྦྱོར་སྣང་འདིར་བསྟན་པ་ལ་བླ་ཆེན་འབྲོག་བཀའ་དྲིན་ཆེ་སྟོང་དུ་རིན་ཆེན་བཟང་པོ་ཆེ་སྟེ་སྟོན་སངས་རྒྱས་དཀར་རྒྱལ་འཛེག་ཁྲི་པ་བྱ་བ་བྱུང་ནས་འཕྲུལ་ཆོས་འདྲ་ལ་ཧི་ས་གནད་བཙོས་པ་བསྟན་པས་འཁམས་ཡན་ཆོད་འདུས་ན་ཆོས་ལོག་ཤཱད་པ་ལ་རིན་བཟང་གིས་མ་བཏུད་པར་ཟླ་བ་དྲུག་ཐུགས་དམ་མཛད་ནས་ཁོ་ཙན་བྱོན་ཐུན་བཏབས་པས་ཁོ་ཁྲི་སྟེང་ནས་ལྷུམ་མོན་ཕྲུག་ཅིག་ཏུ་སོང་གང་པ་ཡིན་བྲུས་པས་ཁྲ་ནུ་བ་ཡིན་ཟེར་ཀླུ་དཀར་རྒྱལ་བྱ་བ་ཁོ་ལ་ཞུགས་པ་ཡིན་ཟེར་ཁོ་མིན་ན་དེང་སང་དུ་འང་ཆོས་ལོག་དར་འགྲོ་གསུང་དེ།

སྐུ་འདའ་ཀར་ངའི་ཕུང་པོ་འདི་ཞག་བདུན་མ་བསྲེག་པར་ཞོག་ཅིག། ཞག་བདུན་ན་རིག་

master [Sa chen] were disciples of each other. When Slob dpon Rin po che went to a Dharma council, [Nags ston] didn't offer the Indian manuscript, but offered a fourteen volume set of the *Śatasāhasrikā prajñāpāramitā*.[66] The handle of [Lord Gayadhara's] bell was broken. So it has been stated. When the lord went to Ru 'tshams, the vajra was in the hands of one called G.yung ston, who said, "I request a single explanation of the *Pañjara*, and I will offer this."[67] But he replied, "I am unable to explain the perilous tantra, except to a Sa skya follower. Because it is perilous, the [root] tantra must first be explained or many spiritual friends would die in the process." He later performed sessions of the hundred-syllable mantra and explained [the *Vajrapañjara*] to get that vajra.[68] Both the painted image and the *Brtag gnyis* were passed down through the translator Nag ston, arrived in Sa skya, and are even now residing in Sa skya. When the lord [Grags pa rgyal mtshan] traveled to Ru 'tshams, one said to be the bell [of Gayadhara] also came into his hands, and is even now in Sa skya.[69]

Those are stated to be the intermediate stories concerning Lord Gayadhara.

'Brog mi Lo tsā ba's Special Qualities, and His Death

What special qualities did the Lord of Mu [gu] lung who obtained the treasury of the Precious Oral Instructions from such a master have? He was a consummate expert, he achieved stability in the creation stage, he could emanate two bodies from one and pick up objects from the furnace of the fire offerings,[70] by the force of the vital winds he was able to hold the crossed-legged position in space, and he had various clairvoyant powers with which to know the thoughts [of others]. It is said that he was able to perform the transference [of consciousness]. In general, the great master 'Brog was the kindest to the Doctrine here in Smad. Rin chen bzang po was the kindest in Stod.[71] Previously, a certain Sangs rgyas dkar rgyal appeared, called "the one on a grass throne," and taught some short-term Dharma at Ti se while fabricating the essential points.[72] He gathered [disciples] from as far away as Khams. Not tolerating these perverse teachings, Rin [chen] bzang [po] practiced meditation for six months and then went to his place. When [Rin chen bzang po] performed an exorcism, he fell from that throne and turned into a Mon youth. When asked, "Who are you?" he said, "I am from Ku nu."[73] It was said that a nāga called Dkar rgyal had possessed him. If not for him [i.e., Rin chen bzang po] the perverse Dharma would have spread even until today. So it has been stated.

པ་འདི་ཉིད་ལུས་འདི་ཉིད་ལ་ཞུགས་ནས་ཕྱག་རྒྱ་ཆེན་པོ་མཆོག་གི་དངོས་གྲུབ་ཐོབ་པར་བྱེད་དོ་
བདེ་མཆོག་ནས་དེ་འདྲ་བཤད་གསུང་བ་ལ།

མི་རྣམས་ཀྱིས་མ་བརྟགས་པར་གློ་བུར་དུ་གནས་ལས་བསྐྱོད་དེ་དྲོད་མ་ཡལ་བར་འདུག་
གསུང་།

At the point of passing away ['Brog mi] said, "Leave this body of mine for seven days without burning! In seven days, this same intrinsic awareness will enter into this same body, and I will achieve the sublime attainment of Mahāmudrā." It is explained like that in the *Cakrasaṃvara*.

But without inspection, the people quickly moved [his body] from the place while the warmth had not faded. So it has been stated.[74]

དེ་ལྟ་བུའི་བླ་ཆེན་དེ་ལ་སྤྱིར་སློབ་མ་ཤིན་དུ་མང་ན་ཡང་སློབ་མའི་མཆོག་དུ་ཡོད་ཅེ་ན་གསུང་ཚོ་ན་ཐོག་མར་གྲུབ་པ་ཐོབ་པ་དེ་ནས་གཞུང་ཚར་བ་དེ་ནས་མན་ངག་ཚར་བ་གསུང་། གཞུང་ཚར་བའི་སློབ་མ་དང་། མན་ངག་ཚར་བའི་སློབ་མ་དང་། གྲུབ་པ་ཐོབ་པའི་སློབ་མ་དང་གསུམ་མོ།།

དེ་ལ་གཞུང་ཚར་བའི་སློབ་མ་ནི་ལྷ་རྗེའི་གྱི་ལྡང་དབུ་དཀར་བ་ཁོང་གིས་གཞུང་ཚར་ནས་གསུང་ངག་ཞུས་པས་ནོར་ཕྱིར་ལ་ཤོག་གསུང་དེར་དབུས་སུ་ཕྱིན་གཡུའ་པད་ཁྱེད་གང་རྙེད་བླ་ཆེན་ལ་ཕུལ་ནས་བླ་མའི་ཆོས་ཀྱིས་བཙལ་བ་མིན་ཕན་བྱ་གཏོད་བྱ་རྙེད་པ་ཡིན་ཟེར་བླ་ཆེན་གྱིས་བསམས་མི་ཁྲབ་ལ་སོགས་པ་ལས་གསུང་ངག་མ་གནང་གསུང་། ཞངས་ཀྱི་བྲག་ཅེ་སོ་ནག་པ། འཕྲང་འོག་གི་དབྲད་སྟོན་དཀོན་མཆོག་རྒྱལ་པོ། ཁོང་གཉིས་ཡིད་ཀྱང་གཙུགས་ས་སྐྱའི་འཁོན་དཀོན་མཆོག་རྒྱལ་པོ། ཕྱི་ཚར་མདའ་རིས་པ་གསལ་བ་སྙིང་པོ་དང་ལྔ་ཡིན་ནོ།

གདམ་ངག་ཚར་བའི་སློབ་མ་གསུམ་ནི་འབྲོམ་དེ་པ་སྟོན་ཆུང་། ལྷ་བཙུན་ཀ་ལི། སེ་སྟོན་ཀུན་རིག་སྟེ་གསུམ་མོ།།

གྲུབ་པ་ཐོབ་པའི་སློབ་མ་ཕོ་གསུམ་མོ་བཞི་སྟེ།

དེ་ཡང་ཕོ་གསུམ་ནི་ཅང་པ་དགྱེར་སེ་འོ། ཧྲ་ནག་པ་གཤེན་སྒོམ་རོག་པོ། དབུས་པ་ཁོང་གྲུག་ཁེར་ཆེད་པོ་ཞིག་ཡིན་རླུང་གི་ནུས་པས་ཟས་མང་པོ་འཛུ་བ་ཞིག་བྱུང་དེ་རླུང་སྦྱུ་གྱི་སྟོབས་སུ་གྱུར་པ་ཡིན། ཕྱིའི་སྦྱུ་གྱི་དང་ནང་གི་གཉིས་ལས་ནང་གི་ཡིན་ནང་གི་ལ་ཡང་ཡོན་ཏན་གཅོད་པར་བྱེད་པ་དང་ཁ་ཟས་གཅོད་པར་བྱེད་པ་གཉིས་ལས་ཁ་ཟས་གཅོད་པར་བྱེད་པའི་སྦྱུ་གྱི་སྟོབས་སུ་གྱུར་པ་ཡིན་ཆོས་རྗེ་པ་གསུང་ཁོ་ལ་འཚོ

TWO
The Disciples of 'Brog mi Lo tsā ba

IN GENERAL, such a great master had very many disciples. How many best disciples were there? The three types were the disciples who fully received the scriptures, the disciples who fully received the esoteric instructions, and the disciples who reached attainment. When this is taught, those who reached attainment are mentioned first, then those who fully received the scriptures, and then those who fully received the esoteric instructions.

There were five disciples who fully received the scriptures.[75] Gyi ljang Dbu dkar ba of Lha rtse:[76] After he had fully received the scriptures, he requested the Oral Instructions [of the Lam 'bras]. ['Brog mi] replied, "Bring riches and come!" He went to Dbus and obtained a sack full of turquoise. Offering it to the great master, he said, "I didn't seek [this] by means of the master's Dharma. I obtained it through beneficial and harmful deeds." The great master didn't bestow the Oral Instructions, except for the *Bsam mi khyab* and so forth. So it has been stated.[77] And there were Brag rtse So nag pa of Shangs,[78] Dbrad ston Dkon mchog rgyal po of 'Phrang 'og[79] and 'Khon Dkon mchog rgyal po of Sa skya, both of whose minds were also in harmony, and Gsal ba snying po of Mnga' ris who fully received them later.[80]

There were three disciples who fully received the oral instructions. These were 'Brom De pa ston chung, Lha btsun Ka li, and Se ston Kun rig.

There were three male[81] and four female disciples who reached attainment.

The Three Male Disciples Who Reached Attainment

Moreover, the three men were Dgyer Se'o from Tsang,[82] Gshen sgom Rog po from Rta nag[83] and, from Dbus a young man of 'Jag thang in 'Phan yul, Drod po che, who had been a great robber. Due to the force of the vital winds, he could

བ་ཡང་བླ་ཆེན་གྱིས་གནང་སྟེ། ནས་ཕུལ་དགུ་ལ་བྱས་པའི་ཟན་རེ། ལུག་ཤ་གཟུག་རེ། ཆང་ཤུ་རེ་བྱིན་གྱིན་བསྒོམ་དུ་བཅུག་པས་གྲུབ་པ་ཐོབ་བྱུང་གསུང་དྭོད་པོ་ཆེའོ་འཕན་ཡུལ་འཇམ་ཐང་པའི་གྲྭ་འོ་ཡིན་ནོ།།

མོ་བཞི་ནི་རྟོད་མོ་རྡོ་རྗེ་མཚོའ། དབྲད་སྒྲོམ་མ་དཀོན་ནེ། ཤབ་པ་མོ་ལྕམ་གཅིག། འཕྲུད་མོ་ནམ་མཁའོ།།

དེ་ལ་རྟོད་མོ་ཡུལ་མང་འགར་དགྲ་འདུལ་མ་ཡིན་ཁམ་བྱུང་ནས་བུ་ཁྲོ་ཙོ་བསད་ནོར་ཁྲེར་བས་རྐྱེན་བྱས་ནས་སྙིང་རླུང་བྱུང་སྟེ། ཤེས་པ་བསྒོ་ནས་ཡོད་ཙམ་ན། དེ་བླ་ཆེན་གྱིས་གསན་ནས་དེ་ངའི་ཙར་བྱུང་ན་སྡུག་བསྔལ་ཉིད་ཏིང་ངེ་འཛིན་དུ་སློལ་ཤེས་པ་ཡིན་ཏེ་གསུང་བླ་ཆེན་གྱི་སྤྱན་སྔར་འོངས་ནས་དབང་བསྐུར་བ་བྱས་གདམ་ངག་བསྟན་པས་བསྒོ་བ་སངས་ནས་སྡུག་བསྔལ་ཉིད་ཏིང་ངེ་འཛིན་དུ་བསླུལ་བས་ཏིང་ངེ་འཛིན་དཔག་དུ་མེད་པ་སྐྱེས་ཏེ། ལས་འཕྲོ་ཅན་རང་གི་ངང་གིས་ཁམས་འདུས་པས་ཚེ་འདི་ཉིད་ལ་ལུས་མ་སྤངས་པར་ཕྱག་རྒྱ་ཆེན་པོ་གྲུབ་པོ་ཨུ་རྒྱན་དུ་གཤེགས།

ཡང་དབྲད་མོ་དཀོན་ནེ་ཡུལ་མང་འགར་ཕུའི་གཡམ་འཁར་མ་ཡིན། དེས་བླ་ཆེན་ལ་དབང་ཞུས་ནས་གདམ་ངག་གསུངས་པ་ནི། བསམ་མི་ཁྱབ་ཀྱི།

མིག་གི་རྣམ་ཤེས་རྟོག་པ་ཡིས།། གཉིས་མེད་ཡེ་ཤེས་རོ་མཚར་ཆེ།།

ཅེས་བསྟན་པའི་ཚིག་ལ་བརྟེན་ནས། མུ་གུ་ལུང་གི་ཆོས་ས་དེ་ཉིད་དུ་ཞག་བདུན་གྱི་བར་དུ་ཏིང་ངེ་འཛིན་ཞིག་དུ་སོང་སྐད་དོ། དེས་ན་མོས་གུས་ཅན་བྱིན་གྱི་བརླབས་ཀྱིས་ཁམས་འདུ་བ་ཚེ་འདིའི་ཟས་གོས་ཀྱི་རྟོག་པ་གང་ཡང་མེད་པར་སྒྲུབ་པ་འབའ་ཞིག་བྱས་དེ་ཡིན་ཏེ། ཁོང་མང་འཁར་གྱི་རི་ལ་བཞུགས་ཙ་ན་བླ་མ་སེས་ལྷོ་ཤེད་ན་ཕར་ཆོས་འཁོར་ལ་བྱོན་འབྱུལ་བ་མང་པོ་བྱུང་ནས་མང་འཁར་ན་མར་བྱོན་ཙ་ན་འདི་ན་ངའི་ཨ་ཆེ་ཞིག་ཡོད་པས་ཕྲད་དུ་འགྲོ་གསུང་ནས་ཁོང་ཅན་བྱོན་པས་ཁོང་ན་རེ་འདི་ན་མར་བན་བུན་འགྲོ་བ་འདི་པ་ཅི་ཡིན་བྱས་པས་བདག་གི་ཡིན་བྱས་པས་ཁྱོད་ཀྱང་རླུང་གིས་ཁྱེར་ཨ་གསུང་དེ་བས་སྐྱིངས་པ་འོང་མ་སྟོང་ཟེར་ཚེ་འདི་ཉིད་ལ་ལུས་མ་སྤངས་པར་ཕྱག་རྒྱ་ཆེན་པོ་གྲུབ

digest great amounts of food. This was because the vital winds had become razor-sharp. From among the outer and inner razors, this was the inner. From among the inner, there is also that which cuts through qualities and that which cuts through food. From among those two, it had become razor-sharp and able to cut through food.[84] So the Dharma Lord stated. The great master provided [Drod po che] with foodstuffs. Given meals composed of nine portions of barley, a sheep carcass, and a vat of beer, and made to meditate, he reached attainment. So it has been stated.[85]

The Four Female Disciples Who Reached Attainment

The four women were Rtod mo Rdo rje mtsho', Dbrad sgom ma Dkon ne, Shab pa mo Lcam gcig, and 'Phyad mo Nam mkha'.

1. Rtod mo Rdo rje mtsho'

Rtod mo was a Dgra 'dul woman in the Mang 'gar region. A robber appeared, murdered her sons and husband, and took the valuables.[86] That acted as a catalyst, causing a state of depression, and her mind became deranged. The great master heard about it and said, "If she comes to me, she will learn how to make the suffering itself into meditative concentration." At that point she came before the great master and requested the bestowal of initiation. When he taught the oral instructions the madness was cured, the suffering itself was made into meditative concentration, and infinite meditative concentrations arose. For one with residual karma the essential constituents are gathered naturally,[87] and she realized Mahāmudrā in this very lifetime, without discarding the body. She went to Uḍḍiyana.

2. Dbrad sgom Dkon ne

Dbrad mo Dkon ne was a G.yam khar woman in the upper valley of the Mang 'gar region.[88] She asked the great master for initiation, and the oral instructions he spoke were from the *Bsam mi khyab:*

> The nondual primordial awareness of the conceptual visual consciousness is so miraculous.[89]

On the basis of those words he taught, it is said that she went into a meditative concentration for seven days right there in the Dharma place

ནས་པོ་དོང་གི་རིའི་བྲེ་བྲག་སླན་ནགས་རྒྱལ་གྱི་གནོད་སྦྱིན་མོའི་མཆོད་གནས་བྲེད་ཅིང་ད་ལྟ་འང་བཞུགས་ཏེ་འགའ་ཞིག་གིས་སྐབས་སུ་མཐོང་བ་ཡང་འབྱུང་ངོ༎

ཡང་གཅིག་ནི་ཤབ་ཀྱི་ཚ་མོ་རོང་པ་ཏུས་རྗེ་མོ་ཡིན་*མིང་པོ་བདུན་གྱི་སྲིང་མོ་ཡིན།* ཁོང་གིས་ཀྱང་སུ་ག་ལུང་དུ་བྱོན་ནས་དབང་གདམས་ངག་ཞུས་པས་གནང་ནས་བསྒྲུབས་པས་ཚེ་འདི་ཉིད་ལ་གྲུབ་སྐད་*དཔལ་གྱི་རི་ལ་གཤེགས*༎

གཅིག་ནི་དབུས་ཀྱི་འཕན་ཡུལ་གྱི་མཆད་མོ་སྐྱེ། དེས་ཀྱང་བླ་མ་འབྲོག་མི་ལ་དབང་སྐུར་ཞུས་བདེ་མཆོག་གི་གདམས་ངག་དང་བསྐྱེད་པའི་རིམ་པ་ཕག་མོ་མཁའ་སྤྱོད། རྫོགས་པའི་རིམ་པ་རྩ་དབུ་མ་ཐུན་མོང་གི་གདམས་ངག་གནོད་སྦྱིན་མོ་དབང་དུ་བྱ་བ། ལམ་གྱི་ཡན་ལག་སྨན་ཆེན་པོའི་བཅུད་ལེན་ལ་སོགས་པ་གནང་ནས། བརྩོན་འགྲུས་དྲག་པོས་བསྒྲུབས་པས་ཐུན་མོང་གི་དངོས་གྲུབ་རྫུ་འཕྲུལ་དང་མངོན་ཤེས་ཅི་རིགས་པ་ཐོབ།

གནོད་སྦྱིན་མོ་གྲུབ་སྐྱེ་དབུས་ཀྱི་*ཤུམ་བྲག་རུམ་བྱ་བའི་*ལམ་སོ་ཞིག་དུ་ལ་མའི་སྤྱིལ་པོ་ཆུང་ངུ་ཞིག་བརྩིགས་ནས། *འགྲོན་པོ་རྣམས་ལ་ཁམ་ཟན་སྦྱོང་གིན་སྒྲུབ་པ་མཛད་པས་གྲུབ་ནས་*སུ་འགྲོ་བ་ལ་ཟན་བྱེ་ན་དང་བཅས་པ་རེ་དང་ཤམ་པོ་ཕོར་པ་རེ་ཐོབ་ངས་སྐད། དེའི་དུས་སུ་འགྲོན་ཟན་ཟོས་པའི་མི་གཅིག་གཉིས་དང་རྗེ་པ་དང་གསུང་གླེང་བྱས་སྐད།

དེ་ལ་སྤྱར་གྱི་གསུམ་ནི་ལུས་མ་སྦྱངས་པར་གྲུབ་*ད་འང་བོད་ཀྱི་གྲུབ་ཐོབ་བཞིན་སྤྱོད་པ་སུ་རྩིང་རྩིང་ལ་གྲུབ་ཐོབ་དུ་བྱེད་པ་མིན་པའི་མཐོང་ལམ་ཡན་ཆད་ཐོབ་པ་འབའ་ཞིག་བྱུང་།* ཕྱིས་ཀྱི་འདི་ལུས་ནི་སྦྱངས་ཏེ། འོན་ཀྱང་བརྩོན་འགྲུས་ཅན་འབད་རྩོལ་གྱིས་ཁམས་འདུས་པའི་དཔེར་མཛད་དོ་*དམ་པ་གླེ་སྟོན་གྱིས་ཕྱུད་མོ་ལ་ཆོས་ཞུས་པས། ལྟ་བ་འདི་ལ་ཡངས་སུ་བཀྲི།། ལྟ་བ་ཡངས་སུ་མི་བཀྲི་རྟ། ཆོས་ཀྱི་དབྱིང་ལ་དོག་པ་མེད།། སྤྱོད་པ་འདི་ལ་དོག་དུ་བཀྲི།། སྤྱོད་པ་དོག་དུ་མི་བཀྲི་རྟ།། རྒྱུ་འབྲས་ནམ་ཡང་སླུ་བ་མེད།། ཅེས་གསུང་ཆོས་རྗེའི་ཞལ་ནས་གྲུབ་ཐོབ་ཀྱི་ཚིག་དུ་ག་རང་འདུག་གསུང་*༎

of Mu-gu lung. Therefore, she was one with devotion for whom the essential constituents are gathered by the blessing.[90] She did only practice, with no thought of the food and clothing of this life. After realizing Mahāmudrā in this very lifetime without discarding the body, she acts as the chaplain for the yakṣinī of Sman Nags rgyal, a certain mountain in Bo dong.[91] When she was living on a mountain in Mang 'khar, master Se[92] had gone off to a Dharma council in the region of Lho and received many offerings. When he passed through Mang 'khar on the way back, he said, "I am going to meet a sister of mine who is here." When he went to her place, she said, "What is all this fuss going on below here?" He replied, "It's mine." She exclaimed, "Even you have been carried away by the wind!" He said that he had never been more embarrassed than that.[93] She remains even now, and on occasion some still see her.

3. Shab pa mo Lcam gcig

One was a Tsha mo rong woman of Shab. She was the sister of seven brothers. Her clan was the Rje. When she also came to Mu gu lung and requested initiation and oral instructions, ['Brog mi] bestowed them.[94] She practiced, and is said to have reached attainment in this very lifetime.[95] She went to Śrīparvata.[96]

4. 'Phyad mo Nam mkha'

One was Mchad mo of 'Phan yul in Dbus.[97] She also requested the bestowal of initiation from the master 'Brog mi. He gave the oral instructions of Saṃvara, and the creation stage of Varāhī Khecarī, the perfection stage of the central channel, the common oral instructions for controlling the yakṣinī, the alchemical extraction of the great medicine, which is a branch of the path, and so forth.[98] When she practiced with intense diligence she also gained various common attainments, magical abilities, and clairvoyance.

It is said that she realized yakṣinī, built a small hut of reeds on a path called Shum brag rum in Dbus, practiced while begging provisions from travelers, reached [attainment], and would hand out spiced food and a bowl of beer to anyone passing by. It is said that one or two people who had eaten her guest food at that time spoke about it with the lord.[99]

In this respect, the first three [women] reached attainment without discarding the body. They all advanced up to the Path of Seeing, unlike Tibetan adepts now who are regarded as adepts just because of their crude and coarse

དེ་ལ་གཞུང་ཚར་བའི་སློབ་མ་ལྔ་ལས།

འཁོན་དཀོན་མཆོག་རྒྱལ་པོའི་ལོ་རྒྱུས་ནི་སད་མི་མི་བདུན་གྱི་གྲྭོར་འཁོན་ཀླུའི་དབང་པོ་བསྲུང་བ་ནས་དགེ་བཤེས་འཁོན་རོག་ཤེས་རབ་ཚུལ་ཁྲིམས་ཡན་ཆད་གསང་སྔགས་སྔ་འགྱུར་བ་ཡིན་ནོ། ཁོང་གི་ཞལ་ནས་ང་ཡན་ཆད་གསང་སྔགས་སྔ་འགྱུར་འདི་ལ་སྦྱངས་པ་ཁོང་གི་ཆོས་སྐྱོང་དཀར་མོ་ཉི་ཟླ་སྟོང་གི་ཐོད་འཕྲེང་ཅན་ཞལ་གཟིགས་ཡིན། ད་ཕྱི་འགྱུར་བྱུ་བ་ཞིག་དར་འདུག་པ་ཁྱོད་ཀྱིས་གསང་སྔགས་ཕྱིས་འགྱུར་འདི་ལ་སློབས་དེ་ལ་སྟོད་ན་རིན་ཆེན་བཟང་པོ་བཞུགས་ཏེ་ཐག་རིངས་འདི་ན་འབྲོག་མི་བཞུགས་པས་དེར་སོང་གསུང་བ་ལ་ཁོང་ལ་ཆོས་ཞུ་བ་ལ་ཀ་ཚོགས་ཆེན་པོ་ཡོད་པས་ནས་འཕྲང་ཕུར་ཁ་བསྟན་བྱོན།

དེ་ན་བཞུགས་པའི་དགེ་བཤེས་ཁྲིམས་ལོ་ཚ་བ་དེ། བླ་ཆེན་འབྲོག་མི་ལ་རྒྱ་གར་དུ་ཆོས་འབྲེལ་ཙམ་ལས་མེད། ཕྱིས་བོད་དུ་བརྟག་གཉིས་ལེགས་པར་ཤེས་པར་བསླབས། དེ་ལ་དགེ་བཤེས་དཀོན་མཆོག་རྒྱལ་པོས་གསན་ཞིང་ཡོད་ཙམ་ན་ཁྲིམས་སྐུ་གཤེགས་ནས། བླ་ཆེན་འབྲོག་གི་སྤྱན་སྔར་བྱོན་ནས་བླ་ཆེན་འབྲོག་གི་ཞལ་ནས་ཕ་ཤི་ནས་མེས་པོ་ལ་བསྙེགས་པ་ཨང་ཁྱོད་ཀྱི་འགྲོ་ས་མ་ལོག་གསུང་།

དེར་གཞུང་གི་བཤད་པ་རྣམས་ཚར་བར་སླབས་ནས། གདམ་ངག་ཞུ་བར་དགོངས་སྟེ་ཡུལ་དུ་བྱོན་གཡག་ལུང་འཇག་ཤོངས་ཀྱི་ཞིང་བཙོང་བར་འོས་པ་བཙོངས། ལྷག་མ་རྣམས་དགེ་འདུན་འཕྲང་པ་ལ་ཕུལ་ནས་ད་ལྟ་ཡང་གནས་རྒྱུན་ཡོད་དོ།

བཙོངས་པའི་རིན་རྟ་བླ་ཁལ་འོག་ཁལ་བཅུ་བདུན་ཙམ་བྱུང་ནས་དེ་རྣམས་ཕུལ་བས་བླ་ཆེན་གྱི་ཞལ་ནས། རྟ་འདི་རྣམས་ལ་ང་ལ་རྟ་རིན་མེད་གསུང་ནས་མ་བཞེས་པ་ལ། ཁོང་རང་གི་རྒྱགས་བྲ་མཛོད་བའི་ནོར་འཕྲེང་བཟང་པོ་ཞིག་ཕུལ་ནས་འདི་ལ་རྟ་རིན་མཛད་པར་ཞུ་བྱས་པས། བླ་ཆེན་གྱི་ཞལ་ནས་དེ་ལ་ཤགས་མེད་གསུང་ནས་བཞེས་སྐད། དེ་ནས་གདམ་ངག་ཞུས་པས་བསམ་མི་ཁྱབ་དང་རྟུམ་མོའི་མངོན་རྟོགས་ཉི་ཤུ་ཙ་བཞི་ལ་སོགས་པ་ལས་མ་གནང་སྐད།།

behavior.[100] This last one discarded the body, but nevertheless, she is used as the example of a diligent one for whom the essential constituents gathered due to energetic effort.[101] When Dam pa Kle ston asked Phyad mo for Dharma, she replied, "Make this view expansive. The reason for this view being expansive is that there is no restriction to the expanse of reality. Restrict this behavior. The reason to restrict this behavior is that cause and effect are totally infallible." The Dharma Lord commented, "These are truly the words of an adept."[102]

The Disciples Who Fully Received the Scriptures

There were five disciples who fully received the scriptures.[103]

1. 'Khon Dkon mchog rgyal po

From among them, this is the story of 'Khon Dkon mchog rgyal po. From 'Khon Klu'i dbang po bsrung ba, who was one of the young men known as the Seven Men on Trial, up to the spiritual friend 'Khon rog Shes rab tshul khrims, who had beheld the face of the Dharma Protectors Dkar mo nyi zla and Stong gi thod 'phreng can,[104] the ['Khon] were followers of the earlier translated secret mantra. He told [Dkon mchog rgyal po] "Up to me, we have studied this earlier translated secret mantra. Now the so-called Later Translations are spreading. You should study this later translated secret mantra! Rin chen bzang po lives in faraway Stod, but 'Brog mi lives here.[105] Go to him." But since it was very difficult to receive Dharma from him [i.e. 'Brog mi], he directed him to the upper valley of 'Phrang, and he went.

Living there was the spiritual friend Khyim Lo tsā ba, who had no more than just a Dharma link in India with the great master 'Brog mi.[106] In Tibet he later studied the *Brtag gnyis* until he knew it well. While the spiritual friend Dkon mchog rgyal po was receiving it from him, Khyim passed away. Then [Dkon mchog rgyal po] went before the great master 'Brog mi. The great master 'Brog said, "After the father dies, you come to the grandfather! You have not come to the wrong place."

Having fully studied the explication of the scriptures there, he decided to request the oral instructions. He went home and sold the fields of 'Jag shongs in G.yag lung that were suitable to sell. He offered the rest to the Saṅgha of 'Phrang, and even now there is a small place.[107]

As the price for selling them he got about seventeen horses with upper and lower loads. When he offered them, the great master said, "I have

གཉིས་པ་མདའ་རིས་པ་གསལ་བའི་སྙིང་པོའི་ལོ་རྒྱུས་ནི། དང་པོ་བྲིས་པ་ཡབ་ཁྲིམ་བཙུན་རེས་རི་ཞིང་དང་ཡོ་སེ་མོར་བཞུགས། དེར་ཁོང་གིས་དོན་གཉེར་དུ་བྱོན་བསླབས་བསླུས་ཤིག་ཀློག་དར་ལ་གཏད་ནས་ཁོང་ལོག་འོངས་ཙ་ན། བུ་ཚ་ཚོ་ཞིག་དང་རྩེད་མོ་བྱེད་ཀྱིན་འདུག་པ་ལ་ཀློག་མི་སློབ་པར་བྱས་པས་ཀློག་བསླབ་རྒྱུ་མི་འདུག་ཅི་ཡིན་བྱས་པས་འཁོར་ཀློག་དུ་བསླབ་བསླུས་བློ་ལ་བྱུང་འདུག་གསུང་དེས་ན་ཆུང་དུ་ནས་ཀློག་ལ་སོགས་པ་ཚེགས་མེད་པར་ལོབས། སྤྱོད་ཕྱོགས་དང་དབུ་མ་ཤར་གསུམ་དུ་མིང་བཏགས་པ་སྙིང་མའི་ཆཤད་པ་ཀུན་སྐྱེ་བ་སྦྱ་མའི་བག་ཆགས་སད་པའི་སྟོབས་ཀྱིས་མ་བསླབས་པར་ལེགས་པར་མཁྱེན་ཏེ། གཞོན་ནུའི་དུས་ནས་ཆཤད་པ་མཛད་པས་གྲགས་པ་ཆེན་པོ་བྱུང་གསུང་།

དེ་ལྟར་ཐོས་པ་འཛིན་པའི་བདག་ཉིད་ཆེན་པོ་དེས། མུ་གུ་ལུང་དུ་བྱོན་དབང་བསྐུར་བ་ཞུས་དེ་ཙམ་ན་མཚོ་སྐྱེས་ལ་ཉན་ཤད་མང་པོ་མཛད་པའི་སྟོབས་ཀྱིས། མཚོ་སྐྱེས་ཚར་བརྒྱད་གསན། བླ་མ་མདའ་རིས་པའི་ཞལ་ནས་གསང་སྔགས་ལ་གདམ་ངག་མེད་ན་མི་ཤེས་ཟེར་ཏེ་བདེན་པར་འདུག། ངས་ཆོས་འགའ་ཞིག་མ་བསླབས་པར་ཤེས་གཞན་ཚར་རེས་མི་ཤེས་པ་མ་བྱུང་བ་ལ། མཚོ་སྐྱེས་ཚར་བདུན་རྒྱུན་ཆད་མཉན་པ་ཟིན་བྲིས་ཀྱི་ཡི་གེ་དམ་དུམ་ཡོད་པ་ཀུན་བླ་ཆེན་གྱིས་བསྐྱོམས་ཀྱིན་ངའི་བུ་ལ་དགོས་གསུང་ལ་རྟོགས་པ་རེ་སྐྱེ་བར་བྱུང་། བདུན་ནས་བརྒྱད་པ་ལ་སྤྱར་དང་ཁྱད་པར་མ་བྱུང་གསུང་།

དེ་ལྟར་གཞུང་གི་ཆཤད་པ་རྣམས་ཚར་བར་ཞུས་ཏེ། གསུང་ངག་ཞུ་བར་བཞེད་ནས་རྐོང་པོར་བྱོན་ནས་བསོད་ནམས་ཆེན་པོ་བྱུང་ནས་ཡོ་བྱད་མང་པོ་ཁྱེར་ནས་ཡར་བྱོན་ཏེ་བླ་ཆེན་ལ་ཕུལ་གདམ་ངག་ཞུས་དབང་ཡང་ཞུས་པས་གནང་སྟེ། སྟ་གོན་གྱི་ནུབ་མོ་རྨི་ལམ་ན་བླ་མ་འབྲོག་མིའི་མཛོད་ཡིན་ཟེར་བ་སྒྲོ་སྐྱ་ཁྲིག་གེ་བ་མང་པོ་འདུག་པ་ལས། དེ་རྣམས་ཀྱི་ནང་ན་སྒྲོ་གཞན་པས་ཆེ་བ་སྐྱ་ཁྲིག་གེ་བ་ཞིག་གི་ལྟེ་མིག་རྟད་པ་རྨི་ནས་རྣལ་སད་དེ། ནང་པར་བླ་མ་ལ་ཞུས་པས་རྗེ་ལ་གསུང་ངག་རིན་པོ་ཆེའི་མཛོད་མདའ་བར་གདའ་ཡང་། དངོས་ལ་ཐམས་ཅད་མི་གནང་བར་གདའ་བྱུས་པས།

nothing to pay for the grass for these horses," and wouldn't accept them. But when he offered a fine string of jewels that he had intended to use for his own provisions, and said, "Please use this to pay for the grass," it is said that the master replied, "Can't argue with that," and accepted them.[108] He then requested the oral instructions, but it is said that ['Brog mi] did not bestow more than the *Bsam mi khyab,* the twenty-four techniques for direct realization of *caṇḍālī,* and so forth.[109]

2. Gsal ba'i snying po

Second is the story of Gsal ba'i snying po of Mnga' ris. His father was a householder-monk who sometimes lived in a mountain field and sometimes with Yo se mo. When he left to apply himself [to meditation], he gave [the child] the *Śikṣāsamuccaya* as a reading assignment. When he returned, his son was playing with some children. "You are not studying reading," he said. "I don't have any reading to study," he replied. When asked, "Why is that?" he recited the *Śikṣāsamuccaya* from memory. Therefore, from when he was first a small child, he learned reading and so forth without difficulty.[110] By the force of the awakened propensities of the previous lifetime, without studying he knew well all the Rnying ma explications concerning conduct, and what are given the name *Dbu ma shar gsum.*[111] Since he taught at a young age, he became very famous. So it has been stated.

The great being who upheld learning in such a way went to Mu gu lung and requested the bestowal of initiation. Because ['Brog mi] was giving much explanation of [the sādhana of] Saroruha at that point, he received [the text of] Saroruha eight times. This master from Mnga' ris remarked, "The saying that secret mantra is not understood if one lacks the oral instructions is true. I understand some Dharma without studying. There hasn't been another that I haven't understood the first time, but when hearing the [*sādhana* of] Saroruha seven times, [further] realization arose each time. Between the seventh and the eight there was no difference from before." All of the piecemeal summarizing notes he had were taken by the great master ['Brog mi], who said, "I need these for my sons."[112]

In that way, having fully received the explication of the scriptures, he decided to request the Oral Instructions [of the Lam 'bras]. He traveled to Rkong po, received great offerings, and returned carrying many possessions. Offering them to the great master, he requested oral instructions, and also requested initiation, which were granted. On the evening of the preliminary [section of the initiation] he had a dream in

བླ་ཆེན་གྱི་ཞལ་ནས་ཇི་ལྟར་འདུག་གསུང་བ་ལ།

སྤྱིར་གྱི་རྗེ་ལམ་རྣམས་ཆཤད་པས་བླ་ཆེན་གྱི་ཞལ་ནས་ཁྱོད་ལ་གདམ་ངག་མི་སྟེར་ན་སུ་ལ་སྟེར་འོན་ཀྱང་ཁྱོད་ངའི་གཞུང་འཛིན་པར་འོང་གསུང་ནས། བསམ་མི་ཁྱབ་ཀྱི་གདམ་ངག་ལ་སོགས་པ་ལས་མ་གནང་སྐད།

གདམ་ངག་ཚར་བའི་སློབ་མ་གསུམ་ནི།

ལྷ་བཙུན་ཀ་ལི་ཧོ་མོའི་མིང་པོ་ཡིན་ཏེ་གདམ་ངག་ཡོངས་སུ་རྫོགས་པར་ཚར་ཡང་གཞན་ལ་འཕེལ་བ་མེད་དོ།

འབྲོམ་ནི་འཕན་ཡུལ་བ་ཡིན་རིགས་དང་སྐྱེ་ས་ཡོངས་སུ་བཟང་ཞིང་ལོངས་སྤྱོད་ཆེ་བ་ཡིན། ཁོང་གིས་བླ་མ་འབྲོག་གི་སྙན་པའི་གྲགས་པ་ཐོས་ནས་དད་པ་སྐྱེས་ཏེ། ནོར་མང་པོ་ཁྱེར་ནས་མུ་གུ་ལུང་དུ་བྱོན་ནས་རྣམ་གཞག་ཆེན་པོ་བྱས་ནས་གཡུ་འབྲོག་མི་ཞོ་སྨྱུངས་བྱ་བ་ཡང་བྱམ་སྙིང་ལ་ཕུལ་དབང་བསྐུར་ཞུས་ཏེ་གསུང་ངག་ཞུ་བ་ལ་ཞབས་ཏོག་རྒྱ་ཆེན་པོ་མཛད་པ་ཡང་ཆོས་ཐུན་རེ་ལ་ནང་གི་མཆོད་པ་རེ། གཏོར་མ་མི་རེས་ཐེག་ཚད་རེ་གསེར་ཞོ་རེའི་མ་ཎལ་ཞབས་ཁྲིས་ལ་དར་ཤམ་རེ་བྱས། དེ་དུས་ཀྱི་དར་བཟང་ཞིང་དཀོན་དེ་ད་ལྟའི་ཟ་འོག་ཤམ་རེ་དང་རིན་མཉམ་གསུང་། དེ་ལྟར་དུས་ཁྱད་པར་ཅན་དང་ནར་མའི་བསྙེན་བཀུར་དཔག་ཏུ་མེད་པ་མཛད་ཅིང་ཡུན་རིང་དུ་བསྟེན་སྟེ།

ཞབས་ཏོག་ཆེ་བས་གསུང་ངག་རིན་པོ་ཆེ་འདི་ཚར་ནས་ཡུལ་དུ་བཞུད་པར་དགོངས་ཏེ། དཔེའ་ཆ་འགྲེལ་བའི་རྟ་ཞིག་གཡར་དུ་ཞུས་པས་བླ་ཆེན་གྱི་ཞལ་ནས་དཔེའ་མི་ཐེག་པ་དང་ཡུལ་དུ་འགྲོ་བ་ཡང་བདེན་ཏེ་བླ་མས་སློབ་མ་ལ་འབུལ་བ་བྱས་པའི་ཁྲིམས་མི་འདུག་བ་མི་ཡོད་གསུང་ནས་མ་གནང་།

དེར་འབྲོམ་སྔར་ཞབས་ཏོག་བྱས་པའི་ཡུས་ཀྱིས་ཐུགས་མུག་སྟེ་མུ་གུ་ལུང་རྡོ་རྗེ་གདན་དུ་སོང་། འབྲོག་མི་ཤཱཀྱ་ཡེ་ཤེས་ཤཱཀྱ་ཐུབ་པར་སོང་ཡང་ད་ཕྱིན་ཆད་འགྲོས་མེད་སྨམ་སྟེ་ལོག་ལྷ་

which there were many bright white doors said to be the treasury of master 'Brog mi. He dreamed that he was given the key to one that was larger and a brighter white than the other doors, and then awoke from the dream. In the morning he said to the master, "The lord possesses the treasury of the Precious Oral Instructions, but will not give them all to me."

The great master replied, "How so?"

When he explained the previous dreams, the great master replied, "If I wouldn't give oral instructions to you, who would I give them to? However, you will be an upholder of my scriptures," and, it is said, did not bestow them, except for the oral instructions of the *Bsam mi khyab* and so forth.[113]

The Disciples Who Fully Received the Oral Instructions

There were three disciples who fully received the oral instructions.

1. Lha btsun Ka li

Lha btsun Ka li was the brother of the Lady, and although he fully received the entire oral instructions, he did not pass them to others.[114]

2. 'Brom De pa ston chung

'Brom was from 'Phan yul. His family and birthplace were excellent, and he had great wealth. Hearing about the reputation of master 'Brog, faith arose, and he traveled to Mu gu lung bringing many valuables. After making great offerings he requested the bestowal of initiation. He also offered in an old vase the turquoise called *'Brog mi's Hoard*.[115] While receiving the Oral Instructions [of the Lam 'bras] he performed vast offerings. He presented at each session of Dharma an inner offering that was a gtor ma as large as could be lifted by a man, a tenth of an ounce of gold as a maṇḍala, and a silk drape on the throne beneath ['Brog mi's] feet. The silk of that time was fine and rare, and each piece was equal in value to a brocade drapery now. So it has been stated. In that way, he performed infinite service, continuously and at special times, and studied under ['Brog mi] for a long time.[116]

After fully receiving these Precious Oral Instructions because of his

སྐྱེས་ཟེར་ནས་

ཡུལ་དུ་མ་ཕྱིན་པར་ལྷོ་སྟོད་དིང་རི་ཤེད་དུ་བྱོན་པས། འབྲོག་མིའི་སློབ་མ་མཆོག་ཡིན་ཟེར་བའི་སྙན་པ་དང་གྲགས་པས་བསོད་ནམས་ཆེན་པོ་བྱུང་ནས་དེར་སློབ་མ་འགའ་ཞིག་ལ། ཕྱག་རྒྱ་ཆེན་པོ་ཡི་གེ་མེད་པའི་བྱིན་རླབས་ཤིག་མཛད་པས། ཞལ་ནས་ཁྲག་དུ་སྐྱུགས་ཏེ་བསྙུང་ནད་ཀྱིས་ཟིན་པ་ལ།

འབྲོམ་ན་རེ་ངའི་བླ་མ་དེ་སངས་རྒྱས་དངོས་ཡིན་ཞིང་ངའི་སྐྱོད་རྟོག་པ་ཡིན་པར་འདུག་པ་ལ། ངས་དེ་ལྟར་མ་ཤེས་པས་ང་ལ་དམ་ཚིག་གི་ཉེས་པ་བག་ཙམ་བྱུང་སྟེ། འོན་ཀྱང་བདག་བླ་མའི་ཐུགས་རྗེས་བར་དོར་རྗེས་སུ་འཛིན་པར་འདུག། ངའི་ཡོ་བྱད་འདི་རྣམས་ཁྱེར་ལ་བླ་མའི་ཕྱག་དུ་ཕུལ། ཁྱེད་རྣམས་གདམས་ངག་སུ་ཞུ་ཡང་ངས་བྱས་པའི་བཀའ་ལས་ཙམ་མི་དགོས་པར་གནང་ནས་འོང་བར་འདུག་གིས་ཞུས་གསུང་ཏེ།

དེའི་དུས་སུ་རྟོགས་པ་ཁྱད་པར་ཅན་སྐྱེས་ནས་གཤེགས་སྐད།

འཁོར་རྣམས་ཀྱིས་པུར་ཞུགས་ལ་བཞུ་སྟེ། གདུང་དང་ནོར་ཧྲ་བཅུ་བདུན་གྱི་བླ་ཁལ་འོག་ཁལ་དང་བཅས་པ་ཁྱེར་ནས། སུ་ག་ལུང་གི་མདའ་ན་ཡར་དུང་འབུད་ཅིང་འོངས་ཙམ་ན། བླ་ཆེན་གྱི་ཞལ་ནས་ངའི་སློང་བཏོན་པ་སློམ་བྱེད་ཀྱིས་སུ་འདུག་ལྟོས་དང་གསུང་ནས་

བལྟས་པས། འབྲོམ་གྱི་འཁོར་དུ་འདུག་པས་ནོར་རྣམས་དང་གདུང་བླ་མའི་ཕྱག་དུ་ཕུལ་བས། གདུང་ཕང་དུ་བཞེས་ནས་བུ་ལ་ཚེ་འདི་ལ་གྲུབ་མཐའ་སློགས་པ་ཞིག་རེ་བ་ཡིན་ཏེ་བྱས་པ་སླགས་པ་ཨང་གསུང་ནས་མང་དུ་བཤུམས།

ཁྱེད་ཚོའི་ནང་ན་གདམས་ངག་སུ་འདོད་པ་ལ་བཀའ་བ་མི་དགོས་པར་བཤད་ཀྱིས་གསུང་བ་ལ་ཞུ་བ་མང་པོ་ཡང་མ་བྱུང་། དེའི་དུས་སུ་སྒོམ་ཆེན་སེ་རོག་གཉིས་ཀྱིས་ཁྲིད་ཞུས་ཅིང་བསྒོམས་པས་ཏིང་ངེ་འཛིན་བཟང་པོ་སྐྱེས་སྐད་དེ། ཕྱིས་གྲུབ་པ་ཐོབ་པོ་སྟེ་པོ་གསུམ་ཀྱི་གཉིས་ཡིན།

དེས་ན་འབྲོམ་ལས་འཕེལ་བ་མེད་དེ། འབྲོམ་ལུགས་ཟེར་བའི་ལམ་འབྲས་དེ་ནི་ཇོ་མོ་འབྲོམ་མོ་ཅེས་པ་དབུས་ཀྱི་འཕན་ཡུལ་བ་བླ་མ་ས་སྐྱ་བ་ཆེན་པོ་དངོས་ཀྱི་སློབ་མ་ཡིན་ཏེ་ལམ་འབྲས་ཡོངས་སུ་རྫོགས་པ་འང་མེད་ལ། དེའང་ཞི་བྱེད་དང་རྫོགས་ཆེན་ལ་སོགས་པ་བསྲེས་པས་ན་གྱི་ན་དེ་བོར་བར་བྱ་ཞིང་གཞན་ཡང་དམ་ཚིག་ཀྱང་མི་སྲུང་ཆབ་ལྷ་ཁང་གི་ཆབ་སྟོན་ཆོས་

great offerings, he decided to return home, and requested the loan of a horse on which to load his texts. The great master replied, "It is true that you can't carry the texts, and are going home, but a master does not make offerings to a disciple, there is no such custom," and did not give one.[117]

Because of his pride from making offerings before, 'Brom became despondent and said, "Mu gu lung had become the Vajrāsana, and 'Brog mi Shākya ye shes had become Śākyamuni, but from now on I have nowhere to go." Thinking this a perverse view arose.

Without going home, he went to the region of Ding ri in upper Lho.[118] The reputation and fame of being called 'Brog mi's best disciple brought great offerings. When he performed the blessing of the *Phyag rgya chen po yi ge med pa* for several disciples there, he vomited blood from the mouth and was stricken ill.[119]

'Brom stated, "That master of mine is truly a buddha, and was testing my worthiness. Since I didn't understand it in that way, a slight infraction of the sacred commitments occurred for me. Nevertheless, in the intermediate state I will be graced by the master's compassion. Take these things of mine and offer them into the hands of the master. Whichever of you request oral instructions, he will grant them without the necessity of hardships such as I performed, so request them."

It is said that an exceptional realization arose at that point, and he passed away.

His followers cremated his body and carried the bones and valuables on seventeen horses with upper and lower loads. At the point when they were blowing a conch and coming up into the lower valley of Mu gu lung, the great master exclaimed, "I think my heart is being torn out. See who it is!"

They looked, and it was the followers of 'Brom. They offered the valuables and bones into the hands of the master. He held the bones in his lap, and saying, "Son, I hoped you would be one who reached the culmination of attainment in this lifetime, but the son has returned to the father!" he wept a great deal.

"Whoever among you wishes oral instructions, I will explain them without need for hardships," he said, but there were not many requests. The two great meditators Se and Rog requested instruction at that time, and when they meditated it is said that a fine meditative concentration arose. They later reached attainment and were two of the three males.[120]

Therefore, there was no dissemination from 'Brom.[121] But there was

དགའ་མདོ་སྡེས་ཞུ་རྟེན་བྱས་ནས་གསུང་ངག་ཞུས་པས་དེ་མ་བླངས་ང་རང་གི་ཆོས་ལ་འབུལ་བ་བྱུང་བ་ཞིག་འདོད་ཟེར་ཕྱིས་ཆབ་སྟོན་གྱིས་ལྷོ་བྲག་དུ་ཕྱིན་པས་དུལ་སྐྲ་ལེགས་པ་ཞིག་འབུལ་བ་བྱུང་འདོད་ཟེར་བ་ལ་མ་ཕུལ་དཔོན་སློབ་མཐུ་རྒྱུས་བྱས་གསུང་། སྡེ། འདིའི་ལོ་རྒྱུས་གཞན་ཡང་ཡོད་མོད་ཆཤད་ཀྱིས་ག་ལ་ལང་།།

Se ston Kun rig

གསུམ་པ་བླ་མ་སེས་གདམ་ངག་ཇི་ལྟར་ཐོབ་ན་སེའི་ཡུལ་མདོག་སྨད་ཀྱི་ཕྱི་འབྲུམས་ལྷུམ་སྡིང་ལྷའི་ལྷ་ཚོགས་པ་ཡིན། གནག་འཚོར་ཕྱིན་ཙ་ན་ཁོང་གི་ཐུགས་དགོངས་ལ་རིགས་སད་པ་བཞིན་དུ། མང་གར་མུ་གུ་ལུང་གི་ཐད་སོར་སྤྲིན་ལྡིངས་པ་མཐོང་ནས། ཡ་གི་འི་འོག་ན་སངས་རྒྱ་བའི་གདམ་ངག་ཅིག་ཡོད་ངེས་སྙམ་པའི་རྣམ་རྟོག་སྐྱེས་ཏེ།

ཡ་གི་ན་སུ་ཡོད་དྲིས་པས།

འགའ་ཞིག་ན་རེ་འབྲོག་མི་ལོ་ཚ་བ་བྱ་བ་ཡོད་ཟེར་རོ།

དེ་ཐོས་པ་ཙམ་གྱིས་རབ་དུ་དད་ནས། གསེར་ཞོ་གཉིས་ཁྱེར་ནས་འོངས་པ་ན་དེའི་རེས་དབང་ཞུ་བ་འདུག་པ་དང་ཕྲད་དེ་འཁར་ཆེ་ཆེ་ནས་གསེར་ཞོ་གཅིག་གིས་ཁྲལ་བྱས། ཞོ་གཅིག་གིས་དབང་ཡོན་བྱས་ནས་དབང་བསྐུར་བ་ཞུས་པས་ཐོབ་སྐད། ཕྱིར་ནི་དེའི་དུས་ན་དབང་བསྐུར་ལ་ཡོད་བྱེད་མང་པོ་དགོས་ཀྱང་མ་འོངས་པ་ན་པན་ཐོགས་འོང་བ་དགོངས་གསུང་།

དེ་ནས་རྗེ་སེ་ལ་དྲན་པ་གཅིག་པའི་བསྒྲུབ་ཐབས་དང་། རྩ་ལྟུང་གི་ཆོས་ཤིག་གསུངས་ནས་ཡང་སྐྱ་འཚམས་ལ་བཞུགས་ཏེ། འཁོར་རྙིང་པ་འགའ་རེ་མ་གཏོགས་པ་སུ་དང་ཡང་མི་འབྱུལ་སྐད། ཁ་པའི་ནང་དུ་ཁྲིད་ལ་སོགས་པ་ཆོས་ཐུན་རེ་ཙམ་ལས་མི་གསུང་། དེ་ཙམ་ན་

a Lam 'bras referred to as the 'Brom tradition. The one known as Lady 'Brom mo was from 'Phan yul in Dbus. She was an actual disciple of the great master of Sa skya [i.e. Sa chen]. She did not even have the complete Lam 'bras, and furthermore, since she mixed it with the Zhi byed, the Rdzogs chen, and so forth, [this tradition] is inferior and should be rejected.[122] Moreover, she also did not maintain the sacred commitments. Chab ston Chos dga' of Chab lha khang made a gift of sūtras and requested the Oral Instructions [of the Lam 'bras], but she didn't accept it, and said, "I want an offering that has come for my own Dharma." When Chab ston later went to Lho brag, [taught the Lam 'bras that he had received from her,] and was offered a fine silver saddle, she said she wanted it, but he didn't offer it. The master and disciple used sorcery [against each other]. So it has been stated.[123] While there are also other stories about this person, why explain them?

3. Se ston Kun rig

Third is how master Se obtained the oral instructions. Se's home was Phyi 'brums in lower Mdog. He was the fifth of five brothers and sisters.[124] His spiritual propensities having been awakened when he went to Gnag 'tsho and saw a cloud floating directly above Mu gu lung in Mang gar, the thought arose, "Below that is certainly one with the oral instructions for buddhahood."

He asked, "Who is up there?"

Several people replied, "The one known as 'Brog mi Lo tsā ba is there."

On merely hearing that he was filled with faith.[125] He brought two tenths of an ounce of gold, and arrived just as an initiation was being requested. Due to his great merit, he [was allowed to] pay the fee with one tenth of an ounce of gold. Using one tenth of an ounce for the initiation offering, it is said that he requested the bestowal of the initiation, and received it.[126] At that time many possessions were generally necessary for the bestowal of initiation, but ['Brog mi] considered the benefit that would come in the future. So it has been stated.

['Brog mi] then taught Lord Se the method for realization in a single [moment] of mindfulness, and an instruction about the root infractions.[127] Again ['Brog mi] stayed in retreat, it is said, not meeting anyone except for several old followers. He did not teach except for instructions and so forth inside his room, in just single Dharma sessions. At that time an offering was necessary at each Dharma session of the Oral

གསུང་དག་གི་ཆོས་ཐུན་རེ་ལ་མཆོད་པ་རེ་དགོས། མི་གཉིས་སུ་ལོངས་པ་ལ་ལམ་འབྲས་མི་གསུང་སྟེ། རྣ་བཞི་པ་ལ་གདམ་ངག་མི་ཆཤད་རྣ་བ་དུག་པ་སྤྱགས་ཀྱིས་དབྱེན་གསུང་ངོ།།

དེའི་དུས་སུ་དགེ་ཆཤེས་དཀོན་མཆོག་རྒྱལ་པོས་ས་སྐྱར་མི་བཅུ་བདུན་ལ་བརྟག་པ་གཉིས་པ་ཆཤད་པས། བླ་མས་འཕྲིན་བསྐུར་ཏེ་རྩ་བའི་རྒྱུད་གཉན་པོ་མི་བཅུ་བདུན་ལ་ཤད་པ་ཁྱོད་ལ་རྡོ་རྗེའི་སྲོག་ཡོད་དམ་ཞེས་བཀའ་བཀྱོན་མཛད།

ཁྱད་པར་དུ་གསུང་ངག་རིན་པོ་ཆེ་འདི་ལ་གཅེས་སྤྲས་སུ་འཛིན་ཏེ། བཀའ་ཤིན་དུ་དམ་པའི་སྟོབས་ཀྱིས་ལོ་གཅིག་དུ་ཆོས་ནི་མ་བྱུང་། འོན་ཀྱང་བླ་མ་སེས་དེར་བསྡད་ནས་ཡོད་ཙམ་ན་ཚོགས་འཁོར་ཞིག་གི་གྲལ་དུ་ཁ་ཅིག་ན་རེ། བྱུང་པའི་རྣལ་འབྱོར་པ་དེ་གླུ་མཁས་པར་གདའ་ནང་དུ་འབོད་དམ་བྱས་པས།

བླ་ཆེན་གྱི་ཞལ་ནས་དེ་སུ་ཡིན་གསུང་བ་ལ་སྔར་ཀྱི་ལོ་རྒྱུས་རྣམས་བསྙད་པས། དེ་ད་རུང་མ་སོང་བར་འདུག་གམ་ནང་དུ་བོས་གསུང་ནས

བོས་པས། ཁྱོད་དེ་ཙམ་དུ་ཅི་ལ་སྡོད་གསུང་བ་ལ

རྗེ་ལ་གསུང་ངག་རིན་པོ་ཆེ་ཞུ་བ་ལགས་བྱས་པས

གདམ་ངག་འདོད་ན་ནོར་ཁྱེར་ལ་ཤོག་གསུང་།

དེ་ནས་རྗེ་སེ་ཡིས་ཡུལ་དུ་བྱོན་ཏེ། ཁོང་པ་རང་གཟའ་ཚོའི་གནག་སྣད་སུམ་བཅུ་ཙམ་སྲི་ལ་ཡོད་པ་དེའི་གནག་རྫི་བྱེད་ཅིང་། ཁོང་མིག་བྲིད་པའི་ཆེད་དུ་རྩ་ཞག་བྱེད་ཟེར་ནས་ཞག་རེ་ཞག་གཉིས་རི་ལ་བསྡད་ཅིང་འོངས་པ་དེ་ལྟ་བུ་ལན་མང་དུ་བྱས་པའི་རྗེས་ལ། གནག་ཚོ་དེད་ནས་ལྷ་རྩེ་ཀོ་ཁ་རུ་གྲུ་བ་ལ་སྒྲོལ་བྱས་པས

གནག་གསུམ་གསུམ་ལ་རེ་རེ་བླ་ལ་འདོད་ཟེར།

དེ་ལྟར་ན་བླ་མ་ལ་སུམ་གཉིས་ལས་དབུལ་དུ་མི་ཡོད་པར་འདུག་སྙམ་ནས། བླ་མ་ཉིད་ལ་གསོལ་བ་བཏབ་ཆོས་སྐྱོང་ལ་གཏོར་མ་བཏང་བས། འབྲི་ག་མ་ཞིག་གིས་སྣ་དྲངས་ནས་ཆུ་ལ་རྐྱལ་ནས་སོང་། བླ་མ་ཉིད་ཀྱིས་ཀྱང་གཡག་ཅིག་གི་རྔ་མ་ལ་འཇུས་ནས་ཕྱིན་པས་ཐར་ཏེ།

མུ་གུ་ལུང་དུ་སྔར་ཀྱི་འབྲི་མོ་དེས་སྣ་དྲངས་ནས་མུ་གུ་ལུང་དུ་ཟིན་སོང་དེར་བླ་ཆེན་གྱི་ཕྱག་དུ་ཕུལ་བས། བླ་ཆེན་གྱི་ཞལ་ནས་ཁྱོད་ཀྱི་འབུལ་བ་འདི་ཆེན་པོ་མིན་ཏེ། འོན་ཀྱང་ང་ཡུལ་ཕུ

Instructions [of the Lam 'bras]. He would not teach the Lam 'bras to as many as two persons, saying "I don't explain oral instructions to four ears and there is no mantra for six ears."

At that time, when the spiritual friend Dkon mchog rgyal po was explaining the *Brtag pa gnyis pa* to seventeen persons in Sa skya, master ['Brog mi] sent a message scolding him, "Explaining the perilous root tantra to seventeen persons; do you have an indestructible life force?"[128]

In particular, he cherished these Precious Oral Instructions [of the Lam 'bras], and by virtue of being extremely strict with the teaching, for one year there was no Dharma. Nevertheless, master Se stayed there. At one point[129] someone in the row of a gaṇacakra said, "That yogin from Byang is an expert at songs. Should I call him in?"

The great master asked, "Who is he?" When his story from before was explained, ['Brog mi] said, "He still hasn't left? Call him in!"

When he was called, [the master] asked, "Why have you stayed so long?"

"I would ask the lord for the Precious Oral Instructions," he replied.

He said, "If you want oral instructions, bring wealth!"[130]

Then Lord Se went home.[131] His own family had about thirty yaks and cows in common, and he worked as their shepherd. In order to trick them, he would say, "We'll spend the day grazing," stay for a day or two on the mountain, and come back. After acting like that many times, he drove the yaks away, and at the ferry landing at Lha rtse he said to the ferryman, "Take us across!"

He replied, "For every three yaks I want one as a toll."[132]

"In that way, there would be no more than two thirds left to offer the master," he thought. He prayed to the master himself, offered a gtor ma to the Dharma guardians, and [the yaks] crossed the river led by a cow with a white mark on its forehead. Grabbing the tail of a yak, master [Se] himself also made it across.

Led by that cow from before, he went straight to Mu gu lung. There he offered them into the hands of the great master at Mu gu lung. The great master said, "This offering of yours is not large. Nevertheless, I control an area of three upper valleys, and it is good for that."[133] He also bestowed various oral instructions.

In that way, his offerings were not great, but he was extremely skilled and devoted in conduct of body and speech, and pleased ['Brog mi] with great undivided faith. Studying under him for seventeen years—

གསུམ་འཛིན་པ་ལ་དམར་གསུང་ནས། གདམ་ངག་ཀྱང་ཅི་རིགས་པར་གནང་ངོ།

དེ་ལྟར་ན་ཞབས་ཏོག་ཆེན་པོ་མིན་ལུས་ངག་གི་སྤྱོད་ལམ་ཤིན་དུ་མཁས་ཤིང་གུས་ལ། མི་ཕྱེད་པའི་དད་པ་ཆེན་པོས་མཉེས་པར་བྱས་ཏེ། སྔར་ལོ་བདུན་ཕྱིས་ལོ་བཅུ་སྟེ་བཅུ་བདུན་དུ་བསྟེན་པས་གསུང་ངག་མ་ལུས་པར་ཐོབ།

བླ་ཆེན་གྱི་ཞལ་ནས་སེ་ལྕེ་ལ་རེ་འདི་ལ་ངའི་གདམ་ངག་རྣམས་མ་ཆོར་བར་ཤོར་གསུང་བ་ལ།

སེ་བཤུམས་ཏེ་དངོས་ཀྱང་བུ་མ་ལགས་སམ་ཞེས་ཞུས་པས།

ངས་ཀ་རེ་བྱས་པ་ཡིན་ཁྱོད་ལ་གདམ་ངག་མི་སྟེར་ན་སུ་ལ་སྟེར་གསུང་།

དུས་ཕྱིས་བླ་མ་སེ་ཡུལ་ན་བཞུགས་ཙམ་ན། ཇོ་སྲས་ཆེ་ཤོས་ཨི་ཀྲ་བྱང་གཡག་དང་སྲུས་པ་ཆེ་འབྲོག་བལྟ་གསུང་ནས་མདོག་དུ་བྱོན་པ་ལ། བསྙེན་བཀུར་ཆེན་པོ་མཛད་ནས་ལོ་རྒྱུས་མཛད་པས། ཇོ་རྗེ་ཅིག་རྐང་གི་སྐད་ཆོ་ཁུངས་ཆོད་ནས་ཧྲ་ཞིག་ཕུལ་ནས་ཟིན་ཐུན་བྱས་ཏེ། ཚར་བའི་རྗེས་ལ་ཇོ་སྲས་ན་རེ་སེ་ལ་ཨ་པོ་ངའི་སྙིང་བཙོན་པ་སླམ་བྱེད། ཉིད་རང་གི་ཧྲ་ཁྲིར་ལ་ངའི་ཆོས་ཚུར་འཁོར་དང་གསུང་བ་ལ།

སེ་ན་རེ་ཁྲིད་ཡབ་སྲས་ལ་འདི་འདྲའི་ལུགས་ཤིག་ཡོད་པ་ཡིན། ཆོས་གློ་ལ་ཟིན་པ་དེ་སྐུག་དུ་ནི་མི་འདོད་ད་ཇི་ལྟར་བྱ་ཟེར་ནས་ཞབས་ཏོག་བསྟན་དེ་ཕྱིས་བླ་ཆེན་ཉིད་ལ་འདང་ལེགས་པར་ཞུས་སོ།

དེ་ལྟར་ལོ་བཅོ་བརྒྱད་ལྷག་ཙམ་གྱི་བར་ལ་གདམ་ངག་རིམས་ཀྱིས་གནང་སྟེ། ཐམས་ཅད་ཚར་ནས་དེའི་རྗེས་སུ་ལམ་བསྡུས་ཏེ་བསྒྲུབ་པའི་ལུང་སྦྱིན་པ་མཛད་པས་བུམ་པ་གང་ཡོའི་ཚུལ་དུ་ཐམས་ཅད་ཡོངས་སུ་རྫོགས་པར་ཐོབ་ཅེས་གྲགས་སོ།།

དེ་ནས་གཞུང་གི་བཤད་པ་ཞུས་པས་བླ་ཆེན་གྱི་ཞལ་ནས་ངས་བླ་མ་ཞིག་གི་དྲུང་དུ་གཞུང་ཚར་བའི་སློབ་མ་ལ་གདམ་ངག་མི་བཤད། གདམ་ངག་ཚར་བའི་སློབ་མ་ལ་གཞུང་མི་བཤད་པའི་དམ་བཅའ་བྱས་པ་ཡིན་པས་ཁྱོད་གཞུང་མཉན་ན་ས་སྐྱར་སོང་གསུང་ནས་མ་གནང་།

སེས་ཀྱང་ས་སྐྱར་ལོ་བཞི་གཞུང་གི་བཤད་པ་དགེ་བཤེས་དཀོན་མཆོག་རྒྱལ་པོ་ལ་ཚར་བར་སླབས་སོ།།

seven years before and ten later—he obtained absolutely all the Oral Instructions [of the Lam 'bras].[134]

The great master said, "Without noticing it, my oral instructions were lost to this smooth-tongued Se."

Se wept, and asked, "Am I not also your son?"

"I'm just joking," he replied, "If I didn't give the oral instructions to you, to whom would I give them?"

At a later time, when master Se was living at home, Indra, ['Brog mi's] eldest noble son, came to Mdog, saying he was looking at the yaks in Byang and the nomads in Mus pa tshe. [Se] provided great honors, asked his story, and found out about the final sections of the *Rdo rje tshig rkang.* Then he offered a horse and observed a period of memorization. After it was finished, the noble son said to Se, "Uncle, I think my heart has been torn out. Take your horse and return my Dharma!"

Se replied, "Father and son, you have this kind of custom. I have memorized the Dharma and don't wish to regurgitate it. Now what can I do?" and added to the honors. Later he also received it well from the great master himself.[135]

In that way the oral instructions were gradually bestowed for more than eighteen years. After they were all completed, ['Brog mi] gave the transmission of the summation of the path and prediction of practice.[136] [Se] is thus famed as having completely obtained everything, in the way a vase is fully [poured into another].

Then he requested the explication of the scriptures. But the great master did not bestow them, and said, "In the presence of one of my masters I promised not to explain the oral instructions to disciples who fully received the scriptures, and not to explain the scriptures to disciples who fully received the oral instructions.[137] So if you would hear the scriptures, go to Sa skya."

For four years Se also completely learned the explication of the scriptures from the spiritual friend Dkon mchog rgyal po at Sa skya.[138]

In that way, what special qualities did this Lord Se have? He obtained some stability in the creation stage.[139] In particular, he gained ability by means of the root mantra, and subdued the malevolent nāga demoness of 'Khar chung, bringing her under control so that she even moved her residence and would listen to whatever he ordered. All who had been harmed by her and suddenly contracted leprosy were healed merely by the touch of the master's hand.[140] He also manifested many physical forms.

དེ་ལྷ་བུའི་རྗེ་སེ་དེ་ལ་ཡོན་ཏན་གྱི་ཁྱད་པར་ཅི་མངའ་ཞེ་ན། བསྐྱེད་རིམས་ལ་བརྟན་པ་ཙུང་ཟད་ཐོབ་ཁྱད་པར་དུ་རྩ་སྦྱུགས་ཀྱི་སྒྲོ་ནས་ནུས་པ་བརྙེས་ཏེ། འཁར་ཆུང་གི་ཀླུ་སྲིན་མོ་ཤེན་དུ་ཕུ་བ་ཞིག་ཡོད་པ་དེ་བཏུལ་ནས་གནས་ཀྱང་སྤྱོས། ཅི་བསྒོ་བ་ཉན་ཞིང་དེ་དབང་དུ་འདུས་སོ། དེས་གནོད་པ་བྱས་ཏེ་གློ་བུར་དུ་འཛེ་བྱུང་བ་ཀུན་བླ་མའི་ཕྱག་གིས་རེག་པ་ཙམ་གྱིས་སོས་སོ་སྐྱུའི་བཀོད་པ་དུ་མ་ཡང་མཛད་སྟོན་མོ་བྱུང་བ་ཐམས་ཅད་ཀྱི་གྲལ་མགོའ་ལ་སེ་སྤྱུན་འདྲེན་པ་ལ་ཉིན་གཅིག་ལ་སྟོན་མོ་དུ་བྱུང་ཡང་ཐམས་ཅད་ཀྱི་གྲལ་འགོར་སེ་འོང་གསུང་།

When Se was invited to be at the head of the rows of all the festivals, even though the festivals fell on the same day, Se came to the head of the rows of them all. So it has been stated.[141]

Zhang ston Chos 'bar

དེ་ལྷ་བུའི་རྗེ་སེ་དེ་ལ་སློབ་མའི་མཆོག་དུ་ཡོད་ཅེ་ན། གདམ་ངག་རབ་དུ་ཐོབ་པ། འབྲིང་དུ་ཐོབ་པ། ཐ་མར་ཐོབ་པ་གསུམ་ཡིན་ནོ།།

དེ་ཡང་རབ་དུ་ཐོབ་པ་ནི་རྩང་སྨད་དིངས་ཀྱི་ཞང་སྟོན་མཆེད་གཉིས་ཡིན་སྟེ་ཁོང་ལ་འབངས་ལ་སོགས་པའི་བྱ་བ་རྒྱ་ཆེན་པོ་ནི་མེད། གསུང་རབས་ཀྱི་རྩི་འགྲུས་བྱེད་པ་ཞིག་ཡིན་ཏེ། བླ་མ་སེས་མདོ་སྡེ་དང་འབུམ་བྲིས་པའི་རྩི་འགྲུས་ལ་བོས་ཏེ། རྩི་འགྲུས་ཚར་ནས་ཡོན་མ་བརྫངས་པ་ལ་ཁོང་གིས་གསུང་དག་རིན་པོ་ཆེའི་ཁངས་ཆོད་ནས་ཁོང་གཉིས་གྲོས་བྱས་ཏེ་ཡོན་རྣམས་ཕུལ་ལ་གདམ་ངག་ཞུ་འམ་བྱས་པས་མཐུན་ཏེ། རྩི་འགྲུས་ཀྱི་ཡོན་རྣམས་ཕུལ་ཏེ་ཞུས་པས། བླ་མའི་ཞལ་ནས་འདི་རྣམས་ཁྱེད་རང་ལག་གི་བླ་ཟ་བས་ཐོབ་པ་ཡིན་པས་ང་མི་འདོད། ཡོ་བྱད་ཡོད་ན་ཡུལ་ནས་ཁྱེར་ལ་ཤོག་གསུང་ནས།

ཡུལ་དུ་ཕྱིན་ནས་ལོངས་སྤྱོད་ཅི་ཡོད་པ་ཁྱེར་ནས་འོངས་ནས་ནས་སུམ་རྒྱ་དང་ཁྲབ་ཅིག་བླ་མ་ལ་ཕུལ་སྤྱོད་ལམ་གྱི་སྒོ་ནས་ཤིན་དུ་མཉེས་པར་མཛད་དོ། ཤེས་རབ་ཀྱང་ཤིན་དུ་ཆེ་བར་བྱུང་བས་བླ་མ་ཐུགས་དགེས་ཏེ་ངའི་ཆོས་འདི་ཞང་སྟོན་མཆེད་གཉིས་ཀྱིས་གོ་དེའི་ནང་ནས་ཀྱང་ཞང་སྟོན་གཟིའ་བརྗིད་འབར་གྱིས་གོ་ཅེས་ཡང་དང་ཡང་དུ་བསྔགས་པ་མཛད་དོ།

THREE
The Disciples of Se ston Kun rig

How many best disciples did this Lord Se have? The three types were the superior recipients of the oral instructions, the middling recipients, and the inferior recipient.

1. The Zhang ston Brothers

The superior recipients were the two Zhang ston brothers of Dings in lower Rtsang.[142] They did not perform extensive acts of servitude and so forth. They were finishers of scriptural works, and master Se summoned them for the finishing of the sūtras and the *Śatasāhasrikā prajñāpāramitā* that were being written.[143] When the finishing was done, they were rewarded with gifts, but they had found out about the Precious Oral Instructions. The two of them discussed it, saying, "Shall we offer the gifts and request oral instructions?" and were in agreement. When they offered the gifts from their finishing work, and made the request, the master said, "These were obtained as wages for your craftsmanship. I don't want them. If you have goods, bring them from home!"[144]

They went home and brought back what possessions they had, which were three hundred [loads of] barley and one suit of armor, offered them to the master, and delighted him with their conduct. They were remarkably intelligent, which pleased the master, who praised them again and again, saying, "This Dharma of mine is understood by the two Zhang ston brothers. And between them, it is understood by Zhang ston Gzi' brjid 'bar."[145]

2. Lady Zha ma and Her Brother

Concerning the middling recipients, there is the supplemental story of

འབྲིང་དུ་ཐོབ་པ་ལས་འཕྲོས་པ་ཞར་ལས་བྱུང་བ་ཞ་མའི་ལོ་རྒྱུས་ནི། ཕོང་ཡུལ་ལྷོ་བསྟོད་པ་དྲུག་པ་ཡིན་ལུམ་སྤྲིན་གཉིས་ཡོད་པ་ལས། སྤྲིན་མོ་རྫོ་མོ་ཞ་ཆུང་མ་ཅེས་ཡོངས་སུ་གྲགས་པ་དེ། སྡུག་བསྔལ་འབབ་ཞིག་གིས་སྔར་ཡང་གཉའ་ཚ་བྱ་བར་ཁྲིམ་ཐབ་ལ་ཕྱིན་ནས་ཁྲོ་ཤི་དེ་ནས་རྨ་ཆོས་འབར་བྱ་བའི་རྫོ་མོ་མཛེད་ཕོང་གྲོངས་པས་རྐྱེན་བྱས་ཏེ་སྙིང་རླུང་བྱུང་ནས་བསྐོ་བ་ལ། དེ་ཙམ་ན་གདམ་ངག་སུ་ཆེ་དྲིས་པས་དིང་རི་བླ་འཁོར་ན་དམ་པ་རྒྱ་གར་ཆེ་ཟེར་བ་ཐོས་ཏེ། དམ་པ་ལ་ཞུས་པས་དམ་པའི་མངོན་ཤེས་ཀྱིས་གཟིགས་པས་ལེགས་པར་མཁྱེན་ཏེ། ཁྱོད་ཀྱིས་དང་པོ་བླ་མ་ལ་དབང་བསྐུར་ཞུས་ནས་དབང་ཡོན་མ་ཕུལ་བར་འདུག་པས་དེའི་སྐྱོན་ཡིན་གསུང་བ་ལ།

དེ་བདེན་ཏེ་བླ་མ་རྨ་ཆོས་འབར་ཞེས་བྱ་བའི་རྫོ་མོ་བྱས་ཏེ་ཉེ་སློམས་ཀྱིས་དབང་ཡོན་མ་ཕུལ་བ་ཡིན་ལ། དེའི་ཞབས་ཐོག་བྱ་བར་འདོད་ན་འདང་བླ་མ་ནི་མི་བཞུགས། བླ་མའི་གདུང་བཞུགས་པའི་མཆོད་རྟེན་ཞིག་ཡོད་པ་ལ་བལ་པོ་ནས་ཀླུ་ཧི་ར་བླན་ཏེ་བཙུགས་པས་ལོ་གཅིག་གི་བར་དུ་ནད་དེ་ལེགས་པར་གྲག་སྐད། ཡང་བྲུ་ནས་དམ་པ་ཅན་ཕྱིན་པས་མདོ་རྒྱུད་ལྡོས་རྒྱལ་འཁམས་སློར་གསུང་དེར་རྟུབས་ཡུལ་རོང་དུ་ཕྱིན་པས་ལྷ་རྗེ་རྟུབས་པའི་བན་ཆུང་ཁ་ཅིག།

ཨེ་མ་ངོ་མཚར་རྨད་ཀྱི་ཆོས། རྫོགས་པའི་སངས་རྒྱས་ཀུན་གྱིས་གསང་།
སྐྱེ་བ་མེད་ལས་ཐམས་ཅད་སྐྱེས། སྐྱེས་ཙམ་ཉིད་ན་སྐྱེ་བ་མེད།

ཅེས་ཟེར་བ་ལ་བརྟེན་ནས་ནང་དུ་ངེས་ཤེས་ཁྱད་པར་ཅན་སྐྱེས་པས་དྲག་དེ་ནས་ཡང་བསྐོ་ནས་དམ་པ་ལ་ཞུས་པས་ཛ་ཞིག་བཏང་ནས་འདི་རྟུངས་ཟེར་

བརྟུངས་པས་སྐད་ཆེན་པོ་ཞིག་བྱུང་སྟེ། ལ་ལ་ན་རེ་ཕྱིས་ཀྱི་གྲགས་པ་ཡོང་བའི་རྟགས་ཡིན་ཟེར་རོ།

འོན་ཀྱང་ནད་ལ་མ་ཕན་ནས་གདམ་ངག་ཞུས་པས་སོང་ཅིག་པའི་ཕྱག་གི་བརྡ་མཛད་ནས་མ་གནང་སྐད།

དེ་ནས་དུས་ཕྱིས་བླ་མ་སེ་ལྷོ་སྟོད་དིང་རི་ཤེད་དུ་ཆོས་འཁོར་ཞིག་ལ་གདན་དྲངས་ཏེ། དེ་ཙམ་ན་འབྲོག་མི་ལོ་ཙ་བ་དངོས་ཀྱི་སློབ་མ་ཡིན་ཟེར་བའི་སྙན་པའི་གྲགས་པ་ཞ་མ་བས་ཐོས་ནས། བྱོན་པའི་ལམ་ཀར་ཞ་མ་ལུམ་སྤྲིན་གཉིས་འོངས་ནས་ཇི་ལྟར་ན་བའི་ལོ་རྒྱུས་རྣམས་བསྙད་པས་

the Zha mas. They were from Pha drug in the region of upper Lho.[146] Between the two, brother and sister, the sister was known everywhere as Lady Zha chung ma.[147] Total misery acted as a catalyst, causing a state of depression, and she became deranged. She had gone before to be a wife in Gnya' tsha, but her husband had died. Then she had been the consort of Rma Chos 'bar, and he had died.[148] At that point, she asked about who had the greatest oral instructions, and heard it said that Dam pa rgya gar in Ding ri Bla 'khor had the greatest.[149] She told Dam pa. Seeing with his clairvoyance, Dam pa understood well, and said, "At the time when you first requested the bestowal of initiation from a master you did not offer an initiation gift. That's the problem."[150]

That was true. She had been the consort of the master known as Rma Chos 'bar, and with the arrogance of close association she had not offered an initiation gift. Even though she wanted to honor him, the master was no longer living. It is said that when she brought an ornamental pinnacle from Nepal and attached it to the stūpa in which the bones of the master rested she was completely cured of that illness for a period of one year. When it became worse again, she went to Dam pa's place. He said, "Look at the sūtras and tantras, and wander around the country."[151] When she went to Rong, in the region of Rnubs, several of Lha rje Rnubs pa's[152] young monks were reciting:

> E Ma! The incredible, miraculous Dharma is the secret of all the perfect buddhas. From a birthless state everything is born. At the very moment of birth they are birthless.

On the basis of that an exceptional certainty arose within, and she was cured.[153] Then she became deranged again. When she told Dam pa, he gave her a drum and said, "Beat this!"

When she beat it there was a great sound, and some said, "It is a sign of fame to come later."

However, when it did not help the illness, she requested oral instructions. He made a gesture for her to go away and did not bestow them.

Then, at a later time, master Se was invited to a Dharma council in the region of Ding ri in upper Lho. At that point the Zha mas heard of his reputation as an actual disciple of 'Brog mi Lo tsā ba, and both brother and sister Zha ma came to the road on which he was traveling. While she told the story of how she had become ill, he was tapping a cane on one of his boots, and commenting, "That is also a meditative concentration, that is also a meditative concentration."

ཁོང་ལྷམ་འབུར་མ་ཞིག་ལ་སྣ་ལྷུག་ཅིག་ཏུག་ཏུག་མཛད་ཅིང་དེ་ཡང་ཉིང་ངེ་འཛོན་ཡིན་དེ་ཡང་ཉིང་ངེ་འཛོན་ཡིན་གསུང་།།

བླ་མའི་ཞལ་ནས་འོ་ན་ཁྱོད་ལ་འདི་འདྲ་བ་མ་བྱུང་ངམ་ཅེས་དྲིས་པས་ཞ་ཆུང་མའི་ཉམས་སྐྱོང་གི་ཐོག་ཏུ་བབས་སྐྱེ། མགོ་བོ་ས་ལ་རྫེབས་ཅིང་ཕྱག་འཚལ་ནས། རྗེ་སངས་རྒྱས་སམ་བྱ་བ་དེ་ལགས་སམ་ཟེར་ཅིང་བྱུང་བ་ལ།

རྗེའི་ཞལ་ནས་ཞ་ཆུང་མ་ལ་སྒོམ་འདུག་སྐེ་གདམ་ངག་མི་འདུག་སེ་འཁར་ཆུང་བ་ལ་གདམ་ངག་ཡོད་དེ་སྒོམ་མི་གདའ། ཁ་ལ་ཚོ་འདི་ལ་སངས་རྒྱས་འོང་དུ་མ་ཐོ་སྤྲང་པོ་པེ་ཀར་འདིས་ཀྱང་གནོད་པ་ཞིག་ཀྱང་སྐྱེལ་དུ་མ་འདོད་ཐ་ན་སྙིང་ཆུང་གཅིག་ཀ་བཏང་དང་ངས་ཉིང་ངེ་འཛོན་དུ་སྤྱོལ་ཞེས་པ་ཡིན་ཏེ་གསུང་ནས། དེའི་རེས་ལ་གདམ་ངག་མ་གནང་སྐད། འཁར་ཆུང་དུ་ཤོག་ཁམས་ངན་པར་འདུག་པས་གྲོགས་ཤིག་ཁྲིད་ལ་ཤོག་གསུང་ནས

ཕྱིས་ཞ་མ་ལྷུམ་སྤྲིང་གིས་ཞབས་ཐོག་ཆེན་པོ་ཁྱེར་ནས་འཁར་ཆུང་དུ་ཕྱིན། དབང་བསྐུར་བ་ཞུས་གདམ་ངག་བསྟན་པས་ཞ་ཆུང་མའི་ནད་དེ་སོས་ནས་ཁྲིད་བྱས་པས་གཞུང་ཚར་བར་ནི་མ་མཉན་གསུང་ངོ་།།

དགེ་བཤེས་ཞ་མས་ནི་གསུང་ངག་རགས་རིམས་ཤིག་མཉན་ནས་སེམས་ཆིམ་ཚོག་ཤེས་པའི་བདུད་བྱུང་སྐེ་ལྷུམ་སྤྲིང་འགྲོ་བར་འདུག་པ་ལ་རྗེའི་ཞལ་ནས་ཞང་སྟོན་པ་གཉིས་ལ་ཁོང་ལྷུམ་སྤྲིང་གཉིས་ནི་འགྲོ་བར་གདའ། གདམ་ངག་ནི་མ་ཚར་བརྒྱུད་པ་འདིའི་ལུགས་ཀྱིས་མ་ཞུས་པར་མི་གནང་བར་གདའ། ཁོང་པ་མི་ཆེན་དུ་འང་གདའ་གདམ་ངག་གི་འང་སྐྱོད་དུ་གདའ་བས་འདི་པ་ལ་གསུང་ངག་འདི་རྫོགས་པར་བཤད་པར་འདོད་ན་ཡང་ཁོང་པ་མི་ཞུ་བར་གདའ་བས། ད་དུང་མ་འགྲོ་བར་གསུང་ངག་ཚར་བར་ཉོན་ཅེས་གྲོས་ཐོབ་གསུང་བས།

ཞང་པ་མཆེད་གཉིས་ཀྱིས་ཁོང་པ་ལ་ད་དུང་རྗེ་ལ་གསུང་ངག་རིན་པོ་ཆེའི་འཕྲོ་བག་ཙམ་བདོག་པར་གདའ་བས་ཞུ་འཚལ། ཞར་ལ་ཁོ་བོ་ཅག་ཀྱང་ཞུ་བ་ལགས་བྱས་པས

ཞ་མ་ན་རེ་ཇོ་ཇོ་འདི་ཅི་གསུང་ངེད་ཅག་གིས་འཁོར་གསུམ་ཡོངས་དག་ལན་གསུམ་བྱས་བྱུང་དང་ར་དང་ཆུང་ཚུན་ཆད་བསྔོར། ཛག་དམར་གི་གོས་རྒྱང་པ་རེ་ལས་མེད་པར་ཕུལ་བས་དྲང་གྲགས་ནས་ལམ་དུ་གཡག་གི་སྐྱིབས་འཛེ་ཞིང་འོངས་ཅི་ཡོད་ཕུལ་ནས་ཞུས་པ་ཡིན།

When the master asked, "Well, didn't it happen like this to you?" it matched Zha chung ma's experiences, and she struck her forehead on the ground and prostrated, exclaiming, "Lord, are you the one known as the Buddha?"

The lord replied, "Zha chung ma has meditation, but not the oral instructions. Se 'khar chung ba has the oral instructions, but not meditation. For me, even this impotent beggar Pe kar can't prevent the occurrence of buddhahood in this lifetime,[154] because I know how to make even just the least state of depression into meditative concentration." It is said that he did not bestow the oral instructions right then. He said, "Come to 'Khar chung. Since you are in bad health, bring a companion."

The Zha mas, brother and sister, later traveled to 'Khar chung bringing large offerings.[155] They requested the bestowal of initiation, and when he presented the oral instructions Zha chung ma's illness was cured. He instructed them, but they did not fully receive the scriptures. So it has been stated.

The Zha ma spiritual friends were satisfied with hearing the Oral Instructions [of the Lam 'bras] in a general way. The māra of contentment arose.[156] When brother and sister were going to leave, the lord told the two Zhang ston pa [brothers], "Both of them, brother and sister, are leaving. The oral instructions are incomplete. It is the custom of this lineage not to bestow them without a request. Because they are fine people, and because they are worthy vessels for the oral instructions,[157] I want to completely explain these Oral Instructions to them, but they are not asking. So you must advise them not to go yet, and to completely listen to the Oral Instructions!"

The two Zhang pa brothers said to them, "Since the lord still has a small amount of the Precious Oral Instructions left, please ask. In which case, we will also receive them."

[Lady] Zha ma replied, "Honored brothers, what is this you are saying? We made [offerings] of threefold purity three times. We went around to Byang, Ra, and Chung, and made offerings, to where we have nothing except a single coarse red garment each, and from the intense cold will have to be satisfied with the bellies of yaks on the path.[158] We offered what we had, and made our request. Even though you may say that the lord still has oral instructions, the lord also kept us close to his heart, and completely granted these Oral Instructions. We certainly don't need any more than these. Even though he says he still has some, the lord himself is lying." They went home without listening.

རྗེ་ལ་གདམས་ངག་ཡོད་ཟེར་ཏེ་འདུག་ཀྱང་འདུག། རྗེས་ཀྱང་ཐུགས་ལ་བཏགས་ནས་གསུང་ངག་འདི་ཚར་བར་གནང་བ་ཡིན། འདི་ཚོ་ལས་མང་བ་དགོས་ཀྱང་མི་དགོས། ད་དུང་ཡོད་པ་སྐད་གསུང་ཡང་རྗེ་ཉིད་བརྟན་གསུང་བ་ཡིན་ཟེར་ནས་མ་ཉན་པར་ཡུལ་དུ་སོང་ངོ།།

དེས་ན་ཡོངས་སུ་རྫོགས་པ་མེད་དེ་ལམ་འབྲས་ཀྱི་ལྟ་བ་འཁོར་འདས་དབྱེར་མེད་ཡིན་པ་ལ་སྒྲེ་སྐྱོད་སྐྱི་མཐུན་ཟེར་ཀྱེ་རྡོར་དབང་སྐུར་ལ་རྣལ་འབྱོར་དབང་ཕྱུག་ནས་རྒྱུད་པའི་དབང་ཆུ་མེད་པར་ནག་པོ་པའི་ལ་བྱེད་མངོན་རྟོགས་རྒྱས་པ་སྙེན་སྒྲུབ་བཞིས་མི་འཆིང་བར་མཚོ་སྐྱེས་དངོས་ཟེར་བ་རྣམས་སོ། གདམས་ངག་འབྲིང་དུ་ཐོབ་ཅེས་གྲགས་སོ།

འོན་ཀྱང་ཇོ་མོ་ཞ་ཆུང་མ་དེས་བསྒོམས་པས་ཏིང་ངེ་འཛིན་དཔག་དུ་མེད་པ་སྐྱེས་ཏེ། ཐུན་མོང་གི་དངོས་གྲུབ་མངོན་ཤེས་བརྟན་པོ་ཡང་ཡོད་སྐད། རྫུ་འཕྲུལ་ལུས་གཅིག་ནས་གཅིག་ཏུ་སྤྲུལ་བ་དང་ནམ་མཁའ་ལ་དཀྱིལ་ཀྲུང་འཆའ་བ་ལ་སོགས་པ་བླ་མ་ཞུ་བྲུས་ཀྱིས་ཀྱང་གཟིགས་སྐད།

རྗེ་དགོན་པ་བའི་ཞལ་ནས་ཞ་ཆུང་མ་འདི་ཚེ་འདི་ལ་ལུས་མ་སྦྱངས་པར་ཕྱག་རྒྱ་ཆེན་པོ་འགྲུབ་པ་ལྷུམ་ལེགས་སྐྱི་ཀ་ར་ཙམ་ཞིག་འོང་བ་ཡིན་པ་ལ། ཉམས་དབྱངས་ལ་དགའ་ཆེས་པས་ལམ་གི་བར་ཆད་དུ་སོང་གསུང་ངོ།།

དེ་ལ་ཐ་མར་ཐོབ་པ་ནི་ཕ་དུག་གི་སྐད་ན་བོང་ཤོད་སེན་ཐོག་བསྒོམ་ཆོའི་དཔོན་ཟེ་སྒོམ་བྱང་སེང་ཅེས་པ་དེ་ལ་བབ་ཙམ་འཕེལ་ཏེ། ཞིབ་ཏུ་ནི་མི་གསུང་བར་གདའོ།།

Therefore, they did not have the complete [teachings], and are known as the middling recipients of the oral instructions.[159] The view of the Lam 'bras is the indivisibility of saṃsāra and nirvāṇa, but they said it was in agreement with the piṭakas in general. Without the stream of initiation transmitted through the Lord of Yogins, they used that of Kṛṣṇa for the bestowal of the Hevajra initiation. Not requiring the fourfold approach and attainment of the extensive method for direct realization, they said the actual practice was that by Saroruha.[160]

Nevertheless, when Lady Zha chung ma meditated, infinite meditative concentrations arose, and it is said that she also had the common attainment of stable clairvoyance. It is said that master Zhu byas also saw miracles, such as the emanation of a body from her body, and holding the crossed-legged position in space.[161]

Lord Dgon pa ba said, "This Zha chung ma would have realized Mahāmudrā in this lifetime without discarding the body, and would have become like Lady Lakṣmiṅkarā, but her excessive fondness for songs of experience became an obstacle on the path."[162]

3. Ze sgom Byang seng

The inferior recipient was known as Ze sgom Byang seng, the leader of the Bong shod Sen thog meditators in lower Pha drug. There was a slight dissemination from him, but it was not mentioned in detail.[163]

དེ་ལྟར་ན་གདམ་ངག་རབ་དུ་ཐོབ་པའི་མཆེད་གཉིས་ལས་གཙེན་པོ་ཞང་སྟོན་ཆོས་འབར་ལ། བླ་མ་ས་སྐྱ་བ་ཆེན་པོ་དེས་གསུང་ངག་ཇི་ལྟར་གསན་ཅེ་ན།།

འདི་ལྟར་ཁམས་ཏེ་ལོ་རྒྱུས་ཙུང་ཟད་རྗོད་ན། ཡབ་དགེ་ཤེས་དཀོན་མཆོག་རྒྱལ་པོ། ཡུམ་ཇོ་མོ་ཞང་མོ་ཅེས་པའི་སྲས་སུ་སྐུ་འཁྲུངས་སྟེ། འཁོན་དཀོན་རྒྱལ་འཛག་ཤོངས་ནི་ཕུལ་ཞིང་བཙོངས་ཁོང་རེས་ཁའུ་ན་བྲའི་བྲུ་བར་བཞུགས་རེས་གྲོལ་མ་ལྷ་ཁང་ན་ཡོད་པའི་དུས་སུ་ས་སྐྱ་ནི་ས་དཀར་ཤིང་སྣུམ་པ་སླང་པོ་ཆེའི་འཁལ་ཁང་འདྲ་བ་ཆུ་གཡས་སུ་འཁོར་བ་ས་སྤྱད་བཟང་བར་འདུག་ཏེ་དགོན་པ་བྱ་སྣམ་ཏེ་ག་ར་བ་འབུལ་ཟེར་ཀྱང་ཕྲུགས་ཟབ་པས་རྐྱོད་མ་ཞིག་ཙལ་དེར་དགོན་པ་མཛད་འཁོར་བན་དེ་སུམ་བཅུ་བཞི་བཅུ་ཙམ་ལ་རྒྱུད་གསུང་བའི་དུས་སུ་ཇོ་མོ་རྗོ་ཕྱུག་མ་ལ་སྲས་མེད་ཞང་མོ་ལ་བླ་ཆེན་འཁྲུངས་རྗོ་ཕྱུག་མ་ན་རེ་ཉིད་ཀྱི་གདུང་འཆད་དུ་ཕངས་པ་ཡིན་ཞང་མོ་ལ་སྲས་ཡོད་པ་བདག་ལ་གསང་བ་མ་ལེགས་ད་བདག་ལ་ནོར་མི་དགོས་བུའི་མ་ལ་དགོས་པས་ཟེར་མདུན་གྱི་ཞིང་མ་གཏོགས་པ་ཙོ་ཞང་མོ་ཡུམ་སྲས་ལ་གཏད་བླ་ཆེན། དགུང་ལོ་བཅུ་གཉིས་ལོན་པ་དང་ཡབ་འདས་ནས་རྩིས་མཁན་ལ་རྩིས་བྱས་པས་གཤེགས་རྫོངས་ཕྱི་རྟེན་གདན་ས་བ་ཞིག་དང་གསུམ་ཉིན་གཅིག་ལ་བྱས་ན་ཤུལ་དུ་ཕུན་སུམ་ཚོགས་པའི་རྟེན་འབྲེལ་དུ་འགྲོ་ཟེར་ནས་འཕྲང་བྲག་དམར་ལ་སེར་ཆགས་བྱས་ཕྱི་རྟེན་གྱི་འགྲམ་དེང་།

མ་གཅིག་ན་རེ། ཁྱོད་ཀྱི་ཕའི་སློབ་དཔོན་ཀུང་ལོ་ཚ་བ་ཡིན་ཉིད་ཀུང་ལོ་ཚ་བའི་སློབ་དཔོན་ཞིག་ལ་ཆོས་སློབ་དགོས་ཟེར་ཏེ།

གཡུང་འཁར་མོ་ནས་བླ་མ་བ་རི་ལོ་ཚ་བ་རིན་ཆེན་གྲགས་པ་སྤྱན་དྲངས་ས་སྐྱའི་ཞིང་མོ་ཆེ་མ་

FOUR
The Life of Sa chen Kun dga' snying po

Sa chen Kun dga' snying po

IN THAT WAY, between the two brothers who were the superior recipients of the oral instructions, just how did that great master of Sa skya receive the Oral Instructions [of the Lam 'bras] from the elder brother Zhang ston Chos 'bar?

This will be summarized and some of the story told in the following way. He was born as the son of the father, the spiritual friend Dkon mchog rgyal po, and the mother, Lady Zhang mo.[164] 'Khon Dkon [mchog] rgyal [po] had sold [the fields of] 'Jag shongs, offered [the wealth to 'Brog mi], and sometimes stayed at a place called Bra'o in Kha'u.[165] Once, when he was at the Sgrol ma lha khang, he thought that Sa skya had a fine topography, with white and glistening earth [shaped] like an elephant's abdomen, and a stream circling to the right. He thought to make a monastery there. Gu ra ba said he would offer it, but [Dkon mchog rgyal po] was far-sighted, and paid with a mare. He made a monastery there, and taught tantra to a following of about thirty or forty monks. At that time Lady Rdo phyug ma had no son. The great master [Sa chen] was born to Zhang mo.[166] Rdo phyug ma said, "It was to save your family line from dying out. But it was not right that you kept from me the secret that Zhang mo had a son. I don't need the wealth now. The child's mother needs it." Except for just the fields in front, she gave [everything] to Zhang mo, the mother with the son. When the great master [Sa chen] reached the age of twelve years, his father passed

རྟོགས་པའི་ཞིང་ཐམས་ཅད་ཕུལ་ནས་གདན་ས་མཛད་པར་ཞུས་པས་ཞལ་གྱིས་བཞེས་ནས། བླ་མ་བ་རི་བའི་ཞལ་ནས་ཁྱོད་ཕ་རྗེ་སྲས་ཀྱི་བུ་ལ་སློབ་གཉེར་བྱེད་དགོས་དེ་ལ་ཤེས་རབ་དགོས་པས། ཤེས་རབ་ཀྱི་ལྷ་འཕགས་པ་འཇམ་དཔལ་ཡིན་པས་ཨ་ར་པ་ཙ་ན་འདི་བསྒྲུབས་གསུང་ནས་

བསྒྲུབས་པས་དང་པོ་བར་ཆད་ཀྱི་ལྟས་ཅུང་ཟད་ཅིག་བྱུང་བ་ལ་ཁྲོ་བོའི་རྒྱལ་པོ་མི་གཡོ་བའི་སྒོ་ནས་བར་ཆད་བཟློག་ནས་འཕགས་པ་འཇམ་དཔལ་གྱི་ཞལ་མཐོང་ཞེས་ལོ་གར་གྲགས་སོ།

དེ་ནས་བློ་གྲོས་ཕུལ་དུ་བྱུང་བའི་བདག་ཉིད་ཆེན་པོ་དེས་དགུང་ལོ་བཅུ་གསུམ་པ་ལ། ཐོག་མར་ཆོས་རྒྱུབ་ཆེ་བས་མངོན་པ་ཞིག་གསན་ན་འཐད་ཟེར་ནས་རོང་གི་དགེ་བཤེས་དྲུར་དམིག་པ་ལ་གཡར་ཆོས་ཤིག་གི་མགོ་ལ་སླེབ་ཁོང་ལ་གྲྭ་པ་ལྔ་བརྒྱ་ཙམ་ཡོད་པས་ཁང་པ་མ་ཐོབ་སྒང་ཀ་ཕུག་རྡུགས་ཤིག་ཏུ་ཕྱུར་བའི་ཡོལ་བ་བྱས་མངོན་པ་གསན་པས་ཚར་གཅིག་གིས་ཁོང་དུ་ཆུད་དེ་ཀུན་གྱིས་ངོ་མཚར་དུ་འཛིན་ཏོ། དེར་བླ་ཆེན་ལ་འབུམ་ནག་བྱུང་ཨ་ཙེ་ཕག་སྟོན་ལ་མཐོང་སྣང་དུ་བྲ་རྒྱུ་གོང་ན་ཡར་བན་དེ་རྟ་སྒྲོ་བོ་ལ་ཞོན་པོད་ཀ་ནག་ལྷུབ་སེ་བ་ཞིག་ཀུན་དགའ་སྙིང་པོ་ན་ཡིན་ཡོད་ཁྱེད་ཅི་མཛོ་ཟེར་འདི་ལྷ་བུ་བྱུང་བྱུས་པ་ཨ་ཙེ་ཟེར་བ་བཞིན་འོང་བ་ཞིག་ཡོད་ཟེར་ནས་ཡུམ་གྱིས་གསེར་བག་ཙམ་སློམས་ནས་བུ་ཤི་ན་ང་ལ་ཡར་འོང་རྒྱུ་ཙམ་མེད་དགོན་པ་ཆོས་དང་མཐུན་པ་འདྲར་བསྡད་སྙམ་ནས་སྐྱེད་འགོ་བ་དང་བཅས་པས་བྱོན་ཙ་ན་ཁམས་ཅུང་གསོས་པ་ལ་སླེབ་བླ་ཆེན་གྱིས་བཤུམས་པས་ཁྲོད་དགེ་འདུན་རྒྱ་མཚོ་ལྟ་བུའི་དབུས་འདིར་ཤི་ཡང་ལེགས་ཕ་རྗེ་སྲས་ཀྱི་བུ་བྱ་བ་ལ་སྙིང་རུས་དགོས་པ་ཡིན་ཟེར་

དེའི་དུས་སུ་བྲང་ཏི་སྐུ་གཤེགས་ཏེ། ཟུར་ཆོས་པ་བྱང་འཆད་ཁྲུང་ལ་ས་སྡེ་མངོན་པའི་ཆ་ལག་ཙོ་ལ་སོགས་པ་གསན་ནོ།། ཚར་གཉིས་ལ་སྐྱིད་མ་བྱུང་སྡེ་གསན

དེ་ནས་ཉང་སྟོད་དུ་ཁྲུང་རིན་ཆེན་གྲགས་པ་ལ་ཚད་མ་རྣམ་ངེས་དང་རིགས་ཐིགས་ལ་སོགས་པ་རྣམ་འགྲེལ་མ་རྟོགས་གཞན་ཐམས་ཅད་གསན་ནོ། ཟུར་ཆོས་ནི་ཙུང་པ་མེ་དིག་པ་ཡིན་དེ་ཙམ་ན་ས་སྐྱའི་གཞི་བ་རྣམས་ཀྱིས་འཕྱིན་བསྐྱིངས་སྟེ་ཚད་མ་ཕྱིས་གསན་པས་ཆོག། བླ་མ་བ་རི་བ་བགྲེས་པས་གསན་ལོང་མི་ཡོང་བས་ཡར་བྱོན་པར་ཞུས་སྟེ། ཡར་བྱོན་ནས་ཕལ་པོ་ཆེ་དཀོན་བརྩེགས་ཏིང་ངེ་འཛིན་རྒྱལ་པོ་གཟུངས་གྲྭ་ལྔ་ལ་སོགས་པ་བླ་མ་བ་རི་བའི་ཆོས་སྐོར་ཐམས་ཅད་ཐུགས་སུ་ཆུད་པར་མཛད་དོ་དེ་ནས་བ་རི་བའི་ཞལ་ནས་ད་ཁྱོད་རང་གདན་ས་གྱིས་ང་ཡང་སྦྱུར་དུ་འགྲོ་འདུག་བྱེད་གསུང་ནས་རིང་པོ་མ་ལོན་པར་སྐུ་གཤེགས།།

away.[167] When the astrologers made calculations they said that if the funeral ceremony, the outer reliquary, and a successor on the monastic seat were all accomplished in a single day, the perfect dependently arisen connections would be formed for the heir. A Dharma council was held at 'Phrang Brag dmar, and the foundation of the outer reliquary was laid.[168]

Early Studies

Ma gcig [Zhang mo] said, "Your father's teacher was a translator.[169] You must also learn Dharma from a teacher who is a translator."

The master Ba ri Lo tsā ba Rin chen grags pa was invited from G.yu' 'khar mo.[170] All the fields except for the great field of Sa skya were offered, and he was asked to take the monastic seat, which he accepted. Then master Ba ri ba said, "Son of a noble father, you must study, and for that you need wisdom. Since noble Mañjuśrī is the deity of wisdom, you should practice this *A ra pa tsa na*."[171]

When he practiced, at first some signs of obstacles occurred, but after repulsing the obstacles by means of Acala, the king of the wrathful, it became known throughout the world that he had "beheld the face of noble Mañjuśrī."[172]

Because it was the great support of the Dharma, it was said that it would be fitting to receive the Abhidharma first. Then, at the age of thirteen, that great being with consummate intelligence received the Abhidharma from the spiritual friend Ngur dmig pa of Rong.[173] He arrived at the beginning of a summer session of Dharma, and since there were about five hundred monks, he did not obtain a room. He hung a curtain up in the end of a hallway.[174] He mastered [the Abhidharma] upon hearing it once, and everyone held him in awe. The great master became infected with smallpox there. A co Phag ston had a vision in which a monk wearing a flapping black robe and mounted on a horse with a white mark on its forehead appeared above Bra chu gong [in Sa skya], and said, "Kun dga' snying po is ill. What are you thinking about?" He told what had happened. The mother said, "Things come to pass like A co says." She took some gold, and thinking, "If my son dies I will have no reason to come back. I will stay in some isolated place in harmony with Dharma," she started off with an escort. She arrived when his health had slightly improved. When the great master wept, she said, "Even to die here in the midst of an ocean-like Saṅgha would be good. To be the son of a noble father you must have courage."[175]

At that point Brang ti passed away, and [Sa chen] received the *Sa sde,*

དེ་ནས་ཁའུར་གནང་ཁ་འུ་བ་དར་མ་རྒྱལ་མཚན་སྐུ་བན་ཚང་སྒོམ་པ་ལ་གསང་བ་འདུས་པ་ལ་སོགས་པ་དང་དེ་ཉིད་བསྡུས་པ་ལ་སོགས་པ་ཡོ་ག་རྣམས་ཀྱང་གསན་ནོ་བླ་མ་གནང་ཁོང་རང་དགེས་པ་དཀོན་མཆོག་ལ་འདང་སྒོམ་པ་ཕྱུལ་ཕྱིན་འོ་བྲུ་འཕུང་པ་འབྲུལ་དུ་འོང་ཙ་ན་སྣེད་ལོང་སྤྱོད་ལ་འཛོན་པ་ཆུང་ཧེ་གཅིག་གིས་གསེར་ཕུལ་བ་ཞིག་ཡིག་ཆའི་ནང་ན་གང་དགར་བཞག་ནས་འདུག་པ་ལ་འདི་ཅི་ལགས་ཞུས་པས་གསེར་རམ་བྲུ་བ་ལགས་ལོ་གསུང་ནས་ཁ་ཡང་མ་ཕྱེ་བར་འདུག་སྐད་འགྲོངས་ཙ་ན་ཆོས་བརྡོ་ལྡའི་ཟླ་བའི་འོད་ལྟ་བུ་ཐམས་ཅད་ཀྱིས་མཐོང་བ་བྱུང་ཅི་འདུག་བལྟས་པས་བླ་མ་གནང་རིན་པོ་ཆེའི་ཁྲི་ཆེན་པོ་ཞིག་གི་སྟེང་ན་བཞུགས་ནས་ལྷའི་བུ་མང་པོ་ཁྲི་འདེགས་པའི་རིན་པོ་ཆེའི་འོད་དུ་འདུག་སྟེ་མཁའ་སྤྱོད་དུ་གཤེགས་གསུང་། ||

དེ་ནས་བགྲེས་པ་ཀུན་གྲོས་བྱས་ནས་དེ་དུས་ཀྱི་སློབ་མ་དེ་པ་མང་པོ་མེད་པར་འདུག་སྟེ་གོ་ཆོད་པོ་ཚོ་ཞིག་ཡོད་པར་འདུག་གསུང་ད་ཕ་ཆོས་ཤིག་རང་གཙོད་བཅད་པ་དགའ་ཟེར་ནས་སུ་མཁས་དྲིས་པས་པུ་རངས་པ་གསལ་སྟིང་ནི་གཤེགས་དེའི་སློབ་མ་འགོན་སྐྱི་ཆུ་བ་མཁས་ཀྱང་ཟེར་གདུང་ཡང་གཅིག་པས་ཟེར་ནས་སྐྱི་ཆུར་བྱོན་

དེའི་དུས་སུ་གཡས་རུ་སྐྱི་ཆུ་རུ་དགེ་ཚ་ཤེས་འགོན་ཀྱི་མཚན་དངོས་དཀོན་མཆོག་འབར་བླ་དགས་འགོན་ཆུང་དགྲ་བླ་འབར་ལ་དགེས་རྡོར་འགྲེལ་པ་དང་བཅས་པ་གསན་ཅིང་ཡོད་ཙམ་ན་མདོག་སྟོད་དུ་ཆོས་འཁོར་ཞིག་ལ་བླ་མ་སེ་བྱོན་པས་བླ་ཆེན་ལ་སོགས་པ་སྐྱི་ཆུ་བའི་གྲྭ་པ་ཁ་ཅིག་གིས་ཞལ་ལྟར་ཕྱིན་པས། རྗེ་སེའི་ཞལ་ནས་ཁྱེད་ཚོ་ཇི་ལྟར་ཡིན་ཅེས་པའི་ལོ་རྒྱུས་སོ་སོར་དྲིས་པས།

བླ་མའི་ཞལ་ནས་དངོས་གྲུབ་སྟོད་པ་ཞིག་ལགས་བྱས་པས

དེའི་གང་ན་ཡོད་གསུང་བ་ལ།

ས་སྐྱ་ན་བདོག་བྱས་པས

དེ་ན་ངའི་བླ་མ་ཞིག་ཡོད་པ་ཡིན་ཏེ་སྐུ་ནི་གཤེགས་ཚོད་འདུག་རྗེས་ན་ཇི་འདྲ་བདོག་གམ། ང་ལ་ཁྲལ་འདོད་པ་ཅིག་ཀྱང་མ་བྱུང་གསུང་བ་ལ

དེའི་སྲས་ཀྱི་དོན་ཞིག་དངོས་ལགས་ཞུས་པས།

ཁྱོད་བརྟུན་མ་ཟེར་ངའི་བླ་མ་ལ་སྲས་མེད་ཡོད་ན་སྐུ་གཤེགས་ཙ་ན་ང་ལ་བརྫ་སྤྲོད་པ་ཅིག

the affiliated texts of Abhidharma, and so forth from the assistant teacher Byang 'chad Khyung. He received the basic texts twice.[176]

Then he received the *Pramāṇaviniścaya*, the *Nyāyabindu*, and so forth, all the other texts except the *Pramāṇavārtikka*, from Khyung Rin chen grags in upper Nyang.[177] The assistant teacher was Me dig pa from Rtsang. At that point the residents of Sa skya sent a message that he could receive epistemology later, but since master Ba ri ba was old there would not be time to receive [his teachings]. They requested that he return. He returned and mastered all the Dharma cycles such as the *Avataṃsaka*, *Ratnakuṭa*, *Samādhirāja*, and the *Gzungs dra lnga* of master Ba ri ba. Then Ba ri ba said, "Now you take the monastic seat. I am leaving soon." Not long after that he passed away.[178]

From Gnang Kha'u pa Dar ma rgyal mtshan, a monk who meditated in retreat at Kha'u, he then received the Guhyasamāja and so forth, and also the yoga [tantras] such as the *Tattvasaṃgraha*.[179] Master Gnang liked garlic, and even offered it to the Triple Gem, but when people from 'O bya 'phrang came to visit, he would hide it.[180] He had little attachment to possessions, and it is said that when someone offered gold he would just leave it anywhere at random among the texts. When asked, "What is this?" he would reply, "They said it was gold or something." He wouldn't have even opened it up. When he died, everyone saw a light like the moon of a fifteenth day. When they looked to see what it was, master Gnang was seated on a great jeweled throne being held up by many divine children in a jeweled light, and going to Khecāra. So it has been stated.[181]

Then all the elders held a discussion. There were not many disciples of his [i.e., Gnang's] at that time, but one reliable one spoke up. "Now it would be good for him to seek out one of the ancestral teachings," he said. When he was asked who was an expert, he answered that Gsal snying of Pu rangs had died, but it was said that his disciple 'Khon Sgyi chu ba was an expert, and that he was also of the same clan. So [Sa chen] went to Sgyi chu.[182]

Meeting Se ston Kun rig

During the time [Sa chen] was receiving the *Hevajra [tantra]* together with the commentaries from the 'Khon spiritual friend whose real name was Dkon mchog 'bar, alias 'Khon chung Dgra bla 'bar, at Sgyi chu in G.yas ru, master Se came to a Dharma council in upper Mdog.[183] The great master [Sa chen] and several of Sgyi chu ba's students went to gaze upon his face. Lord Se asked, "How are you?" and asked about each of their stories.

Master [Sa chen] said, "I am from upper Brom."[184]

ཀྱང་མ་བྱུང་གསུང་བ་ལ།

བླ་ཆེན་སྐྱིངས་ནས་གསུང་མ་ནུས་པ་ལ་གྲོགས་རྣམས་ཀྱིས་ལོ་རྒྱུས་ཞིབ་དུ་བསྙད་པས་སེའི་ཞལ་ནས་མི་གསོན་གཤིན་མི་ཕྲད་ཟེར་ཏེ་ཕྲད་པའི་དུས་བྱུང་གསུང་ནས། ཕར་དུ་བཞེས་སྤྱན་ཆབ་བྱུང་ནས་

ཀྱད་པོ་གོག་པོ་འདིའི་ནང་ན་ཆོས་ཡོད་པ་ཡིན་པས། མྱུར་དུ་སྤྱོན་ཕྱིས་འོང་སྙམ་ན་སང་ཕོད་ནི་ང་འཆི་བ་ཡིན་གསུང་།

དེའི་དུས་སུ་བླ་མ་ཞག་འགའ་ཞིག་བཞུགས་པའི་བར་ལ། རྗེ་སེམས་ལམ་འབྲས་ཀྱི་སྤྱིའི་རྣམ་པར་གཞག་པའི་བབས་དང་། གགས་སེལ་ལ་སོགས་པའི་གདམ་ངག་གི་རྐང་གྲངས་འདི་ཡོད་ཀྱི་ཁུངས་ཐམས་ཅད་ལེགས་པར་གསུངས་སོ།།

དེ་ནས་ཡར་བྱོན་ཏེ་འཁར་ཆུང་དུ་བཞུད་པར་དགོངས་པ་དང་། བླ་མའི་བྲང་གྲོགས་ཡོན་བརྩོན་ར་ཛ་དང་སྟོན་པ་རྡོ་རྗེ་འོད་ན་རེ་ཉིད་ལ་བླ་མ་སྐྱི་ཀྱུ་བ་འདི་ཐུགས་ལ་ཤིན་དུ་འདོགས་པར་གདའ་བས། འགྲོ་བ་ཞུས་ན་ལེགས་ཟེར་བ་ལ་

དེ་བདེན་སྙམ་སྟེ་བླ་མ་སྐྱི་ཀྱུ་བ་ལ། བདག་འཁར་ཆུང་དུ་ཡུག་ཅིག་མཆི་བར་ཞུ་བྱས་པས་

ཁྱོད་ཅི་ལ་འགྲོ་གསུང་བ་ལ་

གདམ་ངག་ཅིག་ཞུ་བ་ལགས་བྱས་པས་

ཁོང་ན་རེ་ཉིད་ཐུགས་ཆོད་མ་ཆུང་དེ་ནི་སེ་ལྷེ་ལ་རེ་བྱ་བ་ངའི་བླ་མ་མངའ་རིས་པའི་ཆོས་ཀྱི་བྲལ་བྲུལ་འདྲ་བ་བསྒྲུགས་ནས་གཞན་ལ་ཤོད་པ་ཡིན། གདམ་ངག་ཅི་ཡང་མེད་མ་འགྲོ་གསུང་ནས་མ་གནང་ངོ།།

དེར་བླ་མས་མ་གནང་ནས་འགྲོ་བ་ཆ་མ་ཡིན་སྙམ་སྟེ། འོན་ཀྱང་སང་ཕོད་འགྲོ་སྙམ་ཙ་ན་སེ་གསུང་བ་བདེན་ཏེ་རྗེ་སེ་སྐུ་གཤེགས་སྐད།

དེ་ནས་དུས་རིང་མོ་ཞིག་འགྱངས་ཏེ་དེ་ནས་ཡང་ཁའུར་བྱོན་ནས་དགེ་བཤེས་གནང་སྐུ་མཆེད་ལ་ཆོས་གསན།

དུས་ཕྱིས་བླ་མ་སྐྱི་ཀྱུ་བ་ས་སྐྱར་སྤྱན་དྲངས་ནས་ཆོས་འཁོར་མཛད་པར་བཞེད་པའི་ཡོ་བྱད་ཐམས་ཅད་སྟ་གོན་ཚར་ནས་ཡོད་ཙམ་ན། སྐྱི་ཀྱུ་བ་བསྐུང་སྟེ་སྐུ་གཤེགས་ཀར་བླ་མ་ཆེན་

"Where up there?" [Se] asked.

"In Sa skya," he said.

"I had a master there," he remarked, "but he has already passed away.[185] What has it been like afterward? I've had no wish to worry."

"I am his son and heir," he said.

[Se] replied, "Don't you lie. My master had no son. If he had, at the point of passing away he would have given me an indication, but he didn't."

The great master was embarrassed and unable to speak, but his companions explained the story in detail. Se exclaimed, "It is said, 'The living don't meet the dead,' but the meeting time has come," held him on his lap, and shed tears.[186]

Then he said, "There is Dharma inside this decrepit old man, so come quickly. If you think 'I'll come later,' by next year I'll have died."

At that time, while the master stayed for a few days, Lord Se carefully spoke about the general structure of the Lam 'bras, and all the sources of these numerous oral instructions, such as those for removing impediments.[187]

Then [Sa chen] returned [to Sgyi chu] with the intention to go to 'Khar chung.[188] The master's roommates Yon btsun Ra dza and Ston pa Rdo rje 'od said, "This master Sgyi chu ba holds you very close to his heart, so it would be good if you asked to go."

He thought that was true, and said to master Sgyi chu ba, "I would ask to go for a while to 'Khar chung."

"Why are you going?" he asked.

"I am requesting an oral instruction," he said.

"You should not have such little judgment. He is called 'Smooth-Tongued Se.' Having gathered up some tattered remnants of my master Mnga' ris pa's Dharma, he explains them to others.[189] He doesn't have any oral instructions. Don't go," he replied, and didn't give permission.

Since the master had not been given permission, he thought it was not right to go. He thought, "Nevertheless, I will go next year," but it is said that Se's words came true, and Lord Se had passed away.[190]

Then, after a long time had passed, he traveled to Kha'u again and received Dharma from the spiritual friend Gnang and his brother.[191]

At a later time he wished to invite master Sgyi chu ba to Sa skya and hold a Dharma council, but just when he had finished the preparations for everything, Sgyi chu ba became ill. At the point of passing away there was no time to invite the great master [Sa chen]. He left a

པོ་སྤྱན་དྲང་ལོང་མ་བྱུང་ནས། ཞལ་ཆེམས་སུ་ཁྲིད་བཙུན་པ་གྱིས་ལ་འགོན་ཚོའི་སྡེ་པ་འདིའི་དཔོན་གྱིས་ལ། ངའི་གདན་ས་འདི་སྐྱོངས་ཤིག་གསུང་ནས་གཏད་ཏེ་སྐུ་གཤེགས།

དེ་ནས་བླ་མས་ཀྱང་བླ་མ་སྐྱི་རྒྱ་བའི་གསུང་མཉན་ནས་རྗེས་ཀྱི་བྱ་བ་རྣམས་ལེགས་པར་མཛད་དེ། རབ་ཏུ་འབྱུང་བར་དགོངས་ནས་ན་བཟའི་སྣ་གོན་རྩུན་ཆད་ཆར་ནས་ཡོད་ཙམ་ན། དེའི་ལོ་རྒྱུས་བླ་མ་ཁའུ་བས་གསན་ནས་འཕྲིན་བསྐུར་ཁྲིད་རབ་ཏུ་བྱུང་ན་དམ་ཚིག་ཉམས་སོ་གསུང་ཏེ་ཁོང་ལ་མངོན་ཤེས་ཡོད་པས་མ་འོངས་པ་ན་འཕྲིན་ལས་རྒྱ་ཆེན་ལ་དགོངས་ཏེ་དེར་བླ་མ་མཉམ་པོ་ལ། གཤིན་པོའི་ངོ་བས་གསོན་པོའི་ངོ་ལྟོས་སླམ་ནས་ལ་རབ་ཏུ་མ་བྱུང་ཅིག་གསུང་ནས་མ་གནང་།

དེར་རབ་ཏུ་མ་འབྱུང་འོན་ཀྱང་འགོན་ཚོའི་དཔོན་མཛད་དོ།

དགེ་བཤེས་སྐྱི་རྒྱ་བ་དེ་བླ་མ་མལ་གྱི་སློབ་མ་ཡིན་ཏེ། སྐྱི་རྒྱ་བའི་བདེ་མཆོག་གི་དཔེའ་རྣམས་སློམས་ཏེ་གང་ཐང་ན་ལ་ཙེ་གནས་གསར་དུ་བྱོན་ནས། བདེ་མཆོག་རྩ་བ་འི་རྒྱུད་དང་བཤད་པའི་རྒྱུད་ཆ་ལག་དང་བཅས་པ་ཐམས་ཅད་གསན་པས་བླ་ཆེན་གྱིས་ཆོས་ཚར་རེས་མཁྱེན་ངས་མི་ཚེ་ཕྱི་བའི་ཆོས་ཚར་རེས་ཤེས་སུ་རེ་བ་གསུང་འཛིགས་བྱེད་ཀྱི་རྟོག་པ་བདུན་པའི་ཡིག་གེ་བརྟ་བ་ཞིག་འཁོར་ཆོས་མ་ཤེས་པ་ལ་བླ་ཆེན་གྱིས་མཁྱེན་པས་ཤེས་ན་དགའ་བས་མི་ཤེས་མ་ཤེས་ཀྱང་ཚོག་པས་ཤེས་ཟེར་བླ་ཆེན་མར་བྱོན་ཁར་ངའི་ཆོས་སངས་རྒྱ་བའི་ཆོས་ཡིན་ར་བར་སླུ་གུ་ལ་བལ་བཀྲིས་པ་མ་བྱེད་གསུང་དེ་འདྲ་ག་ན་བགྱིད་བྱུས་མར་བྱོན་ནས་གཡས་རུ་ནས་གསེར་སྲང་བཅུ་བདུན་ཙམ་རྙེད་སྤྱགས་པ་ཞིག་ལ་བསྐུར་ནས་འབུལ་དུ་བཏང་སློན་མོ་བྱེད་པ་ཞིག་གི་སར་སླེབ་འབྲུལ་བྱུས་པས་ཟས་བྱིན་གསུང་ས་སྐྱ་པའི་འབུལ་བ་ཡོད་བྱུས་པས་ཇི་ཙམ་ཡོད་ཡང་ཡང་དྲིས་བས་སྲང་བཅུ་བདུན་བདོག་བྱུས་པས་བླ་མ་རང་བྱོན་འབུལ་བའི་སྟེང་དུ་འང་བླ་མས་གསེར་སྲང་གང་བསྣན་ནས་ཚོགས་སུ་ཕུལ་ཅིག་གསུང་མཉེས་ནས་ཁོ་དམ་ཚིག་པར་འདུག་ཡར་ཤོག་གྱིས་ཆོས་ཀྱི་གཉམ་ཡོད་ཟེར་ཡར་བྱོན་པས་ཆོས་ཀྱི་གཉམ་ཡན་ལག་བརྒྱད་པ་དཀོན་རྩེགས་ཀྱི་ལུང་འགོན་པོའི་རྗེས་གནང་བསྒྲུབ་ཐབས་གནང་དེའི་རྟེན་དར་ནག་དང་ལྕགས་ཀྱི་རྡོ་རྗེ་གནང་ནག་པོ་ཆེན་པོ་ང་ལ་འདིར་མི་དགོས་འགོན་ས་སྐྱ་པའི་ཆོས་སྐྱོང་ལ་རྒྱུག་གསུང་ནས། ནས་མར་བྱོན་ཏེ།

last testament that stated, "You must become a monk, be the leader of this establishment of the 'Khon, and maintain this monastic seat of mine." Then he passed away.

Obeying the statement of master Sgyi chu ba, the master then carefully performed the final rites, and intending to take ordination, had finished as far as the preparation of the robes when the story was heard by master Kha'u pa. He sent a message stating "If you take ordination your sacred commitments will be damaged." He had clairvoyance and was thinking of the vast enlightened activities in the future. He said, "Masters are equal, but think, and look at the face of the living one more than the face of the dead one. Do not take ordination!" and did not give permission.

He did not take ordination. Nevertheless, he did act as the leader of the 'Khon [establishment].

That spiritual friend Sgyi chu ba had been a disciple of master Mal. [Sa chen] took Sgyi chu ba's Saṃvara texts and traveled to Na la tse gnas gsar in Gung thang. He received the root tantra and the explanatory tantras of Saṃvara, together with all the affiliated [texts].[192] The great master understood a teaching on hearing it once. But [Mal] commented, "You hope to understand on hearing once a teaching that has taken me half a lifetime."[193] When the syllables of [a mantra] in the *Bhairava sapta kalpa* were being recited, the followers [of master Mal] didn't understand, but the great master understood.[194] [Master Mal] exclaimed, "Those who are happy only if they understand, don't understand. Those who are content even though they don't understand, do understand." As the great master was about to leave, [master Mal] said, "My Dharma is a Dharma for buddhahood. Don't wrap wool around a pitcher in a goat pen."[195] "How could I act like that?" he replied. As he was returning [to Sa skya] he received seventeen ounces of gold from G.yas ru. He gave them to a tantric practitioner and sent him to offer them [to master Mal]. He arrived at the place where a celebration was being held and asked for an audience. [Mal] said, "Give him food." He said, "I have an offering from the Sa skya pa." When he was asked again and again how much he had, he said, "I have seventeen ounces." So master [Mal] himself came. The master added a full ounce of gold to the offering, and said, "Offer it to the assembly!" He [i.e., master Mal] was pleased, and said, "He is trustworthy. Tell him to come back! I have some further teachings." When [Sa chen] came back, he bestowed the further teachings of the *Yan lag brgyad pa*, the reading transmission of the *Ratnakuṭa*, and the ritual permission and method for realization of [Pañjara]nātha.[196] As representations of him [i.e. Mahākāla Pañjaranātha] he bestowed black silk and an iron vajra. "Mahākāla," he said, "I don't need you here. Run off and be the Dharma Protector of the 'Khon Sa skya pa!"[197] Then he went back.

སྔར་གྱི་གསུང་དག་གསན་པར་བཞེད་ནས་རྗེ་སེའི་སློབ་མ་ལ་སུ་དྲག་ཅེས་དྲིས་པས། མི་རྣམས་ན་རེ་ཞ་མ་བ་ལ་ནི་ཆོས་རྫོགས་པ་མེད་ཞང་སྟོན་མཆེད་གཉིས་དྲག་སྟེ་ཅུང་པོ་ནི་མི་བཞུགས་གཅེན་པོ་ཆོས་འབར་བཞུགས་ཅེས་ཐོས་སོ།

དེར་བཞུད་པར་བཞེད་ནས་བླ་མ་ཁ་འུ་བ་ལ་འགྲོ་བར་ཞུས་པས། ཁའུ་བའི་ཞལ་ནས་སྒོམ་ཆེན་པ་འདྲ་བརྟན་ཆེ་བ་ཡིན་དང་པོ་སློབ་མར་མི་ཆོད་སྒོག་ཆོད་ནས་དེ་ལས་ཡོད་རི་བ་སྐད་ཟེར་གདམ་ངག་ཅི་ཡང་ཡོད་དེ་མི་མཆི། ཉིད་རང་དད་པ་ཡོད་ན་གསང་བ་འདུས་པའི་སྒྲུབ་ཐབས་ཐ་ག་བས་མཛད་པའི་བསྟན་པའི་ནོར་རྫས་བསྒོམས་གསུང་ནས་མ་གནང་བ་ལ།

དངོས་ལ་ཡིད་ཆེས་ཤིག་བདོག་པ་ལགས་བྱས་པས

འོ་ན་སོང་གསུང་ནས།

དེ་ནས་བླ་མས་ཇ་སྒྲོ་བ་གང་དར་ཡུག་སེར་པོ་ཞིག་ཁྲབ་ཅིག་སྒོམས་ནས་སག་ཐང་དིངས་སུ་རྗེ་དགོན་པ་བའི་སྤྱན་སྔར་ཕྱིན་ནས་འབུལ་བར་ཞུས་པས། རྗེ་དགོན་པ་བ་དེ་སྟབས་པའི་རྣལ་འབྱོར་པ་ཡིན་ཏེ། རྟེན་རབ་དུ་བྱུང་བ་ཡིན་ཡང་ར་ཐུལ་ཞིག་གྱོན་ཡོ་ག་ཞིག་ཡོག་གིན་འཕོ་ལེ་བའི་གསེབ་ན་གཏམ་ཆལ་ཆོལ་མང་པོ་ཟེར་གྱིན་འདུག་པ་ནས་ཕྱིན་ཕྱུང་པ་ལ། ཁྲབ་ཅིག་གིས་ཕྱག་རྟེན་མཛད་ནས་གསུང་དག་ཞུས་པས། རྗེ་ཞང་ན་རེ་ཁྱོད་ནོར་བ་མ་ཡིན་ནམ་ངས་ནི་ཁྱོད་འདོད་པའི་ཆོས་ཀྱང་མི་ཤེས། ཁྱེད་གསང་སྔགས་གསར་མ་བ་བྱ་བ་རྣམ་རྟོག་ཆེ་བ་ཡིན། ངེད་རྫོགས་ཆེན་རྩ་མུན་ཏི་དང་བྲམ་ཟེ་སྐོར་ལ་སོགས་པ་ཤད་པ་ཡིན་གསུང་ནས་མ་གནང་།

ཡང་ནས་ཡང་དུ་ཞུས་པས་ངས་མི་ཤེས་གསུང་ནས་མ་གནང་བ་ལ། བླ་མ་ཆེན་པོའི་ཐུགས་དགོངས་ལ་འོ་ན་མི་ཤེས་པ་རང་ཡིན་ནམ་སྙམ་ནས་ཡར་ལོག་ནས་ཕྱིན་པ་དང་།

ཇོ་སྲས་འོད་མཆོག་གི་ཕ་ན་རེ་རྗེ་ཞང་ལ་དང་པོ་རྗེ་འཁར་ཆུང་བསྒྲི་ཆུ་བའི་གྲྭ་པ་ཞིག་ལ་ངའི་བླ་མའི་སྲས་ཤིག་ཡིན་གསུང་ནས་ཕར་དུ་བླངས་ཏེ་སྤྱན་ཆབ་ཕྱུང་ནས། མི་གསོན་ཤི་མི་ཕྲད་ཟེར་ཏེ་ཕྲད་པའི་དུས་བྱུང་ད་རྒད་པོ་གོག་པོ་འདིའི་ནང་ན་ཆོས་ཡོད་པས་མྱུར་དུ་ཤོག་གསུང་བའི་ཇོ་སྲས་དེ་འདྲ་ན་བྱས་པས།

རྗེ་ཞང་ན་རེ་འོ་ན་དམ་ཚིག་གི་ཉེས་པ་བྱུང་བ་སྲིད་པས་ཡིན་ན་མར་ཀློག་མིན་ན་ཁོ་རང་ཐོང་གསུང་ནས

Zhang ston Chos 'bar and the Lam 'bras

Wishing to receive the previous Oral Instructions [of the Lam 'bras], he asked who was the best of Lord Se's disciples. He heard people say that the Zha mas didn't have the complete Dharma, that the two Zhang ston brothers were the best, and that the younger brother was no longer alive, but that the elder brother Chos 'bar was still living.

Intending to go to him, he asked master Kha'u pa for leave. Kha'u pa replied, "Some great meditators are great liars.[198] He doesn't have any oral instructions. If you have faith, meditate on the *Bstan pa'i nor rdzas,* the method for the realization of Guhyasamāja composed by Tha ga ba,"[199] and did not give permission.

"I believe in him," he said.

"Well, go!" he replied.

Then the master took a full leather bag of tea, a bolt of yellow silk, and a coat of armor, arrived in front of Lord Dgon pa ba at Sag thang in Dings, and requested a meeting.[200] Lord Dgon pa ba was a hidden yogin, and although he was ordained, he was spinning thread and making a lot of random talk in the midst of some vagrants, and came over wearing a goatskin. When [Sa chen] made a gift of the coat of armor and requested the Oral Instructions [of the Lam 'bras], Lord Zhang replied, "Are you not mistaken? I don't even know the Dharma you want. You so-called practitioners of the new secret mantra are very opinionated. I teach the *Rdzogs chen rtsa mun ti,* the *Bram ze'i skor,* and so forth," and didn't agree.[201]

[Sa chen] asked again and again, but he said, "I don't know it," and didn't agree. Then the great master thought, "Well, does he really not know it?" turned around, and left.

The father of Jo sras 'Od mchog said to Lord Zhang, "At first Lord 'Khar chung ba said to a disciple of Sgyi chu ba, 'You are my master's son,' took him on his lap, and while weeping, exclaimed, 'It is said that the living do not meet the dead, but the meeting time has come. Now there is Dharma inside this decrepit old man. Come quickly!' That noble son to whom he spoke was like this one."[202]

Lord Zhang replied, "Well, it is possible that damage to my sacred commitments has occurred.[203] If it is he, bring him back. If not, let him go."

He was brought back from 'O lu.[204] His story was discussed in detail. The lord said, "Not recognizing who you were, I lied just now. Now, I have not ever explained the Lam 'bras before, so I must also consider what the Dharma is about. A

འོ་ལུ་ནས་བཟློག་སྟེ། ལོ་རྒྱུས་ཞིབ་ཏུ་གསུང་གླེང་མཛད་ནས། རྗེའི་ཞལ་ནས་ད་ཅི་ཙོ་མ་ཤེས་པར་བརྟུན་བྱས་ད་སྔར་ལམ་འབྲས་བཤད་པ་འང་མེད་པས་ཆོས་ཀྱང་ག་ན་ཅི་འདུག་བལྟ་ཉིད་རང་དང་དུས་ཆོས་མ་ཆག་པར་བཤད་པ་ལེགས་པས་ཕར་སོང་། ད་ལྟ་འདི་ན་པན་ཆེན་དང་པན་ཆུང་དང་མར་ལོ་ལ་སོགས་པ་མར་ལོ་རིན་ཆེན་བཟང་པོ་དང་ཁ་ཆེ་པན་ཆེན་པཎ་ཆུང་སྤྱན་དྲངས་ཆོས་འཁོར་བྱེད་པའི་དུས་སུ། སྒོམ་ཆེན་པའི་ཉན་ཤད་ཚུལ་དང་མི་མཐུན་པས། སང་ཕོད་རྒྱུན་སྤྱོན་ཆོས་ཆོ་ལེགས་པར་ཚར་བ་བགྱི་གསུང་།

དེས་ན་བླ་ཆེན་གྱི་ཞལ་ནས་འོད་མཆོག་གི་ཕ་འདི་ང་ལ་དྲིན་ཆེ་གསུང་ངོ་།།

དེ་ནས་ཡར་བྱོན་ཏེ་ཕྱིས་རྒྱུན་རིངས་སུ་བྱོན་ནས་དབང་བསྐུར་བ་ཞུས། གསུང་ངག་ཉན་པའི་སྔོན་དུ་མ་ཀཱ་ལ་དང་ཡིག་གེ་བརྒྱ་པའི་ཁྲིད་ལེགས་པར་ཚར་ནས། ནང་པར་གསུང་ངག་གསུང་བའི་ནུབ་མོ་རྗེ་ཞང་གི་ལྗགས་བསྐུང་ནས་ཆོས་གསུང་བ་མ་བྱུང་བ་ལ།

རྗེའི་ཞལ་ནས་ཁུ་ཙག་གཉིས་ཀྱི་བར་ན་དམ་ཚིག་གི་ཟེལ་ཞིག་ཡོད་པར་འདུག་པས་ད་དུང་ཡི་གེ་བརྒྱ་པ་ཐོན་གསུང་།

བླ་མའི་ཐུགས་དགོངས་ལ་གཞན་ནི་ཉེས་པ་མེད་སྔར་ཞུ་བའི་དུས་སུ་དེད་རྫོགས་ཆེན་པ་ཡིན་ལམ་འབྲས་མི་ཤེས་གསུང་བ་ལ། འོ་ན་མི་ཤེས་སམ་སྙམ་པའི་རྟོག་པ་ཞིག་བྱུང་བས་དེས་ཉེས་སམ་དགོངས་ནས་

དེ་ལ་དམིགས་ཏེ་ཡི་གེ་བརྒྱ་པ་བཏོན་པས་བླ་མའི་ལྗགས་བསྐུང་བ་དེ་གདངས་ནས། ཆོས་གསུང་བའི་དུས་སུ་ཡི་གེ་ནི་མེད་ཀཱའ་བའི་གནས་འགག་ཞིག་ལ་རྗེ་བའི་རྩེ་མོས་ཕྱག་ལ་ཟིན་བྲིས་བྱས་པས་རྗེའི་ཞལ་ནས། སྙན་རྒྱུད་ཟབ་པོ་ལ་དེ་རྩུག་མ་མཛད་ཐུགས་དམ་ལ་གནོད་པ་ལགས་གསུང་ནས་མ་གནང་།

དེ་ལྟར་སྒོམ་པས་ལོ་བཞིའི་བར་དུ་གསུང་ངག་རིན་པོ་ཆེ་རྩ་བ་དང་ཡན་ལག་དུ་བཅས་པ་ཡོངས་སུ་རྫོགས་པར་བླ་མ་བརྒྱུད་པའི་དམ་ཚིག་གི་རིམ་པ་ལ་དགོངས་ནས་གནང་སྟེ། དེའི་རྗེས་ལ་ལམ་བསྡུས་ཏེ་བསྒྲུབ་པའི་ལུང་སྦྱིན་པ་མཛད་ནས། བཀའ་རྒྱ་བཏབ་པ་ནི་ལོ་བཅོ་བརྒྱད་ཀྱི་བར་དུ་ཆོས་འདི་གཞན་ལ་སྟོན་པ་ལྟ་ཞོག་གི་ངས་ཤེས་ཅེས་པའི་མིང་ཙམ་ཡང་བསྟན་པར་མི་བྱའོ།། དེ་ནས་ལོ་བཅོ་བརྒྱད་ལོན་ནས་གཞན་ལ་འཆད་དམ། ཡི་གེར་འདྲི་འམ་

period of uninterrupted explanation of the Dharma would also be best for you, so go away." [He also said,] "Now, while a Dharma council is being held here with great paṇḍitas, lesser paṇḍitas, Mar Lo and so forth, Mar Lo Rin chen bzang po, and great and lesser Kashmiri paṇḍitas had been invited, the explanations of a great meditator would be inappropriate, so come in the winter next year.[205] I will carefully complete the teachings."

Therefore, the great master said, "This father of 'Od mchog was very kind to me."[206]

Then he went back. The next winter he returned to Dings and requested the bestowal of initiation. Before listening to the Oral Instructions, the instructions of the maṇḍala and the hundred-syllable [mantra] were carefully completed. The night before the morning on which the Oral Instructions were to be taught, the tongue of Lord Zhang became swollen, and he could not speak the Dharma.[207]

Lord [Zhang] said, "Between the two of us there is something to be cleared away in regard to the sacred commitments, so you must still recite the hundred-syllable [mantra]."

The master thought, "There is no other transgression, but when I asked before, and he said, 'I am a practitioner of the Rdzogs chen. I don't know the Lam 'bras,' I had the thought, 'Well, does he not know it?' Did that cause a transgression?"

Focusing on that, he recited the hundred-syllable [mantra], and the illness of the master's tongue cleared up. During the time [Lord Zhang] was teaching the Dharma for which there was no written text, [Sa chen] made notes of some difficult points on his hand with the tip of a stone. The lord said, "Don't treat the profound oral transmission like that. It will damage your meditation," and did not give permission.[208]

In that way, for four years in total, [Zhang ston] completely bestowed the Precious Oral Instructions [of the Lam 'bras], the root with the branches, in consideration of the sequence of the sacred commitments of the lineal masters. After that he gave the summation of the path and the prediction of practice. Then he sealed it, stating, "For eighteen years you should not even reveal the name, and say 'I know it,' let alone teach this Dharma to others. Then, after eighteen years have passed, whether you explain it to others or write it in texts, you will be the owner of this Dharma. I was thinking this Dharma needed an owner, and you appeared. Now my mind is at ease. What you do with it depends on you."[209]

He prophesied, "In general, if you chiefly practice meditation you

ཉིད་རང་ཆོས་ཀྱི་བདག་པོ་ཡིན་པས་ཆོས་འདི་ལ་བདག་པོ་ཞིག་དགོས་སྙམ་སྟེ་ཁྱོད་བྱུང་ད་གློ་བདེ་གསུང་ཅི་བྱེད་ལ་རག་གསུང་།

སྤྱིར་ཁྱོད་ཀྱིས་བསྒྲུབ་པ་རྩོར་བྱས་ན་ཚེ་འདི་ཉིད་ལ་ལུས་མ་སྤངས་པར་ཕྱག་རྒྱ་ཆེན་པོ་མཆོག་གི་དངོས་གྲུབ་ཐོབ་རྣལ་འབྱོར་དབང་ཕྱུག་ཙམ་ཞིག་འོང་བ་ཡིན། ཉན་ཤད་བྱས་ན་གདུལ་བྱ་དཔག་ཏུ་མེད་པའི་དོན་དུ་འགྱུར་མོད་ཀྱི། འོན་ཀྱང་ཁྱོད་ལ་ལུས་མ་སྤངས་པར་ཕྱག་རྒྱ་ཆེན་པོ་གྲུབ་པའི་སློབ་མ་གསུམ། བཟོད་པ་ཐོབ་པའི་རྣལ་འབྱོར་པ་བདུན་འབྱུང་ཅེས་པའི་ལུང་བསྟན་ནོ།།

དེ་ལྟ་བུའི་བླ་མ་ཞང་དེ་ལ་ཡོན་ཏན་གྱི་ཁྱད་པར་ཏིང་ངེ་འཛིན་དཔག་ཏུ་མེད་པ་མངའ་ཞིང་མངོན་པར་ཤེས་པ་བརྟན་པོ་ཡོད་བྱ་དང་རི་དགས་གཉིས་ནས་གསུམ་ལ་སོགས་པར་སྤྲུལ་བའི་རྫུ་འཕྲུལ་ཡང་ཅི་རིགས་པ་མངའ་སྟེ། ལུས་ཀྱི་བཀོད་པ་འགའ་ཞིག་བླ་ཆེན་གྱིས་ཀྱང་གཟིགས་སྐད་དེ་སྐུ་ལུས་བདུན་ཙམ་དུ་སྤྲུལ་ནས་ངས་ཀྱང་སློམས་མ་བྱུང་སྟེ་འདི་ཙམ་ཡོད་གསུང་གཞན་མི་རྒྱུད་ལ་སོགས་པ་འདི་ལྟར་འབྱུང་ཞེས་པའི་ལུང་བསྟན་ཡང་མཛད།།

བླ་ཆེན་གྱིས་སག་སྟོན་དང་ཞང་པོ་སྟོན་པ་ལ་སོགས་པ་ལ་ལ་གསུང་ངག་གསུང་བར་ཞུ་བྱས་པས་སག་སྟོན་ཤམ་པོ་སྟོད་ཡིན་ཞང་པོ་སྟོན་པ་སྟོད་དུ་རུང་བ་ཙམ་འདུག་སྟེ་ཞུར་མི་འདོད་འདུག་ཁྱེད་ཀྱིས་ཞུས་ཀྱིས་དང་གསུང་ནས་རྗེ་ལ་གདམས་ངག་ཁྱད་པར་ཅན་འདུག་པ་ཞུས་བྱས་པས་ཤེས་ཟིན་བརྗེད་ཟིན་ད་མི་ཞུ་ཟེར་མ་ཉན་དེ་ནས་བླ་ཆེན་གྱིས་ཡར་བྱོན་ནག་སྟོན་ལ་ཙ་བ་ཅན་ནུབ་མོ་བཞུགས་པས་ཁོང་ན་རེ་ཁྱོད་སྒྲི་ཆུ་བའི་གྲ་པ་བརྒྱ་བཅུ་ན་དགའ་བ་ཞིག་ཞང་ཆུང་བ་ལ་ཉན་པ་ཟེར་བས། སྙན་བཀབ་ནས་དེ་སྐད་མི་གསུང་བར་ཞུ་བདག་རང་ལ་དགོངས་པ་ཞིག་བརྡོག་གིས་གསུང་།

ཕྱིས་བླ་མ་སྐུ་གཤེགས་ཁར་ས་སྐྱ་བ་བོས་ལ་ཞོག་གསུང་ནས་མི་བཏང་བས་བླ་ཆེན་ཀྱིས་ཀྱང་རིངས་པར་བྱོན་ཏེ།། དེངས་ཀྱི་ཕུར་སླེབ་ཙམ་ན་སྤྱང་དུག་པས་བླ་མ་དབུ་བསྙུང་ནས་དེར་ནུབ་མོ་བསྡད། ནང་པར་བྱོན་ཙམ་ན་དེའི་ནུབ་མོ་སྐུ་གཤེགས་ནས་འདུག། དེ་ནས་གདུང་བཞུ་བ་ལ་སོགས་པ་རྗེས་ཀྱི་བྱ་བ་རྣམས་ཚར་ནས། ཕྱག་དཔེ་ཀུན་མ་གཟིགས་པར་བླ་མ་ཞང་གི་མ་གཅིག་ན་རེ་ཨ་པོ་བྱ་བ་འདི་འདྲ་ལ་དགའ་བ་ཡིན་ཁྱེར་ཟེར་ནས་ཤོག་ཀ་ལི་ཞིག་ན་ཆོས་བྲལ་བྲུལ་མང་རབ་ཞིག་གཏད་ནས་བལྟས་པས་རྩ་གནས་འདིར་རླུང་སེམས་འདུས་ན་ཉམས་འདི་འབྱུང་ཞེས་པའི་རྡོ་རྗེ་

will reach the sublime attainment of Mahāmudrā in this very lifetime, without discarding the body, and become like the Lord of Yogins. If you engage in teaching, it will benefit countless trainable beings. However, you will have three disciples who realize Mahāmudrā without discarding the body, and seven yogins who obtain Forbearance."[210]

This master Zhang was endowed with the exceptional qualities of infinite meditative concentrations and had stable clairvoyance. He was also endowed with various magical abilities, such as emanating two or three birds or mountain creatures, and it is said that the great master [Sa chen] also saw several physical manifestations. He emanated about seven bodies, and then said, "I haven't even meditated and I have this much [ability]." He also made other prophecies about [Sa chen's] descendants, and so forth, saying, "It will happen like this."

The great master said, "Please teach the Oral Instructions to some such as Sag ston and Zhang po ston pa." [Master Zhang] replied, "Sag ston sham po is worthy. Zhang po ston pa is just barely worthy. But they don't want to request it. You must speak to them!" When [Sa chen] told them that the lord had exceptional oral instructions, [Zhang po] replied, "I already learned them. I already forgot them. I'm not requesting them now," and wouldn't listen.[211] Then the great master left, and stayed one night at Nag ston Lo tsā ba's place. [Nag ston] said, "You were the best among Sgyi chu ba's one hundred and ten students, and yet you listen to little Zhang." [Sa chen] covered his ears and said, "Please don't talk like that. He has been kind to me.[212]

Later, when master [Zhang] was at the point of passing away, he sent a man, telling him, "Call the Sa skya pa to come!" The great master also came quickly. But when he arrived in the upper valley of Dings, the master's head was hurting because of the altitude of the pasture and he spent the night there. When he arrived in the morning, [Lord Zhang] had passed away that night.[213] Then he completed the last rites, such as the cremation of the body. Master Zhang's consort said, "Sir, take these if such things please you," and gave him a large amount of tattered Dharma texts in a wrapped bundle. When he looked, there was a text that presented the true state of the vajra body, saying, "If the vital winds and mind gather in this channel location, this experience will arise." Afraid that if there was Dharma that had not been bestowed before, he would lose respect for the master, he wrapped them in a roll of yellow silk.[214] It is said that he put all the manuscripts[215] in the stūpa in which the bones resided, without looking at them.

The prophecy of Lord Dgon ba ba, and [Sa chen's] dream the night of the preliminary when requesting the bestowal of initiation from

ལུས་ཀྱི་གནས་ལུགས་སྟོན་པའི་དཔེའ་འདུག་སྟེ་སྒྱུར་མ་གནང་བའི་ཆོས་བྱུང་ན་བླ་མ་ལ་མ་གུས་པ་སྐྱེས་ཀྱིས་དོགས་ནས་དར་ཡུག་སེར་པོ་ཞིག་གིས་དྲིལ་ནས་གདུང་བཞུགས་པའི་མཆོད་རྟེན་དུ་བཞུགས་སྐད།

རྗེ་དགོན་པའི་ལུང་བསྟན་དང་བླ་མ་སྒྲི་ཆུ་བ་ལ་དབང་བསྐུར་ཞུས་པའི་སྟ་གོན་གྱི་ནུབ་མོའི་རྨལ་ལམ་གཉིས་མཐུན་པར་བྱུང་སྟེ། དེ་ཡང་སྟ་གོན་གྱི་དུས་སུ་རྨལ་ལམ་དུ་ཆུ་བོ་ཆེན་པོ་ཞིག་ལ་སྲིད་པའི་རྒྱ་མཚོ་ཡིན་ཟེར་བའི་འཚོ་དམར་པོ་ཞིག་ཟམ་པ་གསུམ་འདུག་པ་ལ་བསྒྲལ་རྒྱུ་མི་མང་པོ་འདུག་པའི་ཚུ་རོལ་ནས་ངེད་ཅག་ཆུ་འདི་ལས་བསྒྲལ་བར་ཞུ་ཟེར་བ་ལ། བླ་ཆེན་གྱིས་མི་མང་པོ་ཞིག་ཟམ་པ་གཅིག་ལ་བསྒྲལ། ཡང་མི་བདུན་ཙམ་ཟམ་པ་གཉིས་ལས་བསྒྲལ། མི་གསུམ་ཟམ་པ་གསུམ་ཀའི་ཕ་རོལ་དུ་བསྒྲལ་བ་དང་ཙུང་ཟད་བསྒྲེལ་ཏེ་མ་ལ་ཡའི་རི་ཡིན་ཟེར་བ་ཞིག་ལ་ཉི་མ་ལ་དལ་བསོ་བ་སློམ་བྱེད་པ་ཞིག་རྨི་ནས

བླ་མ་སྒྲི་ཆུ་བ་ལ་ཞུས་པས་ཁོང་གི་ཞལ་ནས། ཁྱོད་ཀྱི་འཁོར་ཀས་མི་གསུམ་ལས་གང་ན་སྒྲོལ་ཅེས་ཀུ་རེ་འདང་གསུང་།

དེ་འདང་ཟམ་པ་གསུམ་ལས་མི་གསུམ་བསྒྲལ་བ་ནི་ལུས་མ་སྤྱངས་པར་གྲུབ་པ་ཐོབ་པ་གསུམ་སྟེ།

གཅིག་སེང་ག་ལའི་གླིང་ཕྲན་ནས་མཁན་པོ་དགྲ་བཅོམ་པ་ཞིག་གིས་ཉན་ཐོས་སེན་ཐ་བ་ཞིག་ཁ་བསྟན་ནས། བོད་ན་རྣལ་འབྱོར་དབང་ཕྱུག་གི་སྤྲུལ་པ་ས་སྐྱ་པ་བྱ་བ་ཡོད་ཀྱིས་སོང་ཟེར་ནས་ཨ་ཙ་ར་གཉིས་འོངས་པ་ལ་གཅིག་བལ་པོ་ནས་ལོག་གཅིག་གིས་བླ་ཆེན་གུང་ཐང་ན་ལ་ཙེ་གནས་པོ་ཆེ་ན་བཞུགས་ཙམ་ན་སླེབ་ནས་དབང་བསྐུར་བ་ཞུས། དབང་ཡོན་དུ་ག་གུ་ཡ་ཅེས་པའི་ཟབ་ཆེན་གྱི་བླ་རེ་བཟང་པོ་ཞིག་ཕུལ། དེ་ནས་ཁྲིད་ལ་སོགས་པ་རིམས་ཀྱིས་ཞུས་པས་དེའི་ནང་ནས་ཀྱང་སྤྲུས་ཆད་བསྟན་པས་ཟླ་བ་གཅིག་ཙམ་ནས་ཏིང་ངེ་འཛིན་དཔག་དུ་མེད་པ་སྐྱེས་ནས་བདེན་པ་མཐོང་སྟེ་ཨུ་རྒྱན་དཔལ་གྱི་རི་ལ་སོང་སྐད།།

གཅིག་ནི་འཕྲང་འོག་གི་སྒོམ་པ་ཀྱི་འབར་ཅེས་པ་སྟེ། དེས་ཀྱང་དབང་དང་གདམས་ངག་ཞུས་

master Sgyi chu ba, were both in agreement. Furthermore, at the time of the preliminary he had dreamed that there were three bridges over a great body of water that was a red lake said to be the sea of existence, and on the near side of the water there were many people to be taken across, who had said, "Please take us across this water." The great master had taken many people across one bridge. He had also taken about seven people across two of the bridges. He had taken three people across to the far side of all three bridges, and somewhat exhausted, had thought to rest in the sun on what was said to be Mt. Malaya.[216]

He had told master Sgyi chu ba, who had also joked in reply, "With your strength how could you take across more than three people?"[217]

Sa chen's Three Disciples Who Reached Attainment Without Discarding the Body

Moreover, the three people taken across the three bridges were the three who reached attainment without discarding the body.

1. The Ceylonese Mendicant

As for the first, at the direction of an arhat abbot, a śrāvaka sendhapa who said, "In Tibet there is an emanation of the Lord of Yogins, known as the Sa skya pa, so you must go!" two mendicants came from the island of Ceylon, but one turned back in Nepal.[218] One arrived when the great master was staying at Na la tse gnas po che in Gung thang, and requested the bestowal of initiation.[219] As an initiation gift he offered a fine brocade canopy known as a *gaguya.* Then the instructions and so forth were gradually imparted, and from among them, when the *Sbas bshad* was taught, after about one month infinite meditative concentrations arose, he perceived the truth and, it is said, traveled to Śrīparvata in Uḍḍiyana.[220]

2. Sgom pa Kyi 'bar

One was known as Sgom pa Kyi 'bar of lower 'Phrang. He also requested initiation and oral instructions, and when he meditated, numerous meditative concentrations arose.[221] At the point when [Kyi 'bar] had stable clairvoyance and various magical abilities, the great master [Sa chen] passed away. The spiritual friend Gnyan Phul chung ba imparted

ནས་བསྒོམས་པས་ཏིང་ངེ་འཛིན་དུ་མ་སྐྱེས། མངོན་ཤེས་བརྟན་པོ་དང་རྫུ་འཕྲུལ་ཅི་རིགས་པ་ཡོད་ཙམ་ན། བླ་ཆེན་སྐུ་གཤེགས་ནས་ཁྲིད་ཀྱི་འཕྲོ་དགེ་བཤེས་གཉན་ཕུལ་ཆུང་བ་ལ་བསྐྱངས་པས། ཕྱིས་ཁོ་བོ་ལྷོ་ཕྱོགས་དཔལ་གྱི་རི་ལ་འགྲོ་ཟེར་ནས་སོང་གསུང་།།

གཅིག་ནི་བྱང་ཆུབ་སེམས་དཔའ་སྟག་ཡིན་གསུང་སྟེ་བོད་རྒྱལ་ཁྲིམས་ལམ་ཁྲིམས་འགྲོ་བ་ཉམས་སྐྱོན་མེད་ཁོ་ན་སྐྱེ་བ་མཆོ་སྒྲིང་མ་ཧཱ་ཧྲིའུར་གཤེགས་སྐུ་ནི་རེ་ཤིག་བོར་ཕྱིས་ལུས་དེ་ཉིད་ལ་ཞུགས་ནས་ལུས་མ་སྤྱངས་པར་གྲུབ་པ་ཐོབ་ཅེས་ཟེར་རོ།

དགེ་བཤེས་གཉག་གིས་བཟང་རྒྱུད་ཀྱི་འབྲོག་གསེབ་དུ་བྱོན་ཙ་ན་ལ་ལ་ན་རེ་བླ་མ་ཆེན་པོ་ཚར་གར་བཞུགས་པའི་དུས་ཀྱི་སློབ་མ་ཡིན་ཟེར་བའི་བཟང་རྒྱུད་ཀྱི་འབྲོག་པའི་གསེབ་ན་རྣལ་འབྱོར་པ་ཞིག་ལ་རྒྱུ་མཐུན་ལྡན་སྐྱེས་དང་། རྣམ་སྨིན་གྱི་འབྲས་བུའི་རྟགས་ཤར་བ་ཚེ་གཞུག་ལ་བདེན་པ་མཐོང་དུ་རུང་བ་ཞིག་འདུག་སྟེ། དེ་ཡིན་ཟེར་འཚར་ཀ་གང་ཐང་ས་སྐུ་རུ་འཚམས་བཞིར་སྐུའི་བཀོད་པ་བཞི་མཛད་དེ་འཚི་མོ་ཐུག་མ་ཆོར་གསུང་། སྐད་

ཡང་གཅིག་ཀློ་ཏ་རུ་ཏུ་ལའི་སློབ་མས་རྣལ་འབྱོར་དབང་ཕྱུག་ལ་གསོལ་བ་བཏབ་པས་ཀླུང་གི་དམིགས་པ་ཞིག་དང་གསེར་འགྱུར་རྩི་གནང་ནས་བོད་ན་ཟངས་རྒྱ་རྡོག་འདྲ་བ་ཡོད་ཀྱིས་དེར་སོང་ལ་གསེར་འགྱུར་རྩིས་སེམས་ཅན་ལ་ཕན་ཐོགས་གསུང་ནས་འོངས་པས་བླ་ཆེན་དང་འཕྲུལ་ནས་གདམ་ངག་ཞུས་པས་ཡོན་ཏན་ཁྱད་པར་ཅན་སྐྱེས་ནས་ཡང་རྒྱ་གར་དུ་གཤེགས་དེ་ཡིན་ནམ་ཟེར་འདི་དང་རྒྱུ་མཐུན་རྟགས་ཤར་བ་དང་ཀྱི་འབར་གསུམ་གདམ་ཀ་ཡིན

ཡང་ཟམ་པ་གཉིས་པ་ལ་མི་བདུན་བསྒྲལ་བ་ནི་བཟོད་ཐོབ་བདུན་ཡིན་ཏེ། རྗེ་བཙུན་ཆེན་པོ་དང་བླ་མ་ཞུ་ཡས་ལ་སོགས་པ་སྒོམ་པ་འོད་གྲགས་སྒོམ་རྡོ་ལྕགས་མང་ཆུང་མ་གནས་བརྟན་བསོད་ཤེས་བྱང་སེམས་ཟླ་རྒྱལ་རྒྱ་སྟོན་ཡིན་ཀྱང་ཟེར་བདུན་བྱུང་ངོ། ཟམ་པ་གཅིག་ལས་མང་པོ་བསྒྲལ་བ་དེ་ཕྱིར་སློབ་མ་དཔག་དུ་མེད་པ་བྱུང་ངོ།

the remaining instructions.[222] [Kyi 'bar] later said, "I am going to Śrī-parvata in the south," and left. So it has been stated.

3. Byang chub sems dpa' Stag

One was Byang chub sems dpa' Stag. So it has been stated. He advanced by the path of direct transcendence, and only the flawless experiences arose. He went to Mtsho snying Ma hā dhe'u. It is said that he abandoned the body for a while, later entered into that same body, and so reached attainment without discarding the body.[223]

When the spiritual friend Gnyag was traveling among the Bzang rgyud nomads some said that [Byang chub sems dpa' Stag] was the yogin among the nomads of Bzang rgyud who said, "I am a disciple of the great master [Sa chen] when he stayed at Tshar ka."[224] People were not aware that [Sa chen] had manifested physical bodies at the four locations of 'Tshar ka, Gung thang, Sa skya, and Ru 'tshams. So it has been stated. The signs of the result simultaneously arisen in correspondence to the cause, and of full maturation, had appeared for him indicating that he would see the truth at the end of his life.[225]

Also, a disciple of Bho ta Rāhula supplicated the Lord of Yogins and was granted a visualization practice of the vital winds, and a gold transforming tincture. He was told, "In Tibet there are some deposits of copper.[226] Go there and benefit sentient beings with the gold transforming tincture." He came, and after meeting the great master [Sa chen] and requesting oral instructions, exceptional qualities arose. Then he returned to India. Was that he [i.e., Stag]? There is a choice between three: this one, [the 'Tshar ka nomad] for whom the signs corresponding to the cause arose, and Kyi 'bar.

The Seven Who Reached the Stage of Forbearance

The seven people taken across the second bridge were the seven who reached Forbearance.[227] There were seven, such as the great Rje btsun and master Zhu yas.[228] It is also said that they were Sgom pa 'Od grags, Sgom Jo lcags, Mang chung ma, Gnas brtan Bsod shes, Byang sems Zla rgyal, and Rga ston.[229] In general, there were infinite disciples. These were the many taken across one bridge.[230]

བླ་ཆེན་གྱི་སྐུ་ཚེའི་སྟོད་ཡན་ཆད་སྣང་བརྒྱུད་འབབ་ཞིག་ཡིན་སྟེ། ཡི་གེ་མེད་པའི་སྟོབས་ཀྱིས་ཐུགས་བསྐྱེལ་གྱིས་དོགས་ནས། ཞག་རེ་ལ་རྡོ་རྗེ་ཚིག་རྐང་ཚར་རེ་ཟེར་ཀྱང་བདུན་ཟླ་བ་རེ་ལམ་རྒྱུས་པ་ཆ་ལག་དང་བཅས་པ་ཚར་རེ་ཐུགས་བསམ་དུ་མཛད་གསུང་ངོ༎

བླ་མ་མལ་གཤེགས་སར་བྱོན་གཞི་ཙོ་བླ་ཆེན་ལ་གཏད་མར་བྱོན་ཙ་ན་བར་སྤྱུག་རོང་གི་གྲང་ཆུང་དུ་བསྟུང་ནད་དྲག་པོ་ཞིག་བྱུང་དེར་ཆོས་ཙོ་བརྗེད་ཁྱད་པར་དུ་གསུང་ངག་བརྗེད་དེར་ཐུགས་མ་བདེ་ས་སྐྱ་རུ་བྱོན་འཇམ་དབྱངས་ཞལ་གཟིགས་སར་སྐུ་འཚམས་བཅད་ནས་གསོལ་བ་བཏབ་པས་ཆོས་ཐམས་ཅད་སྔར་བཞིན་ཐུགས་ལ་བྱུང་། བླ་མ་ཞང་བྱོན་ནས་ཆོས་མང་དུ་གསུངས། རྣལ་འབྱོར་གྱི་དབང་ཕྱུག་བྱོན་ནས་ས་དཀར་པོ་ལ་རྒྱབ་ཡོལ་བྱས་དཀྱིལ་དཀྱུངས་ཤིག་གིས་ས་སྐྱ་ཁྲིབས་པར་མཛད་ནས་འདི་ཐམས་ཅད་ང་དབང་གསུང་ནས་རྒྱུད་སྡེ་བདུན་བཅུ་རྩ་གཉིས་ཀྱི་ལུང་གནང་། སྔས་ཕྱད་རྣལ་འབྱོར་དབང་ཕྱུག་གི་བསྲུང་འཁོར་འབིར་འཇོམས་སོགས་མང་དུ་གནང་བའི་ལོ་རྒྱུས་སྔས་ཏེ་གསུང་བས་ཞིབ་དུ་གཞན་དུ་ཤེས་པར་བྱའོ༎

དེ་ནས་བཀའ་རྒྱའི་ལོ་བཅོ་བརྒྱད་ཐིམ་པ་དང་། བླ་མ་རང་གི་སློ་མ་འཁམས་པ་ཨ་སེང་གིས་ལམ་འབྲས་ཁུངས་ཆོད་ནས་ཉིད་ལ་གསུང་ངག་རིན་པོ་ཆེ་མངའ་བར་གདའ་བས། བདག་ཚར་གཅིག་ཞུ་ལ་ཡི་གེ་ཞིབ་པ་ཞིག་ཐུགས་ལ་ཐོགས་ཞུས་པས།

ཚར་གཅིག་གསུངས་ནས་སྔར་ཡི་གེ་ཅིག་ཀྱང་མེད་པ་ལ་ལམ་འབྲས་མདོར་བསྡུས་མ་མཛད་དེ་གནང་ངོ༎

དེ་ནས་ལོ་བཞིར་མ་གསུངས་པ་ལ་ཕྱིས་གསོལ་བ་འདེབས་པ་འགའ་ཞིག་གི་ངོར་གསུང་ངག་རྒྱས་པ་འདི་མི་རེ་རེ་ཙམ་ལ་གསུང་ངོ༎ དེ་ནས་ལྷ་གྲངས་བཞིན་དགུ་དང་དབང་བཞིན་ཉི་ཤུ་རྩ་ལྔ་དང་སོ་བདུན་དང་། དེ་ནས་འདིའི་ཏིང་ལ་ང་ཡོད་ལ་མ་འཆམ་པར་ཕྱིས་སྐུ་ཚེའི་སྨད་ལ་མ་ངེས་པར་གསུངས་སོ༎

དེའི་དུས་སུ་རྡོ་རྗེའི་ཚིག་རྐང་གི་དབུ་ཞབས་གཉིས་དང་བར་དུ་གཉིས་སྟེ་མཆོད་པ་བཞི་མཛད། ཕྱིས་དབུ་ཞབས་གཉིས་དང་ཉམས་ཆག་བསྐང་བའི་སྐབས་སུ་གཅིག་སྟེ་གསུམ་མཛད། དེ་ནས་གཉིས་དང་གཅིག་དུ་ཡང་མཛད་དོ༎

དེ་ནས་འཁམས་པ་དཀའ་ཐེང་ལ་སོགས་པ་ལན་མང་དུ་གསོལ་བ་འདེབས་པའི་དོན་དུ་རྡོ

Sa chen's Bestowal of the Lam 'bras

Through the early part of the great master's lifetime [the Lam 'bras] was only an oral transmission.[231] Because there was no text, he was afraid of forgetting it, and mentally reviewed the *Rdo rje tshig rkang* once it is said, but it was seven times every day, and the extensive path together with the affiliated teachings once every month. So it has been stated.

The great master went to where master Mal had passed away, and the estates were given to him. When he was returning he was stricken with a severe illness at Bar spug, a small village in Rong, and forgot the Dharma teachings.[232] In particular, he forgot the Oral Instructions. Distraught about this, he returned to Sa skya and went into retreat at the place where he had beheld the face of Mañjughoṣa.[233] He made supplications, and all the Dharma appeared in his mind like before. Master Zhang came and taught much Dharma. The Lord of Yogins came, used the white earth as a backdrop, covered Sa skya with a single crossed-legged position, said, "I control all this," and bestowed the reading transmission of seventy-two tantras.[234] Since the story of the bestowal of many teachings, such as the *Sbas bshad,* the *Rnal 'byor dbang phyug gi bsrung 'khor,* and the *'Bir 'joms,* has been concealed and taught, it should be known in detail elsewhere.[235]

Then the eighteen-year restriction expired. A seng, one of the master's own disciples from 'Khams, found out about the Lam 'bras, and said, "Since you possess the Precious Oral Instructions [of the Lam 'bras], I request it once, and please honor me with a detailed text."[236]

He taught it once, and although there had not been a single text before, he composed the *Lam 'bras mdor bsdus ma* and gave it to him.[237]

Then he did not teach it again for four years. Later, in response to several requests, he taught these extensive Oral Instructions to single individuals alone. Then he taught it to nine like the number of deities, then to twenty-five like in the initiation, and to thirty-seven.[238] Then there was not agreement as to who had [received] it after this. Later, toward the end of his life, he taught it to unspecified numbers.

At that time he performed four offerings: two at the beginning and end of the *Rdo rje tshig rkang,* and two in between. Later he performed three: two at the beginning and end, and one at the point of the renewal of damaged [sacred commitments].[239] Then he performed two, and even one.

Then, for the benefit of Dga' theng from 'Khams, and the others who prayed for them many times, the master himself composed about eleven

རྗེ་ཆིག་རྐྱང་ལ་བླ་མ་ཉིད་རང་གིས་སྔ་ཕྱིར་རྣམ་འགྲེལ་བཅུ་གཅིག་ཙམ་མཛད་རྒྱ་ཐེང་ནི་བླ་ཆེན་ཡུན་རིང་དུ་བསྟེན་ཏེ་འཚམས་སུ་ཕྱོན་ཙ་ན་རྒྱ་ཐེང་གི་ཟིན་བྲིས་མཐོང་མང་དུ་མཉན་པས་བཏབ་པ་ཡོད་དམ་སྙམ་ཙ་ན་ནོར་བ་ལས་མི་འདུག་འོ་ན་ང་ཤི་ནས་ཆོས་འདི་རབས་འཆད་པར་འདུག་སྙམ་ནས་རྒྱ་ཐེང་གི་དོན་དུ་རྒྱ་ཐེང་མ་བྱུ་བ་དེ་མཛད་པ་ཡིན་གསུང་ཞུའི་དོན་དུ་ཞུ་ས་མཛད་དེ། དེ་འདང་ཐམས་ཅད་ཀྱི་རྗེས་ལ་དགེ་ཤེས་གཉག་གིས་ཞུས་པའི་ངོར་མཛད་པ་གཉག་མ་ནི། ཚིག་ཉུང་ཞིང་དོན་རྒྱས་ལ་བསྡེབ་ལེགས་ཏེ། འཐད་པར་དགོངས་ནས་དེ་སང་གི་བར་དུ་ཕྱག་དཔེར་མཛད་དོ།། བཞི་པོ་དེ་ཡོངས་སུ་གྲགས་གཞན་ཡུམ་དོན་མ་དང་སྲས་དོན་མ་ལ་སོགས་པ་ཡོད་ཟེར་ཀྱང་འདི་ཡིན་མ་འཐོང་གསུང་།

དེ་ལྟ་བུའི་བླ་མ་ཆེན་པོ་ཀུན་དགའ་སྙིང་པོ་དེ་ལ་ཡོན་ཏན་དཔག་ཏུ་མེད་པ་མངའ་ཞང་གི་འགྲོན་ལར་རབ་གནས་ལ་སྤྱན་དྲངས་པ་ན་འཛམ་དཔལ་དྲི་མེད་ཀྱི་དཀྱིལ་འཁོར་བཞེངས་ནས་ཆོ་ག་མཛད་པས་དགེ་བཤེས་མང་པོ་འཚོགས་པ་ཙོའི་བློ་རུ་མི་ཆུད་པ་ཙམ་བྱུང་སློ་ལྟར་ཆོས་འཁོར་ཞིག་ལ་ཕྱོན་པས་འཁོར་དགེ་བཤེས་གདུགས་ཕུབ་པ་རང་ལྷ་བརྒྱ་ཙམ་བྱུང་གསུང་སྟེ། འདིའི་རྣམ་ཐར་རྒྱས་པ་རྗེ་བཙུན་རིན་པོ་ཆེས་མཛད་པར་བལྟའོ།།

མདོར་ན་ཁ་བ་ཅན་གྱི་ཁྲོད་འདིར་གདུལ་བྱའི་དོན་དཔག་ཏུ་མེད་པ་རིམ་དང་ཅིག་ཆར་གྱིས་གྲོལ་བར་མཛད་དོ། གཡས་རུ་སྟག་རིས་ཀྱི་སའི་ཆ་སྐྱོ་བོ་ཁ་གདངས་ཀྱི་རྩུག་ལག་ཁང་དུ་རྒྱང་ལོ་དྲུག་བཅུ་རྩ་གཅིག་པ་ལ་ངོ་མཚར་གྱི་ལྟས་དཔག་ཏུ་མེད་པ་མངོན་སུམ་དུ་བསྟན་ནས་སྐུ་གཤེགས་པའི་ཚུལ་བསྟན་ཏོ། ཕུར་སྦྲུངས་པའི་མིའི་སྒྲ་ཐམས་ཅད་བདེ་མཆོག་རྩ་སྔགས་སུ་བྱུང་མེའི་གསེབ་ན་བདེ་མཆོག་ཞལ་བཞི་ཕྱག་བཅུ་གཉིས་པ་རྣམ་པར་སྣང་མཛད་ཀུན་དུ་ཞལ་ལྟ་བུར་ཐམས་ཅད་ཀྱིས་མཐོང་གཟང་རི་ཕུག་པས་གར་ཕྱིན་པར་ཞལ་འགྱུར་བར་མཐོང་།

འོན་ཀྱང་དེའི་སྲས་ཀྱི་ཐུ་བོ་རྗེས་འབྲང་དང་བཅས་པས་དེང་སང་གི་བར་དུ་ཐུབ་པའི་བསྟན་པ་ཤིན་དུ་རྒྱས་པར་མཛད་དོ།།

དེ་ཡང་བླ་མ་ཆེན་པོ་དེས་པར་རྡོ་རྗེ་འཆང་དང་མི་གཉིས་པའི་ཐུགས་མངའ་བ་དེའི་སྐུ་གསུང་ཐུགས་ཀྱི་སྲས་བཞི་བྱུང་ཆེན་པོ་ཀུན་དགའ་འབར་རེ་ཙད་ཚ་ཡིན་ཏེ་རྒྱ་གར་དུ་ཕྱོན་མཁས་པ་ཞིག་བྱུང་སྟེ་མུ་སྟེགས་པ་དང་བརྩོད་པས་དུག་གིས་སྐུ་གཤེགས་དེ་ནས་འགྲོ་ཚ་གསུམ་ནི་སློབ་དཔོན་རིན་

earlier and later commentaries on the *Rdo rje tshig rkang.*[240] Rga theng studied under the great master for a long time. When [Sa chen] came to Ru 'tshams he saw Rga theng's summarizing notes. He thought, "He has received it many times; will it be reliable?" It was nothing but errors. He thought, "Well, after I have died this Dharma will be gone," and for the benefit of Rga theng he composed the *Rga theng ma*. So it has been stated. For the benefit of Zhu [byas] he composed the *Zhu [byas] ma*.[241] Moreover, last of all, the *Gnyag ma,* composed in response to the request by the spiritual friend Gnyag, is succinct in words but extensive in meaning and well formulated. Considered suitable [by later masters], it has been used as the teaching manual up until the present.[242] [Rin po che] stated, "Those four are widely known, and although it is said that there are others, such as the *Yum don ma* and the *Sras don ma*, I have not seen them."[243]

Sa chen's Special Qualities, and His Death

In this way, the great master Kun dga' snying po was endowed with infinite qualities. When he was invited to Zhang gi 'gron la for a consecration, he constructed the maṇḍala of 'Jam dpal dri med.[244] While he performed the rite, [things] happened that were incomprehensible to the many spiritual friends who had gathered. When he went to a Dharma council at Sgo lnga, he had an entourage of about five hundred spiritual friends for whom parasols would be raised. So it has been stated.[245] One should consult the extensive life story of this [master] composed by Rje btsun Rin po che.[246]

In brief, he gradually and instantaneously liberated infinite trainable beings in these snowy ranges. At the age of sixty-one, in the temple of Skya bo kha gdangs in the region of Stag ris in G.yas ru,[247] he directly manifested infinite miraculous signs and displayed the manner of passing away. All the sounds of the fire in which his body was cremated arose as the root mantra of Saṃvara. In the midst of the fire everyone saw Saṃvara with four faces and twelve arms, like the Vairocana with faces all around. Gzang ri phug pa saw the faces turn wherever he went.[248]

However, his elder sons and followers have greatly expanded the Doctrine of the Sage up to the present day.

Moreover, there were four sons of the enlightened body, speech, and mind of that great master whose state of mind was certainly no different from Vajradhara. The eldest, Tsad tsha's [son] Kun dga' 'ba', went to India and became an expert, but he debated with a tirthika and died of poisoning.[249] Then there were the three [sons] of 'Bro tsha. Slob dpon Rin po [che], whose name was

པོ་མཚན་བསོད་ནམས་ཙེ་མོ་རྒྱུད་གསུམ་གདམ་ངག་དང་བཅས་པ་ཡབ་ཉིད་ལ་གསན་ཤིང་ཐུགས་སུ་ཆུད་པར་མཛད། ཕྱི་བ་ལ་ཚད་མ་དང་སྤྱོད་འཇུག་གསན་ཤིང་ཐུགས་སུ་ཆུད་པར་མཛད་དེ་ཡོན་ཏན་བསམ་གྱིས་མི་ཁྱབ་པ་མངའ་བ་མི་ཐུབ་ཟླ་བའི་སྤྲུལ་པར་བཞེད་གུང་ལོ་ཞི་གཉིས་པ་ལ་གཤེགས་དེ་ནས་རྗེ་བཙུན་པ་དེ་ནས་ཆོས་རྗེ་པའི་ཡབ་སློབ་དཔོན་ཅུང་འཚན་དཔལ་ཆེན་འོད་པོ།

རྗེ་བཙུན་རིན་པོ་ཆེ་འདིས་བླ་ཆེན་དང་སློབ་དཔོན་རིན་པོ་ཆེ་པ་དང་དགེ་བའི་བཤེས་གཉེན་གཞན་དང་གཞན་ལས་ཀྱང་། གསང་སྔགས་ཀྱི་རྒྱུད་སྡེ་མཐའ་དག་ཡན་ལག་དང་བཅས་པ་ཐམས་ཅད་གསན་ནས། ཐུགས་སུ་ཆུད་པར་མཛད་དེ། གསུང་ངག་རིན་པོ་ཆེ་འདི་ཞུ་བའི་དུས་སུ་ཀ་བ་དཔག་ཏུ་མེད་པས་ལན་མང་དུ་གསོལ་བ་བཏབ་ཏེ། གསན་ཞིང་ཐུགས་སུ་ཆུད་པར་མཛད་ནས། སྐབས་འགའ་ཞིག་ཏུ་བསྒྲུབ་པ་ལ་སྙིང་པོར་མཛད་ནས་ཡོན་ཏན་གྱི་ཆ་དཔག་ཏུ་མེད་པ་ལ་མངའ་བརྙེས་སོ།

དུས་ཕྱིས་ཀ་བའི་གནས་འགའ་ཞིག་རྣལ་ལམ་གྱི་རྣམ་པས་རྣལ་འབྱོར་གྱི་དབང་ཕྱུག་ཉིད་ལ་ཞུས་པས། ཐེ་ཚོམ་གྱི་མདུད་པ་དྲལ་ཞིང་བླ་ཆེན་དང་སློབ་དཔོན་རིན་པོ་ཆེ་གཉིས་ལས་ཀྱང་རྣལ་ལམ་དུ་ཞལ་ཡང་ཡང་འབྲུལ་ཞིང་དོན་འགའ་ཞིག་ཞུས་པས་གནང་ཏེ། མི་ཤེས་པའི་དྲི་བ་རྣམ་པར་བསལ་བས་ན་མི་མཚུངས་པའི་བློ་གྲོས་ཆེན་པོ་དེ། ཐུན་མོང་དུ་སློབ་མ་ལ་རྒྱལ་བའི་གསུང་རབ་འགྲེལ་པ་ཡན་ལག་དང་བཅས་པ་མན་ངག་དུ་བཅས་པ་ལ་འཆད་པ་དང་རྩོམ་པ་ལ་སོགས་པ་གཞན་དོན་འབའ་ཞིག་མཛད་དེ།

གུང་ལོ་བདུན་བཅུ་བཞེས་པ་དང་དཔལ་ས་སྐྱའི་ཙུག་ལག་ཁང་དུ་མེ་བྱི་བའི་ལོ་ཁྲ་ཟླ་ཡི་ཡར་ངོའི་ཚེས་བཅུ་གཉིས་ཀྱི་ནུབ་མོ། ངོ་མཚར་གྱི་ལྟས་སྣ་མང་བྱུང་བའི་ཆོས་ཀྱིས་ངེས་པའི་རྣམ་པར་འཕྲུལ་པ་བསམ་གྱིས་མི་ཁྱབ་པ་བསྟན་ནས་བདེ་བ་ཅན་དུ་སྐུ་གཤེགས་སོ།

འདིའི་རྣམ་པར་ཐར་པ་རྒྱས་པར་ཁོ་བོས་བཤད་པར་ག་ལ་ནུས། དེ་ཉིད་ཀྱི་གདུང་དང་ཉེ་བའི་ཆོས་སྲས་མཆོག་ཏུ་གྱུར་པའི་བདག་ཉིད་ཆེན་པོ་བཟང་པོའི་ཞབས་ཀྱིས་མཛད་པར་བལྟའོ།།

Bsod nams tse mo, received the *Rgyud gsum* and the oral instructions from his father, and mastered them. He received epistemology and the *Bodhicaryāvatāra* from Phya ba, and mastered them. He had inconceivable qualities, and was accepted as an emanation of Durgacandra. He passed away at the age of forty-two. Then there was Rje btsun pa. Then the Dharma Lord's father, the teacher, the younger brother, whose name was Dpal chen 'od po.[250]

Rje btsun Grags pa rgyal mtshan

This Rje btsun Rin po che received all the tantras of the secret mantra [tradition], together with all the branches, from the great master, from Slob dpon Rin po che, and also from other different spiritual friends, and mastered them.[251] At the time he requested these Precious Oral Instructions, he endured infinite hardships, prayed for [the instructions] many times, and received and mastered them. On several occasions he made practice the essential act, and acquired control over infinite qualities.

At a later time, through dream images, when he asked the Lord of Yogins himself about several difficult topics, the knot of doubt was untied.[252] He also met both the great master and Slob dpon Rin po che again and again in dreams, and when he asked about several points, they replied.[253] Because the web of unknowing was completely removed, he possessed a great matchless intelligence. For disciples in common he carried out explication, composition, and so forth, concerning the works of the Victor, the commentaries, the affiliated [texts], and the esoteric instructions, only for the benefit of others.[254]

At the temple of glorious Sa skya, on the evening of the twelfth day of the waxing moon in the second month of the fire-mouse year [1216], when he had reached the age of seventy, he displayed miraculous signs, inconceivable miracles certifying that phenomena are illusory, and passed away into Sukhāvati.

How could I explain his extensive life story? One should consult the composition of the honorable Bzang po, the great being who is of the same family line and is his close and sublime Dharma son.[255]

དེ་ལྟ་བུའི་རྡོ་རྗེ་བཙུན་ཆེན་པོ་དེ་ལ། བླ་མ་ལོ་ཙ་བ་སྐུ་མཆེད་ཀྱིས་ཀྱང་ཉེ་འབྲེལ་གྱི་རྟོག་པ་སྤངས་ཏེ་རྡོ་རྗེ་འཆང་དང་མི་གཉིས་པའི་གུས་པ་ཆེན་པོས་མཉེས་པར་མཛད་ནས། རྒྱུད་དང་གསུང་ངག་ལ་སོགས་པ་མ་ལུས་པ་ཐམས་ཅད་ཇི་ལྟ་བ་བཞིན་དུ་ཐུགས་སུ་ཆུད་པར་མཛད་དོ།།

དེ་ཡང་ཞིབ་དུ་བརྗོད་ན་འདི་ལྟར་ཐོས་ཏེ། བླ་མ་ལོ་ཙ་བ་འདིའི་རྣམ་པར་ཐར་པ་ནི་དང་པོ་ཆོས་རྗེ་པའི་རྣམ་ཐར་ནི་རིན་པོ་ཆེ་པའི་ཞལ་ནས་སློབ་དཔོན་མ་ཏི་ཙི་ཏྲས། ཀུན་མཁྱེན་མ་ལགས་ཀུན་མཁྱེན་ཁྱོད། ཀུན་མཁྱེན་ཁྱོད་ཀོ་ཇི་ལྟར་རྟོགས། གསུངས་པ་བཞིན་ཁོང་གི་ཡོན་ཏན་བརྗོད་པ་ལ་ཁོང་དང་མཉམ་པ་ཞིག་གིས་རྗོད་དགོས་ཀྱི་གཞན་གྱིས་རྗོད་མི་ནུས་ཀྱང་བྱིན་རླབས་འབྱུང་བས་ཅུང་ཟད་རྗོད་ན་ཆོས་རྗེ་པ་འདི། ཡུམ་གྱི་ལྷུམས་སུ་ཞུགས་པའི་དུས་སུ་ཡ་མཚན་གྱི་རྨི་ལྟས་བསྟན་ཀླུའི་རྒྱལ་པོ་རིན་པོ་ཆེའི་འགོ་རྒྱན་ལ་སོགས་པས་བརྒྱན་པར་མཛད་ནས་བྱོན་པ་ཡིན་གསུང་ལྷུམས་ན་བཞུགས་ཙ་ན་ཡུམ་ལ་ཏིང་ངེ་འཛིན་བཟང་པོ་ལ་སོགས་རྨི་བལྟས་བཟང་པོ་བྱུང་། ཅིང་། ལྟམས་པ་ནས་བྱང་ཆུབ་སེམས་དཔའ་ལྟམ་པའི་ལྟས་ཚོ་བྱུང་ དང་སྐྱེད་ཅུང་ཟད་བསྐྱིངས་ཏེ་རིང་པོ་མ་ལོན་པ་ན་བག་ཆགས་སད་པའི་སྟོབས་ཀྱིས་ལེགས་པར་བཤད་པའི་སྐད་དུ་གསུངས་པས་ཡུམ་ན་རེ་འདི་ལ་གུ་བ་ཞིག་རང་མཆི་བ་ལགས་སམ་ཟེར་བས་རྗེ་པས་སངས་ཏེ་ངའི་སྐད་མཁྱེན་པས་ཁྱོད་ཀྱི་བུ་ལ་གུ་བ་བྱུང་དོགས་མེད་གསུང་ཡང་གོག་ཐུལ་ཐུལ་བའི་དུས་ན་ས་ལ་ཕྱག་འཛུག་གིས་ན་ག་ར་དང་ལན་ཚ་ལ་སོགས་པའི་རྒྱ་ཡིག་བྲིས་ཀྱིན་ཀློག་པའི་ཚུལ་མཛད་ཀྱིན་བསྐུབས་ཀྱིན་གཏོང་བ་བྱུང་གསུང་རྒྱ་ཡིག་བོད་ཡིག་གཉིས་མ་སླབས་པར་ཤུ་མོར་ཤེས་འདུག་ཏེ་ཐོག་མར་འདི་ཤེས་དྲན་པ་མི་འདུག་གསུང་། བག་རེ་ཤེས་པར་ནུས་ཅེས་ཐོས་སོ།

གཞན་ཡང་སྤྱོད་ལམ་ཕུན་སུམ་ཚོགས་པ་ནི་ཀུན་གྱི་ཡིད་དུ་འོང་སྟེ་ཞི་བ་དང་། དུལ་བ

FIVE
The Life of Sa skya Paṇḍita

Sa skya Paṇḍita

THE MASTER TRANSLATOR, the relative of this great Rje btsun, abandoned the concept of family relation, and [viewing] him as no different than Vajradhara, pleased him with great devotion.[256] He precisely mastered absolutely all the tantras, the Oral Instructions [of the Lam 'bras], and so forth.

Moreover, the life story of this Master Translator, if expressed in detail, I have heard to be like this:[257] In regard to the Dharma Lord's life story, Rin po che commented, "Ācārya Mātṛceṭa stated, 'Not being omniscient [myself], while you are omniscient, how can I understand you, Omniscient One?' Likewise, the expression of his [i.e. Sa skya Paṇḍita's] qualities must be spoken by one equal to him. Others are not able to express them. Nevertheless, since blessings will come, I will express a little. This Dharma Lord,"[258] at the time he first entered into the womb of his mother, displayed incredible dream signs. A nāga king adorned with a jeweled headdress and so forth came. So it has been stated. While he was residing in the womb, fine dream signs, such as fine meditative concentration, came to the mother. I have heard that at birth,[259] after which the signs of the birth of a bodhisattva occurred, and not long after, when he had been somewhat reared, he was able to understand a little of the Sanskrit language by the force of awakened propensities. When he spoke in [Sanskrit], the mother exclaimed, "Is this one actually retarded?" The lord[260] replied, "He knows Sanskrit, so have no fear that your son is retarded." Also, when he was just able to crawl, he would write Indian letters in nāgara, lañcana,[261] and so forth, on the ground with his finger, act like he was reading

དང་དང་རྒྱུད་བཟང་བ་དང་། འཇམ་པ་དང་རན་པར་སྨྲ་བ་ཡིད་གཞུངས་པ་དང་། ཡོན་ཏན་ལ་ཆེད་ཆེར་འཛིན་པ་དང་། བླ་མ་དང་རྒན་རིམས་ལ་གུས་པ་དང་ཞེ་ས་དང་རིམ་གྲོ་ཆེ་ཞིང་དབང་པོ་མི་རྒོད་པ་དང་། སེམས་ཅན་ལ་སྙིང་བརྩེ་བར་གྱུར་ཏོ།།

དེ་ནས་ཆེར་སྐྱེས་པ་དང་ཡི་གེའི་རིགས་དང་རྒྱ་གློག་དང་བོད་གློག་དང་རྩིས་ཀྱི་བྱེ་བྲག་དང་། གསོའ་སྤྱད་དང་རི་མོ་ལ་སོགས་པ་བཟོའི་བྱེ་བྲག་སྣ་ཚོགས་པ་དག་མ་སླབས་པར་ཕུལ་དུ་བྱུང་བ་མཁྱེན་ནས་འཇིག་རྟེན་པ་ཀུན་ངོ་མཚར་དུ་གྱུར་ཅིང་ཀུན་གྱིས་སྔགས་སོ།།

དེ་ནས་ཆོས་ཀྱི་རྗེ་དེ་ཉིད་ལ་ཡབ་མེས་ཀྱི་ཆོས་ཐམས་ཅད་ལེགས་པར་གསན་ཞིང་ཐུགས་སུ་ཆུད་པར་མཛད་ནས་ཀྲུང་ལོ་དགུ་ལོན་པ་བརྒྱད་པ་ཟེར་ལ་མཆོ་སྐྱེས་གསུངས། བཅུ་གཉིས་པ་ལ་བརྟག་གཉིས་གསུངས། བཅུ་བཞི་པ་ལ་སཾ་བྷུ་ཊི་གསུངས། བཅོ་ལྔ་ལོན་པ་དང་ཡབ་མེས་ཀྱི་ཆོས་ཐམས་ཅད་ཐུགས་སུ་ཆུད་སློབ་གྲྭའི་སྐྱེ་བོ་ཕལ་པོ་ཆེ་ཐམས་ཅད་ངོ་མཚར་དུ་གྱུར་ཏོ།།

དེ་ནས་བཟུང་སྟེ་གཞུང་ཆེན་པོ་རྣམས་ཀྱང་ཇི་ལྟ་བ་བཞིན་གསུངས་པས་རང་གི་སློབ་མ་རྣམས་ལ་བློ་གྲོས་ཀྱི་མིག་རྣམ་པར་བཀྲལ་ཏོ།

དེ་ནས་ཀྲུང་ལོ་བཅོ་བརྒྱད་པའི་དུས་སུ་རྣལ་ལམ་དུ་ས་སྐྱའི་ལྷག་གི་བླ་ཆེན་གྱི་ཡུམ་གྱི་མཆོད་རྟེན་གྱི་དྲུང་དུ་སློབ་དཔོན་གཡིག་གཉེན་ཡིན་ཟེར་བའི་དགེ་སློང་སྤོ་བསངས་དར་ཡོལ་བ་ཞིག་ལ་ཆོས་མངོན་པ་མཛོད་ཆར་གཅིག་གསན་སྐད།

ཡང་དུས་གཞན་ཞིག་དུ་རྣལ་ལམ་དུ་སློབ་དཔོན་ཕྱོགས་ཀྱི་གླང་པོའི་ཕུག་ཡིན་ཟེར་བ་ཞིག་དུ་ཕྱིན་ནས། ཚད་མའི་པོ་ཏི་མང་པོ་འདུག་པ་འདི་དག་གི་སྒོའི་ལྡེ་མིག་ཁྱོད་ལ་གཏོད་ཟེར་བ་དང་། ཐོག་མར་ཀུན་ལས་བཏུས་བལྟ་སྙམ་ཙ་ན་ཅིག་གིས་ཐེན་པ་ཞིག་བྱུས་པས་རྣལ་སད་དེ་ཕྱིས་མཐའ་འཁོབ་དུ་གཟིགས་པ་ལ་ལྟ་གསུང་དེའི་རྗེས་ལ་རྟོགས་པ་ཁྱད་པར་ཅན་སྐྱེས་སོ།།

དེ་ནས་དགུང་ལོ་བཅུ་དགུ་པའི་དུས་སུ་འཕྲང་དུ་དགེ་བཤེས་ཞུ་རྟུལ་ལ་བྱམས་ཆོས་དང་། ཚད་མ་ཅུང་ཟད་གསན་ནོ།།

ཀྲུང་ལོ་ཉི་ཤུ་པའི་དུས་སུ་ཉང་སྟོད་རྒྱང་ཐུར་དུ་དགེ་བཤེས་མཆུར་སྟོན་གཞོན་ནུ་སེང་གེ་ལ་རྣམ་ངེས་སྟོད་ཚར་བཞི་སྨད་ཚར་གཉིས་གསན་པས་ཚིག་དོན་མ་ལུས་པ་ཐུགས་སུ་ཆུད་ནས།

them, and then erase them. So it has been stated. He stated that he understood early both the Indian and Tibetan scripts, without studying, and didn't remember which one he understood first.

Furthermore, his excellent behavior was pleasurable to everyone. He was calm and disciplined, and had a fine disposition. He was gentle, moderate in speech, and bright, and fully upheld good qualities. He was devoted to his masters and elders, and very polite and respectful. His sense faculties were restrained, and he was compassionate to sentient beings.

Early Studies

He then grew older, and without studying, perfectly understood the types of scripts, the reading of Indian script and the reading of Tibetan script; the specifics of astrology; and the various specifics of the arts, such as medical diagnosis and painting. The entire world was amazed, and everyone praised him.

Then he carefully received all the Dharmas of his ancestors from that same Dharma Lord, and mastered them.[262] When he reached the age of nine, eight is also said, he taught the [text by] Saroruha.[263] At twelve he taught the *Brtag gnyis.* At fourteen he taught the *Sampuṭa.* By the age of fifteen he had mastered all the Dharma of his ancestors. All the many people in the institute [at Sa skya] were amazed.

Thereafter he also precisely taught the great treatises, fully bestowing the eye of discernment on his disciples.

When he was eighteen years old, it is said he dreamed that in front of the stūpa of the great master [Sa chen's] mother, up above Sa skya, he received the *Abhidharmakoṣa* once from a pale blue young monk, who said, "I am the teacher Vasubandhu."[264]

Also, at another time, in a dream he went to a cave that was said to be the teacher Dignāga's. There were many volumes of epistemology, and he was told, "The door keys for these are given to you." When he thought to first look at the *Pramāṇasamuccaya*, someone shook him and he awoke from the dream. He looked at it later when he traveled to a foreign borderland. So it has been stated.[265] Following that an exceptional realization arose.

Then, at the age of nineteen, he also received the *Byams chos* and some epistemology from the spiritual friend Zhu Rul in 'Phrang.[266]

When he was twenty years old he received the first section of the

རྒྱང་ཕུར་ན་བཞུགས་ཙམ་ན་ཡབ་སློབ་དཔོན་གཙུང་སྐུ་བསྟུང་ནས་ཡར་བྱོན་པ་དང་སློབ་དཔོན་གཙུང་སྐུ་གཤེགས་རྗེས་ཀྱི་བྱ་བ་ཅི་རིགས་པ་མཛད་དེ་མཆོར་ལ་ཆོས་ཞིག་འགའ་འཐེན་པར་ཞུས་པས་གྲུ་པ་རྣམས་འཇིགས་ཁྲིད་པར་དུ་ཡ་མ་སྐུག་ཐེང་འཇིགས་པས་ཇོ་སྲས་ས་སྐྱ་བས་གྲུ་པ་ཚོག་ན་ཉིད་ཚོས་ཀྱེས་སོ་དེ་མེན་ན་ཆོས་ཤོད་ཟེར་ནས་ཆཤད། དེའི་རྗེས་སུ་ཡོ་བྱད་མང་པོ་སྣོམས་ནས་རྒྱང་ཕུར་དུ་བྱོན་ཙམ་ན་དབྱར་ཆོས་བ་འཁོར་དུ་བྱུང་ནས་དེར་རྣམ་གཞག་རྒྱ་ཆེན་པོ་མཛད་བཀའ་རྒྱས་འབྲིང་གསུམ་ཕུལ་ནས། ཆོས་དབུ་ནས་བསྐྱུར་རམ་གསུང་བ་ལ་མི་འཆལ་ཟེར་ནས་རྣམ་ངེས་དབུ་དང་གཞན་དོན་ནས་དབུ་བཙུགས་ཏེ་ཉིན་རེ་ལ་ཆོས་ཐུན་གཉིས་གཉིས་བཤད་ནས་གཞུང་དབུ་ཞབས་རྫོགས་པར་ཚར་གཅིག་ཐུགས་ལ་གསུངས་པས་ཐམས་ཅད་ངོ་མཚར་དུ་འཛིན། དེ་ཉིད་ལ་དུས་ཕྱིས་དབུ་མ་རིགས་ཚོགས་ཀྱང་གསན་ནོ།

དེ་ནས་ས་སྐྱར་བྱོན་ནས་སློབ་དཔོན་ཙུང་གི་ལྷུད་ལ་སོགས་པ་རྗེས་ཀྱི་བྱ་བ་ཚར་ནས། རྒྱང་ཕུར་དུ་གསེར་མང་བ་ཞིག་གིས་སྣ་དྲངས་པའི་དབུལ་བ་སྐྱེལ་དུ་བྱོན་པའི་ལམ་ཀར། ཆུ་དམིག་དུ་བླ་མ་ཤཱཀྱ་ཤྲཱི་དང་འཇལ་ཏེ་ཆོས་མཆོག་གསུང་བའི་འཕྲོ་ལ་སླེབ་ནས། སློབ་དཔོན་གྱིས་བོད་དཔེའ་བཀྲམ་ནས་གསན་པཎ་ཆུང་ཙོ་ཁོང་ལ་ཁྲེལ་ནས་རྐྱོད་པས་བླ་མའི་ཞལ་ནས་བོད་དཔེའ་བཀྲམ་པས་ཅི་ལ་ཕན་ཅེས་གསུངས་སྐད།

བླ་མས་འཚམས་གླགས་ནས། དེའི་རྗེས་སུ་ཁྲིད་གླེགས་དང་གསུང་བ་ལ

སློབ་དཔོན་གྱིས་བོད་དཔེའ་ལ་རྒྱ་གླེགས་སྤངས་ཀྱི་ཏའི་སྐད་ཀྱིས་བླགས་པས་ཤིན་དུ་མཉེས་ཁྲེད་ཙོ་ཅི་ལ་རྐྱོད་ས་སྐྱ་པ་ཁོ་རང་གིས་ཤེས་ཀྱིན་འདུག་པ་གསུང་། སྐད།།

དེའི་དུས་སུ་བླ་མའི་སློབ་མ་པཎྜི་ཏ་རྟོག་གེ་བ་ཆེན་པོ་དཱ་ན་ཤཱི་ལ་ལ་ཚད་མ་གསན། བལ་པོ་སང་གྷ་ཤྲཱི་ལ་སྒྲ་དང་ཚད་མ་རྣམ་འགྲེལ་ལ་སོགས་པ་གསན་ནོ།། ཆོས་རྗེ་པའི་ཞལ་ནས་ང་བསོད་དེ་ཆེ་བར་བྱུང་རྒྱ་གར་ཤར་ནུབ་ན་སཾ་གྷ་ཤྲཱི་བས་སྒྲ་མཁས་པ་མེད་པར་འདུག་སྟེ་དེ་ངའི་ཚོར་བྱུང་བ་ཡིན་གསུང་།

དེ་ནས་སློབ་དཔོན་གྱིས་རྒྱང་ཕུར་དུ་བྱོན་ནས་སློབ་དཔོན་ལ་སྔར་གྱི་འབུལ་བ་རྣམས་ཕྱག་དུ་ཕུལ་ནས་ཡར་བྱོན་པ་ན། བླ་མ་ཤཱཀྱ་ཤྲཱི་དབུས་སུ་གཤེགས་ཏེ་སློབ་དཔོན་གྱིས་པཎྜི་ཏ་སུ

Pramāṇaviniścaya four times and the last section twice, from the spiritual friend Mtshur ston Gzhon nu seng ge at Rkyang thur in upper Nyang, and mastered absolutely all the meaning of the words. While he was staying in Rkyang thur, his father, the teacher, the younger brother [Dpal chen 'od po], became ill, and he went back. After the teacher, the younger brother [Dpal chen 'od po], passed away, he performed the various final rites.[267] He asked Mtshur to delay the Dharma teachings for several days, but the students insisted. In particular, Ya ma stag theng insisted, saying, "If the noble son of Sa skya is student enough, we are leaving. If not, teach the Dharma!" Then [Mtshur] taught.[268] After that he took many things, and when he arrived in Rkyang thur, there was a summer Dharma council. He made vast offerings there. He offered the three extensive, medium, and [brief *Prajñāpāramitā*] scriptures. [Mtshur] asked, "Shall I repeat the Dharma from the beginning? He replied, "Please do not."[269] [Sa skya Paṇḍita] began the *Pramāṇaviniścaya* from the beginning and [from the section on] benefit for others. Teaching in two Dharma sessions every day, he completely taught the treatise by heart, from beginning to end, and everyone held him in awe. At a later time he also received the *Dbu ma rigs tshogs* from that same [master].[270]

Meeting Mahāpaṇḍita Śākyaśrī

After then returning to Sa skya, he completed the final rites, such as the funeral ceremony, for the teacher, the younger brother [Dpal chen 'od po]. On the road, when he was going to Rkyang thur to deliver offerings, the foremost of which was much gold, he met master Śākyaśrī at Chu dmig. He arrived while the teaching of the Dharmottara [commentary] was in progress.[271] When the teacher [Sa skya Paṇḍita] spread out his Tibetan texts and listened, the lesser paṇḍitas ridiculed him, and laughed, and master [Śākyaśrī] said, "What use is it to spread out Tibetan texts?"

Master [Śākyaśrī] read to a stopping point, and after that said, "You read!"

When the teacher [Sa skya Paṇḍita] read out the Tibetan text in the Sanskrit language, [as though he were] reading an Indian [manuscript], it is said that [Śākyaśrī] was extremely pleased and exclaimed, "What are you laughing at? The one from Sa skya understands."[272]

At that time he received [teachings on] epistemology from Dānaśīla, a disciple of master [Śākyaśrī], who was a paṇḍita and a great dialectician.[273] From the Newar Saṃghaśrī he received grammar, the

ལྷ་ཏ་ཤྲི་ས་སྐྱར་སྤྱན་དྲངས་སྒྲ་དང་ཚད་མ་དང་སྙན་ངག་སྡེབ་སྦྱོར་ལ་སོགས་པ་གསན་ཞིང་ཐུགས་སུ་ཆུད་པར་མཛད་དོ།།

དེ་ནས་དུས་ཕྱིས་བླ་མ་ཤཱཀྱ་ཤྲི་རྩང་དུ་བྱོན་ཏེ་ཉངས་ཆུང་དུ་བཞུགས་པའི་དུས་སུ་སློབ་དཔོན་ཆོས་གསན་དུ་བྱོན་པ་ལ་རབ་ཏུ་འབྱུང་བར་དགོངས་སྟེ། དེ་ལྟར་ཞུ་བའི་ཡི་གེ་རྗེ་བཙུན་གྱི་ཕྱག་དུ་ཕུལ་བས་གནང་སྟེ། རྒུང་ལོ་ཉི་ཤུ་རྩ་བདུན་བཞེས་པའི་དུས་སུ་བླ་མ་ལ་མཁན་པོ་ཞུས་སློབ་དཔོན་སྤྱི་བོ་ལྷས་པ་ལ་ལས་ཆོག་ཞུས་དགེ་ཚཤེས་ཞུས་གསང་སྟེ་སྟོན་པ་མཛད་ནས། ཉང་སྨད་རྒྱན་གོང་གི་གཙུག་ལག་ཁང་དུ་ཟེར་ཀྱང་དེར་དབུ་སྐྲ་བཞར་ན་བཟའ་གསོལ་བ་མ་གཏོགས་པ་སྡོམ་པ་ཉངས་ཆུང་དུ་བླངས་དགེ་སློང་གི་དགེ་འདུན་རྒྱ་མཚོའི་དབུས་སུ་རབ་ཏུ་བྱོན་སྟེ། རྙོག་པ་མེད་པའི་ཚུལ་ཁྲིམས་ཀྱིས་མཛེས་པར་བྱས་སོ། རྗེ་པ་ཡང་རབ་ཏུ་བྱུང་བ་ལ་མཉེས་པས་ད་རབ་དུ་བྱུང་ནས་བྱ་བ་དང་བསྲུང་སྡོམ་ལ་བརྩོན་པར་གྱིས་གསུང་ནས་ཆོས་རྗེ་པའི་དྲུང་དུ་ཛོ་བདན་ཕྲུ་མོ་ཞིག་བཞག་ནས་འཕྲུལ་གྱི་གསོལ་ལུགས་བཞུགས་ཚུལ་ཚུན་ཚོད་ལ་སྐྱོན་གཏོང་བ་ཞིག་ཡོད་གསུང་།

ཡང་མཁན་པོ་དེ་ཉིད་ལ་སྤྱི་ཕྱིར་ཆོས་གསན་པ་ནི་ཚད་མ་རབ་ཏུ་བྱེད་པ་སྡེ་བདུན་ལ་སྡེ་གསུམ་རྒྱན་དང་ཆོས་མཆོག་ལ་སོགས་པའི་འགྲེལ་པ་ཆེན་པོ་ཡན་ལག་དང་བཅས་པ་ཐམས་ཅད་གསན། རྒྱན་དང་ཆོས་མཆོག་ཅུང་མ་རྫོགས་པ་ཕྱིས་པཎ་ཊི་ཏ་གཞན་ལ་གསན། ཡང་བླ་ཆེན་དེ་ཉིད་ལ་མངོན་པ་མཛོད་དང་འདུལ་བ་མདོ་རྩ་དང་། སོ་སོར་ཐར་པ་དང་དགེ་སློང་གི་ཀ་རི་ཀ་ལ་སོགས་པ་འདུལ་བའི་སྤྲན་དང་བཅས་པ་ཐམས་ཅད་གསན་ཏོ།།

ཡང་དེ་ཉིད་ལ་དཔལ་དུས་ཀྱི་འཁོར་ལོའི་འགྲེལ་པ་དྲི་མ་མེད་པའི་འོད་སྟོང་ཕྲག་བཅུ་གཉིས་པ་ལ་སོགས་པ་ཡན་ལག་དང་བཅས་པ་གསན་ཏོ།། གཞན་ཡང་བདེ་མཆོག་དང་གསང་བ་འདུས་པ་འཕགས་སྐོར་དང་ཡེ་ཤེས་ཞབས་ཀྱི་སྐོར་ལ་སོགས་པ་ཡང་གསན་ཏེ། དེ་རྣམས་ཀྱི་དབང་བསྐུར་བ་ཡང་ཞུས་ཤིང་ཐམས་ཅད་ཐུགས་སུ་ཆུད་པར་མཛད་དོ།

དེའི་རྗེས་སུ་སློབ་དཔོན་སྤྱི་བོ་ལྷས་པ་ལ་ཕ་རོལ་ཏུ་ཕྱིན་པ་བརྒྱད་སྟོང་པ་དང་ཉི་ཁྲི་འགྲེལ་པ་མན་ཆད་དང་། མངོན་པ་ཀུན་ལས་བཏུས་པ་ལ་སོགས་པ་སྤྱོད་ཕྱོགས་དང་དང་གསང་སྔགས་ཀྱི་གདམ་ངག་ཕྲ་མོ་འགའ་ཞིག་དང་། བཀའ་གདམས་ལ་སོགས་པ་ཐམས་ཅད་གསན་ཏོ།།

Pramāṇavārttika, and so forth. The Dharma Lord stated, "I have great merit. From the east to the west of India there is no one more expert in grammar than Saṃghaśrī, and he has come to my place.[274]

Then the teacher [Sa skya Paṇḍita] traveled to Rkyang thur and presented the earlier offerings into the hands of the teacher [Mtshur]. When he returned,[275] master Śākyaśrī went to Dbus. The teacher [Sa skya Paṇḍita] invited paṇḍita Sugataśrī to Sa skya, and received and mastered grammar, epistemology, poetics, metrics, and so forth.[276]

Taking Ordination

Then, at a later time, master Śākyaśrī returned to Rtsang and stayed at Nyungs[277] chung. At that point, when the teacher [Sa skya Paṇḍita] came to receive Dharma, he decided to take ordination. Accordingly, he offered a letter into the hands of Rje btsun requesting permission, which was granted.[278] When he had reached the age of twenty-seven, he requested the master [Śākyaśrī] to be abbot and the teacher Spyi bo lhas pa to be master of ceremonies. The spiritual friend Zhus acted as the secret preceptor. In the midst of a Saṅgha sea of monks in the temple of Rgyan gong in lower Nyang, he was ordained, it is said, but except for shaving his head and dressing in the robes there, he took the vows at Nyungs chung, and was beautified with unsullied moral discipline. Lord [Grags pa rgyal mtshan] was also pleased at the ordination, and said, "Having now taken ordination, you must be diligent in your conduct and in guarding the vows." He placed a strict monk in the presence of the Dharma Lord, one who found faults down to his usual way of eating and manner of sitting. So it has been stated.[279]

He received Dharma from that same abbot [Śākyaśrī], both before and later. He received all the great commentaries, such as the *Alaṃkāra* and the [commentary of] Dharmottara, together with the affiliated [texts], for the Set of Three from among the Seven Sets on Epistemology.[280] He later received from another paṇḍita the [sections] of the *Alaṃkāra* and Dharmottara's [commentary] that had not quite been completed.[281] From that same great master [Śākyaśrī] he also received the *Abhidharmakoṣa,* the *Vinayamūlasūtra,* the *Pratimokṣa,* the *Bhikṣukārika,* and so forth, as well as the *Vinayakṣudrakavastu.*

From the same [master] he also received the twelve thousand-line *Vimalaprabhā* commentary of Śrī Kālacakra and so forth, together with the branchs.[282] He also received Saṃvara,[283] and the cycles of

གཞན་ཡང་ཐུགས་དམ་ལ་གཞོལ་བས་ཏིང་ངེ་འཛིན་དུ་མ་ལ་མངའ་བརྙེས་ཏེ། ཕྱི་ནང་གི་རྟེན་འབྲེལ་ཟབ་མོའི་འགྲོས་ཐུགས་སུ་ཆུད་པའི་སྟོབས་ཀྱིས་མ་འོངས་པའི་དོན་འགའ་ཞིག་འདི་ལྟར་འབྱུང་ཞེས་ལུང་སྟོན་པ་རྣམས་ནི་སློབ་མ་ཉུང་སེ་ལས་མེད་དུས་སུ་ང་དུས་ཕྱིས་སྐད་རིགས་མི་གཅིག་པའི་ས་ཞིག་ཏུ་ཕྱིན་ནས་བསྟན་པ་ལ་བག་ཙམ་ཕན་པ་ཞིག་འོང་བྱ་བ་གསུང་སྐྱེ་ཐོག་ཏུ་བབ་དེ་ཁོ་ན་བཞིན་དུ་འབྱུང་བ་མཐོང་བ་དང་གཞན་ཡང་འཇམ་དབྱངས་མཉེས་པའི་མཛད་པའི་རྟགས་ཐུན་མོང་མ་ཡིན་པ་སྐབས་འགའ་ཞིག་ཏུ་ཐུགས་དམ་མཛད་པས་ཏིང་ངེ་འཛིན་བསམ་གྱིས་མི་ཁྱབ་པ་བྱུང་ཏེ་ཐ་མལ་གྱི་རྟོག་པ་ཡེ་མ་བྱུང་བ་དང་མི་མང་པོའི་གསེབ་ཏུ་གཟིགས་རྟོགས་ལ་སོགས་པ་གང་མཛད་ཀྱང་གཞན་རྐྱེན་གྱིས་གཡེང་བར་མི་ནུས་པ་ལ་སོགས་པ་ཡོན་ཏན་བསམ་གྱིས་མི་ཁྱབ་པ་མངའ་འོ། དང་བྱིན་རླབས་ཀྱི་ཤུགས་ཤིན་ཏུ་ཆེ་བ་སྟེ། གསོལ་བ་བཏབ་ན་འདོད་པའི་དོན་འགྲུབ་པའི་མཐུ་ཕུན་སུམ་ཚོགས་པ་དང་ཡང་ལྡན་ནོ།།

མདོར་ན་རིག་པའི་གནས་ལྔ་མཁྱེན་པ་རྒྱ་མཚོའི་ཕ་རོལ་དུ་ཕྱིན་པས་ཡོངས་སུ་རྫོགས་པའི་པཎྜི་ཏ་ཆེན་པོར་གྱུར་ཏེ། རྟོགས་པའི་ཏིང་འཛིན་དུ་མ་བརྙེས་པས་སྙན་པའི་གྲགས་པས་ཕྱོགས་ཀུན་དུ་ཁྱབ་ཅིང་གདུལ་བྱའི་སྐྱེ་བོ་དཔག་ཏུ་མེད་པ་སྨིན་ཅིང་གྲོལ་བར་མཛད་ལ།

གཞན་ཡང་འཆད་པ་དང་རྩོད་པ་དང་རྩོམ་པ་ལ་སོགས་པ་མཁས་པའི་བྱ་བ་གསུམ་ལ་རབ་ཏུ་མཁས་པའི་བདག་ཉིད་ཆེན་པོ་འདི་ནི་རབ་ཏུ་གུས་པས་བསྟེན་པར་བྱའོ། དེ་ནས་དགུང་ལོ་བདུན་བཅུ་བཞེས་པ་དང་ཤིང་པོ་ཕག་སྨྲུལ་པོའི་ཟླ་བའི་ཚེས་བཅུ་བཞི་ལ་རྒྱལ་ས་བྱང་ཆོས་སུ་བདེ་བར་གཤེགས་སོ

འདིའི་རྣམ་པར་ཐར་པ་རྒྱས་པར་བརྗོད་ཀྱིས་མི་ལང་སྟེ་གདོན་མི་ཟ་བར་མགོན་པོ་འཇམ་པའི་དབྱངས་ཉིད་དུ་རིག་པར་བྱའོ།།

མི་དབང་གསུང་རབ་ཟས་ཀྱི་དགའ་སྟོན་ལ།།
དོན་གཉེར་རྣ་བའི་སློང་མོས་ཉེར་བླངས་ཏེ།།
རྣམ་སྤྱོད་ལྕེ་འིས་མྱངས་པས་བདག་བློའི་ལུས།།
སོམ་ཉིའི་རྒྱུད་ལས་རྣམ་གྲོལ་རབ་བརྟས་གྱུར།།

Guhyasamāja according to Ārya [Nāgārjuna], according to Jñānapāda, and so forth. He also requested the bestowal of their initiations, and mastered them all.

After that, from the teacher Spyi bo lhas pa he received the *Prajñāpāramitā,* through the commentaries on the *Aṣṭāsāhasrikā* and the *Viṃśatisāhasrikā,* the *Abhidharmasamuccaya,* and so forth, the texts concerning conduct, several minor oral instructions of secret mantra, and all the [teachings] of the Bka' gdams pa and so forth.

Sa skya Paṇḍita's Special Qualities

Furthermore, by engaging in meditation he gained control of numerous meditative concentrations. I have seen his prophecies that several future events would "happen like this," happen exactly like that, due to the force of his mastery of the movements of the profound outer and inner dependently arisen connections. At a time when there were none but a few disciples, he stated, "At a later time I will go to a place where there is a different kind of language, and some benefit will come to the Doctrine." That happened exactly.[284] Moreover, he is endowed with uncommon signs of having pleased Mañjughoṣa. On several occasions when he engaged in meditation, inconceivable meditative concentrations arose. He never had ordinary thoughts, and whatever he did in the midst of many people, such as considering something, he could not be distracted by other influences. He had inconceivable such qualities. He has enormous blessing, and the perfect power to achieve the desired goal if it is prayed for.

In brief, by reaching the far shore of knowing the five fields of knowledge, he has become a great consummate paṇḍita.[285] Obtaining numerous realized meditative concentrations, the fame of his reputation has filled all directions, and he has brought infinite trainable beings to spiritual maturation and liberation.

Furthermore, with true devotion we should study under this great being who is truly expert in what is done by experts, such as the three activities of explication, disputation, and composition.[286] Then, when he had reached the age of seventy, he passed into bliss at the capital Liang-chou, on the fourteenth day of the eleventh month in the wood-pig year [1251].[287]

The extensive life story of this being cannot be expressed. It should be known that he is without doubt Mañjughoṣanātha himself.

གང་ཞིག་སྤེལ་ལེགས་སྣན་ཚིག་ཤས་ཆུང་ཡང་།།
དོན་དང་མི་འགལ་ཅུང་ཟད་བྲིས་པ་ལས།།
ཚིག་གི་གཏེར་མངའ་མཁས་པའི་ཚོགས་རྣམས་ཀྱིས།།
རེ་ཞིག་བཟོད་པར་གསོལ་ལ་གཟུའ་བོས་དཔྱོད།།

འདིར་ནི་རང་ཉིད་དྲན་པ་གསོའ་ཕྱིར་དང་།།
དམ་པའི་གྲོགས་འགས་བསྐུལ་ནས་བརྟའ་སྤྲོད་པ།།
དཔལ་ལྡན་བཟང་པོའི་ཞབས་སོགས་བླ་མ་ཡི།།
རྣམ་ཐར་བྲིས་པའི་དགེ་དེས་མཆོག་ཐོབ་ཤོག།།

བླ་མ་བོད་ཀྱི་བརྒྱུད་པའི་རྣམ་ཐར་ཞིབ་མོ་ཪྡོ་རྗེ་ཞེས་བྱ་བ་མང་དུ་མཉན་ཞིང་ཞལ་ལས་བྲིས་ཏེ་ལེགས་པར་རྣྗེད་པ་འདི་ནི་ཤཀྱའི་དགེ་སློང་ཆོས་ཀྱི་རྒྱལ་པོ་ཞེས་བྱ་བས། གུང་ཐང་ན་ལ་ཅོ་གནས་པོ་ཆེའི་རྩུག་ལག་ཁང་དུ་སྦྱར་བ་འདི་ཡོངས་སུ་རྫོགས་སྷོ།།

ལོ་རྒྱུས་ཀྱི་ཡི་གེ་འདི་བླ་མ་ལོ་ཙ་བ་ཆེན་པོའི་ཕྱག་དུ་ཕུལ་བས་མཉེས་སྟེ་རབ་དུ་བཏགས་པས་ན་ཐེ་ཚོམ་མེད་པར་གུས་པས་ལོང་ཤིག།

ཡུལ་དབུས་ཀྱི་བློ་གསལ་དམར་གྱིས་ཡི་གེ་འདི་དཔྱི་བསླན་མེད་པར་བྲིས་པ་ཡིན་ནོ།

དགེ་འོ།།
དགའ་གོ།།

Colophon

At a celebration feast of the teachings of the monarch, a seeker with begging ears partook,
And tasting with the tongue of discernment, my mental body was nourished and liberated from the weakness of doubt.
Although lacking in fine composition and poetic words, what little I have written does not contradict the truth.
May it be tolerated for a while and properly examined by groups of experts endowed with the treasury of words.
This has been composed to nourish my own memory, and after being urged by several excellent companions.
By the virtue of writing the life stories of the masters, such as the splendid and honorable Bzang po, may the sublime be obtained![288]

These life stories of the lineal masters in Tibet, known as the *Zhib mo rdo rje,* were carefully acquired through much listening to and questioning of [Sa skya Paṇḍita] in person. Composed by the Śākya monk known as Chos kyi rgyal po, in the temple of Na la tse gnas po che in Gung thang, this is complete.[289]

When this text of stories was offered into the hands of the great Master Translator [Sa skya Paṇḍita], he was pleased and praised it highly, so it should be respectfully accepted without doubts.[290]

This text was written by the clear-minded Dmar of the central region, without omissions or additions.[291]

Good Fortune!
This is accurate.

Notes to Part One

1 See 'Jam mgon Kong sprul, *Sgrub,* 645. Notice was first made of this verse in Kapstein (1996), 277. See Kapstein's article for general information and references to the following eight great systems.

2 For example, see the comments in 'Jam mgon Kong sprul, *Sgrub,* 635–36. Kong sprul specifically states that the teachings of the Shangs pa Bka' brgyud, Zhi byed, and Rdo rje gsum gyi bsnyen sgrub had nearly disappeared. See Smith (1970) for information about Mkhyen brtse'i dbang po, 'Jam mgon Kong sprul, and the nineteenth-century *ris med* movement.

3 See Karmay (1988), 17, 206–15, and 'Jam mgon Kong sprul, *Sgrub,* 647.

4 See 'Jam mgon Kong sprul, *Sgrub,* 635.

5 The problem of the dates of Mar pa and his disciple Mi la ras pa are still unresolved. I am following the opinions of Kaḥ thog Rig 'dzin Tshe dbang nor bu (1698–1755), expressed in his study of the chronology and dates of the early Bka' brgyud masters. See Tshe dbang nor bu, *Mar.*

6 See 'Jam mgon Kong sprul, *Sgrub,* 635.

7 See Stearns (1999), especially 70–79.

8 See part two, 142–43.

9 See 'Jam mgon Kong sprul, *Sgrub,* 661.

10 For example, see Grags pa rgyal mtshan, *Bla ma brgyud pa rgya,* 582.

11 This text has been preserved in a number of variant editions. See Virūpa, *Lam,* which may represent a xylograph descendent of one of the oldest manuscripts. In translating the title of this work, I understand *tu bcas pa* to be an alternate form of *dang bcas pa.*

12 Grags pa rgyal mtshan specifically gives the original Indian name as Kahna (Kahna pa), which is also found in a number of Indian siddha lists. See Grags pa rgyal mtshan, *Rgyud,* 5. For the other information about Kahna, see 'Jam dbyangs mkhyen brtse'i dbang phyug, *Byung,* 217, and *Snang,* 268.

13 The mention of Ācārya Śraddhākaravarman in connection with the Lam 'bras is interesting in light of the fact that he was sometimes identified with Gayadhara, who originally brought the Lam 'bras to Tibet. This issue will be discussed at length below.

14 This is presumably a reference to the **Caryāgītikoṣavṛtti* of Munidatta, which has been studied and reproduced in Kvaerne (1986). I have not been able to locate any quotes from the *Rdo rje tshig rkang* in this work. Kun dga' bzang po, *Lam,* 110.3, cites both Ācārya Munidatta and the great adept *Vīraprabhāsvara (Dpa' bo 'od gsal) as Indian authors who quoted Virūpa. 'Jam dbyangs mkhyen brtse'i dbang phyug, *Gdams,* 31, does not mention Munidatta, but does cite "the commentary on *Vīraprabhāsvara's [compilation of] the spiritual songs of the one hundred *[sic!]* great adepts." *Vīraprabhāsvara's work is the *Grub thob brgyad cu rtsa bzhi'i rtogs pa'i snying po,* no. 3140 in the Peking edition of the Tibetan Tripitaka, 69: 139.4–141.5. The commentary, by Abhayadattaśrī, is the *Grub thob brgyad cu rtsa bzhi'i rtogs brjod do ha 'grel pa dang bcas pa,* no. 5092 in the Peking edition of the Tibetan Tripitaka, 87: 201.3–219.5. A note in Ngag dbang blo bzang rgya mtsho, *Zab,* 2: 77, states that the paṇḍita Sūryarasmi was also called Dpa' bo 'od gsal.

15 See Mus chen Dkon mchog rgyal mtshan, *Lam,* 448. Kun dga' bzang po, *Lam,* 110.3, also mentions the paṇḍita Darpaṇa Ācārya as an Indian author who cited the esoteric instructions of Virūpa. Ngag dbang blo bzang rgya mtsho, *Zab,* 2: 25ff, provides much information about Darpaṇa Ācārya ('Gro ba'i me long) and his collection. Darpaṇa Ācārya was a disciple of many masters, such as Lalītavajra, and was said to have lived for twelve hundred years! His *Kriyāsamuccaya* was very widely known in India. The first Sanskrit manuscript was brought to Tibet by a Newar trader, and came into the hands of the Sa skya throne-holder 'Jam dbyangs don yod rgyal mtshan (1310–44). Under the sponsorship of the Jo nang master Kun spangs Chos grags dpal bzang, it was then translated by the Indian paṇḍita Mañjuśrī and Sa bzang Ma ti paṇ chen Blo gros rgyal mtshan (1293–1376). However, the transmission line had been broken, and Sa bzang 'Phags pa gzhon nu blo gros had to travel to Nepal to receive the initiations from the paṇḍita Mahābodhi.

16 Mang thos klu sgrub refers to a partial knowledge of the Lam 'bras by these two Indian masters and notes that a certain Rngog, who refuted the Lam 'bras, did so in ignorance of the evidence of their knowledge and due to the fact that he had never received the teachings himself. See Mang thos klu sgrub, *Bstan,* 94. See note 209 in part one for more about Rngog Lba ba can and his refutation of Gayadhara's teachings.

17 See 'Jam dbyangs mkhyen brtse'i dbang phyug, *Gdams,* 31. The two Indian authors were Darpaṇa Ācārya and Abhayadattaśrī.

18 'Brog mi's dates, and those for Gayadhara's arrival in Tibet and his death, are found in Mang thos klu sgrub, *Bstan,* 83, 92, and 94.

19 See 'Jam dbyangs mkhyen brtse'i dbang phyug, *Byung,* 210. Cf. Yuthok (1997), 139–40, who strangely enough claims that since 'Brog mi translated the *Rdo rje tshig rkang* into Tibetan it must have been placed in writing before his time.

20 Mang thos klu sgrub, *Bstan,* 130, gives this as the date when Sa chen first taught the Lam 'bras and wrote the first brief verse commentary for his disciple A seng. In this first text Sa chen specifically states that the *Rdo rje tshig rkang* had not yet been recorded in writing. See Sa chen Kun dga' snying po, *Thams,* 191. Also see Dmar ston, *Gzhung,* 4, who states that the tradition was only oral up until Sa chen. 'Jam dbyang mkhyen brtse'i dbang phyug, *Byung,* 211, states that Sa chen also first wrote down the *Rdo rje tshig rkang* in the same period that he wrote the first commentary for A seng. Shākya mchog ldan, *Lam,* 631, also says that the tradition was only oral until the *Rdo rje tshig rkang* was first placed in writing by Sa chen.

21 See Virūpa, *Lam,* 10.

22 See Cha rgan, *Cha,* 9a: *rdo rje tshig rkang rjed thor yi ger btab.* I am grateful to Leonard van der Kuijp for a copy of Cha rgan's rare text. The fourteenth-century author Bar ston Rdo rje Rgyal mtshan also referred to a time when the text was written *(bri bar bya ba'i dus)* by Virūpa. See Bar ston, *Bar,* 3b. I am grateful to Mkhan po A pad Rin po che and Guru Lama for a copy of this rare manuscript.

23 See 'Jam mgon Kong sprul, *Theg,* 1: 522.

24 See Kun dga' bzang po, *Lam,* 114.1–2.

25 See Kun dga' bzang po, *Lam,* 117.1 and 117.4–118.1.

26 See 'Jam mgon A mes zhabs, *Yongs,* 99–100, who also says that the *Lung skor lnga* are mentioned many times in the Zha ma tradition, but without any precise identification. 'Jam mgon A mes zhabs' information seems to be based on Cha rgan, *Cha,* 11b, although Cha rgan describes these texts as the *Lung skor gsum* extracted from the one hundred thousand-line tantra. But elsewhere Cha rgan also refers to the texts as the *Lung skor lnga.*

27 See Cha rgan, *Lam,* 27a–b, and also 'Jam mgon A mes zhabs, *Yongs,* 134–35, who copied Cha rgan.

28 See 'Jam dbyangs mkhyen brtse'i dbang phyug, *Gdams,* 7. The *Kye rdor rgyud gsum (The Tantra Trilogy of Hevajra)* is composed of the basic text of the *Hevajra tantra rāja* (*Kye'i rdo rje shes bya ba rgyud kyi rgyal po),* Peking Tripitaka, vol. 1, no. 10, 210.2–223.1; the uncommon explanatory tantra *(thun mong ma yin pa'i bshad rgyud)* of the *Ārya ḍākinī vajrapañjara*

('Phags pa mkha' 'gro ma do rje gur), Peking Tripitaka, vol. 1, no. 11, 223.1–238.5; and the common explanatory tantra *(thun mong bshad rgyud)* of the *Sampuṭa nāma mahātantra (Yang dag par sbyor ba shes bya ba'i rgyud chen po),* Peking, vol. 2, no. 26, 245.5–280.2. The term *rgyud gsum* in this context should not be confused with the same term when it is used to designate the second of the seven sections within the first major part of the *Rdo rje tshig rkang.*

29 All three works are found in volume 11 of the *Sa skya Lam 'bras Literature Series* (Dehra Dun: Sa skya Centre, 1983). Sa chen's work, the *Lung mtha' dag dang mdor bsdus su sbyar ba,* is on pp. 529–81.

30 See Sa chen Kun dga' snying po, *Gzhung bshad,* 22. The definition is found in the annotations to the text, which were written by Grags pa rgyal mtshan.

31 See 'Jam dbyangs mkhyen brtse'i dbang phyug, *Byung,* 197–98.

32 See Grags pa rgyal mtshan, *Gsung,* 7: *yi ges shes pa'i chos ma yin pas bsam mno la shin tu 'bad par bya'o.*

33 See Cha rgan, *Cha,* 9a: *rdo rje tshig rkang rjed thor yi ger btab.*

34 Cha rgan, *Lam,* 84a–b: *nges spun gyi lo bco rgyad kyi bar du 'bad rtsol mang du byas kyang lan gsum spros pa bcod du 'gro dgos pa byung/ kho yis tha snyad la 'bungs nga yis sgom la 'bungs pas lam 'bras 'phral bla ma'ang khong la mnyes ste/ phyi rdo rje tshig rkang gi stengs nas go ba'i yul ma mnyam pas/ khong gis kyang nga bla mar bzung/ chos 'di la sgom nyams kyi spros pa nang nas ma chod na/ tshig tha snyad kyi mdud pa phyi nas grol ba mi srid pas/ nyan 'jur ba dang sgom la 'bungs ba gnad du che ba yin/ [yas la bla ma'i thugs rje zhugs/ yi dam gyi byin gyis rlabs/ ngas kyang bdag pas gzhan gces par byas pa'i rten 'brel 'dzoms pas/ da nga bas nyid mi zhan pas/] spros pa chod la lo bco rgyad kyi bar du gdam pa ming kyang ma smos par sgrubs [84b] pa 'bungs cig/ de nas yi ge bri 'ang khyed rang chos kyi bdag po yin no// chos zab mo 'di rabs 'chad par 'dug pa la bdag po khyed la 'phrod pas nga'i bsam pa rdzogs so// gsang sngags gsang bas 'grub/ nyams rtogs sbas pa'i rnal 'byor gyis kyang dgos pa yin te/.*

35 See Sa skya Paṇḍita, *Rten,* 238: *glegs bam tsam la brten pa yi/ lam 'bras pa yis 'di ma shes.* Here Sa skya Paṇḍita is specifically concerned with the esoteric significance of dependently arisen connections *(rten 'brel).* The impossibility of comprehending the *Rdo rje tshig rkang* without the esoteric instructions of a teacher is also emphasized by Grags pa rgyal mtshan, who is quoted in Bar ston, *Bar,* 3a–3b.o

36 Cf. Davidson (1991), 218, who seems offended by what he terms the "pugnaciously secretive" tradition of the Lam 'bras.

37 See part two, 118–19. According to Cha rgan, *Lam,* 36b, 'Brog mi sent this letter while Dkon mchog rgyal po was still living at his first hermitage in the Bra bo valley before founding Sa skya monastery in 1073. The surviving text of the *Hevajra tantra* is often referred to as the *Brtag pa gnyis pa (The Second Fascicle),* indicating that it is the second fascicle *(brtag pa)* of the huge original root tantra, most of which has been lost.

38 See Cha rgan, *Lam,* 47b–48a.

39 See Kun dga' grol mchog, *Khrid brgya'i brgyud,* 333–35.

40 See the *Sa skya Lam 'bras Literature Series* (Dehra Dun: Sa skya Centre, 1983).

41 See Stearns (1997) for a translation of the sections in 'Jam dbyang mkhyen brtse'i dbang phyug, *Gdams,* which describe Sa chen's quest for the Lam 'bras. The dates for Sa chen's studies with Zhang ston are taken from Mang thos klu sgrub, *Bstan,* 129–30. 'Jam mgon A mes zhabs, *Gsung ngag rin po che lam,* 567–68, follows Klu sgrub.

42 The dates of Sa chen's vision and the first teaching of the Lam 'bras are found in Mang thos klu sgrub, *Bstan,* 130.

43 See Grags pa rgyal mtshan, *Gsung,* 3.

44 See Gung ru ba, *Lam,* 119.3. For information on Gung ru ba, see Jackson (1989), 13–16.

45 See Grags pa rgyal mtshan, *Gsung,* 3: *rje bla mas mdzad pa bcu gcig tsam zhig snang ba.* Rdo rje rgyal mtshan, *Man,* 240, notes that Grags pa rgyal mtshan chose not to use a definitive phrase *(nges gzhung gi tshig).*

46 Also see 'Jam mgon A mes zhabs, *Yongs,* 187, who dismisses various accounts of different masters rumored to have had the reading transmission of all eleven commentaries, or even more.

47 See Rdo rje rgyal mtshan, *Man.* The modern publishers of this anonymous text have indicated in the marginal notation that it is the work of Mang thos klu sgrub *(klu sgrub gsung).* However, the list of the eleven commentaries given in this text differs from that given by Mang thos klu sgrub in another work of undoubted authorship. See Mang thos klu sgrub, *Bstan,* 131. It is also known that Mus srad pa wrote four "clarifications" *(gsal byed),* the second of which was entitled *Man ngag gsal byed.* See Mang thos klu sgrub, *Bstan,* 223. This title matches the title of the anonymous work. Not only that, several of the surviving manuscripts of the eleven commentaries are books that actually belonged to Mus srad pa. Finally, the only other writer to give the same list for Sa chen's eleven

works is another author of the Rdzong tradition, Nyi lde ba Nam mkha' dpal bzang. See Nam mkha' dpal bzang, *Untitled*, 295. For a short but extremely informative sketch of Mus srad pa's life, see Mang thos klu sgrub, *Bstan*, 222–25.

48 These eleven texts were only available in manuscript form until the twentieth-century Sde dge edition collected and prepared for publication by Bla ma 'Jam dbyangs rgyal mtshan (1870–1940), the uncle of the late Sde gzhung Rin po che, Kun dga' bstan pa'i nyi ma. See Sde gzhung Rin po che, *Rje*, 36. The most detailed discussions of these commentaries as a group, and the problem of identification, are found in Rdo rje rgyal mtshan, *Man*, and 'Jam mgon A mes zhabs, *Yongs*, 185–87. See also Gung ru ba, *Lam*, 119.2–3. The *Don bsdus ma* (*A seng ma*) is found in vol. 11 of the *Sa skya Lam 'bras Literature Series* (Dehra Dun: Sa skya Centre, 1983), 189–91, as is the *Gnyags ma*, 21–128. The *Sras don ma* is found in vol. 12 of the *Sa skya Lam 'bras Literature Series*, 11–446. The remaining eight commentaries are found in vols. 27–29 of the *Sa skya Lam 'bras Literature Series.* In the Sde dge edition informative colophons to most of these eight were composed by the editor, Bla ma 'Jam dbyangs rgyal mtshan.

49 The three surviving manuscripts that belonged to Mus srad pa are of the *'A 'u ma*, the *Zhu byas ma*, and the *Jo gdan ldan bu ma*. Each of these has a final annotation saying, "Rtsang Rdo rje rgyal mtshan's book" *(rtsang rdo rje rgyal mtshan gyi dpe'o).* These three commentaries are found in a three-volume collection of *dbu med* manuscripts of eight of Sa chen's commentaries. All three volumes, with the titles *Sa skya pa'i lam 'bras rnam 'grel skor*, were purchased from the Sa skya Centre in Rajpur, but have no date or place of publication. In the Sde dge collection only the *Jo gdan ldan bu ma* has a notation stating that the original was "Rtsang Rdo rje rgyal mtshan's book." See the *Sa skya Lam 'bras Literature Series* (Dehra Dun: Sa skya Centre, 1983), 29: 497.

50 For example, see 'Jam dbyangs mkhyen brtse'i dbang phyug, *Gdams*, 128, and 'Jam mgon A mes zhabs, *Yongs*, 187.

51 The information about Bla ma Blo dga' was related to me by H. H. Sa skya Trizin in Vancouver, Canada, on August 1, 2000. The secret autobiography of Rdzong gsar Mkhyen brtse Rin po che records the dream of Sa chen bestowing the blessing of the eleven commentaries, and another of Ngag dbang legs pa Rin po che (1864–1941) urging Rdzong gsar Mkhyen brtse to revive the reading transmission of the eleven commentaries. See 'Jam dbyangs chos kyi blo gros, *Khyab*, 24, 253.

52 See Sa chen Kun dga' snying po, *Thams*, and Gung ru ba, *Lam*, 119.3.

53 See 'Jam dbyangs mkhyen brtse'i dbang phyug, *Gdams,* 128.

54 See Nam mkha' dpal bzang, *Untitled,* 295.

55 See Rdo rje rgyal mtshan, *Man,* 240. 'Jam dbyangs mkhyen brtse'i dbang phyug, *Gdams,* 127, also notes the existence of both a larger and smaller work.

56 Gung ru ba, *Lam,* 122.4, refers to Spru lung pa's commentary and says he was 'Phags pa's disciple. The spellings Sru lung pa and Spro lung pa are also found. Go rams pa's commentary is available. See Go rams Bsod nams seng ge, *Gsung.*

57 See Zhang G.yu grags pa Brtson 'grus grags pa, *Dpal,* 378, 391–92, and Roerich (1976), 556.

58 See 'Jam mgon A mes zhabs, *Yongs,* 186–87.

59 See part two, 154–55.

60 See 'Jam mgon A mes zhabs, *Yongs,* 187.

61 See Rdo rje rgyal mtshan, *Man,* 237.

62 See Tāranātha, *Jo,* 243–44, and 250.

63 For example, see 'Jam mgon A mes zhabs, *Yongs,* 188, and Mang thos klu sgrub, *Bstan,* 131. Gung ru ba Shes rab bzang po, *Lam,* 119.2, does not mention the *Bande ma* at all, but lists an untitled commentary written for Stod sgom Byang chub shes rab. Gung ru ba otherwise agrees with the list of the Rdzong tradition. 'Jam dbyangs mkhyen brtse'i dbang phyug, *Gdams,* 128, does not mention the *Bande ma* at all.

64 See Roerich (1976), 557, 561, 1024–25, etc.

65 See Sa skya Paṇḍita, *Bla,* 656–57. 'Jam mgon A mes zhabs, *Yongs,* 186, seems to say that Zla ba rgyal mtshan first received the vows himself from Sa chen, and then transmitted them to Rje btsun Grags pa.

66 See Rdo rje rgyal mtshan, *Man,* 237.

67 See Sa skya Paṇḍita, *Lam,* 310. Sindhu presumably refers to the large district in west India also known as Sindh.

68 See Rdo rje rgyal mtshan, *Man,* 237, and Nam mkha' dpal bzang, *Untitled,* 295. Gung ru ba Shes rab bzang po, *Lam,* 119.2; Mang thos klu sgrub, *Bstan,* 131; 'Jam dbyangs mkhyen brtse'i dbang phyug, *Gdams,* 127–8; and 'Jam mgon A mes zhabs, *Yongs,* 186, do not mention the *Ldan bu ma* among the eleven commentaries or among the others written by Sa chen's disciples.

69 See 'Jam dbyangs mkhyen brtse'i dbang phyug, *Gdams,* 127.

70 See 'Jam mgon A mes zhabs, *'Dzam,* 50 and 62, and Mang thos klu sgrub, *Bstan,* 131.

71 See 'Jam mgon A mes zhabs, *Yongs,* 186.

72 See 'Jam dbyangs mkhyen brtse'i dbang phyug, *Gdams,* 127, and 'Jam mgon A mes zhabs, *Yongs,* 186.

73 See 'Jam dbyangs mkhyen brtse'i dbang phyug, *Gdams,* 127–8.

74 See Rdo rje rgyal mtshan, *Man,* 239, and Gung ru ba, *Lam,* 119.3.

75 See the *Sa skya Lam 'bras Literature Series* (Dehra Dun: Sa skya Centre, 1983), 29: 1. The manuscript of the *Yum don ma* is found in vol. 1 of the *Sa skya pa'i lam 'bras rnam 'grel skor,* n.d.n.p.

76 See Mang thos klu sgrub, *Bstan,* 131.

77 See Rdo rje rgyal mtshan, *Man,* 239, and 'Jam dbyangs mkhyen brtse'i dbang phyug, *Gdams,* 127.

78 See the *Sa skya Lam 'bras Literature Series* (Dehra Dun: Sa skya Centre, 1983), 27: 394.

79 See Mang thos klu sgrub, *Bstan,* 131, and 'Jam dbyangs mkhyen brtse'i dbang phyug, *Gdams,* 130–31. Bla ma dam pa, *Bla,* 67–68, also tells several stories about Zhu byas, as does Bar ston, *Bar,* 21a.

80 See Rdo rje rgyal mtshan, *Man,* 238.

81 See the *Sa skya Lam 'bras Literature Series* (Dehra Dun: Sa skya Centre, 1983), 27: 187. Also see Rdo rje rgyal mtshan, *Man,* 238, who uses this verse to verify Bsod nams rtse mo's involvement in the recording of the commentary.

82 See Rdo rje rgyal mtshan, *Man,* 238, and Gung ru ba, *Lam,* 119.2.

83 See Mang thos klu sgrub, *Bstan,* 131. Also see note 222 in part two for more information about Gnyan Phul byung ba.

84 See Gung ru ba, *Bstan,* 119.2.

85 See Rdo rje rgyal mtshan, *Man,* 238.

86 For example, see Sa chen Kun dga' snying po, *Lam,* 445.

87 See 'Jam dbyangs mkhyen brtse'i dbang phyug, *Gdams,* 128.

88 See 'Jam mgon A mes zhabs, *Yongs,* 186.

89 See Rdo rje rgyal mtshan, *Man,* 238.

90 See 'Jam dbyangs mkhyen brtse'i dbang phyug, *Gdams,* 128.

91 Jo mo Mang chung ma, another of Sa chen's female disciples for whom he is said to have written a commentary, also had a similar experience, but as a yak. See 'Jam dbyangs mkhyen brtse'i dbang phyug, *Gdams,* 133–34. For some explanation of a similar meditative experience of rebirth in the hell realms by the Lam 'bras master Ko brag pa Bsod nams rgyal mtshan (1170–1249), see Stearns (2000), 23 n. 24.

92 See Rdo rje rgyal mtshan, *Man,* 238. The unavailable *Mang chung ma* will be mentioned again below.

93 Gung ru ba, *Lam,* 119.2, gives the name Dbang phyug dpal.

94 See Grags pa rgyal mtshan, *Gsung,* 3.

95 'Jam mgon A mes zhabs, *'Dzam,* 74, states that Grags pa rgyal mtshan was the author of the annotations in the *Gnyags ma.*

96 See Grags pa rgyal mtshan, *Gsung,* 3, and the *Pod ser* itself in the *Sa skya Lam 'bras Literature Series* (Dehra Dun: Sa skya Centre, 1983), 11: 128–91. Some authors, such as Bdag chen Blo gros rgyal mtshan and Mang thos klu sgrub, said that there were twenty-two clarifying texts *(gsal byed).* These masters did not include the *A seng ma* among the group. For example, see Mang thos klu sgrub, *Gsung ngag slob bshad khog,* 165–66. Also see Rdo rje rgyal mtshan, *Man,* 240–41, for an identification of the nine points in the *Gnyags ma* and which texts in the *Pod ser* are meant to clarify each point. Rdo rje rgyal mtshan, *Lam,* 301–2, also states that twenty-three texts are for the clarification of the *Gnyags ma.*

97 Spru lung pa's work is noted in Gung ru ba, *Lam,* 122.4. See Rdo rje rgyal mtshan, *Lam,* 306, and Ngag dbang blo bzang rgya mtsho, *Zab,* 461, for mention of the *Gzhung bshad gsal byed bar ston zin bris,* which has survived. See Bar ston Rdo rje rgyal mtshan, *Bar.* The work by Ngag dbang chos grags is mentioned in his biography. See Bsod nams rgyal mtshan, *Dpal,* 357: *rdo rje'i tshig 'grel gnyag ma'i dgongs gsal.*

98 See part two, 154–55.

99 Also see Dmar ston, *Gzhung,* 4.

100 See 'Jam mgon A mes zhabs, *Yongs,* 187.

101 See Gung ru ba, *Lam,* 119.2.

102 See Mang thos klu sgrub, *Bstan,* 131, and 'Jam dbyangs mkhyen brtse'i dbang phyug, *Gdams,* 127–28.

103 See also 'Jam mgon A mes zhabs, *Yongs,* 185–86.

104 I have used the spellings found in 'Jam dbyangs mkhyen brtse'i dbang phyug, *Gdams,* 128, who also gives more information about Jo mo Mang chung ma on 133–34. Mang thos klu sgrub, *Bstan,* 131, refers to the two disciples as Zangs ri phug pa and Jo mo Mang chung ma of Mang mkhar, as does 'Jam mgon A mes zhabs, *Yongs,* 186.

105 Rdo rje rgyal mtshan, *Man,* 238–39, also records two further lists of Sa chen's eleven works, which he rejects as mistaken. Gung ru ba, *Lam,* 119.3, also mentions some of the same mistakes by other authors.

106 See 'Jam dbyangs mkhyen brtse'i dbang phyug, *Gdams,* 127, and 'Jam mgon A mes zhabs, *Yongs,* 188, who is apparently following Mkhyen brtse's explanation.

107 See Rdo rje rgyal mtshan, *Man,* 239.

108 See Mang thos klu sgrub, *Bstan,* 131, and 'Jam mgon A mes zhabs, *Yongs,* 188, who follows Mang thos klu sgrub in his discussion.

109 According to Mang thos klu sgrub, *Gsung ngag slob bshad khog,* 163, Zhang zed Mar pa also put together a volume *(glegs bam)* of texts using the *Gnyags ma* as the basic work, and supplementing it with other small writings. But Gung ru ba, *Lam,* 123.2, says this collection was compiled by Zhu brag Dmar pa and gives extra information about it, as well as quoting from it on 126.1–2. Also see Gung ru ba, *Lam,* 119.3.

110 See Mang thos klu sgrub, *Bstan,* 131.

111 See 'Jam mgon A mes zhabs, *Yongs,* 188.

112 I am grateful to Dan Martin, E. Gene Smith, David Jackson, and Jan-Ulrich Sobisch for copies of Phag mo gru pa's unpublished writings on the Lam 'bras. All references given below are from the 1507 manuscript edition of Phag mo gru pa's writings prepared by the 'Bri gung master Kun dga' rin chen (1475–1527). This identification of Kun dga' rin chen was made by Dan Martin.

113 See Bde chen rdo rje, *'Gro,* 403, who says that Phag mo gru pa was twenty-seven years old shortly before he traveled to Sa skya. See Kun dga' bzang po, *Lam,* 118.2, and 'Jam dbyangs mkhyen brtse'i dbang phyug, *Gdams,* 152, who both state that Phag mo gru pa remained at Sa skya for twelve years. The relationship between Sa chen and Phag mo gru pa has previously received some attention in Broido (1987), whose misinterpretations were largely corrected in Jackson (1990a).

114 See Kun dga' bzang po, *Lam,* 118.1–2.

115 See Padma dkar po, *Bka',* 461, and *Chos,* 403.

116 See Bsod nams dbang po, *Dpal,* 30a: *khrid yig gcig kyang khong gi don du gsungs/ de yi ming la gzhung bshad phag gru la/ zer ba ding sang mkhas blun yongs la grags/.* I am grateful to Jan-Ulrich Sobisch for a copy of this manuscript.

117 See Bsod nams dbang po, *Dpal,* 30a–b.

118 See Sangs rgyas phun tshogs, *Dam,* 305.

119 See Ngag dbang rnam rgyal, *Brgyud,* 609. I am grateful to David Jackson for this reference. The original passage is quite difficult and may allow other interpretation.

120 See Bsod nams dpal, *Bde,* 149–50. According to Sprul sku Gsang sngags Rin po che, Seattle, March 16, 2000, the term *skye tshang* is an archaic form of *ke'u tshang,* "cave." The published text actually contains the reading *rtas skye tshang,* but another manuscript of the same biography does not have the superfluous *rtas,* and I have translated accordingly.

121 See Dpa' bo Gtsug lag phreng ba, *Chos,* 2: 1165. I am grateful to David Jackson for this reference.

122 See Padma dkar po, *Bka',* 462, and Tāranātha, *Stag,* 573.

123 See Phag mo gru pa, *Lam 'bras gzhung,* 155b: *Dpal phag mo gru bas mdzad pa'i lam 'bras dpe mdzod ma.*

124 See Phag mo gru pa, *Lam 'bras bu,* Grags pa rgyal mtshan, *Gsung,* 4, and Sa chen Kun dga' snying po, *Byung.*

125 See Phag mo gru pa, *Lam 'bras bu,* 194a: *rje sa skya pa'i zhal gdams zab mo btsun pa rdo rje gyal pos bris pa'o.*

126 See Phag mo gru pa, *Lam 'bras kyi 'phrin* and *Lam 'bras kyi yan.*

127 See Grags pa rgyal mtshan, *Phrin,* 292.

128 See Grags pa rgyal mtshan, *Gsung,* 6–7, and the *Pod ser* itself in the *Sa skya Lam 'bras Literature Series* (Dehra Dun: Sa skya Centre, 1983), vol. 11.

129 See 'Jam mgon A mes zhabs, *Yongs,* 193–94.

130 See Grags pa rgyal mtshan, *Gsung,* 6–7.

131 See Gung ru ba Shes rab bzang po, *Lam,* 120.1 and 3; 'Jam dbyangs mkhyen

brtse'i dbang phyug, *Byung,* 211; and Mang thos klu sgrub, *Gsung ngag slob bshad khog,* 163.

132 See Gung ru ba Shes rab bzang po, *Lam,* 120.1 and 3; 'Jam dbyangs mkhyen brtse'i dbang phyug, *Byung,* 211; and Mang thos klu sgrub, *Gsung ngag slob bshad khog,* 163.

133 See Mang thos klu sgrub, *Gsung ngag slob bshad khog,* 163.

134 See Grags pa rgyal mtshan, *Gsung,* 8.

135 See 'Jam dbyangs mkhyen brtse'i dbang phyug, *Byung,* 211. The vajra signifies impenetrability, and the jewel is a wish-fulfilling gem. The term *gsung ngag,* "Oral Instructions," is a special honorific form of the term *gdams ngag* specifically used to refer to the Lam 'bras.

136 See Mang thos klu sgrub, *Gsung ngag slob bshad khog,* 164.

137 See Sa chen Kun dga' snying po, *Thams* and *Rten.*

138 See Grags pa rgyal mtshan, *Kun* and *'Khor.*

139 See Grags pa rgyal mtshan, *Kun,* 194 and *'Khor,* 242.

140 See Grags pa rgyal mtshan, *Gsung,* 5.

141 See Grags pa rgyal mtshan, *Gsung,* 4 and *Sa skya Lam 'bras Literature Series* (Dehra Dun: Sa skya Centre, 1983), 11: 128–91.

142 See Grags pa rgyal mtshan, *Kun,* 194 and *'Khor,* 242.

143 See Grags pa rgyal mtshan, *Gsung,* 4–5 and *Sa skya Lam 'bras Literature Series* (Dehra Dun: Sa skya Centre, 1983), 11: 260–92.

144 See Grags pa rgyal mtshan, *Gsung,* 5.

145 See Grags pa rgyal mtshan, *Gsung,* 5 and *Sa skya Lam 'bras Literature Series* (Dehra Dun: Sa skya Centre, 1983), 11: 292–300.

146 See Grags pa rgyal mtshan, *Gsung,* 5–6 and *Sa skya Lam 'bras Literature Series* (Dehra Dun: Sa skya Centre, 1983), 11: 300–344.

147 See *Sa skya Lam 'bras Literature Series* (Dehra Dun: Sa skya Centre, 1983), 11: 344–45.

148 See note 30 in part two for some discussion of the Lam skor brgyad (Eight Cycles of the Path).

149 See *Sa skya Lam 'bras Literature Series* (Dehra Dun: Sa skya Centre, 1983), 11: 481–581.

150 See Grags pa rgyal mtshan, *Bla ma brgyud pa rgya.* The Tibetan term *lo rgyus* has usually been translated in this book as "story." The more usual translations of this term are "history," "chronicle," "account," and so forth. However, the word *lo rgyus* was also used simply to mean "story" or "tale."

151 See *Sa skya Lam 'bras Literature Series* (Dehra Dun: Sa skya Centre, 1983), 11: 593–94.

152 See Grags pa rgyal mtshan, *Bla ma brgyud pa bod.*

153 See Mang thos klu sgrub, *Gsung ngag slob bshad khog,* 163.

154 See Tāranātha, *Stag,* 571.

155 For a brief discussion of Sa skya Paṇḍita's Lam 'bras works, see Gung ru ba, *Lam,* 120.4–121.1. For a list of his writings later received by the Fifth Tā la'i bla ma, see Jackson (1987), 2: 526–27.

156 See Mang thos klu sgrub, *Gsung ngag slob bshad khog,* 164.

157 See Tāranātha, *Stag,* 571.

158 The Five Supreme Masters of Sa skya *(Sa skya gong ma lnga)* were Sa chen, Grags pa rgyal mtshan, Bsod nams rtse mo, Sa skya Paṇḍita, and Chos rgyal 'Phags pa.

159 The *Pod nag* of Bla ma dam pa is contained in vol. 16 of the *Sa skya Lam 'bras Literature Series* (Dehra Dun: Sa skya Centre, 1983). The *Man ngag gter mdzod,* a commentary on the *Rdo rje tshig rkang,* was composed in 1342. The *Ngo mtshar snang ba,* a history of the Lam 'bras, was written in 1344. The *Sbas don kun gsal,* an instruction manual for the *snang gsum* and *rgyud gsum* practices of the Lam 'bras was recorded in 1347. See Bla ma dam pa, *Lam 'bras bu dang bcas pa'i gdams,* 423; *Bla,* 121; and *Lam 'bras bu dang bcas pa'i gzhung,* 543. Since all this information is provided by Bla ma dam pa himself, his biographer Lo chen Byang chub rtse mo (1302–80) must have been mistaken in mentioning that the *Gzhung bshad, 'Khrid,* etc., were composed in 1344. See Byang chub rtse mo, *Chos,* 19b.

160 See Mang thos klu sgrub, *Gsung ngag slob bshad khog,* 163.

161 For example, most of Grags pa rgyal mtshan, *Kun,* and Sa skya Paṇḍita, *Rten,* are incorporated into Bla ma dam pa's work.

162 Annotations to the *Man ngag gter mdzod* were written by Bla ma Dam pa's main disciple, Chos rje Dpal ldan tshul khrims (1333–99), but do not seem to have survived. A brief work dealing only with specific difficult

points in the *Rdo rje tshig rkang* was later composed by Paṇ chen Shākya mchog ldan (1428–1507). See Shākya mchog ldan, *Rdo.*

163 See Bla ma dam pa, *Lam 'bras bu dang bcas pa'i gzhung.* According to the Lam 'bras teachings, all phenomena are mental appearances *(sems kyi snang ba).* The "three appearances" *(snang gsum)* are the impure appearances *(ma dag pa'i snang ba)* of ordinary living beings, the experiential appearances *(snyams kyi snang ba)* that arise for a yogin, and the pure appearances *(dag pa'i snang ba)* experienced by a buddha. The "three continuums" *(rgyud gsum)* are the cause continuum of the universal ground *(kun gzhi rgyu rgyud),* the method continuum of the body *(lus thabs rgyud),* and the result continuum of Mahāmudrā *(phyag rgya chen po 'bras bu rgyud).*

164 See Tāranātha, *Stag,* 572.

165 See Bla ma dam pa, *Bla.*

166 This feature of Bla ma dam pa's work is discussed in 'Jam dbyangs mkhyen brtse'i dbang phyug, *Gdams,* 6, where it is contrasted with the work of Ngor chen.

167 See 'Jam mgon A mes zhabs, *Yongs,* 311. Mus srad pa's text on the identification of Sa chen's eleven commentaries has been drawn upon in the discussion above. He is also known to have composed at Sa skya a text on the removal of impediments *(gegs sel)* in 1476 and a work on the Hevajra system of practice in 1483. See Ngag dbang blo bzang rgya mtsho, *Zab,* 465. Mus srad pa transmitted the Lam 'bras teachings to Bdag chen Rgya gar Shes rab rgyal mtshan (1436–94). Several of Mus srad pa's personal manuscripts *(phyag dpe)* of the commentaries by Sa chen have survived and been recently published.

168 See Grags pa rgyal mtshan, *Gsung,* 6, and also Kun dga' dbang phyug, *Zab,* 2, who refers to Grags pa rgyal mtshan's statement.

169 See 'Jam dbyangs mkhyen brtse'i dbang phyug, *Byung,* 214. Although this text has the spelling *Po ti dmar chung,* and others also have just *Pod dmar ma,* or *Pod dmar,* I am following the spelling found in the original catalogue to the collection. The *Pusti dmar chung,* according to the list of texts in the catalogue, is found in the *Sa skya Lam 'bras Literature Series* (Dehra Dun: Sa skya Centre, 1983), 13: 5–446.

170 See Gung ru ba, *Lam,* 125.1.

171 See Kun dga' dbang phyug, *Zab.*

172 See Gung ru ba, *Lam,* 125.1, and Mang thos klu sgrub, *Gsung ngag slob bshad khog,* 163–64.

173 See the collection itself, 5–410; Kun dga' dbang phyug, *Zab,* 3–5; the comments in 'Jam dbyangs mkhyen brtse'i dbang phyug, *Byung,* 214; and Mang thos klu sgrub, *Gsung ngag slob bshad khog,* 171–73.

174 See *Sa skya Lam 'bras Literature Series* (Dehra Dun: Sa skya Centre, 1983), 13: 410–46; Kun dga' dbang phyug, *Zab,* 5; the comments in 'Jam dbyangs mkhyen brtse'i dbang phyug, *Byung,* 214; and Mang thos klu sgrub, *Gsung ngag slob bshad khog,* 173.

175 See See *Sa skya Lam 'bras Literature Series* (Dehra Dun: Sa skya Centre, 1983), 13: 446–69.

176 See Grags pa rgyal mtshan, *Gsung,* 6, and Rdo rje rgyal mtshan, *Lam,* 301–2, who, in his catalogue to the *Glegs bam phra mo,* refers to Grags pa rgyal mtshan's statement.

177 See Rdo rje rgyal mtshan, *Lam.* The Fifth Tā la'i bla ma later received the transmission of the *Glegs bam phra mo,* and in his record of the teachings he received he reproduces much of Mus srad pa's work, with some interesting additions. See Ngag dbang blo bzang rgya mtsho, *Zab,* 454–64. For another catalogue of the Rdzong lineage, see Nam mkha' dpal bzang, *Untitled.*

178 See Tshar chen Blo gsal rgya mtsho, *Khams,* 74ff. The Bdag chen traveled in secret to avoid possible obstacles from some prejudiced and sectarian people.

179 See Tshar chen Blo gsal rgya mtsho, *Khams,* 79.

180 See Ngag dbang blo bzang rgya mtsho, *Gsung,* 552.

181 See 'Jam mgon A mes zhabs, *Yongs,* 294, who notes that open reference to the Slob bshad was first made by Bdag chen Blo gros rgyal mtshan.

182 The texts by Bdag chen Blo gros rgyal mtshan and Kun spangs Rdo ring pa are found in the *Sa skya Lam 'bras Literature Series* (Dehra Dun: Sa skya Centre, 1983), 18: 1–113.

183 See Grags pa rgyal mtshan, *Gsung,* 7: *yi ge med pa'i snyan brgyud kyi man ngag mang du thos shing gzhan la bsnyan pa dang ma bstan pa mang du yod.* Also see Ngag dbang blo bzang rgya mtsho, *Zab,* 451, who repeats this quote within a longer passage, but with considerable variants from that found in the *Pod ser.*

184 See Sa skya Paṇḍita, *Rten,* 238: *glegs bam tsam la brten pa yi/ lam 'bras pa yis 'di ma shes.*

185 For example, see Ngag dbang blo bzang rgya mtsho, *Zab,* 451–52.

186 See Ngag dbang blo bzang rgya mtsho, *Rigs,* 466–78.

187 See Tshar chen Blo gsal rgya mtsho, *Dpal ldan,* 236–37.

188 See Tshar chen Blo gsal rgya mtsho, *Dpal kye.*

189 See Mang thos klu sgrub, *Rang,* 420–21.

190 See Mang thos klu sgrub, *Rang,* 421. Tibetans consider the fat to be the choicest part of a piece of meat, and so Tshar chen is saying that Mang thos klu sgrub is the best of his disciples. Also see Ngag dbang blo bzang rgya mtsho, *Rigs,* 586, who describes the same events.

191 The instruction manual on the *snang gsum* was composed in 1587; the explanation of the *'khor 'das dbyer med* was written in 1588; and the remaining works were finally recorded in 1589. See Mang thos klu sgrub, *Gsung ngag slob bshad snang,* 151; *'Khor,* 240; and *Skyon,* 403. In his autobiography, Mang thos klu sgrub also mentions beginning the composition of these instruction manuals in 1587. See Mang thos klu sgrub, *Rang,* 547.

192 See Ngag dbang blo bzang rgya mtsho, *Rigs,* 596.

193 See 'Jam dbyangs mkhyen brtse'i dbang phyug, *Bla,* 178. Curiously enough, Ngag dbang blo bzang rgya mtsho, *Rigs,* 602–3, gives the date 1557 for these teachings. The set of texts composed by Mkhyen brtse'i dbang phyug is found in the *Sa skya Lam 'bras Literature Series* (Dehra Dun: Sa skya Centre, 1983), vol. 14.

194 See Mang thos klu sgrub, *'Khor.*

195 See 'Jam dbyangs mkhyen brtse'i dbang phyug, *Gdams.*

196 See 'Jam mgon A mes zhabs, *Yongs.*

197 This apparently was the case from soon after the death of Mkhyen brtse'i dbang phyug. The master Dbang phyug rab brtan (1559–1636) stated that for the final sections of the teaching Mkhyen brtse'i dbang phyug's work should be supplemented with the *Sbas don kun gsal* of Bla ma dam pa and the instructions on the dream yoga, intermediate state *(bar do),* and so forth, from the manuals of Mang thos klu sgrub. See Tshe dbang lhun grub rab brtan, *Gsung,* 146–47. This is still the practice today when the Lam 'bras Slob bshad is taught.

198 See Ngag dbang blo bzang rgya mtsho, *Gsung,* and *Za,* 1: 303–4.

199 See Ngag dbang blo bzang rgya mtsho, *Gsung.*

200 In addition to Mang thos klu sgrub's own texts, see especially the work recorded by his disciple Bsod nams rin chen, which is found in 'Jam mgon

A mes zhabs, *Gsung ngag rin po che slob bshad.* Another important defense by a disciple of Klu sgrub is Anonymous, *Gsung.*

201 See Tshar chen Blo gsal rgya mtsho, *Dpal,* 229–30.

202 See Mang thos klu sgrub, *Bum,* 312–13. For the original source of the quotations given by Klu sgrub, see Sa skya Paṇḍita, *Brda,* 211.

203 This statement is found in a record of Mang thos klu sgrub's teachings written down by his disciple Bsod nams rin chen and proofread by Klu sgrub himself. See 'Jam mgon A mes zhabs, *Gsung ngag rin po che slob bshad,* 12b: *sgyu lus kyi khrid 'di gong ma'i gsung na yod pa ma mthong yang/ bdag gi yongs 'dzin gong mas gsal bar gzigs pa'am don gyis thob pa gang rung du nges so.* I am grateful to Mkhan po A pad Rin po che and Guru Lama for a copy of this rare text.

204 See Ngag dbang blo bzang rgya mtsho, *Zab,* 451–53.

205 For example, see Ngag dbang blo bzang rgya mtsho, *Zab,* 452–53, who quotes a verse from Dkon mchog lhun grub's *Rgyud gsum mdzes rgyan* that clearly makes this point: *dam pa'i drin las chos 'di'i zab pa'i gnad/ mang po'i don la kho bo blo gsal yang/ thun mong ngag tu brjod rung 'ga' zhig tsam/ 'chad par 'gyur gyis mkha' 'gros skabs phye zhig.*

206 For example, see 'Jam dbyangs mkhyen brtse'i dbang phyug, *Gdams,* 31.

207 Unless the verse in praise of the master called Sprin gyi shugs ldan that was composed by Vajrāsanapāda is considered to refer to Gayadhara. This question will be discussed below.

208 The five translators were 'Brog mi Shākya ye shes, 'Gos Khug pa lhas btsas, Pu rang Lo chung Gzhon nu shes rab, Gyi jo Zla ba'i 'od zer, and Gnyos 'Byung po, whose personal name was Yon tan grags. Also see 'Jam mgon A mes zhabs, *Gsung ngag rin po che lam,* 564.

209 For example, Mang thos klu sgrub, *Bstan,* 94, quotes the *Gze ma ra mgo* by a certain Rngog: "Gayadhara's golden Dharmas came from jumbled quotations of the *Mātaraḥ tantra.*" This Rngog is also known as Rngog Lba ba can, whose personal name was Nyi ma seng ge, and who was apparently a disciple of 'Gos Lo tsā ba. According to the title cited in Lokesh Chandra, *Materials for a History of Tibetan Literature* (New Delhi, 1963), no. 12442, Rngog's text was a refutation of the Hevajra and Lam 'bras teachings. I am grateful to Dan Martin for this reference. In Dudjom (1991), 1: 930, the same quote is also attributed to 'Gos Lo tsā ba Khug pa lhas btsas, where it is specifically interpreted as a refutation of the Lam 'bras. This quotation has not been located in 'Gos Lo tsā ba, *'Gos,* the text in which it is supposedly found.

210 See Mang thos klu sgrub, *Bstan,* 81–83, 92–94.

211 See Grags pa rgyal mtshan, *Bla ma brgyud pa rgya,* 593. The two historical sketches related to the Zha ma and 'Brom traditions have almost the same exact information and wording as in Grags pa rgyal mtshan's text. See Anonymous, *Bhir,* 392–93, and Ko brag pa, *Lam,* 435.

212 For example, see Shastri (1931). A hundred years after Gayadhara came to Tibet there was another member of the *kāyastha* caste named Surapāla who was a tantric master. His disciple Vairocanavajra then came to Tibet and became the teacher of Zhang G.yu brag pa (1123–93). See Roerich (1976), 844.

213 See Bla ma dam pa Bsod nams rgyal mtshan, *Lam,* 379.

214 For a striking description of the practice of *grong 'jug* by Pha dam pa, see Edou (1996), 33–34.

215 'Jam mgon A mes zhabs, *Gsung,* 566–67, states that Cha rgan is considered to represent the Zha ma *bsres brgyud* tradition, which combined teachings from both the Sa skya and the Zha ma lineages. The significance of the Zha ma versions of events in the lives of the early teachers of the Lam 'bras will be discussed below. For some information on Cha rgan, see van der Kuijp (1994a).

216 The three syllables *sa ta si* are appended to Gayadhara's name in the original text. The meaning is obscure, and they have not been included in the translation. The king's name is spelled Ru pa tsaṇḍa akṣe. 'Jam dbyangs mkhyen brtse'i dbang phyug, *Gdams,* 31, when basically summarizing the information from Cha rgan, gives the king's name as Tsaṇḍa ru pa a kṣi. Mkhyen brtse also specifies that Gayadhara was born in Bhaṃ ga la. It has not been possible to identify this king with any known ruler in the Bengal region.

217 See Cha rgan, *Cha,* 12a–b. The two syllables *sa si* are appended to Gayadhara's name in the original text. The meaning is obscure, and they have not been included in the translation. 'Jam dbyangs mkhyen brtse'i dbang phyug, *Gdams,* 31 and 49–50, incorporates the essential points from Cha rgan, and Ngag dbang blo bzang rgya mtsho, *Rigs,* 413, later took his information from Mkhyen brtse.

218 See Kun dga' bzang po, *Lam,* 111.1–2. 'Jam mgon A mes zhabs, *Gsung ngag rin po che lam,* 587, mentions that Gayadhara's personal name was Ratnaśrī.

219 See Dpa' bo Gtsug lag phreng ba, *Chos,* 1: 512. See also the cover of Snellgrove (1987), vol. 2. Gayadhara is always depicted wearing a white robe, in

spite of the fact that many of his nicknames indicate that he wore a red robe during his first visit to Tibet.

220 See Padma dkar po, *Chos,* 221. On 212 Padma dkar po further identifies Gayadhara's son Ti pu as Nāropa's disciple who was otherwise known as Ham bu Spyi thod. Also see Karma chags med, *Ri,* 73, who identifies the Indian teacher Śraddhākaravarman as the father of Ti pu pa, but says Śraddhākaravarman later went by the name Gayadhara. This problem will be discussed in detail below. See also Nālandā Translation Committee, (1982), 176; Chang, (1962), 2: 397–401; and Lhalungpa (1977), 91–92.

221 See Dpa' bo Gtsug lag phreng ba, *Chos,* 1: 512. No other accounts mention either of these famous masters as teachers of Gayadhara. Perhaps the Avadhūti in the Lam 'bras tradition, whose secret name was Mi mnyam rdo rje, was identified by Dpa' bo with the more well known Maitrīpa, who was also known as Avadhūti, and whose secret name was Gnyis med rdo rje.

222 See Grags pa rgyal mtshan, *Slob dpon nag,* 457, and *Nag,* 461. See also Bu ston Rin chen grub, *Bla,* 68–69. The Lam skor dgu (Nine Cycles of the Path) are listed and briefly discussed in note 30 in part two.

223 See Kun dga' grol mchog, *Zab,* 418–19.

224 See Dpa' bo Gtsug lag phreng ba, *Chos,* 1: 512.

225 See Grags pa rgyal mtshan, *Bla ma brgyud pa bod,* 595–97, and Dmar ston's history in part two, 90–97.

226 See Cha rgan, *Lam,* 22b–23a. The same story, with even more detail, is found in 'Jam dbyangs mkhyen brtse'i dbang phyug, *Gdams,* 43–44, and 'Jam mgon A mes zhabs, *Yongs,* 129–130. Both these masters accepted it as authentic, but it is refuted in the original annotations to Dmar ston's history in part two, 90–91, and it is not found in Bla ma dam pa, *Bla.*

227 Pu rang Lo chung Gzhon nu shes rab was a teacher of both Sa chen Kun dga' snying po and an ancestor of Dmar ston who was also known as Dmar Chos kyi rgyal mtshan. See Grags pa rgyal mtshan, *Dpal,* 26, and Glo bo mkhan chen, *Bla,* 2a. According to Mang thos klu sgrub, *Bstan,* 93, the Zha ma tradition says that during the first of Gayadhara's four trips to Tibet he was invited by the translator Gzhon nu shes rab. The tale of Pu rang Lo chung's miraculous disappearance is recorded in all the Cakrasaṃvara and Vajrayoginī histories, beginning with Bu ston, *Bde,* 108–11. According to this source, Pu rang Lo chung spent many years in Nepal, and received tantric transmissions from teachers such as the Indian master *rājaputra*

Bhīmadeva (*rgyal po'i sras* 'Jig med lha), and the Newar masters Hang du dkar po and Bhadanta. He then accompanied Bhadanta, who was also known as Sumatikīrti, to Tibet as his translator. Later he went into an isolated retreat to meditate on Khecarī (Mkha' spyod ma), and took his disciple Dmar Chos kyi rgyal mtshan with him to impart the esoteric instructions between sessions of meditation. They made a pathway up to the top of a cliff, where a cave was dug out for Pu rang Lo chung. Below that another was dug for Bla ma Dmar, and below that a cave for a kitchen and a place for an attendant to sleep. The opening to Pu rang Lo chung's cave was sealed with mud except for a small hole to pass food through. One day the master told Bla ma Dmar that some people would be coming to see him in the morning and should be admitted. At sunrise a paṇḍita and eight women appeared. They sat in a row outside the sealed entrance to Pu rang Lo chung's cave, having a steady conversation in the Indian language. Bla ma Dmar crept up to see what was happening, but Pu rang Lo chung noticed and sent him away. Then the conversation stopped for a moment, and Bla ma Dmar could not contain his curiosity. When he went to look he saw that the nine visitors were no longer outside the sealed cave. Peeking through the small hole in the sealed entrance, he saw the visitors sitting inside the cave, with the paṇḍita at the head of the row and Pu rang Lo chung now at the end. The paṇḍita passed some golden syllables glowing with light from hand to hand down the row to Pu rang Lo chung. When he swallowed them, his body became a mass of light and the cave was also filled with light. Bla ma Dmar's hair stood on end and he began to weep. He experienced an exceptional state of authentic meditative concentration at that instant, but ran back to his own cave, afraid that he would be discovered. After a moment he heard the sound of the master's hand cymbals, and went to look. The nine visitors were sitting outside the cave as before and the hole in the entrance was untouched. After they left, Bla ma Dmar confessed to his master that he had witnessed the scene. Pu rang Lo chung prophesied that Bla ma Dmar would in the future directly behold the face of Cakrasaṃvara. That night Pu rang Lo chung ascended to Vajrayoginī's paradise of Khecara. When Bla ma Dmar went to check on him the next morning there was no reply. He looked through the small opening and saw only the master's few garments and Sanskrit manuscripts scattered on the yak-hair mat. According to tradition, the man dressed like a paṇḍita was really Cakrasaṃvara, and the eight women were the eight goddesses who guard the directions in his maṇḍala. The golden syllables he had passed to Pu rang Lo chung were the root mantra of Cakrasaṃvara. In the Sa skya tradition this event is still referred to as a prime example of the result to come from Vajrayoginī practice.

228 See Cha rgan, *Lam,* 23b–24b. 'Jam dbyangs mkhyen brtse'i dbang phyug, *Gdams,* 43–46, has used Cha rgan's version, with some deletions and expansions, as has 'Jam mgon A mes zhabs, *Yongs,* 129–130.

229 See 'Jam dbyangs mkhyen brtse'i dbang phyug, *Gdams,* 46; 'Jam mgon A mes zhabs, *Gsung ngag rin po che lam,* 564; and Mang thos klu sgrub, *Bstan,* 93.

230 For some information on this master, see Ruegg (1984), 376. Also see Vitali (1996), 238 n. 336. But it should be noted that Prajñāgupta is actually the correct form of this master's name, not Guhyaprajñā or Prajñāguhya, as it has been rendered in modern scholarly works. This is clear in the colophons to Prajñāgupta's works in the Tibetan canon.

231 For example, see Grags pa rgyal mtshan, *Slob dpon indra,* 479, and *Dpal,* 20–21. The Lam skor dgu are discussed in more detail in note 30 in part two.

232 See 'Jam dbyangs mkhyen brtse'i dbang phyug, *Gdams,* 46.

233 The late Sde gzhung Rin po che first mentioned to me years ago that there was information about Gayadhara in this work, although I did not locate it until recently.

234 In this context it is of special interest that a work translated by Prajñāśrīgupta and Lo chen Rin chen bzang po has been preserved in the Peking edition of the Tibetan Tripitaka, 62: 146.2–147.4. This text is entitled *Dad pa smra ba shes bya ba'i bstod pa.*

235 See Karma Chags med, *Ri,* 73 and 75. Actually, by the time of Gayadhara's last visit to Tibet 'Brog mi had already passed away.

236 See Cha rgan, *Lam,* 24b–25b.

237 See Mang thos klu sgrub, *Bstan,* 93.

238 See 'Jam dbyangs mkhyen brtse'i dbang phyug, *Gdams,* 50.

239 See 'Jam mgon A mes zhabs, *Gsung ngag rin po che lam,* 564, and Mang thos klu sgrub, *Bstan,* 93.

240 See Dmar ston's text in part two, 93–97.

241 See Mang thos klu sgrub, *Bstan,* 93–94. A work by Ā tsār ya Sprin gyi shugs can entitled *Nag po chen po'i srog tig ye shes kyi spyan,* which the author translated with Lo tsā ba Mgos, has survived. It is found in vol. 4, 99–101, of the *Bya rog ma bstan srung bcas kyi chos skor* (Palampur: Sungrab Nyamso Gyunphel Parkhang, 1973). Several works translated by Sprin gyi shugs can and 'Gos Lo tsā ba are also preserved in the Tibetan canon.

242 See Kun dga' bzang po, *Lam,* 111.2. Vajrāsana's verse is quoted as: *Rgyal rigs rig pa'i gnas lnga mkhas/ nam mkha'i lha la the tshom gcod/ sprin gyi shugs can zhes bya ba'i/ bla ma de la phyag 'tshal lo/.* The original verse is found in Vajrāsanapāda, *Grub,* 239.3–4. 'Gos Lo tsā ba Gzhon nu dpal (1392–1481) also identified the teacher Sprin gyi shugs can as the prince of Koṅ ka ṇa. See Roerich (1976), 360. In his history of the Lam 'bras, 'Jam dbyangs mkhyen brtse'i dbang phyug, *Gdams,* 48–49, accepts the identification of Gayadhara as Prince Sprin gyi shugs can during this visit, and also quotes the same verse from Vajrāsana's text.

243 See 'Jam mgon A mes zhabs, *Dpal gsang,* 116–17.

244 See 'Jam mgon A mes zhabs, *Gsung ngag rin po che lam,* 564.

245 For example, see Mang thos klu sgrub, *Bstan,* 93, who states that this was the opinion in the Zha ma tradition; 'Jam mgon A mes zhabs, *Gsung ngag rin po che lam,* 564; and Karma chags med, *Ri,* 75, although the latter mistakenly states that 'Brog mi was Gayadhara's disciple during this visit.

246 See Kun dga' bzang po, *Lam,* 114.1. Also see note 60 in part two.

247 Mang thos klu sgrub, *Bstan,* 94, says that Gayadhara died in the *chu mo lug* year of 1103, when Sa chen Kun dga' snying po was eleven years old.

248 The "globe of light transference" *('od kyi gong bu'i 'pho ba)* is one of the transference techniques associated with the practice of the Vase Initiation *(bum dbang)* in the Lam 'bras. See Dmar ston Chos kyi rgyal po, *Gzhung,* 60–61.

249 See Dmar ston's text in part two, 96–97. This episode in the *Zhib mo rdo rje* is based on Grags pa rgyal mtshan, *Bla ma brgyud pa bod,* 597. Cha rgan, *Lam,* 30b, states that the figure of Heruka, by which is meant Hevajra, was clearly visible in the globe of light.

250 The dates for Se ston are from Mang thos klu sgrub, *Bstan,* 89. Roerich (1976), 215, provides information which would indicate the dates 1029–1116.

251 See 'Jam dbyangs mkhyen brtse'i dbang phyug, *Gdams,* 154, and 'Jam mgon A mes zhabs, *Yongs,* 174 and 187. The earliest surviving systematic list of all these different lineages is by the Jo nang master Kun dga' grol mchog (1507–66). See Kun dga' grol mchog, *Untitled.* Also see Mang thos klu sgrub, *Bstan,* 132–33; Tāranātha, *Stag,* 570–71; and 'Jam mgon A mes zhabs, *Yongs,* 173–76. There are significant differences in the lists of these authors.

252 This woman may be identical to the Ceylonese yoginī mentioned above who was also one of Gayadhara's teachers. A number of tantric works translated by 'Brog mi and Candramālā are found in the Tibetan canon.

253 Ratnaśrīmitra may be another of Gayadhara's names, since 'Jam mgon A mes zhabs, *Gsung ngag rin po che lam,* 587, gives Gayadhara's personal name as Ratnaśrī.

254 Although it is certain that 'Brog mi studied with Prajñāgupta (Shes rab gsang ba), the uncertainty about translation work with him comes from a curious colophon to the *Sarvabuddhāsamayogatantra* found in the *Rnying ma rgyud 'bum* collection. This colophon states that the text was translated in the Nepal Valley (Bal yul) by the Indian paṇḍita Gu hya gsang ba and the Tibetan lo tsā ba 'Brog mi 'bral gyi ye shes. Both names have obviously been garbled. *Guhya* is one of the Sanskrit equivalents for the Tibetan *gsang ba.* Other editions, which I have not examined, apparently have Sangs rgyas gsang ba, the Tibetan for Buddhaguhya. See Kaneko (1982), 255. However, the mistake in 'Brog mi's name seems quite certain. There were, to my knowledge, no other Tibetan translators named 'Brog mi, and whose personal names ended with *ye shes.* Buddhaguhya, however, was active long before 'Brog mi's birth.

255 'Brog mi's teacher Amoghavajra studied with both Vāgīśvarakīrti and Devākaracandra. See Grags pa rgyal mtshan, *Slob dpon ngag,* 406. There may have been several Indian masters known as Amoghavajra. It is unlikely that 'Brog mi's teacher is to be identified with the Amoghavajra who was an important early master of the Vajrabhairava and Yamāntaka practices, and whose own teachers were Lalītavajra and Jetāri. It is also unlikely that the Amoghavajra of the Vajrabhairava lineage is the same as the Amoghavajra who later came to Tibet in the twelfth century and was a teacher of Ras byung pa. Also see Tshe dbang nor bu, *Mar,* 696–97. The Amoghavajra who traveled to Tibet was also responsible for spreading the *Amṛitasiddhi* cycle of practices that go back to a Virūpa who is *not* the same as the Virūpa of the Lam 'bras tradition.

256 See especially Rdo rje rgyal mtshan, *Gnas.*

257 See Rdo rje rgyal mtshan, *Gnas,* 297 and 299. Mang thos klu sgrub, *Bstan,* 83, also dates Gayadhara and 'Brog mi's translations of the *Kye rdor rgyud gsum (The Tantra Trilogy of Hevajra)* and other texts to the *chu mo lug* year of 1043, when 'Brog mi was fifty-one years old.

258 For Vīravajra's statement see Cha rgan, *Lam,* 15a–15b: *gsang sngags kyi rten 'brel sgrig pa la longs spyod dgos.* Gayadhara's instructions are also found in Cha rgan, *Lam,* 27b. On 70a, 'Brog mi specifically states that he had

only demanded gold to test the sincerity of disciples and stress the value of the teachings.

259 I have already discussed the eccentric or "crazy" behavior of certain Buddhist tantric adepts at some length elsewhere. See Stearns (1980), especially 150–73.

260 See for instance the famous story of Mar pa ordering Mi la ras pa to build a tower for him, and subjecting him to other ordeals as described in Lhalungpa (1977), 48–71.

261 See Mang thos klu sgrub, *Bstan,* 83.

262 See Cha rgan, *Lam,* 27b.

263 See Dmar ston's text in part two, 98–101. Mang thos klu sgrub, *Bstan,* 83, says that 'Brog mi died at the age of eighty-five, which corresponds to the year 1077. But Cha rgan, *Lam,* 70b, says that 'Brog mi was sixty-nine when he passed away, and 'Jam dbyangs mkhyen brtse'i dbang phyug, *Gdams,* 65, mentions accounts which state that he died at the age of eighty-two or even ninty-five. Tshe dbang nor bu, *Mar,* 701, says that 'Brog mi died in the *me stag* year of 1066.

264 See Cha rgan, *Lam,* 70b–71b.

265 See Kun dga' grol mchog, *Untitled,* and Mang thos klu sgrub, *Bstan,* 132–33, both of whom list a transmission through 'Brog mi's sons. Also see part two, 120–21. There the story is told of Se ston receiving the last portions of the *Rdo rje tshig rkang* from Indra, which clearly indicates that Indra had received the Lam 'bras from his father.

266 See Dmar ston's text in part two, 114–17, and Kun dga' bzang po, *Lam,* 114.4. Cha rgan, *Lam,* 53b, simply states that although 'Brom wrote explanatory texts concerning the Lam 'bras, his tradition did not spread. The anonymous *Bhir ba pa'i lo rgyus,* 403–4, also traces a lineage from 'Brom which contains many of the same names as the list in Ngor chen's text. 'Jam dbyangs mkhyen brtse'i dbang phyug, *Gdams,* 82, also says the *Zhib mo rdo rje* is wrong about this because the lineage from 'Brom lasted for six or seven generations. However, as usual, Bla ma dam pa, *Bla,* 32, agrees with Dmar ston's *Zhib mo rdo rje.*

267 See Cha rgan, *Lam,* 49b–51b, and 'Jam dbyangs mkhyen brtse'i dbang phyug, *Gdams,* 79–80.

268 Se mkhar chung ba is merely a pseudonym for Se ston Kun rig. Cf. van der Kuijp (1994), 192 n. 39.

269 See Cha rgan, *Lam,* 54a.

270 Dates for Ma gcig and her brother are given in Roerich (1976), 220 and 226–29.

271 For example, see Kun dga' grol mchog, *Untitled,* and Mang thos klu sgrub, *Bstan,* 133.

272 See part two, 126–29.

273 See Cha rgan, *Lam,* 79b–80a

274 See Stag tshang Lo tsā ba Shes rab rin chen, *Dpal,* 10b. I am grateful to Jeffrey Schoening for a copy of this rare manuscript.

275 See 'Jam mgon A mes zhabs, *'Dzam,* 21–22.

276 See Stearns (1997) for a translation of the sections in 'Jam dbyang mkhyen brtse'i dbang phyug, *Gdams,* which describe Sa chen's quest for the Lam 'bras. The dates for Sa chen's studies with Zhang ston are taken from Mang thos klu sgrub, *Bstan,* 129–30.

277 Cha rgan, *Lam,* 77 and 78b, states that the Zhang ston brothers learned the Rdzogs chen teachings of the *Bram ze'i skor* and the *Rtsa mun ti* from their grandfather, and were experts in their practice. The *Bram ze'i skor (The Cycle of the Brahmin)* is a group of Rnying ma tantras of the Atiyoga class which were introduced into Tibet by Padmasambhava and Vimalamitra. The brahmin *(bram ze)* referred to is apparently Bram ze Bde mchog snying po, who received the lineage from Dga' rab rdo rje and passed it to Śrīsiṃha. The *Bram ze'i skor* comprises nos. 112–28 in Kaneko (1982), 127–49. The *Rdzogs chen rtsa mun ti (The Great Perfection of Rtsa mun ti)* is unidentified.

278 See part two, 142–43.

279 The dates are found in Mang thos klu sgrub, *Bstan,* 130.

280 Dmar ston refers the reader to the primary source on Grags pa rgyal mtshan's life, the biography written by his nephew and disciple Sa skya Paṇḍita. See Sa skya Paṇḍita, *Bla.*

281 See Kun dga' grol mchog, *Untitled;* Mang thos klu sgrub, *Bstan,* 133; Tāranātha, *Stag,* 570–71; and 'Jam mgon A mes zhabs, *Yongs,* 173–76. Phag mo gru pa is sometimes referred to by the name Mtha' rtsa ba in these sources.

282 See Jackson (1987), 1: 16–18, for information on early biographies by Sa skya Paṇḍita's personal disciples. He gives a list of lost biographies by disciples,

one of which is by Dmar ston Chos kyi rgyal po. This can now be identified as the section concerning Sa skya Paṇḍita in the *Zhib mo rdo rje*. This identification is made even more certain when it is noticed that the list of independent biographies of Sa skya Paṇḍita given in the *Mdo smad chos 'byung* does not include a work by Dmar ston, which would be expected if his had been a separate biography. See Dkon mchog bstan pa rab rgyas, *Yul,* 10.

283 But see the excellent comments about Sa skya Paṇḍita's tantric studies and practice in Jackson (1994), 85–90.

284 See Tāranātha, *Rdo,* 754.

285 See Bar ston, *Bar,* 17b–18a.

286 See Glo bo mkhan chen, *Grub,* 6b.

287 See Glo bo mkhan chen, *Grub,* 6b.

288 See Rin chen ldan, *Rin,* 76–78, for a fascinating description of Yang dgon pa's studies and relationship with Sa skya Paṇḍita. They first met when Sa skya Paṇḍita was returning from a visit to Gung thang, and later at Sa skya itself. Yang dgon pa received many extraordinary tantric teachings from Sa skya Paṇḍita on both occasions, including some of the rarest instructions of the Lam 'bras. Sa skya Paṇḍita was extremely impressed with him, and expressed the hope that his nephew 'Phags pa would turn out as well! For information about how some of Sa skya Paṇḍita's Lam 'bras instructions later entered into the Sa skya tradition via Yang dgon pa's writings, see Stearns (2000), 25 n. 36.

289 For more about Ko brag pa and a translation of his spiritual songs, see Stearns (2000).

290 For information on Cha rgan, see especially Kun dga' bzang po, *Lam,* 117.1–2, and 'Jam dbyangs mkhyen brtse'i dbang phyug, *Gdams,* 153. For some information about Cha rgan's surviving commentary on the *Rdo rje tshig rkang,* see van der Kuijp (1994), 197–98.

291 The most information on these two Jo nang systems is found in Kun dga' bzang po, *Lam,* 117.2–118.1. Also see 'Jam dbyangs mkhyen brste'i dbang phyug, *Gdams,* 153–54. Tāranātha, *Stag,* 576, makes it clear that in addition to the early fundamental works of the *Pod ser,* the works of Bla ma dam pa Bsod nams rgyal mtshan were specifically valued for the practice of the Lam 'bras in the Jo nang tradition.

292 For information on Mang lam Zhig po and his system see Kun dga' bzang po, *Lam,* 116.4–117.1, and 'Jam mgon A mes zhabs, *Gsung ngag rin po che*

lam, 585. For Lce sgom, see Kun dga' bzang po, *Lam,* 118.1, and 'Jam dbyangs mkhyen brtse'i dbang phyug, *Gdams,* 152. For a detailed examination of Lce sgom and his literary output, see Sørensen (1999).

293 Both Mang thos klu sgrub, *Bstan,* 149, and 'Jam mgon A mes zhabs, *Gsung ngag rin po che lam,* 570, state that Dmar ston and Lho pa Rin chen dpal were the two who upheld the lineage of esoteric instructions *(man ngag brgyud 'dzin)* passed down by Sa skya Paṇḍita.

294 See Glo bo mkhan chen, *Bla.* Glo bo mkhan chen also wrote short biographies of Grub chen Yon tan dpal, who was perhaps the foremost meditator among Sa skya Paṇḍita's disciples, and Yon tan dpal's disciple La ru ba Bsod nams seng ge. See Glo bo mkhan chen, *Grub.* Glo bo mkhan chen's texts were never published in Tibet.

295 'Jam mgon A mes zhabs, *Dpal sa,* 136, mentions the early death of Dmar ston's father. Bu ston, *Bde,* 112.5, states Dmar ston was sixteen years old when he went to Sa skya. Also see Glo bo mkhan chen, *Bla,* 2b, and 'Jam mgon A mes zhabs, *Dpal sa,* 137.

296 The assistant teacher *(zur chos pa)* Nub pa Rig 'dzin grags was an important disciple of Grags pa rgyal mtshan. A short text by him recording Grags pa rgyal mtshan's teachings on the *Zhen pa bzhi bral* has survived. See Nub pa Rigs 'dzin grags, *Nub.* According to Go rams Bsod nams seng ge, *Bde,* 56.2, Nub pa Rig 'dzin grags wrote a commentary to simplify Gnyan Gtsug tor rgyal po's commentary on the *Cakrasaṃvara mūla tantra,* and also a commentary on the meditation practice of Cakrasaṃvara according to the system of Lūhipa.

297 The Five Divisions of the *Yogacaryābhūmi (Sa sde)* of Ārya Asaṅga are: (1) *Yogacaryābhūmi, Śrāvakabhūmi,* and *Bodhisattvabhūmi,* (2) *Yogacaryābhūmi viniścayasaṃgraha,* (3) *Yogacaryābhūmi vastusaṃgraha,* and *Yogacaryābhūmi vinayasaṃgraha,* (4) *Yogacaryābhūmi paryāyasaṃgraha,* and (5) *Yogacaryābhūmi vivaraṇasaṃgraha.*

298 An edition of Sa skya Paṇḍita's auto-commentary to the *Tshad ma rigs gter* was also proofread and corrected by Dmar ston. See Mkhan po A pad, *Dkar,* 34. Dmar ston also corrected and rewrote Lho pa kun mkhyen Rin chen dpal's commentary on Sa skya Paṇḍita's famous *Legs par bshad pa rin po che'i gter.* See Dmar ston, *Legs.*

299 See Glo bo mkhan chen, *Bla,* 2b.

300 See Glo bo mkhan chen, *Bla,* 2b.

301 See part two, 168–69.

302 Bu ston, *Bde,* 112, states that Dmar ston studied under Grags pa rgyal mtshan and Rig 'dzin grags pa for three years, and with Sa skya Paṇḍita for three years. But Mang thos Klu grub rgya mtsho, *Bstan,* 150, says that he studied with Sa skya Paṇḍita for eight years. An annotation in the published edition of Dmar ston, *Gzhung,* 295, also mentions eight years as the time he studied with Sa skya Paṇḍita. The original manuscript this edition was copied from apparently belonged to Brag phug pa Bsod nams dpal (1277–1346), and the annotations seem to be arranged in a manner indicating they were not added after the writing of the manuscript. This is uncertain, however, because the text was recopied by hand for the published edition. The annotation in question is not present in another old manuscript in my own collection.

303 See Dmar ston, *Gegs sel glengs,* 129.

304 See Glo bo mkhan chen, *Bla,* 3a

305 'Jam mgon A mes zhabs, *Yongs,* 194, identifies this man as Sgang ston Sher 'bum, also known as Gye re Sgang ston and as Snar thang Sgang ston. The main transmission of all of Dmar ston's Lam 'bras texts seems to have gone through him to Dkar po brag pa Rin chen seng ge, who is said to have lived to the age of 105. The same basic information is also found in 'Jam dbyangs mkhyen brtse'i dbang phyug, *Gdams,* 142. Dkar po brag pa's verse autobiography is found in the *Sa skya Lam 'bras Literature Series,* 1: 345–362. He passed the transmission of Dmar ston's Lam 'bras works to Dpal ldan tshul khrims, and the transmission line was then unbroken at least to the time of 'Jam mgon A mes zhabs.

306 Because of the family name Dmar, and the unambiguous term used for "son" *(sras)* in several instances in Dmar ston's biography, it seems that Shākya dbang phyug was Dmar ston's actual son, and not just a "spiritual son" *(thugs sras).*

307 See Glo bo mkhan chen, *Bla,* 3b–4a.

308 The Dmar Shākya grub found after Dmar Dharmarāja in the transmission line of the Mahācakra initiation is perhaps to be identified with Dmar Shākya dbang phyug. See Bu ston, *Bla,* 17. Bu ston received at least eleven texts written by Dmar ston concerning the Mahācakra cycle. See Bu ston, *Bla,* 18. Two of these works have survived with some recent editorial modifications and are still used today for the transmission of the initiations and practice of Vajrapāṇi Mahācakra. See 'Jams dbyangs blo gter dbang po, *Phyag* and *Dpal.*

309 Dmar ston is known to have composed a commentary on the *Cakrasaṃvara*

tantra, an explication of the method for practice according to the great adept Lūhipa, and a collection of the life stories of the masters in the lineage, all of which seem to have been lost. See 'Jam mgon A mes zhabs, *Dpal sa,* 137.

310 This disciple can probably be identified as Cha rgan Dbang phyug rgyal mtshan, author of the Lam 'bras history which combines historical information from both the Sa skya and Zha ma traditions. Cha rgan is known to have received the Vajrapāṇi Mahācakra from Dmar ston. See Ngag dbang blo bzang rgya mtsho, *Zab,* 2: 288. Cha rgan is also known as Grub thob Dkar po. See 'Jam dbyangs mkhyen brtse'i dbang phyug, *Gdams,* 153, and Kun dga' bzang po, *Lam,* 117.1–2.

311 Rin chen 'bar was one of the four men who requested Dmar ston to compose the *Gzhung bshad dmar ma* commentary on the Lam 'bras. Only the final portion of his name, *'bar,* is given in the verses of the colophon, but an annotation in a manuscript of the text in my own collection adds *Rin chen.* The other three men were Grags pa rdo rje, Ye shes 'od zer, and 'Od zer grags pa. See Dmar ston, *Gzhung,* 294. From among them, Grags pa rdo rje is mentioned in the lineage of the Rnam 'joms dkar po, which passed through Dmar ston. See Bu ston, *Bla,* 22. Another text written by Dmar ston for the benefit of Glen sgom Rin chen 'bar is Dmar ston, *Lam bsdus.*

312 'Jam mgon A mes zhabs, *Yongs,* 194, lists five of Dmar ston's works transmitted without break down to him: (1) *Gzhung bshad dmar ma,* (2) *Chos 'byung zhib mo rdo rje,* (3) *Gegs sel bka' rgya ma,* (4) *Lam bsdus 'dod pa'i lcags kyu,* and (5) *Bla ma rin chen 'byung.* From among these works accepted by A mes zhabs, the Rdzong master Mus srad pa Rdo rje rgyal mtshan doubted Dmar ston's authorship of the *Gegs sel bka' rgya ma* and the *Bla ma rin chen 'byung.* He believed the *Gegs sel bka' rgya ma* to be the work of Sa chen. See Rdo rje rgyal mtshan, *Lam,* 303 and 306. Glo bo mkhan chen, *Bla,* 4a, mentions an extensive ritual work for initiation into the body-maṇḍala of Vajra Nairātmyā, which has apparently been lost. Jo nang Kun dga' grol mchog mentions that he received the explanatory reading transmission *(bshad lung)* for what seem to be all of Dmar ston's known works. See Kun dga' grol mchog, *Zhen,* 309. From among these works, Ngag dbang blo bzang rgya mtsho, *Zab,* 449, says Dmar ston only wrote *notes* to the *Lung sbyor,* but Dmar ston's authorship of this text was accepted by Kun dga' grol mchog. In the Slob bshad tradition, Dmar ston was also accepted as the author of this work. See Mang thos klu sgrub, *Gsung ngag slob bshad khog,* 172, and also 164, where it is mentioned that although Dmar ston wrote many texts they were never gathered together

into a separate volume *(glegs bam)*. With the exceptions of the *Gsung sgros ma* and the *Zhib mo rdo rje,* all of Dmar ston's surviving works on the Lam 'bras are found in the *Pusti dmar chung*. See the bibliography for a full list of Dmar ston's extant works.

313 See Dmar ston, *Gzhung*. An *dbu med* manuscript copy of this work, in 178 folios, with the title *Gzhung rdo rje'i tshig rkang gi 'grel pa 'jam mgon bla ma'i gsung sgros ma zhes dmar chos rgyal gsung,* is in my own collection. I am grateful to Mkhan po Bstan 'dzin of Khra rigs Monastery for the kind gift of this text. Van der Kuijp (1994), 194–195, notes the existence of another manuscript of the *Gsung sgros ma* in the library of the Cultural Palace of Nationalities, Beijing. His identification of a second manuscript as yet another copy is doubtful, since its title would seem to indicate a collection of small texts concerned with the practice of the Lam 'bras.

314 See Glo bo mkhan chen, *Bla,* 4b.

315 The transmission of the *Gsung sgros ma,* or *Gzhung bshad dmar ma,* continued for at least several centuries. It was received and taught by 'Jam dbyangs mkhyen brtse dbang phyug. See 'Jam dbyang mkhyen brtse'i dbang phyug, *Bla,* 217. Jo nang Tāranātha also taught the Lam 'bras using the *Gzhung bshad dmar ma* commentary, for which he gave the reading transmission in 1591. See Tāranātha, *Rgyal,* 165.

316 See Glo bo mkhan chen, *Bla,* 4a.

317 The date of Grags pa rgyal mtshan's death in 1216 is mentioned in the text itself. As noted above, Dmar ston requested a specific Lam 'bras related instruction from Sa skya Paṇḍita in 1222 while still in Sa skya. This means he had already received the Lam 'bras by this point, and the most reliable sources say that he studied with Sa skya Paṇḍita for eight years after Grags pa rgyal mtshan's death.

318 See Grags pa rgyal mtshan, *Bla ma brgyud pa bod.*

319 See the opening verses of Dmar ston's text in part two, 80–81: *'brog mi la swo dpal ldan bla ma'i/ bod kyi lo rgyus gsal bar mdzad zin mod/ 'on kyang chos rje'i gsung la rab dad nas/ ji bzhin bris pa 'di yang gus pas long//.*

320 This is not the case with Cha rgan's history, which incorporated information from the Zha ma tradition. The study by Ngor chen and Gung ru ba makes no attempt to tell the complete stories of the different teachers, and is not really in the same genre as the works of Grags pa rgyal mtshan, Dmar ston, Bla ma dam pa, 'Jam dbyang mkhyen brtse'i dbang phyug, and 'Jam mgon A mes zhabs.

321 'Jam mgon A mes zhabs, *Yongs,* 311–12, discusses his sources for research into the history of the Lam 'bras. He gives an interesting list of the works that he considered essential for his study. The *Bla ma rgya bod gyi lo rgyus* of Rje btsun chen po are listed first, followed by the *Zhib mo rdo rje* of Dmar, the *Zhib mo rnam dag* of Bar ston, the *Ngo mtshar snang ba* of Bla ma dam pa, a clarification of that work by Mus srad pa, the *Chos 'byung bstan pa rgyas pa'i nyi 'od* by Rje Ngor pa, and its supplement by Kun mkhyen Go ram pa. These seven works obviously follow the Sa skya tradition. But A mes zhabs also utilized other rare sources such as a *Lo rgyus chen mo* of the Zha ma tradition, the *Chos 'byung* of Dpang Rje, a *Chos 'byung* of the 'Brom tradition, the *Bla ma rgya bod kyi lo rgyus* of Cha rgan, and the *Chos 'byung khog phub zin bris* of Rje Klu sgrub rgya mtsho. A mes zhabs also mentions a number of other works. Some otherwise unknown histories of the Lam 'bras are also listed in Dkon mchog bstan pa rab rgyas, *Yul,* 3–15.

322 For example, see Eimer (1978) for comments concerning sources for the study of the life of the Indian master Atiśa, and unfavorable events preserved in some of the earliest biographies which are not found in later works.

323 In the early Sa skya tradition the respectful pseudonyms for the five great masters *(gong ma lnga)* were quite fixed. Kun dga' snying po is most frequently referred to as Sa chen, Sa skya pa chen po, or Brtse ba chen po. Bsod nams rtse mo is Slob dpon Rin po che. Grags pa rgyal mtshan is Rje btsun, Rje pa, or occasionally Sa skya pa chen po. Kun dga' rgyal mtshan is Sa skya Paṇḍita, Chos rje, Bla ma 'Jam pa'i dbyangs, or in the earliest sources, Lo tsā ba chen po. Blo gros rgyal mtshan is 'Phags pa, Chos kyi rgyal po, and 'Gro mgon.

324 See part two, 156–57.

325 The date of Sa skya Paṇḍita's death is mentioned in the annotations to Dmar ston's text in part two, 166–67.

326 See part two, 158–59. The Indian master Mātṛceṭa is known for his eulogies. Our text gives this verse as *kun mkhyen ma lags kun mkhyen khyod/ kun mkhyen khyod ko ji ltar rtogs.* The quote is from Mātṛceṭa's praise to Buddha Śākyamuni. See Mātṛceṭa, *Sangs,* 42.1, where the lines read *kun mkhyen ma lags gang gis kyang/ kun mkhyen khyod ko ji ltar rtogs.*

327 For example, see part two, 86–87, 166–67.

328 As will be discussed below, one of Tshogs sgom Rin po che's main disciples was named Gnyag Snying po rgyal mtshan. His disciple in turn was Bar

ston Rdo rje rgyal mtshan, who wrote summarizing notes to Sa chen's *Gnyags ma,* which have recently come to light embedded in a text by 'Jam mgon A mes zhabs. In this text Bar ston sometimes mentions his teacher Gnyag (14a), and frequently refers to a Rin po che pa or Rin po che (7b, 8a, 11a, 14a, and 16b), who is specifically identified in an annotation as Tshogs sgom pa (7b) and as belonging to the circle of Chos rje pa (7b). See Bar ston, *Bar.*

329 This fragment is transliterated in van der Kuijp (1994), 181.

330 See the incomplete text reproduced in van der Kuijp (1994), 181: *chos kyi rje nyid thugs kyi sras/ bla ma rin po che pa'i rnam thar kyang gong du gsung ba bzhin khong pa rang dang mnyam po zhig gis brjod par rigs pa la 'on kyang bsod nams 'phel bas cung zad brjod na/.*

331 See Anonymous, *Chos,* 338. Cf. Van der Kuijp (1994), 181.

332 See Dkon mchog bstan pa rab rgyas, *Yul,* 10. Van der Kuijp (1994), 177–78, provides a transliteration of a passage added to the end of a manuscript of Tshog sgom Rin po che's biography in the library of the Cultural Palace of Nationalities in Beijing that could conceivably concern the author of the work.

333 See Mang thos klu sgrub, *Bstan,* 182. The Fifth Tā la'i bla ma mentions a text on the Lam 'bras written by Gnyag Snying po rgyal mtshan according to the teachings of Bla ma Rin po che. He also gives the lineage of the Lam 'bras transmitted from Sa skya Paṇḍita to Tshogs sgom, by him to Gnyag Snying po rgyal mtshan, and by him to Bar ston Rdo rje rgyal mtshan. See Ngag dbang blo bzang rgya mtsho, *Zab,* vol. 1, 462 and 482. The same text by Gnyag Snying po rgyal mtshan is mentioned in the 1474 *(shing pho rta)* catalogue of Lam 'bras literature by Mus srad pa, which is the original source of the Fifth Tā la'i bla ma's information. See Rdo rje rgyal mtshan, *Lam,* 306, and also 308, where a text on the *Yi ge med pa* by Gnyag is mentioned.

334 See Glo bo mkhan chen, *Bla,* 4a.

335 For example, this may be seen in part two, 90–91. There an episode that can be identified as coming from the Zha ma tradition is mentioned and refuted in the annotations. This shows an awareness of the Zha ma version, but an attempt to maintain a strictly Sa skya line of interpretation. This episode, and many others, were later accepted in the eclectic works of 'Jam dbyangs mkhyen brtse'i dbang phyug and 'Jam mgon A mes zhabs. Also see note 43 in part two.

Notes to Part Two

1 Virūpa's instructions in the Lam 'bras are unique in presenting a fivefold scheme of dependently arisen connections *(rten 'brel).* These five are the outer, the inner, the secret, thatness *(de kho na nyid),* and the ultimate *(mthar thug).* These five dependently arisen connections must be brought into alignment for a sentient being to become a buddha. These are presented in great detail in the Lam 'bras and are a central theme of the whole system. For example, see Dmar ston, *Gzhung,* 166–70. It is of special interest to note that Sa skya Paṇḍita states that the profound esoteric significance of dependent origination, or dependently arisen connections, is not clearly explained anywhere except in the Lam 'bras. He also says that there was no talk of dependent origination, or dependently arisen connections, among serious meditators in Tibet until the Lam 'bras teachings spread. See Sa skya Paṇḍita, *Rten,* 238. He also mentions that Virūpa himself reached attainment by bringing all the dependently arisen connections into alignment. See Sa skya Paṇḍita, *Sdom,* 45.

2 "The Powerful Lord " (Mthu stobs dbang phyug) is a common pseudonym for Virūpa. These opening verses present several problems. How the five figures mentioned in the verses relate to the five dependently arisen connections is unclear. Perhaps the arhat Aṅgulimāla represents the outer dependently arisen connections, the bodhisattva Mañjuśrī represents the inner, the great adept Virūpa represents the secret, the buddha Vajradhara represents thatness, and the guru, who embodies all sources of refuge, represents the ultimate. I thank Jeffrey Schoening for this suggestion. On the other hand, Mkhan po A pad Rin po che suggested that Aṅgulimāla might be one of the names of Vajra Nairātmyā.

3 The earlier work referred to by Dmar ston is Rje btsun Grags pa rgyal mtshan's brief *Bla ma brgyud pa bod kyi lo rgyus,* the only text dealing with the lives of the early Tibetan masters written before Dmar ston's *Zhib mo rdo rje.* The epithet "Dharma Lord" (Chos rje) is used throughout Dmar ston's text to refer to Sa skya Paṇḍita.

4 Sørenson (1994), 276–77, gives Dri ma med pa rnam dag as the supplementary name for the Rgyang temple and, in note 842, mentions that the chronicle of Nel pa has the name Rnam dag sgrib med.

5 The names and locations of these four temples are spelled in many different ways. The temples were originally constructed in the sixth or seventh

century by King Srong btsan sgam po and his Chinese queen Kong jo as part of an elaborate geomantic scheme to bring the raw energy of the Tibetan landscape under control. The topography of Tibet was divined by Kong jo to be in the form of an enormous supine rākṣasī demoness who had to be pinned down and neutralized by the strategic placement of temples on parts of her body. Grom pa Rgyang was built to suppress her left hip, Gtsang 'phrang to suppress her right hip, Khram 'brug to suppress her left shoulder, and Ka tshal to suppress her right shoulder. As mentioned in our text, these four are usually referred to as the "Four Temples to Suppress the Horns." The term "horn" *(ru)* was used to designate ancient districts in Tibet. For a translation of a traditional Tibetan chronicle that describes these events see Sørensen (1994), 251–64, 275–77, and 561–77. Also see Aris (1980), 15–33. Bla ma dam pa, *Bla,* 13, has incorporated into his Lam 'bras history all this information concerning the construction of the four temples, except for that found in the annotation mentioning Padmasambhava. Bla ma dam pa's acceptance of the fact that the four temples were built for the purpose of "Suppressing the Horns" *(ru gnon)* is of special interest. They are identified as the four temples for "Taming the Border" *(mtha' 'dul)* in the *Rgyal rabs gsal ba'i me long,* which some sources doubt that Bla ma dam pa wrote. As pointed out by Sørensen (1994), 261 n. 770, the *mtha' 'dul* identification is certainly incorrect. This discrepancy between what is found in the uncontested Lam 'bras history by Bla ma dam pa, and in the questionable *Rgyal rabs,* is at least curious, and at most another reason to doubt his authorship of the latter work.

6 "Divine venerable" *(lha btsun)* is usually a term reserved for members of royalty who have taken ordination. However, in this case it should probably be understood to mean "prince," since it is clear that these brothers were not monks. Cha rgan, *Lam,* 10b, identifies the three brothers as Dpal lde, 'Od lde, and Skyid lde, who were the sons of Khri Bkra shis rtsegs pa dpal, the eldest son of Dpal 'khor btsan (869?–899?), who was in turn the son of prince 'Od srungs. These descendants of the ancient Tibetan royal line are discussed in detail in Sørenson (1994), 435–81. According to Mang thos klu sgrub, *Bstan,* 66, quoting Slob dpon Bsod nams rtse mo's *Chos la 'jug pa'i sgo,* Dpal 'khor btsan had already made the royal residence in Grom pa Lha rtse. His three grandsons, who are mentioned in our text, and their descendants are specifically treated in Sørensen (1994), 465ff. According to the Lam 'bras tradition, 'Brog mi Lo tsā ba later took a daughter of this royal family as his tantric consort. Mang thos klu sgrub, *Bstan,* 71, also states that Dpal lde and his descendants controled the Lha rtse region.

7 Lo ston Rdo rje dbang phyug was one of the seven men of Dbus and

Gtsang who took monastic vows in Khams and then returned to Central and Western Tibet to revive the transmission of the Vinaya there. He was originally from 'Gur mo rab kha, and built the temple of Rgyan gong after his return to Gtsang. See Sørenson (1994), 448–49 n. 1634. Cha rgan, *Lam,* 10b–11a, states that Lo ston sent seven *dge slong,* including Rgya Shākya gzhon nu, Se Ye shes brtson 'grus, and Nyang Rdo rje rgyal mtshan, as well as two *dge tshul* and one *dge gnyen* to Grom pa Rgyang. They gathered about 250 monks there. Bla ma dam pa, *Bla,* 13, says that the three princes asked both Lo ston and Tshong btsun for monks to be sent to Grom pa Rgyang. Tshong ge Shes rab seng ge was one of Lo ston's companions in seeking ordination in Khams. See Sørenson, 449 n. 1633. 'Jam dbyangs mkhyen brtse'i dbang phyug, *Gdams,* 50, refers to him as Lce btsun Shes rab seng ge, signifying that he was a member of the Lce clan of Zhwa lu, where the temple of Rgyan gong was located. Mang thos klu sgrub, *Bstan,* 82, follows the information in Cha rgan's text.

8 According to Mang thos klu sgrub, *Bstan,* 83, 'Brog mi was born in the *chu mo sbrul* year of 993. The Skye and the Ban were apparently divisions within the 'Brog mi clan.

9 Cha rgan, *Lam,* 10b–11a, relates that the abbot Rgya favored a third student named Leng, and sent him off with much gold and supplies to get a head start on Stag and 'Brog mi. The teacher Se took a special interest in Stag and 'Brog mi, and explaining the situation to the three princes of Lha rtse, gathered many offerings for them to make the trip. 'Jam dbyangs mkhyen brtse'i dbang phyug, *Gdams,* 51–52, follows Cha rgan's version, but with more detail. The apparent rivalry between Rgya and Se is not found in Dmar ston's or Bla ma dam pa's telling of the story, and probably comes from the Zha ma tradition.

10 These orders are found in all the chronicles of the Lam 'bras, beginning with Rje btsun Grags pa rgyal mtshan's *Bla ma brgyud pa bod,* 594–95. The Dharma Lord (Chos rje) is Sa skya Paṇḍita.

11 The term used here is *big pa rta,* which is spelled *bid pa ta* in manuscript N, 2a, and *big pa ta* in manuscript B1, 2a. Cha rgan, *Lam,* 12a, has *bhig pa ta,* and on 89a, speaks of it as a script *(yi ge big pa ta)* that was studied together with the Kashmiri language *(kha che'i skad)* by the group of young men sent to study in India by Lha bla ma Ye shes 'od. This is clearly a transliteration of an otherwise unknown Indian word. The context in both texts indicates that it was the term for a script currently in use in the Indian subcontinent. 'Jam dbyangs mkhyen brtse'i dbang phyug, *Gdams,* 52, just uses the common term *phal skad,* "vernacular, colloquial," when describing these events. The same cryptic term is also found in

Roerich (1976), 205 and 226, as *bi wa rta,* which has been translated as "*vivarta* script" and further glossed as *vartula.* Dudjom (1991), vol. 2, n. 892, does the same. *Vartula* is a rounded form of the *lañcana* script. Cha rgan, *Lam,* 12a, also mentions that while the funds were being raised for the trip to India, 'Brog mi went into retreat for seven months with one or two Indian mendicant *(a tsa ra)* beggars, and learned the vernacular from them. 'Jam dbyangs mkhyen brtse'i dbang phyug, *Gdams,* 52, says the retreat was for two months, after which no translator was necessary for the trip.

12 The pass known as "The Door of Brahmā" (Tshangs pa'i sgo) is unidentified.

13 Cha rgan, *Lam,* 12b, says that Stag and 'Brog mi each traveled with an attendant, and that one of the itinerant Indian yogins *(a tsa ra 'dzo ki)* also accompanied them. They made the trip to Skyid grong disguised as beggars, and stayed there a while to study and get used to the water. 'Jam dbyangs mkhyen brtse'i dbang phyug, *Gdams,* 52, mentions that they stayed in Mang yul for two months and met their fellow student Leng there, with whom they then continued on into Nepal.

14 The translation follows the reading *chu,* which is found in every other manuscript and version of this story, and not the reading *chung,* which is actually found in the reproduced text of the *Zhib mo rdo rje.*

15 According to Cha rgan, *Lam,* 12b, 'Brog mi and his companions traveled to Nepal disguised as traders. They went to Pham 'thing (modern Pharping), where they received initiation from Śāntabhadra, also called Bha ro Haṃ thung, Tsa haṃ, Mahākaruṇika (Thugs rje chen po), Bādan ta warma, and Ci ther ba. Nyang ral Nyi ma 'od zer (1136–1204), *Chos,* 473, refers to 'Brog mi's teacher Hang du dkar po Shan ta bha dra, and to Pham 'thing pa as a different teacher. 'Jam dbyangs mkhyen brtse'i dbang phyug, *Gdams,* 52, specifies that the Newar master Dzaḥ huṃ, or Śāntabhadra, was the elder of the four Pham 'thing brothers. These brothers were very important for the transmission of a number of tantras to Tibet, but there is considerable confusion about their identification. The earliest extended discussion of all four is Bu ston, *Bde,* 101–5, which was largely copied into later histories, such as the *Deb ther sngon po* translated by Roerich (1976), 380–81, and Thu'u bkwan Blo bzang chos kyi nyi ma, *Rje,* 31–33. None of these sources provide the name Śāntabhadra for any of the four brothers, and all give Dharmakīrti as the eldest brother's name. Mar pa Lo tsā ba also studied with two Newar brothers known as Spyi ther ba and Paiṇḍapa (i.e., Pham 'thing pa). See Nālandā Translation Committee (1982), 10–11, 107, etc. It is of particular interest that Nyang ral refers to Śāntabhadra as Hang du dkar po, and that Dmar ston calls him Haṃ thung, another varient of

the same name. A certain Hang du dkar po was the teacher of many of the Tibetan translators who went to Nepal during this period, but other sources identify him as the Newar paṇḍita Varendraruci. Roerich (1976), 394, says that the real name of Ha mu dkar po was Bsod nams 'byung gnas bzang po (Puṇyākarabhadra), and that his name as a scholar *(yon tan gyi ming)* was Varendraruci. In the biography of Chag Lo tsā ba Chos rje dpal (1197–1264), who was in Nepal almost two hundred years after 'Brog mi, the *hang du* are described as Newar tantric priests who attended to the image of Red Machendranāth during the annual chariot procession in the Nepal Valley. See Roerich (1959), 54–55. Although it seems clear from various sources that the *hang du,* also spelled *haṃ thung, ha ngu, ha mu,* and so forth, were a class of medieval Newar priests, the precise identification of the master (or masters?) known as Hang du dkar po remains uncertain. Whatever the case, during a year of instruction under this master 'Brog mi learned grammar, epistemology, writing, and astrology. He also studied the tantras of Guhyasamāja, Saṃvara, Hevajra, Mahāmaya, and Bhairava. By the end of this period he had received the title *Lo tsā ba,* "Translator." Leng had also become fluent in the vernacular, and could listen to teachings in Sanskrit. But Stag had learned nothing except how to read the Indian script.

16 Cha rgan, *Lam,* 12b–13a, gives the impression that initially Stag wanted to go to India alone, but 'Brog mi felt it would not be good to break up their original group. As a result they asked Śāntabhadra for advice on where to go in India, and to provide them with a guide. He advised them to first go to the Vajrāsana at Bodhgayā and pay their respects to the famous Mahābodhi image of the Buddha.

17 According to Cha rgan, *Lam,* 12b–14a, after telling them about the six great masters at Vikramaśīla, Śāntabhadra sent them off with his own younger brother, the mahāpaṇḍita Abhayakīrti (Paṇ chen 'Jigs med grags pa), as their guide. 'Jam dbyangs mkhyen brtse'i dbang phyug, *Gdams,* 53, says the same, but calls him Bal po A des pa, another name found in almost all sources. They first went to Bodhgayā, and then on to Vikramaśīla.

18 As later mentioned in our text, Stag was overcome with devotion to the shrines at Bodhgayā and stayed there performing circumambulations. This is also stated in Nyang ral Nyi ma 'od zer, *Chos,* 473. It is unclear what became of Leng from this time on. In any case, Cha rgan, *Lam,* 14a, specifies that 'Brog mi went to study with Śāntipa at Vikramaśīla.

19 Some texts state that the "six expert gate keepers" were at Nālandā. For example, see Mang thos klu sgrub, *Bstan,* 83. For a discussion of the lives of the six gate keepers see Tāranātha, as translated in Chimpa and

Chattopadhyaya (1990), 294–300. Śāntipa is the master with whom 'Brog mi's Newar teacher urged him to study. More details about 'Brog mi's studies with him are given below. See Chimpa and Chattopadhyaya (1990), 296–99, for the story of the gate-keeper Vāgīśvarakīrti, who was born in Vārāṇasī and was later active in Nepal. Although it is tempting to identify this master with the Vāgīśvarakīrti who received the teachings of the *Phyag rgya chen po yi ge med pa* directly from holy Tārā, this does not seem to be the case. 'Brog mi received the *Yi ge med pa* from Lord Amoghavajra, who had himself received it from Vāgīśvarakīrti and his disciple Devākaracandra. See Grags pa rgyal mtshan, *Slob dpon ngag,* 406. The youngest of the four Newar Pham 'thing brothers was also known as Vāgīśvarakīrti, but Bu ston, *Bde,* 102–3, does not make a connection between him and the Vikramaśīla gate-keeper. Prajñākaramati is the author of a well-known commentary to the *Bodhicaryāvatara,* as well as several other works preserved in the Tibetan canon. See Chimpa and Chattopadhyaya (1990), 295–96, for information on his life. Bla ma dam pa, *Bla,* 15, states that 'Brog mi also received tantric teachings from the great Nāropa. See Guenther (1963), for the translation of a biography of Nāropa, and for a discussion of his tantric teachings.

20 It is interesting to note that Nyang ral Nyi ma 'od zer, *Chos,* 473–74, has virtually the exact same wording for these events in 'Brog mi's life. See Chimpa and Chattopadhyaya (1990), 301–2, for Ratnavajra's life and, 302–3, for Jñānaśrīmitra's life.

21 Bu ston, *Bde,* 99–100, is an early source for information about Śāntipa's life, and mentions a number of his compositions. The story of Śāntipa is also told by Tāranātha in his history of Indian Buddhism. See Chimpa and Chattopadhyaya (1990), 299–300. Ratnākaraśānti, which is Śāntipa's full name, was a famous and prolific author. Bu ston, *Bde,* 100, also mentions several works by him, such as a commentary on the twenty thousand-line *Prajñāpāramitā,* known in Tibetan as the *Nyi khri.* The annotation in the *Zhib mo rdo rje* refers to a *Nyi khri dag ldan,* which must be the *Mngon par rtogs pa'i rgyan gyi tshig le'ur byas pa'i 'grel pa dag ldan,* no. 5199, in vol. 91 of the Peking edition of the Tibetan Tripitaka. But this is a commentary on the *Abhisamayālaṃkara,* not the twenty thousand-line *Prajñāpāramitā.* The *Snying po mchog* is the *'Phags pa shes rab kyi pha rol tu phyin pa brgyad stong pa'i dka' 'grel snying po mchog,* no. 5200, in vol. 92 of the same collection. The *Kye rdor rgyud gsum* is explained in note 28 in part one.

22 The brief teachings that 'Brog mi received from all six masters as he was later about to return to Tibet have been preserved. They are found in a

group of texts with the common title *Mkhas pa sgo drug la rje 'brog mis chos 'brel du zhus pa'i gdams ngag,* in vol. 13 of the *Sa skya Lam 'bras Literature Series* (Dehra Dun: Sa skya Centre, 1983) 395–410. The teaching of Śāntipa (395–98) is known by three different names: *Mdo rgyud bsre ba'i nyams len, Snying po don gyi rang 'gros,* and *Snang rig* [or *Snang srid*] *byin gyis brlab pa'i man ngag.* The teaching of Prajñākaragupta, who is referred to as Prajñākaramati in our text, is the *Phyi rol gyi gdon gsum bsrung ba'i man ngag* (398–99). Jñānaśrī's instructions are known as the *'Byung ba lus 'khrugs bsrung ba'i man ngag* (399–400). Ratnavajra's teaching is the *Ting nge 'dzin sems kyi bar chad bsrung ba'i man ngag* (400–401). These three are thought of as a set. Vāgīśvarakīrti's instruction is the *Gnyug ma dran gsal* (401–2), which is also known as the *Rim pa gnyis dbyer med du bsgom pa'i man ngag* and as the *Dbang bzhi'i lam gdan thog gcig tu bsgom pa'i man ngag.* An anonymous commentary to it is also included (402–6). Nāropa's teaching is the *Phyag rgya chen po sdug bsngal gsum sel* (406–10).

23 *Gra 'dos pa* is an obscure phrase. Mkhan po A pad Rin po che did not understand the meaning, but felt it was not a name.

24 The phrase "conduct of the renunciation of duality" *(gnyis spangs kyi spyod pa)* refers to the advanced practice of renouncing all distinctions of duality, such as filth and cleanliness, good and bad, etc., which would be considered pretentious if engaged in by a mere beginner.

25 The famous Khasarpaṇa image figures in the lives of numerous Indian and Tibetan masters of this period. Virūpa himself had also visited it and received prophecy. Cha rgan, *Lam,* 14a, mentions that this image was brought from Potala by *Ajitaguptamitra (Mi pham sbas pa'i bshes gnyen), which would also appear to be one of the names of the Indian master Mitrayogin. See Roerich (1976), 1031. According to Tatz (1987), 701, the famous image was probably located in the Puṇḍravardhana forest of the Vārendra district of northern Bengal. In note 31, Tatz lists a number of sources where it is mentioned and possible locations for it. Rāḍha is a district of Bengal just south of Puṇḍravardhana. See the reference cited in Tatz (1987), 702. Whereas our text locates the image in eastern India, 'Jam dbyangs mkhyen brtse'i dbang phyug, *Gdams,* 54, says that it was located in the Devikoṭa gorge in south India. Cha rgan, *Lam,* 14b, states that 'Brog mi received a very important prophecy from Avalokiteśvara when he was worshipping the Khasarpaṇa image. The deity told him he would meet a master on the road and should practice his instructions. Later another master would appear at his door in Tibet and great benefit would come to many people from his teachings. He later understood these words to be prophecies of his meetings with Vīravajra and Gayadhara. This event is also

found in 'Jam dbyangs mkhyen brtse'i dbang phyug, *Gdams,* 54, with somewhat more detail, and in 'Jam mgon A mes zhabs, *Yongs,* 125.

26 The Newar is Śāntabhadra, with whom 'Brog mi first studied in Nepal. The Dharma Lord Sa skya Paṇḍita's comment at the end of this annotation refers to the opinion that a student of tantric meditation should receive both initiation and the oral instructions for practice from the same master.

27 Mu gu lung was later 'Brog mi's main residence in Tibet. According to Cha rgan, *Lam,* 30b–31a, Vīravajra magically came to Tibet to visit 'Brog mi, and stayed for about one month at Mu gu lung. During that time the two of them translated a number of texts, such as the *Bzang po yongs bzung, Rin chen 'bar ba,* and *Bstod pa nyi shu.* Bla ma dam pa, *Bla,* 17, says that Vīravajra stayed in Tibet for three years. The *Bzang po yongs bzung* (To. no. 1240) is a text for the maṇḍala rite of initiation in the Hevajra tradition of Ḍombi Heruka. See Tshar chen, *Dpal kye,* 335. The *Ratnajvāla (Rin chen 'bar ba),* also in the Hevajra tradition of Ḍombi Heruka, is by Prajñendraruci. It is found in the Peking Tripitaka, 56: 182.5–198.1, but several pages have been omitted. The *Bstod pa nyi shu* is from the Hevajra tradition of Padmavajra. See Tshar chen, *Dpal kye,* 335.

28 Ḍombi Heruka was one of the most important disciples of Virūpa. He did not receive the transmission of the *Rdo rje tshig rkang* of the Lam 'bras from Virūpa, but did receive the extensive teachings of the *Hevajra tantra,* which have been passed down to the present day. Also see the next two notes.

29 As discussed at length in part one, the basic text of the Lam 'bras is the *Rdo rje tshig rkang* of Virūpa, which 'Brog mi did not receive from Vīravajra. The teaching known as *Sahajasiddhi (Lhan cig skyes grub),* which was composed by Ḍombi Heruka and is one of the Lam skor dgu (Nine Cycles of the Path), is also referred to as "the Lam 'bras without the basic text" *(rtsa ba med pa'i lam 'bras).* See the anonymous notes to Grags pa rgyal mtshan, *Ḍombi,* 395. An edition of the Sanskrit original of Ḍombi Heruka's text, with the Tibetan translation, has been published in *Guhyādi-aṣṭasiddhi-saṅgraha,* (Sarnath, Central Institute of Higher Tibetan Studies, 1988), 185–91 and 275–83.

30 The Lam skor dgu (Nine Cycles of the Path) are the most important tantric legacy of 'Brog mi Lo tsā ba. The first of the nine is the Lam 'bras itself. The remaining eight teachings by other Indian masters have traditionally been transmitted in the Sa skya tradition when the Lam 'bras is given. The Lam skor brgyad (Eight Cycles of the Path), and the com-

mentaries by Rje btsun Grags pa rgyal mtshan, are found in the *Sa skya Lam 'bras Literature Series,* 11: 347–479. The eight are (1) *Bsam mi khyab (Acintyādvaya),* by Kuddālapāda (Tog tse pa); (2) *Lhan cig skyes grub,* by Ḍombi Heruka; (3) *Mchod rten drung thob,* by Nāgārjuna; (4) *Phyag rgya chen po yi ge med pa,* by Vāgīśvarakīrti; (5) *Bskyed rim zab pa'i tshul dgu,* by Padmavajra, who is also known as Saroruha; (6) *Gtum mo lam rdzogs,* by Kṛṣṇacaryā (Nag po spyod pa); (7) *Yon po bsrang ba,* by Nag po U tsi ṭa 'chi ba med pa; and (8) *Phyag rgya'i lam skor,* by Indrabhūti. The identification and authors of the Lam skor brgyad, about which there is some controversy, are discussed by 'Jam dbyangs mkhyen brtse'i dbang phyug, *Gdams,* 6–9, and on 42, their transmission to 'Brog mi is discussed. The most informative single elucidation of the Lam skor brgyad (Eight Cycles of the Path) is by Paṇ chen Shākya mchog ldan, *Lam.* Also see Bla ma dam pa, *Bla,* 103–4, and 'Jam mgon A mes zhabs, *Gsung ngag rin po che lam,* 565.

31 The *Bsam mi khyab (Acintyādvaya, The Inconceivable)* of Tog tse pa (Kuddālapāda) seems to have always been considered the most important of the Lam skor brgyad (Eight Cycles of the Path). A Sanskrit edition of this text has also been published in *Guhyādi-aṣṭasiddhi-saṅgraha* (Sarnath, Central Institute of Higher Tibetan Studies, 1988), 196–208. In the translation of 'Brog mi Lo tsā ba, which was used in the Sa skya tradition, there are approximately 130 quatrains of verse. The text is basically concerned with the realization of Mahāmudrā as the result of tantric practice. The *Bsam mi khyab* is also one of the texts in the collection known as the *Snying po skor drug,* which includes the *Do hā mdzod* of Saraha and four other works. In the Lam 'bras tradition the *Bsam mi khyab* has been the text most often chosen as a vehicle for granting essential tantric teachings when the entire Lam 'bras itself is not given. This can be seen in several instances in the *Zhib mo rdo rje.* See also Sa skya Paṇḍita, *Rtogs,* which is a teaching on Mahāmudrā granted by Sa skya Paṇḍita to a disciple after bestowing the Hevajra initiation, the instructions of Ḍombi Heruka's *Lhan cig skyes grub,* and Tog tse pa's *Bsam mi khyab.* According to 'Jam dbyangs mkhyen brtse'i dbang phyug, *Gdams,* 42, 'Brog mi received three of the Lam skor brgyad from Vīravajra. These were the *Bsam mi khyab,* the *Mchod rten drung thob,* and the *Lhan cig skyes grub.* Bla ma dam pa, *Bla,* 104, says 'Brog mi received only the *Bsam mi khyab* from Vīravajra.

32 This is the famous Khasarpaṇa image that 'Brog mi visited before meeting Vīravajra.

33 All the histories of the Lam 'bras agree that 'Brog mi spent a total of thirteen years in Nepal and India. He spent one year in Nepal with Śāntabhadra, eight years in India with Śāntipa and the other five masters

at Vikramaśīla, and four years in India with Vīravajra. As just mentioned in our text, the early Sa skya tradition maintained that 'Brog mi spent four years with Vīravajra when they first met. This is also the case with Bla ma dam pa, *Bla,* 16. Nevertheless, there is another tradition that 'Brog mi only met Vīravajra for a very brief period in the forest, and later made a second trip to India during which he stayed with Vīravajra for four years. Mang thos klu sgrub, *Bstan,* 84, says that this version comes from the Zha ma tradition of the Lam 'bras. This extensive story is first found in Cha rgan, *Lam,* 15a–b and 16/17b–21b (the Tibetan text has the numbers 16 and 17 on a single folio.) According to this version Vīravajra advised 'Brog mi to return to Tibet to gather offerings for the extensive tantric teachings he wished to receive, and to return after three years. Vīravajra said that he would be in the court of the king Tsa na ka, and would teach him there. 'Brog mi did as he was told, and later returned to stay for four years and received in full detail the *Kye rdor rgyud gsum (The Tantra Trilogy of Hevajra)* as transmitted through the lineage of Ḍombi Heruka to *Durgacandra (Mi thub zla ba), who was Vīravajra's teacher. This version of the story was later accepted and incorporated into the works of 'Jam dbyangs mkhyen brtse'i dbang phyug and 'Jam mgon A mes zhabs. In translating the name Mi thub zla ba back into the original Sanskrit, I am following the form found in Ngag dbang blo bzang rgya mtsho, *Zab,* vol. 1, 518, in preference to the more common hypothesis of the spelling *Durjayacandra.

34 According to the Zha ma tradition, 'Brog mi first returned to where Stag and Leng had been staying. Then they showed their gratitude to their teachers by making great offerings at Vikramaśīla, and then at Pham 'thing in Nepal. Then they returned to Tibet by way of Skyid grong, where they sent messengers to the abbot, the teacher, and the three princes at Lha rtse. They were welcomed home, and everyone, including the three princes and their families, requested initiations and many teachings from 'Brog mi. See Cha rgan, *Lam,* 15b–16/17a (the Tibetan text has a double page number).

35 Cha rgan, *Lam,* 15b, states that Stag Lo knew the practice of the Vinaya, the commentaries on the *Heart Sūtra (Prajñāpāramitāhṛdaya),* and some texts necessary for practice. Leng had become a skilled translator.

36 This no doubt indicates that 'Brog mi lived for some time as a wandering *kapalika yogin* in India, truly living the tantric lifestyle as well as studying the texts and engaging in the practices.

37 This is all that is known about Stag Lo. Cha rgan, *Lam,* 16/17b, says that Leng was disgusted with the ignorance in Tibet, and after six months

returned to the Vajrāsana in India. He studied for two more years there, and then came back to Tibet and founded a monastery. He also made some translations, but did not have a great deal of success.

38 Mang thos klu sgrub, *Bstan,* 83, states that 'Brog mi chiefly studied and taught the Buddhist Doctrine until the age of sixty-two, and then chiefly practiced meditation for the rest of his life.

39 Lha lcam gcig, whose real name was Mdzes ldan 'od chags, was 'Brog mi's main consort. She was the daughter of Dpal lde, the eldest of the three ruling princes of Lha rtse, and thus of the ancient royal Tibetan family. Her parents offered her to 'Brog mi as his consort during a celebration in gratitude for the many initiations he bestowed on them soon after his return from India. She was a *jñānaḍākinī,* and according to the Zha ma tradition of the Lam 'bras, accompanied 'Brog mi on his second trip to India. They remained together the rest of their lives. See Cha rgan, *Lam,* 16/17b and 22a. According to Cha rgan, *Lam,* 70b, Mdzes ldan 'od chags passed away at the age of sixty-five, before 'Brog mi's death. But 'Jam dbyangs mkhyen brtse'i dbang phyug, *Gdams,* 67, says she died after 'Brog mi, as a result of various relatives and disciples of 'Brog mi breaking the sacred tantric commitments following his death. Little is known about 'Brog mi's sons. Nyang ral Nyi ma 'od zer, *Chos,* 480, refers to Rdo rje as Jo sras Ye shes rdo rje and as Tsad tsa Ye shes rdo rje. He was a translator like his father, and invited the paṇḍita Vajrapāṇi to Tibet. He also made some translations. According to Bcom ldan Rig pa'i ral gri (1227–1305), *Bstan,* 28b, Jo sras Rdo rje prepared a translation of the group of texts known as the *Snying po'i skor.* The only extant translation that can certainly be identified as his is the *Bla ma brgyud pa'i rim pa'i man ngag,* translated by the Indian master *Dhīriśrījñāna and 'Brog mi Jo sras. See no. 4539 in vol. 81 of the Peking edition of the Tibetan Tripitaka. Not long after the death of his father, Rdo rje died at a young age, soon after hearing of the tragic death of his older brother Indra. Cha rgan, *Lam,* 71b, says that sometime after 'Brog mi's death Indra traveled to Central Tibet where he met Gnyan Lo tsā ba at Dar lung. They quarreled, and Gnyan Lo tsā ba placed a curse on Indra. After going to Rong, where he gave some teachings, Indra burned to death in a bizarre accident. Gnyan Lo tsā ba is important for the transmission of certain Mahākāla teachings to Tibet. This story is also found in 'Jam dbyangs mkhyen brtse'i dbang phyug, *Gdams,* 67. Jo nang Tāranātha, *Rgyud,* 100–101, tells much the same story of Indra's death, but he attributes it to the magic of Rwa Lo tsā ba, not Gnyan Lo tsā ba, whom Indra met in Rong on the way to Central Tibet. Furthermore, he says that Indra died in Central Tibet, after three months of bloody dysentery.

40 Cha rgan, *Lam,* 25a, mentions that Gnam thang dkar po was between 'Gos yul and 'Bring 'tshams.

41 According to Mang thos klu sgrub, *Bstan,* 92, Gayadhara first came to Tibet at 'Brog mi's invitation in 1041, a *lcags mo sbrul* year. Mang thos klu sgrub, *Bstan,* 92, calculates that Gayadhara was 289 years old when he arrived in Tibet!

42 The *Gurupañcāśikā (Bla ma lnga bcu pa)* of Aśvaghoṣa is a famous text describing the correct manner of relating to a spiritual master in the practice of Buddhism. It has been translated as *Fifty Verses of Guru Devotion* (Dharamsala: Translation Bureau of the Library of Tibetan Works and Archives, 1976).

43 Cha rgan, *Lam,* 22b–23a, first records the story which is here rejected as corrupt. See chapter two in part one, where the story is related from this source. Also see note 226 in part one.

44 In 1479 *(sa mo phag)* Gtsang byams pa Rdo rje rgyal mtshan, also known as Mus srad pa, stated that 436 years had passed since Gayadhara and 'Brog mi came to Mu gu lung and worked on translations. 'Brog mi, his consort, and his disciples lived in a complex of thirteen caves at Mu gu lung. According to Mus srad pa's calculation, Gayadhara and 'Brog mi's translations of the *Kye rdor rgyud gsum (The Tantra Trilogy of Hevajra)* and other texts, which were done in the "Translation Cave" (Sgra sgyur Lo tsā phug), can be dated to the year 1043. See Rdo rje rgyal mtshan, *Gnas,* 297 and 299. Mang thos klu sgrub, *Bstan,* 83, also dates Gayadhara and 'Brog mi's translations of the *Kye rdor rgyud gsum* and other texts to the *chu mo lug* year of 1043, when 'Brog mi was fifty-one years old.

45 Zur po che Shākya 'byung gnas (1002–1062) was one of the great masters of the Rnying ma school, and is particularly important for the Sems sde Rdzogs chen (Mind Series of the Great Perfection). The story of his life is translated in Dudjom (1991), 1: 617–35, and a brief mention of the following events in our text is found on 633. With the exception of Bla ma dam pa, *Bla,* 18–19, all the later historical sources, who follow Cha rgan, *Lam,* 26b–27a, state that Zur po che had been invited to the cave of Sram pa wa gdong in the upper valley of Shangs, and was practicing meditation there. Whereas the annotation in the *Zhib mo rdo rje* seems to say that Zur po che was a native of Sram pa wa gdong, it could also be understood as saying that he was living at that place. Roerich (1976), 112, also mentions Thag as the location of Zur po che's retreat, as does our text. Yang dag Heruka is one of the eight great Mahāyoga deities of the Rnying ma tradition. Cha rgan, *Lam,* 45a–b, states that Zur po che was a serious disciple of 'Brog mi's from before, and had stayed with him for four years studying

the *Kye rdor rgyud gsum (The Tantra Trilogy of Hevajra),* which he mastered. He was especially expert in the *Sampuṭa.* Cha rgan even counts him as one of those who received the complete transmission of the Hevajra scriptures from 'Brog mi.

46 See note 31 in part two for information about the *Bsam mi khyab (Acintyādvaya, The Inconceivable).* Cha rgan, *Lam,* 26b, gives considerably more detail about what 'Brog mi taught Zur po che. When he received the Hevajra initiation and then the instructions of the *Bsam mi khyab,* Zur po che found it to be in agreement with the Rdzogs chen. When he received the *Bskyed rim zab pa'i tshul dgus brgyan pa* of Saroruha (another one of the Lam skor dgu), he saw that it agreed with the creation stage of the *Māyājāla.* And when he received the twenty-four visualizations of *cāṇḍālī,* as well as the explanation of the twenty-two infractions of the tantric sacred commitments, he realized that they were in agreement with the stages of the path according to the *Māyājāla.* This pleased him greatly, and he spoke the following lines that are found in our text. This episode is also recorded in several Rnying ma histories, the most interesting of which is Sog bzlog pa Blo gros rgyal mtshan (b.1552), *Gsang,* 481–82. Sog bzlog pa notes that this was a period in which there was a great deal of uncertainty among many Rnying ma masters as to the authenticity of their own eighteen scriptures known as the Sems phyogs or the Sems sde (Mind Series). At the time when 'Brog mi's message arrived Zur po che was having doubts about his own Dharma. Sog bzlog pa claims that 'Brog mi bestowed on Zur po che all of Gayadhara's teachings, such as the Lam 'bras, the *Phyag rgya chen po Bsam mi khyab,* and the Lam skor dgu (Nine Cycles of the Path). This is of course somewhat garbled, because the Lam 'bras and the *Bsam mi khyab* are two of the Lam skor dgu, and 'Brog mi did not receive all nine from Gayadhara, but from four different Indian masters. Nevertheless, when Zur po che carefully contemplated the teachings he realized that they were profound and elevated paths which were the same in meaning as the Sems phyogs (Mind Series), and so he gained new certainty in his own teachings. As a result he made the statement about 'Brog mi's teachings on the *Bsam mi khyab* enriching his own Sems phyogs (Mind Series). He also felt that if he had not come to 'Brog mi he might have made the horrible mistake of rejecting his own authentic Dharma teachings. Then he was filled with devotion for 'Brog mi and performed the services that are mentioned in our text. Although Sog bzlog pa says that he has taken this story from the histories of the Lam 'bras, it should be noted that none of the available histories mention Zur po che receiving the Lam 'bras from 'Brog mi. Another example of a Rnying ma version of this story is found in Rig 'dzin Padma phrin las

(1640–1718), *Bka'*, 189–90. He states that Zur po che received the Hevajra initiation and various teachings from both Gayadhara and 'Brog mi. The Sems phyogs (Mind Series) in the text (more often spelled Sems sde) is one of the three classes of the Atiyoga teachings of the Rdzogs chen. See Dudjom (1991), 1: 538–53, for information on its lineage, and see 319–26 for the nature of its teachings. The *Māyājāla sūtra (Mdo sgyu 'phrul),* which is actually a tantra of the Mahāyoga class in the Rnying ma tradition, is found listed as no. 222 in Kaneko (1982), 276.

47 Cha rgan, *Lam,* 27a–b, states that 'Brog mi requested Gayadhara to write a short mnemonic text *(rjed tho'i yig chung)* about the *Rdo rje tshig rkang* and the *Lung skor lnga,* because of the danger of their loss if his memory was affected through illness or other severe circumstances. He invited Gayadhara to the secluded site of Phu dur dgon pa. They went into retreat together for one month and Gayadhara composed the text. This clearly shows that Cha rgan believed the teaching had been completely oral up to this point, and is especially interesting in light of the Sa skya tradition that nothing was written of the Lam 'bras until the time of Sa chen. Cha rgan's story probably originates in the Zha ma tradition, since it is not found in our text or that of Bla ma dam pa. 'Jam mgon A mes zhabs, *Yongs,* 134–35, repeats the information from Cha rgan. See note 134 in part two for more information about the identity of the *Lung skor lnga.*

48 Cha rgan, *Lam,* 27b, says that Gayadhara made some prophecies before his departure, which are important for understanding certain events later in 'Brog mi's life. He told 'Brog mi that there would be problems with his sons, and that his family line would end with them. He urged 'Brog mi himself to practice the techniques for the transference of consciousness at death *('pho ba),* and that he would then be able to proceed directly to the pure land of Khecara without experiencing the intermediate state *(bar do)* between lives. He instructed 'Brog mi to require that disciples who received the oral instructions not teach them until after they had practiced them for thirteen years, and finally impressed on him the importance of examining the worthiness of potential disciples by demanding food and wealth from them. 'Brog mi then accompanied Gayadhara as far as La stod Thang chung, and sent escorts with him as far as Skyid grong near the Tibetan border with Nepal.

49 Mar Lo is Mar pa Chos kyi blo gros, the future teacher of Rje btsun Mi la ras pa. It is well known that Mar pa studied Sanskrit grammar and Indian colloquial language with 'Brog mi, but was unsuccessful in receiving tantric teachings from him. However, he continued to have the greatest respect for 'Brog mi, as expressed in one of his spiritual songs. See Nālandā Translation

Committee (1982), 142–3. Roerich (1976), 399, states that Mar pa first went to 'Brog mi at the age of fifteen. According to Rig 'dzin Tshe dbang nor bu, who accepts that Mar pa was born in the year 1000, the period of Mar pa's study at Mu gu lung with 'Brog mi began in 1014 and lasted for three years. See Tshe dbang nor bu, *Mar,* 674.

50 The more common spelling of 'Gos Lo tsā ba's name is 'Gos Khug pa Lhas btsas, the meaning of which is explained in Mang thos klu sgrub, *Bstan,* 86–87, and 'Jam mgon A mes zhabs, *Dpal gsang,* 115. According to 'Jam mgon A mes zhabs, *Dpal gsang,* 115–16, 'Gos was born from an incestuous union between brother and sister. He first tried to receive teachings from the Rnying ma master Zur po che Shākya 'byung gnas. When he was only given work to do he left Zur po che and went to 'Brog mi for teachings. Then he decided to go to India himself instead of offering the gold necessary to receive tantric instructions from 'Brog mi. He first traveled to India with the translator Gyi jo Zla ba'i 'od zer. He made several trips to India, spent many years in study there with seventy-two different teachers, and specialized in the *Guhyasamāja tantra.* Unlike Mar pa Lo tsā ba, who remained respectful of his teacher 'Brog mi, 'Gos Lo tsā ba apparently held a grudge against him and competed with him for many years. Cha rgan, *Lam,* 27b, specifies that 'Gos Lo tsā ba wanted to invite the famous Maitrīpa in order to humiliate 'Brog mi. This will be touched on again below.

51 According to Tatz (1987), 704, and note 34, Śrīparvata is a range of mountains and a settlement up river (or northwest) of Dhānyakaṭaka, which is in southeast India in Cālukya-Kākatīya country near the delta of the Kṛṣṇa River. Its inhabitants were called Śabara, and it was already a sacred practice site for the Śaivite tradition in the sixth century. But Hirakawa (1990), 242, 253, mentions that inscriptions have been recovered indicating that Śrīparvata, a mountain where Nāgārjuna is said to have lived, was at Nāgārjunakoṇḍa in south India and was the site of the Culadhammagiri monastery. See Tatz (1987), for a study of the life of Maitrīpa (1007–1085), who is also known as Advayavajra (Gnyis med rdo rje), and details on the events referred to here. It is well known that Maitrīpa is said to have received teachings on Mahāmudrā from Śabaripa. Maitrīpa's teachings are often connected with the set of texts known as the *Snying po skor drug.* These six texts are (1) Saraha's *Dohā mdzod,* (2) Nāgārjunasāra's *Phyag rgya bzhi gtan la dbab pa,* (3) Aryadeva's *Sems kyi sgrib sbyong,* (4) Devacandra's *Shes rab ye shes gsal ba,* (5) Sahajavajra's *Gnas pa bsdus pa,* and (6) the *Bsam mi khyab* of Kuddālapāda (Tog tse pa). See Tshul 'khrims rin chen, *Kun,* 694–95. The debate was with 'Brog mi's former teacher Ratnākaraśānti, which is described in Tatz (1987), 708.

52 Manuscript B1, 5a, has "Bon" *(bon)* instead of "Tibet" *(bod).*

53 Cha rgan, *Lam,* 28a, says that Gayadhara was accompanied by one man holding a peacock feather parasol and a fan, and another carrying his cushion and baggage. An annotation in manuscript N, 5a, says that 'Gos Lo asked "about Maitrīpa's story."

54 Cha rgan, *Lam,* 28a, mentions that 'Gos Lo and his servant had gone ahead to prepare a welcome for Gayadhara, and when they arrived in Tshong 'dus lung pa there were many Tibetan traders who told them the news about the Mon people waiting to ambush them on the trail.

55 Cha rgan, *Lam,* 28b, notes that 'Gos Lo tsā ba, with ten horsemen, welcomed Gayadhara at Phag ri. Then they traveled to Gad, where 'Gos discovered who Gayadhara really was when the Indian master began to ask about 'Brog mi's whereabouts.

56 Cha rgan, *Lam,* 28b–29a, adds some important details here. When 'Gos accused Gayadhara of lying, Gayadhara repeated to him a number of insulting remarks 'Gos had made about both Gayadhara and 'Brog mi when Gayadhara had previously spent time at 'Brog mi's place. 'Gos apologized and said that he had meant no disrespect to the master; his comments had been because of the personal animosity he held for 'Brog mi. Gayadhara pointed out to him that 'Brog mi had been his teacher, and that not keeping the proper attitude for his former teacher would cause his own Dharma work to bring little benefit to others. Gayadhara stayed with 'Gos for two years and they translated many texts, such as the *Guhyasamāja tantra* and all the associated texts according to the system of Nāgārjuna. 'Gos is also said to have offered 'Brog mi sixty ounces of gold to apologize for his competitive attitude. 'Gos is especially important for the transmission of Nāgārjuna's system of the *Guhyasamāja tantra* in Tibet. See Nyang ral Nyi ma 'od zer, *Chos,* 475, for much detail on which Indian masters he studied with and invited to Tibet, and what texts he translated. Roerich (1976), 363–64, also lists a number of his translations. 'Gos Lo is also known for having composed a refutation of wrong mantra *(sngags log sun 'byin).* See 'Gos Lo tsā ba, *'Gos.*

57 Cha rgan, *Lam,* 29a–b, relates that Gayadhara, 'Gos, and 'Brog mi were all invited to a Dharma council at Nya ri by Zur po che Shākya 'byung gnas, who knew Gayadhara and 'Brog mi from before. During this time Gayadhara directed 'Brog mi to act as his oral translator, which deeply offended 'Gos and his followers. Gayadhara then explained to 'Gos how he had done so to prevent embarrassment to 'Gos, because 'Brog mi was the superior translator and would have found many faults with any translation

'Gos made. He told 'Gos that if he was not afraid of 'Brog mi's criticism he could do all the oral translating from that time on. 'Gos did not dare to do so. 'Brog mi's accusation was in regard to Gayadhara's earlier promise not to teach the Lam 'bras to anyone else in Tibet.

58 This would happen because 'Brog mi was falsely accusing Gayadhara of having broken his previous promise not to teach the Lam 'bras to any other Tibetan.

59 'Gos Lo's translations of the *Kye rdor rgyud gsum* do not seem to have survived, although a number of his other translations with Gayadhara have. 'Brog mi's translations of the *Rgyud gsum* are found in the Peking Tripitaka. Cha rgan, *Lam,* 29b, states that 'Gos Lo tsā ba escorted Gayadhara as far as Skyid grong.

60 The translator Gyi jo Zla ba'i 'od zer is credited with making the first Tibetan translation of the *Kālacakra tantra* and the *Vimalaprabhā.* Cha rgan, *Lam,* 30a, mentions that these translations were made with Gayadhara. Other sources say that Gyi jo's translation of the *Kālacakra tantra* and the *Vimalaprabhā* were made with the Indian master Bhadrabodhi, who succeeded the great Nāropa as the northern gate-keeper of Vikramaśīla monastery. See Nyang ral Nyi ma 'od zer, *Chos,* 468, and Chimpa and Chattopadhyaya (1990), 300–1. A number of translations made by Gyi jo and Gayadhara are preserved in the Peking Tripitaka, the most significant of which are probably their translations of the *Buddhakapāla tantra* (no. 63) and various texts associated with this cycle. There is some controversy in the tradition about whether or not Gayadhara taught Gyi jo the Lam 'bras during this trip. 'Jam mgon A mes zhabs, *Yongs,* 139–40, points out that Grags pa rgyal mtshan, Dmar ston, Cha rgan, and Bla ma dam pa are all in agreement that Gayadhara did not give the Lam 'bras during his last two trips to Tibet. Kun dga' bzang po, *Lam,* 114.1, which is the earliest extended discussion of this problem, states that the Zha ma and 'Brom traditions also said that Gayadhara did not teach the Lam 'bras to Gyi jo. But then Ngor chen continues to give some strong evidence to the contrary. He points to the existence of a translation of the *Rdo rje tshig rkang* by Gyi jo, a history of the lineage that continued with Gyi jo's disciples, a summary and extensive commentary to the *Rdo rje tshig rkang,* and various texts concerning esoteric aspects of practice. He also lists the names in Gyi jo's lineage of the Lam 'bras and concludes that Gyi jo and his followers did possess the complete teachings of the Lam 'bras. By Ngor chen's time, however, all that remained of this tradition were some texts for which no one had received the transmission. Mang thos klu sgrub, *Bstan,* 93, also mentions evidence that Gyi jo and his disciples had some of the Lam 'bras, but concludes that only 'Brog mi received it all.

61 According to Mang thos klu sgrub, *Bstan,* 83, 'Brog mi passed away at the age of eighty-five, which would correspond to the year 1077. The reference to Gayadhara picking up gold entrusted to 'Brog mi may refer to a story found in Cha rgan, *Lam,* 23bff.

62 Gnyos Lo tsā ba Yon tan grags (b. 961?) was one of the main disciples of Gyi jo Zla ba'i 'od zer. For the most detailed treatment of his life see Anonymous, *Kha,* 6–16, where Gnyos is said to have been thirty-nine years older than Mar pa Lo tsā ba and to have lived to be more than 140 years old! Over a period of several years Gayadhara and Gnyos translated texts such as the *Guhyasamāja* teachings according to the system of Jñānapāda, and the *Kṛṣṇa Yamāri (Dgra nag).* See Cha rgan, *Lam,* 30a. This Gnyos Lo tsā ba is identical to the Gnyos Lo tsā ba in Gtsang smyon He ru ka's well-known life of Mar pa Lo tsā ba, where he is cast as the jealous villain who caused Mar pa's books to be thrown into the Ganges River. Decleer (1992), 20–22, has conclusively proven this story to be a later fabrication. Nyang ral Nyi ma 'od zer, *Chos,* 476–77, also provides substantial information about Gnyos Lo, his translation work, and his sons. Gnyos spent some twenty years studying in India. As with his teacher Gyi jo, there is some question in the tradition as to whether Gnyos Lo tsā ba received the Lam 'bras. Recording the opinion of his master Ngor chen Kun dga' bzang po, Mus chen Dkon mchog rgyal mtshan states that Gnyos Lo himself composed what are known as the thirty-two *Ra li tantras*, which belong to the Cakrasaṃvara system. He says that Gnyos had clearly received some of the Lam 'bras, because many specific technical terms *(brda' chad)* from the Lam 'bras are found in those works. See Mus chen Dkon mchog rgyal mtshan, *Lam,* 449. Go rams Bsod nams seng ge (1429–89) also claims that both the greater and lesser *Nam mkha' dang mnyam pa,* as well as the *Ra li nam mkha' dang mnyam pa,* which are all said to have been translated by Gayadhara and 'Brog mi, were actually fabricated by Gnyos Lo tsā ba and should be rejected as false. See Go rams Bsod nams seng ge, *Bde,* 55.2. These opinions were perhaps based on the knowledge that Sa skya Paṇḍita had earlier mentioned "the twenty-four *Ra li*" among works he felt were bogus compositions by Tibetans. See Sa skya Paṇḍita, *Chag,* 546. Although this was the opinion of these four Sa skya masters, Bcom ldan Rig pa'i ral gri (1227–1305) had listed the *Bde mchog rwa lo'i (sic!) rgyud* as translations made by 'Brog mi, and then stated, "Gayadhara also taught the *Ra li tantras,* for which there are Indian manuscripts, to Kha rag Gnyos kyi Lo tsā ba." See Bcom ldan Rig pa'i ral gri, *Bstan,* 28a–28b. Cha rgan, *Lam,* 21a, mentions the *Ra li* among the sixty short tantras that 'Brog mi received in India from Vīravajra. Bu ston also considered the *Ra li* collection to be authentic tantras translated by

Gayadhara and 'Brog mi. See Obermiller (1932), 2: 216 n. 1605. The *Ra li saṃvara tantras* are all found in vol. 3 of the Peking edition of the Tibetan Tripitaka.

63 Cha rgan, *Lam,* 30a, identifies Se and Rog as disciples of ('Brom) De ba Shak rgyal (sic!), and says that 'Brog mi's disciple 'Phags pa Chos snang was also present. They later received some teachings from 'Brog mi after 'Brom's death. The question of their identity is discussed in note 120 in part two.

64 The "globe of light transference" *('od kyi gong bu'i 'pho ba)* is one of the transference techniques associated with the practice of the Vase Initiation *(bum dbang)* in the Lam 'bras. See Dmar ston Chos kyi rgyal po, *Gzhung,* 60–61. Cha rgan, *Lam,* 30b, states that the figure of Heruka, by which is meant Hevajra, was clearly visible in the globe of light. Mang thos klu sgrub, *Bstan,* 94, says that Gayadhara died in the *chu mo lug* year of 1103, when Sa chen Kun dga' snying po was eleven years old.

65 The *Brtag gnyis* is the surviving text of the *Hevajra tantra,* referred to as the *Brtag pa gnyis pa (The Second Fascicle)* because it was originally the second fascicle *(brtag pa)* of the huge root tantra, most of which has been lost. As mentioned in note 63 in part two, 'Phags pa Chos snang was one of the three men who received teachings from 'Brog mi after the death of 'Brom, and one of those present at the passing of Gayadhara. Also see note 120 in part two. See Bla ma dam pa, *Bla,* 32, and Cha rgan, *Lam,* 30a.

66 This annotation has been incorporated into the text of Bla ma dam pa, *Bla,* 23. Slob dpon Rin po che is Bsod nams rtse mo, the second son of Sa chen Kun dga' snying po. The *'Bum* is the *Śatasāhasrikā prajñāpāramitā (The Perfection of Transcendent Knowledge in One Hundred Thousand Lines).*

67 Here the term "lord" (Rje pa) refers to Sa chen's son Rje btsun Grags pa rgyal mtshan. The *Vajrapañjara* is one of the *Kye rdor rgyud gsum (The Tantra Trilogy of Hevajra).*

68 The root text of the *Hevajra tantra* itself must be explained before or in conjunction with the explanatory tantra of the *Vajrapañjara.* The contents of both annotations in the *Zhib mo rdo rje* have been absorbed into the main text of Bla ma dam pa, *Bla,* 23, where crucial details are added. The hundred-syllable mantra of Vajrasattva is used for purposes of purification and for the mending of damaged vows.

69 Almost all this paragraph is found *only* in the manuscript reproduced here.

70 This annotation has been absorbed into the main text of Bla ma dam pa, *Bla,* 23.

71 In this context the regional designations of Smad and Stod would seem to refer to Gtsang and Mnga' ris respectively. The second spread of Buddhism in Tibet is usually reckoned to have begun with the translation works of Lo chen Rin chen bzang po. Tucci first studied the biography of this immensely important figure in 1932. His work has recently been republished in an English translation as Tucci (1988). A translation and study of a biography of Rin chen bzang po is also found in Snellgrove and Skorupski (1980), 2: 83–118.

72 The translation of this clause is uncertain. The identity of Sangs rgyas dkar rgyal (usually spelled Sangs rgyas skar rgyal) has proved to be elusive. Martin (1991), 274–93, and (1996), has devoted the most attention to the problem and carefully examined a large number of sources. Skar rgyal's story is most well known from the biographies of Lo chen Rin chen bzang po and the *Sdom gsum rab dbye* of Sa skya Paṇḍita. The following account is found in Sa skya Paṇḍita, *Sdom,* 80–81 (Lhasa, 1992).

> During the life of Rin chen bzang po there was one known as Sangs rgyas skar rgyal, from whose forehead light shone, who could sit in midair with his legs crossed, and who sometimes sat on a throne of grass.
>
> He presented teachings about emptiness, and appeared to have great love and compassion. His teachings even caused meditative concentration to arise in others, and all the people were devoted to him.
>
> He taught a fabricated [doctrine] somewhat different than the Doctrine of the King of the Śākyas. His doctrine spread widely.
>
> At that time, Rin chen bzang po practiced for six months and then went before him with firm meditative concentration. When Sangs rgyas skar rgyal was seated in midair and explaining his teachings, it is known that Rin chen bzang po caused him to fall to earth and faint by just looking at him.
>
> It has been stated that if the sublime being known as Rin bzang had not been living at that time Sangs rgyas skar rgyal's doctrine of perverse teachings would have survived.
>
> It has been stated that a great nāga called Skar rgyal, who delighted in the dark side, entered into an evil man and disguised himself as a buddha.
>
> It is possible for some types of māras like that to take the forms of people or of noble individuals. In order to spread a perverse doctrine they combine their perverse teachings with the essential points, and teach them in combination with the Dharma.

73 Sa skya Paṇḍita's own notes to the *Sdom gsum rab dbye* also state that Skar rgyal was from Khu nu (also spelled Ku nu). See Sa skya Paṇḍita, *Sdom gsum rang mchan,* 133. As Martin (1991), 279, points out, Ku nu is the present day Kinnaur district on the upper Sutlej River, now in India. Cha rgan, *Lam,* 91a, says that the malevolent nāga was from Si rib, and that the doctrine proclaimed by Skar rgyal was one of nihilistic emptiness *(stong pa nyid ci'ang med pa'i chos).* Si rib, more often spelled Se rib, corresponds to the district known as Thak-khola, south of Mustang in present day Nepal. See Snellgrove (1987), 2: 417.

74 Mang thos klu sgrub, *Bstan,* 83, says that 'Brog mi died at the age of eighty-five, which corresponds to the year 1077. But Cha rgan, *Lam,* 70b, says that 'Brog mi was sixty-nine when he passed away, and 'Jam dbyangs mkhyen brtse'i dbang phyug, *Gdams,* 65, mentions accounts that state that he died at the age of eighty-two or even ninty-five. Tshe dbang nor bu, *Mar,* 701, says that 'Brog mi died in the *me stag* year of 1066. Cha rgan, *Lam,* 70b–71b, has the most detailed story of the tragic events surrounding 'Brog mi's death. These events have been related from this source in part one, chapter two.

75 In this context, the term *gzhung,* "scripture," is specifically used to refer to the *Kye rdor rgyud gsum (The Tantra Trilogy of Hevajra),* which are the scriptures of this tradition. Only the lives of 'Khon Dkon mchog rgyal po and Gsal ba'i snying po are explained later in our text. This is no doubt because they are the two through whom the transmission of 'Brog mi's line of the *Kye rdor rgyud gsum* was transmitted. Even in Bla ma Dam pa, *Bla,* 24–25, Gyi ljang Dbu dkar ba is given only four lines, while there is no information provided on Brag rtse So nag pa and Dbrad ston. Cha rgan, *Lam,* 45a–b, says there were six disciples who received the complete scriptures from 'Brog mi, adding the great Rnying ma master Zur po che Shākya 'byung gnas to the group of five mentioned in our text.

76 Only the last page explaining the life of Gyi ljang Dbu dkar ba has been preserved in Cha rgan, *Lam,* 44a. According to Bla ma dam pa, *Bla,* 24–25, from among the *Kye rdor rgyud gsum (The Tantra Trilogy of Hevajra),* Dbu dkar ba was especially expert in the *Sampuṭa.* He later went to China by a southern route through Khams and became a royal priest to a Chinese king. Cha rgan, *Lam,* 44a, refers to this king as Rgya nag rgyal po Khri don chen. 'Jam dbyangs mkhyen brtse'i dbang phyug, *Gdams,* 68, does not give his name, but states that the ruler was the king of Gtsong kha in the Kokonor region of Mdo smad. Dbu dkar ba concentrated on meditation, and his explanation of the scriptures did not spread. According to 'Jam

mgon A mes zhabs, *Dpal rdo*, 1: 150–58, this disciple was also known as Gyi ljang Lo tsā ba. He traveled to India and met the mahāpaṇḍita Lalītavajra who lived in a charnel ground and was also known as Dur khrod Nag po ro 'dzin. Gyi ljang received many teachings from this master, such as the *Phyi nang thig le'i skor,* which are related to the Hevajra, but he especially received and practiced certain Mahākāla transmissions that have been passed down in the Sa skya tradition ever since. After he went to Mdo smad he was attacked by a jealous man named Lha 'chang ston pa Thogs med, who denigrated the *Thig le'i skor* and said it was not Dharma. They ended up in a sorcery duel and Lha 'chang died within the year. Gyi ljang's Mahākāla transmission was later passed on by Mal Lo tsā ba to Sa chen Kun dga' snying po. The *Dpal nag po chen po'i rgyud dur khrod nag po le'u gsum pa,* translated into Tibetan by the Indian paṇḍita Nag po ro langs, or Nag po ro 'dzin, and the Tibetan translator Gyi ljang Dbu dkar, is preserved in 2: 111–62, of the *Bya rog ma bstan srung bcas kyi chos skor* (Palampur: Sungrab Nyamso Gyunphel Pharkhang, 1973).

77 This entire annotation is found in the main text of Bla ma dam pa, *Bla,* 24–25. See note 31 in part two for information about the *Bsam mi khyab.*

78 The section in Cha rgan, *Lam,* dealing with the life of So nag pa is unfortunately missing. Bla ma dam pa provides no information. Thus the earliest source for detailed information is 'Jam dbyangs mkhyen brtse'i dbang phyug, *Gdams,* 69–70. So nag pa was the son of a wealthy merchant who knew 'Brog mi Lo tsā ba. On one occasion So nag pa's father told 'Brog mi that he would very much like his son to receive teachings, but that he was married and would have to leave his wife to do so. 'Brog mi was delighted and said that there was no need for So nag pa to leave his wife, both of them could receive his Dharma. They both came to Mu gu lung with sumptuous offerings. 'Brog mi granted them the complete explanation of the *Kye rdor rgyud gsum (The Tantra Trilogy of Hevajra),* as well as some oral instructions such as the *Bsam mi khyab.* They returned home, and although they gave some teachings of the tantras, they primarily devoted themselves to meditation.

79 The pages on the life of Dbrad Dkon mchog rgyal po are unfortunately missing from Cha rgan's text, and Bla ma dam pa provides no information. 'Jam dbyangs mkhyen brtse'i dbang phyug, *Gdams,* 70–71, is thus the earliest available source with information about him. Dbrad Dkon mchog rgyal po was from a wealthy family and became a disciple of the Rnying ma master Zur po che Shākya 'byung gnas. Once some wandering yogins arrived at his place, and while he served them food and drink he asked who had the best reputation as a great teacher in Dbus and Gtsang. They

mentioned 'Brog mi Lo tsā ba, who lived very near to where Dkon mchog rgyal po was. He became quite interested in meeting 'Brog mi, and with his parent's permission he took many precious offerings and went to Mu gu lung. He first met 'Brog mi's consort, Mdzes ldan 'od chags, who helped him meet 'Brog mi. He received the explanation of the *Kye rdor rgyud gsum (The Tantra Trilogy of Hevajra),* as well as some oral instructions such as the *Bsam mi khyab.* After returning home he mostly devoted himself to meditation.

80 The lives of 'Khon Dkon mchog rgyal po and Gsal ba'i snying po will be given below.

81 Cha rgan, *Lam,* 31b, lists five males who reached attainment, adding the names Cog ro bzhong pa 'Bring rje bshag brtson, and Pha drug pa Phyug tshang 'thong dge to the three found in our text. All other works mention only three.

82 Cha rgan, *Lam,* 60a–b, is the earliest story of Dgyer Se'o, whose name is often spelled Sgyer Se'o. Dgyer Se'o was the son of a very wealthy man, and came to 'Brog mi at Mu gu lung riding a fine horse, wearing precious armor, and loaded down with very expensive swords and other weapons. He was also faithful, compassionate, and energetic. When he offered his horse and requested the Lam 'bras, 'Brog mi considered it an auspicious dependently arisen connection and said, "You will be victorious in the battle of saṃsāra. I will give you oral instructions." After offering everything to 'Brog mi and receiving the instructions over a period of three years, Dgyer Se'o meditated in a number of isolated sites and had great success. He finally stated that there were no disciples for him in Tibet and went to Śrīparvata.

83 Cha rgan, *Lam,* 60b–61a, is the earliest story of Gshen sgom Rog po. As the element Gshen in his name signifies, he was from a Bon po family. He is also known as Gshen ston G.yung drung. When his uncle, who was a Bon po master, passed away, Gshen sgom Rog po gathered a vast amount of offerings from his uncle's disciples, patrons, and so forth, and performed the funeral services. He was left with about ten *mdzo* and horses, and more than thirty ounces of gold. Not believing in the Bon po teachings, he went with six attendants to request teachings from 'Brog mi at Mu gu lung. He offered the *mdzo* and horses and requested the Lam 'bras. 'Brog mi bestowed teachings on him for five years. Then Gshen offered all his gold and meditated in isolated sites for thirteen years with great success. He is said to have finally traveled to Mt. Ti se on a path of sunbeams one evening to teach the authentic instructions that would enable the many Bon po *rig 'dzin* living there to reach the pure land of Khecara.

84 The term "razor-sharp," literally "razor-strong" *(spu gri stobs),* is used in the Lam 'bras to refer to certain stages when the vital winds expand in the subtle channels and increase in strength.

85 This entire annotation has been absorbed into the text of Bla ma dam pa, *Bla,* 37–38. The usual spelling of this man's name is Grod po che, "the Great Barbarian." Once again, the earliest detailed information about him is found in Cha rgan, *Lam,* 61a–64a. His personal name was Bkra shis seng ge. He was a wicked and violent young man with great physical strength who led a group of a hundred other similar men. When he was twenty-five years old and his beautiful sister was twenty, they committed incest and she became pregnant. This event finally caused him to change his ways, and after giving his sister and child, along with his estates, into the care of a friend, he set off alone to wander the land. On one occasion some meditators told him that his violent ways would only lead him to hell. They said he should go to Mu gu lung and request teachings from the master known as 'Brog mi Lo tsā ba, who possessed instructions that could enable even a great sinner to gain buddhahood. When Grod po che heard 'Brog mi's name, he fainted. When he awoke, he realized that he had to do as they said. When he arrived in Mu gu lung, he offered precious turquoise and gold and requested the Lam 'bras from 'Brog mi. 'Brog mi agreed. Grod po che could consume prodigious amounts of food and drink, which 'Brog mi told his consort Mdzes ldan 'od chags to provide for him. When he practiced the teachings he experienced excellent meditative concentration, and 'Brog mi was very pleased with him. There are several interesting episodes relating his athletic abilities. He once sang, "I am the famous strongman of Mang 'khar. I am the great pillar that supports the great master. I am the beloved son of Mdzes ldan 'od chags. I am the Dharma protector of great meditators." The word spread through Tibet that 'Brog mi had enslaved a great rakṣāsa demon. Grod po che achieved great success in meditation, especially through the practice of the yogic exercises that opened the knots in the subtle channels. In the end he offered all the rest of his turquoise to 'Brog mi and went to Śrīparvata. In an examination of the cave complex of Mu gu lung, written in 1479, Mus srad pa mentions the "Phyag chen Bkra shis Cave" that was the dwelling of Dbus pa Grod po che Bkra shis seng ge, and the place where his realization of Mahāmudrā was achieved. See Rdo rje rgyal mtshan, *Gnas,* 297.

86 See Cha rgan, *Lam,* 68b, and Bla ma dam pa, *Bla,* 38. Cha rgan, *Lam,* 68b, says Rtod mo had seven sons. When her sons and husband were murdered she went into shock and remained unconscious for five days. Her father and brothers carried her to 'Brog mi, who revived her.

87 The idea of a "gathering of the essential constituents" *(khams 'dus pa)* is a crucial theme in the practice of the Lam 'bras. Briefly, there are three ways in which the "essential constituents" (i.e. the vital winds and "mind") may be "gathered" into specific locations within the practitioner's vajra body (i.e. the network of subtle channels), thereby causing advancement on the path to enlightenment according to the doctrine of the tantras. These three ways are due to residual karma, due to intense devotion, and due to great diligence. In this tradition, Rtod mo Rdo rje mtsho is cited as an example of one who gained realization due to the awakening of residual karma from a previous life. For such an individual, realization can occur without a great deal of effort in this life. See Sa chen Kun dga' snying po, *Lam (=Sras don ma),* 258, and *Gzhung rdo (=Sga theng ma),* 350. Also see Dmar ston, *Gzhung,* 201.

88 Dbrad sgom Dkon ne's full story is found in Cha rgan, *Lam,* 66a–68a. Dkon ne's husband suddenly died and she fell into a state in which she would constantly weep and wail, then fall unconscious, and on waking call out her husband's name and begin to weep and wail once more. 'Brog mi was traveling on a nearby road and heard her as he was leaving and on his return. He asked about her and was told the story. He instructed her brother to bring her to him, which he did. There is a detailed account of the skillful and compassionate manner in which 'Brog mi gradually brought her back to consciousness. Then he granted her the Hevajra initiation and taught her the *Bsam mi khyab.*

89 This quote is from the translation of 'Brog mi and Ratnavajra, found in Tog tse pa, *Dpal,* 352. These lines are missing in all four extant Sanskrit manuscripts of this text, as are many others found in the translations by both 'Brog mi and 'Gos Lo. This quote is used in the context of what is known as "reliance on the nectar of various objects" *(yul sna tshogs kyi bdud rtsi bsten pa),* which is an important theme in the Lam 'bras teachings. For example, see Sa chen Kun dga' snying po, *Gzhung rdo,* 285.

90 Dbrad sgom Dkon ne is traditionally cited as the example of one for whom the essential constituents gather due to intense devotion. For example, see Sa chen Kun dga' snying po, *Lam,* 259, and *Gzhung rdo,* 350.

91 Sman Nags rgyal is the mountain where the hermitage of Jo nang is located. According to Ngag dbang blo gros grags pa, *Dpal,* 20–21, the protecting spirit was the goddess Nags sman rgyal mo, whom he also refers to as the foremost of the twelve *brtan ma* spirits. She later invited Kun spangs Thugs rje brtson 'grus (1243–1313) to build the monastery of Jo nang there. In Tāranātha, *Jo,* 243, Dbrad sgom Dkon ne is called Srad sgom Dkon mchog, and is said to have been the foremost of 'Brog mi's four female

disciples who reached attainment. She first lived for a while on the eastern slope of Mt. Nags rgyal and then moved to Jo nang itself where she remained for a long time. Finally she attained the adamantine form of a rainbow body *('ja' lus rdo rje'i sku brnyes pa).* Her residence was still preserved there in the seventeenth century.

92 Se is Se ston Kun rig, 'Brog mi's main disciple and lineage holder of the Lam 'bras. His story will be related below.

93 In her statement Dkon ne means Se ston has been carried away by the winds of fame and fortune. This annotation has been incorporated into the main text of Bla ma dam pa, *Bla,* 39. According to 'Jam dbyangs mkhyen brtse'i dbang phyug, *Gdams,* 97, the commotion was from all the offerings being brought by Lady Zha ma and her brother passing by on the road on their way to Se ston's residence to request the Lam 'bras.

94 Cha rgan, *Lam,* 68b–69b, provides the most information about Lcam gcig. This woman is also known as Jo jo Rgyan ne and, as indicated by her nickname Lcam gcig, "Single Sister," she was the only sister of seven brothers. Her family was very rich and she was very beautiful. From the age of thirteen she was filled with passion and worked as a prostitute for all the young men of the area. She had exceptional skills in the erotic arts. 'Brog mi heard about her and sent a message to her and her family telling them that it was a great waste for such a *jñānaḍākinī* to just offer herself to everyone. Her oldest brother and a number of servants brought Lcam gcig, two female servants, and much wealth to Mu gu lung. 'Brog mi bestowed initiation on both brother and sister. He gave gifts to the brother and servants and sent presents to the relatives. When introduced to the experience of primordial awareness in the Initiation of Primordial Awareness Dependent on an Embodiment of Transcendent Knowledge *(shes rab ye shes dbang),* Lcam gcig went into a state of meditative concentration for a long period. When she came out of it she prostrated to her brother and exclaimed, "Elder brother, you have been very kind. I have met a master who is a buddha. The blessing entered me on the spot. Realization has been actualized. I discovered buddhahood in the mind. Without rejecting it, saṃsāra has faded into space. You have accomplished great benefit for me, so please leave in good health." Her brother and the servants returned home. The word spread in Tibet that the great master 'Brog mi had instantaneously liberated a prostitute. Lcam gcig stayed and acted as 'Brog mi's initiation consort *(dbang rten)* for five years. She gained clairvoyance and magical abilities at the age of twenty-five and traveled to Uḍḍiyana.

95 Manuscript N, 7b, has "She practiced, and having attained a cessation specifically designated for the body, and stability in both the creation and

perfection [stages], is said to have realized the sublime and common [attainments] in that very lifetime." This description invokes the phrase "a cessation specifically designated for the body," which is found toward the end of Virūpa's *Rdo rje tshig rkang.* It refers to liberation through what is termed the inferior path in the Lam 'bras. See Dmar ston, *Gzhung,* 293.

96 As noted above, Cha rgan says she went to Uḍḍiyana (U rgyan).

97 According to Cha rgan, *Lam,* 48b and 65a, this woman's name was Nam mkha' ye shes and she was the sister of 'Brom De pa ston chung, one of 'Brog mi's three disciples who received the complete Lam 'bras. His story will be told below. Her elder brother had a dream in which many women appeared and told him that he should send his sister, along with a fine amount of valuables, to 'Brog mi Lo tsā ba in Mang 'khar, who would then send her to the pure land of Khecara. Otherwise the women would take her there immediately. At the same time, 'Phyad mo Nam mkha' also fell unconscious for three days, and when she awoke she knew all about the life of master 'Brog mi. Her family asked her what she wanted to do, and she replied that she would go to 'Brog mi. At the age of fifteen, and accompanied by family members, servants, and many offerings, she went to the cave in the region of Gnam thang dkar po where 'Brog mi was staying. She offered everything to 'Brog mi and asked him to send her to Khecara when the time was right. Then he bestowed the initiation, and so forth, as mentioned in our text.

98 These are all practices connected with the special form of Vajrayoginī, or Vajravārāhī, known as Khecarī (Mkha' spyod ma). Short texts for all the practices mentioned here were later written by Grags pa rgyal mtshan and are found in *The Complete Works of the Great Masters of the Sa skya Sect of Tibetan Buddhism,* vol. 3, (Tokyo: the Toyo Bunko, 1968).

99 The lord is Rje btsun Grags pa rgyal mtshan.

100 This annotation has been absorbed into the main text of Bla ma dam pa, *Bla,* 41.

101 'Phyad mo Nam mkha' is cited in the tradition as the prime example of how the essential constituents can be gathered due to great diligence. For example, see Sa chen Kun dga' snying po, *Lam,* 242, and *Gzhung rdo,* 350.

102 In the translation of 'Phyad mo's words I have followed the suggestions of Mkhan po A pad Rin po che, who interpreted *mi bgyi ru* as meaning *rgyu mtshan.* The Dharma Lord is Sa skya Paṇḍita. Most of this annotation has been incorporated into the main text of Bla ma dam pa, *Bla,* 41.

103 Only the lives of 'Khon Dkon mchog rgyal po and Gsal ba'i snying po are

discussed in the *Zhib mo rdo rje*, certainly because it was through these two that 'Brog mi's transmission of the *Kye rdor rgyud gsum (The Tantra Trilogy of Hevajra)* passed. For information on Gyi ljang Dbu dkar ba see note 76 in part two and also the annotation in the *Zhib mo rdo rje* on pp. 102–3. For information on Brag rtse So nag pa see note 78 in part two. For information on Dbrad Dkon mchog rgyal po see note 79 in part two.

104 Dkon mchog rgyal po was born in 1034. An early member of the 'Khon family, Klu'i dbang po bsrung ba, who is also known by the Sanskrit form of his name, Nāgendrarakṣita, was a direct disciple of Guru Padmasambhava. He was one of the first seven men to take Buddhist ordination in Tibet. These seven were known as the "Seven Men on Trial" *(sad mi mi bdun)*. Shes rab tshul khrims was Dkon mchog rgyal po's elder brother. The Dharma Protectors Dkar mo nyi zla (White Lady of Sun and Moon) and Stong gi thod 'phreng can (One with a Rosary of a Thousand Skulls) are the specific protectors of Vajrakīlaya, who has been an important meditation deity for members of the 'Khon lineage since it was first received by Klu'i dbang po bsrung ba from Padmasambhava.

105 See notes 71 and 72 in part two for information on the great translator Rin chen bzang po and his activities in far west Tibet, or Stod.

106 The more usual spelling of this man's name is 'Khyin. Manuscript B1, 8a, has 'Tshur Lo tsā ba. In the Peking edition of the Tibetan Tripitaka there are a number of translations by Mtshur ston Jñānākara, or Mtshur ston Ye shes 'byung gnas. 'Khyin was also known as 'Tshur Lo tsā ba, and as Sbal ti Lo tsā ba. But Mang thos klu sgrub, *Bstan,* 132, gives 'Khyin Lo tsā ba's personal name as 'Od kyi snang ba.

107 In particular, Dkon mchog rgyal po mastered the *Kye rdor rgyud gsum (The Tantra Trilogy of Hevajra)* under the instruction of 'Brog mi Lo tsā ba. Both G.ya' lung and 'Phrang are places not far to the southwest of Sa skya.

108 Manuscript B1, 8b, adds, "Then the four noble sons *(jo sras)* offered the estate of Sa skya, and he took Sa skya." See Cha rgan, *Lam,* 36b–37a; Yar lung Jo bo, *Jo,* 145; and 'Jam mgon A mes zhabs, *'Dzam,* 19, for identification of the men whom Dkon mchog rgyal po dealt with to aquire the land for the future monastery of Sa skya.

109 See note 31 in part two for identification of the *Bsam mi khyab*. The techniques of *cāṇḍālī* are practiced in connection with the Secret Initiation *(gsang dbang)* in the Lam 'bras. According to Dkon mchog rgyal po's grandson, Rje btsun Grags pa rgyal mtshan, *Dpal,* 20–21, Dkon mchog rgyal po also received many transmissions and teachings of the Guhyasamāja from 'Gos Lo tsā ba Khug pa Lhas btsas. He received many

treatises and esoteric instructions, such as the five *Thig le'i rgyud* of the Hevajra system, from the Uḍḍiyana paṇḍita Prajñāgupta (Shes rab gsang ba), who was also known as the Red Paṇḍita. And he received many of the Cakrasaṃvara scriptures and esoteric instructions from Rma Lo tsā ba.

110 According to Bla ma dam pa, *Bla,* 28, Yo se mo was Gsal ba'i snying po's mother. But Cha rgan, *Lam,* 45b, gives his mother's name as Mon mo Dgos skyid. This is yet another clear indication that Bla ma dam pa is following only Dmar ston and not Cha rgan in his account. The *Śikṣāsamuccaya (Bslab bsdus)* is a compendium of early Mahāyāna teachings compiled by the Indian master Śāntideva. The annotation in the *Zhib mo rdo rje* has also been absorbed into the main text of Bla ma dam pa, *Bla,* 28.

111 "Concerning conduct" translates *Spyod phyogs,* which is a term used to designate texts concerned with proper conduct, apparently including sūtras such as the *Avataṃsaka.* See Stag tshang Lo tsā ba, *Dpal,* 11b. I am grateful to Jeffrey Schoening for this reference. The *Dbu ma shar gsum (Three Madhyamaka Texts from the East)* are three texts on Madhyamaka composed by three authors from East India. They are the *Satyadvayavibhaṅga* of Jñānagarbha, the *Madhyamakālaṃkāra* of Śāntarakṣita, and the *Madhyamakāloka* of Kamalaśīla. These are usually considered a trilogy of Svātantrika treatises. See Ruegg (1981), 68 n. 223.

112 Saroruha (Mtsho skyes), also known as Padmavajra, was one of the greatest Indian adepts. The text referred to is his *Śrī Hevajra sādhana* (*Dpal dgyes pa rdo rje'i sgrub thabs,* To. 1218). Cha rgan, *Lam,* 47b–48a, has the most detail about 'Brog mi taking the commentary written by Gsal ba'i snying po. Gsal ba'i snying po had invited 'Brog mi and his wife to his own residence for a feast and to make offerings in gratitude for 'Brog mi's explanation of the tantras. 'Brog mi saw by the side of Gsal ba'i snying po's seat a large and detailed manuscript that he had written on the outer, inner, secret, and ultimate meaning of the *Kye rdor rgyud gsum (The Tantra Trilogy of Hevajra).* He was astonished at the quality of the work and exclaimed, "You are really like Vajragarbha!" (The bodhisattva Vajragarba was the requester of the *Hevajra tantra* itself and wrote a famous commentary to it.) But 'Brog mi was very displeased that Gsal ba'i snying po had essentially "torn out the living hearts of the ḍākinīs" to give to others. Although Gsal ba'i snying po tried to explain that it was only for his own personal use so that he would not forget the instructions, and vowed not to show it to others, 'Brog mi was not convinced. He said that the text was too wonderful and contained points even he did not know. He kept it, saying such wealth was not allowed to go beyond his own residence. This story is also followed in 'Jam dbyangs mkhyen brtse'i dbang phyug, *Gdams,*

76, with some extra details. It is not found at all in Bla ma dam pa, *Bla,* 28–30.

113 'Brog mi had made the vow in India to keep the transmission of the scriptures (i.e. the *Kye rdor rgyud gsum*) separate from that of the Lam 'bras by not teaching both to anyone. See Cha rgan, *Lam,* 48a–48b. These lineages stayed separate until the time of Sa chen Kun dga' snying po, who taught both to the same disciples. See note 31 in part two for identification of the *Bsam mi khyab.*

114 The term Lha btsun indicates that Lha btsun Ka li was a royal monk. Cha rgan, *Lam,* 16/17b, states that he was the son of Lha btsan po'i Dpal sde, and the brother of 'Brog mi's wife, Lady Mdzes ldan 'od chags. Dpal sde was the eldest son of the royal prince Khri Bkra shis brtsegs pa dpal. It is interesting to note that all sources on royal genealogy say that Dpal lde had two sons, although there is some confusion as to their names. The eldest was named either 'Od zer lde or Dpal lde, or according to some sources, Dmar po btsan or Dmar po lde. The second son was named Dharmacakra or Bde spyod lde. See Sørenson (1994), 466 n. 1740. Neither of these sons can be identified as Lha btsun Ka li. If Bla ma dam pa was the author of the *Rgyal rab gsal ba'i me long,* as Sørenson insists, it is curious that he makes no mention in that text of Lha btsun Ka li among the sons of Dpal lde, while doing so in his history of the Lam 'bras. See Bla ma dam pa, *Bla,* 17, 32. Cha rgan, *Lam,* 22a, mentions that Lha btsun Ka li's royal parents first sent him to study with 'Brog mi soon after the master's return from India and Nepal. Cha rgan, *Lam,* 48b,says Lha btsun Ka li was expert in the Lam 'bras but died young.

115 The translation of the word *zho spungs* is uncertain.

116 The historical texts of the Lam 'bras generally agree that 'Brom's name was De pa ston chung, although Cha rgan, *Lam,* 48b, also refers to him as De pa se ral. Cha rgan, *Lam,* 48b, and Bla ma dam pa, *Bla,* 30, agree that 'Brom was from 'Phan yul. An annotation in Bla ma dam pa, *Bla,* 30, also mentions Bla ma Dmar's statement (in the *Zhib mo rdo rje*), but says that the *'Brom la phyi ring mo* states that 'Brom was from Mdo smad. Kun dga' bzang po, *Lam,* 114.1–114.2, also notes that the *Zhib mo rdo rje* says 'Brom was from 'Phan yul, but points out that in the stories of the 'Brom tradition itself he is said to have been from Mdo smad. The only extant text that says that 'Brom was from Mdo smad is the anonymous *Bhir ba pa'i lo rgyus,* 399, which is indeed an account from the 'Brom tradition. 'Brom was at first a great and famous sorcerer who became wealthy from his sorcery. Bla ma dam pa, *Bla,* 30, and Kun dga' bzang po, *Lam,* 114.2, say that he was expert in the *Ma mo srog thig.* Cha rgan, *Lam,* 49a–b, refers to this

teaching as the *Ma mo yang snying 'dus pa* and quotes some verses from it. This text is unidentified. Cha rgan, *Lam,* 50a–51b, gives more detail about the events described here. Also see part one, chapter two.

117 Manuscript N, 9b, contains an annotation stating that 'Brog mi refused 'Brom's request in order to test 'Brom and see whether he had become proud because of the great offerings he had made *('bul ba zhabs tog chen po byas pas yus yod med rtag pa'i phyir du).*

118 Kun dga' bzang po, *Lam,* 114.2., places the following events later in 'Brom's life after he had taught the Lam 'bras to many students. Ngor chen also mentions how 'Brom gave extensive commentary on the *Rdo rje tshig rkang* to many students without translating it from the Indian language. This information is clearly from the stories of the 'Brom tradition to which Ngor chen had access. The anonymous *Bhir ba pa'i lo rgyus,* 400–401, which may well be the text Ngor chen was using, contains these same details. But there are some confusing spellings and phrasing which make it seem that 'Brog mi was the one teaching the *Rdo rje tshig rkang* to 'Brom without translating from the Indian language, which would make more sense, unless 'Brom had memorized the *Rdo rje tshig rkang* in the original Indian language. A further indication that 'Brom knew Sanskrit is found in the work of 'Jam mgon Kong sprul, who states that 'Brom also translated the *Rdo rje tshig rkang* himself. See 'Jam mgon Kong sprul, *Theg,* 1: 522.

119 The *Phyag rgya chen po yi ge med pa (The Unwritten Great Seal)* by the Indian master Vāgīśvarakīrti is one of the Lam skor brgyad (Eight Cycles of the Path). See Grags pa rgyal mtshan, *Slob dpon ngag.*

120 According to Cha rgan, *Lam,* 53a–53b, 'Brog mi gave these two men the Hevajra initiation and related teachings for five days. They also received about two-thirds of the Lam 'bras, up through what is termed "the middle gathering of the essential constituents." One of the six special instructions which 'Brog mi received from the Six Gatekeepers at Vikramaśīla in India has come down to the present in a lineage through Se and Rog. This is the *Ting nge 'dzin sems kyi bar chad bsrung ba'i man ngag* of Ratnavajra. It was passed from Se and Rog to Gnyos Lo tsā ba. See Ratnavajra, *Ting,* 400. The "three males" mentioned in the *Zhib mo rdo rje* annotation are 'Brog mi's three male disciples who reached attainment and whose stories were related above. They are Sgyer sgom Se bo, Gshen sgom Rog po, and Dbus pa Grod po che. There is a good deal of discussion about the identity of the Se and Rog who requested teachings from 'Brog mi after 'Brom's death. In the anonymous *Bhir ba pa'i lo rgyus,* 403, a historical account according to the 'Brom tradition, it is specifically stated that the

two disciples of 'Brog mi named Sgyer Se'o and Gshen sgom Rog po were also disciples of 'Brom. Cha rgan, *Lam,* 50b, mentions two disciples of 'Brom who were also from 'Phan yul, and later came to 'Brom for instructions on sorcery but changed their minds after seeing how 'Brom himself had changed. They are only identified as noble sons *(jo sras),* one of whom had a yellow mustache *(sma ra ser po can)* and one of whom had a black one *(nag po can).* On 53a–53b, Cha rgan mentions Se and Rog returning to Kha rag to meditate and staying there with 'Phags pa Chos snang. Bla ma dam pa, *Bla,* 32, identifies the three men who requested teachings from 'Brog mi after 'Brom's death as Skyer sgom Se bo, Gshen sgom Rog po, and 'Phags pa Chos snang. As mentioned above, these three men were later present at Gayadhara's death at Kha rag. However, Mang thos klu sgrub, *Bstan,* 83, thinks that the two disciples named Se and Rog who requested teachings from 'Brog mi after the death of 'Brom are not to be identified with Sgyer sgom Se'o and Gshen sgom Rog po, two of 'Brog mi's three male disciples who reached attainment. Mang thos klu sgrub would identify the Se and Rog at this point with the two men who had yellow and black mustaches, which he says is the explanation found in the stories of the Zha ma tradition, but does not make the connection found in Cha rgan. Once again, we see evidence of the Zha ma tradition in Cha rgan's work. 'Jam dbyangs mkhyen brtse'i dbang phyug, *Gdams,* 82, agrees with Mang thos klu sgrub.

121 The question of whether there was any transmission of the Lam 'bras from 'Brom became quite controversial within the historical tradition. Cha rgan, *Lam,* 53b, simply states that although 'Brom De ba se ral wrote explanatory texts concerning the Lam 'bras, his tradition did not spread. But Kun dga' bzang po, *Lam,* 114.4, traces two different lineages of the Lam 'bras transmitted from 'Brom, one of which continued for eight generations and the other for five. Therefore, Ngor chen says, the statement in the *Zhib mo rdo rje* is totally wrong. The anonymous *Bhir ba pa'i lo rgyus,* 403–4, also traces a lineage from 'Brom which contains many of the same names as the list in Ngor chen's text. 'Jam dbyangs mkhyen brtse'i dbang phyug, *Gdams,* 82, also says the *Zhib mo rdo rje* is wrong because the lineage from 'Brom lasted for six or seven generations. However, as usual, Bla ma dam pa, *Bla,* 32, agrees with Dmar ston's *Zhib mo rdo rje.*

122 The Zhi byed (Pacification) system was brought to Tibet in the eleventh century by the Indian master Pha dam pa Sangs rgyas. For information on Pha dam pa and his system of meditation, which combined the teachings of the tantras and the *Prajñāpāramitā,* see Roerich (1976), 867–981, and Edou (1996), 31–38. The Rdzogs chen (Great Perfection) teachings are a specialty of the Rnying ma tradition.

123 It is very interesting that the early anonymous *Bhir ba pa'i lo rgyus,* which is an account according to the 'Brom lineage, says that 'Brom De pa ston chung bestowed the Lam 'bras on Chab ston Chos dga', who then gave it to Rgya Lho brag pa. Kun dga' bzang po, *Lam,* 114.4, also mentions Rgya Lho brag pa and Chab ston Chos dga', respectively, after 'Brom in the transmission line. Is it possible that some confusion about the obscure lineages of 'Brog mi Lo tsā ba's disciple 'Brom De pa ston chung and Sa chen's disciple Jo mo 'Brom mo (Lady 'Brom) occurred early in the tradition? Were their identities somehow partially conflated? All of the information from this annotation in the *Zhib mo rdo rje* is found in Bla ma dam pa, *Bla,* 32, but with more detail.

124 According to Mang thos klu sgrub, *Bstan,* 89, Se ston, who is also known as Se mkhar chung ba, was born on the *shing mo glang* year of 1025. Cha rgan, *Lam,* 72a, says that Se ston was specifically from Mkhar chung, which was in lower Mdog in the region of Byang in G.yas ru.

125 Cha rgan, *Lam,* 54a, says that Se was a young shepherd out one day herding the livestock. When some people hoeing their field told him about 'Brog mi, he lost consciousness for a moment. When he was revived, he decided to go to Mu gu lung. Cha rgan gives a detailed description of how Se discussed his idea with a young relative who knew where his mother had hidden some gold. They secretly took it to provide them with funds for food during their trip and joined together with about twenty young tantric practitioners they met who were also going to Mang 'khar just to see the face of the great 'Brog mi Lo tsā ba. When Se first saw 'Brog mi tears cascaded down his face, a great warmth spread through his body, all phenomena seemed to shimmer and swirl about him, and he cried out and began to shake. Everyone looked around to see what had happened, and 'Brog mi asked him what was wrong. Se replied that something had happened that he couldn't explain. 'Brog mi was pleased and said that his blessings had entered into him, and made some further auspicious comments. After a while the other young travelers left, but 'Brog mi's consort, Mdzes ldan 'od chags, advised Se to stay and request initiation because of the auspicious things the master had said.

126 According to Cha rgan, *Lam,* 55b, Se told Lady Mdzes ldan 'od chags that he and his relative were simple herders and didn't even know what an initiation was. They begged for her help, which she kindly gave. They gave her the gold they had and she made the request for them. Then she loaned them cushions and blankets, and gave them a place to sleep.

127 Cha rgan, *Lam,* 55b, says that Se ston also received ten days of teachings in connection with the Hevajra initiation, and the explanation of the six-

branch method for meditation on Hevajra. Se then began to act as a servant for Mdzes ldan 'od chags. But it also occurred to him that he might not ever receive the complete esoteric instructions if he were just regarded as a servant. Since he was an expert singer and story-teller he began to earn some food and so forth by doing those things in nearby places.

128 The *Brtag pa gnyis pa* is the surviving text of the *Hevajra tantra,* referred to as the *Brtag pa gnyis pa (The Second Fascicle)* because it was originally the second fascicle *(brtag pa)* of the huge root tantra, most of which has been lost. According to Cha rgan, *Lam,* 36b, 'Brog mi sent this letter while Dkon mchog rgyal po was still living at his first hermitage in the Bra bo valley before founding Sa skya monastery in 1073.

129 Manuscript N, 10b, has "The master said, 'Someone who knows a song must sing a song!'"

130 Cha rgan, *Lam,* 56a–b, provides many more details here. After 'Brog mi had noticed that Se was still hanging around, and had asked Mdzes ldan 'od chags who he was, she advised Se to wait by the door to the master's retreat cell and then make an offering and ask for teachings when he came out. He did as she told him, and 'Brog mi gave him further initiation, instructions on practice, and the transmission of the *Bzang po yongs bzung, Rin chen 'bar ba,* and the Dharma cycle of Saroruha. Then 'Brog mi told Se to leave. When Se asked to be allowed to come back the next year 'Brog mi told him not to come. When he insisted, 'Brog mi asked what he wanted. Then Se declared that he wished to request the Lam 'bras, and was told to come back only if he brought much wealth.

131 Cha rgan, *Lam,* 56b, mentions that Se performed the full Hevajra retreat while back at home.

132 Manuscript N, 11a, says the toll was one yak for every two.

133 According to Mkhan po A pad Rin po che, the term *dmar* here means "good." Manuscript N, 11a, has *'kho,* while manuscript B1, 11b, and the manuscript reproduced here, have *dmar.* Cha rgan, *Lam,* 57, has *mkho.*

134 Manuscript N, 11a, has seven years before and seventeen later, totaling twenty-four years, but manuscript B1, 11b, has seven years before and ten later, totaling seventeen years, as does Bla ma dam pa, *Bla,* 35. Cha rgan, *Lam,* 57b, says that Se listened to the teachings and meditated on them for eight years. Then 'Brog mi instructed him to practice them for thirteen years before teaching them only to worthy disciples. Finally Se received the Lam skor (phyi ma brgyad) for another four years. One year had passed before he began to receive the Lam 'bras, so in all he spent thirteen years

with 'Brog mi. Cha rgan, *Lam,* 57b, again makes reference to the *Lung skor lnga,* in conjunction with which Se received the *Rdo rje tshig rkang.*

135 See also Bla ma dam pa, *Bla,* 35. This episode is also given in Dpa' bo Gtsug lag 'phreng ba, *Chos,* 2: 1364. It is interesting that Indra had clearly received the entire Lam 'bras from his father, but is not usually listed among 'Brog mi's Lam 'bras disciples in the historical texts of the Sa skya tradition. The first mention of a transmission through 'Brog mi's sons is found in a brief list by Jo nang Kun dga' grol mchog, *Untitled,* 63b. Mang thos klu sgrub, *Bstan,* 132, also lists a transmission through 'Brog mi's sons. 'Jam mgon Kong sprul, *Theg,* 1: 522, seems to follow Kun dga' grol mchog in describing a transmission of the Lam 'bras through both Indra and his brother Rdo rje.

136 The "summation of the path and prediction of practice" (*lam bsdus te bsgrub pa'i lung sbyin pa*) is performed at the end of the Lam 'bras. Briefly, a single quatrain of verse, which sums up the teachings of the Lam 'bras on many levels, is spoken by the master together with a strong injunction to keep the oral instructions secret. See Grags pa rgyal mtshan, *Untitled,* 298–300, and Sa skya Paṇḍita, *Sgrub pa* and *Sgrub pa'i.* But also see 'Jam dbyangs mkhyen brtse'i dbang phyug, *'Byung,* 224, who emphasizes the prediciton of practice.

137 An annotation in manuscript N, 11b, says 'Brog mi had made this promise to his teacher Vīravajra in India.

138 Cha rgan, *Lam,* 58a–60a, gives much detail about Se ston's studies with Dkon mchog rgyal po. In particular, when Se first went to Sa skya, 'Brog mi sent the following letter with him for Dkon mchog rgyal po.

> You are the best of those who fully received my [teachings] on the tantras. Se ston Kun rig is the best of those who fully received the esoteric instructions. I am the best of both your masters. The best has given the best to the best. So accomplish the best benefit for others by means of this best dependently arisen connection!

When Dkon mchog rgyal po read the letter he was delighted, and they held a great celebration. After going home to gather offerings Se returned to Sa skya and received the Cakrasaṃvara and Hevajra initiations from Dkon mchog rgyal po. For a period of six years he then studied and became an expert in the *Kye rdor rgyud gsum.* Cha rgan, *Lam,* 59b–60a, further mentions that Se was under oath not to teach the Lam 'bras for thirteen years, but he did give the complete reading transmission *(lung)* of the *Rdo rje tshig rkang* to Dkon mchog rgyal po, as well as make an outline *(sa bcad)* of it for him, all during a period of twenty-one days in joint retreat. This does not agree with the strictly Sa skya versions of the events, and probably comes from the Zha ma tradition.

139 The expression "some stability in the creation stage" *(bskyed rim la cung zad brtan pa)* refers to the state of realization when meditative concentration is balanced and all appearances actually dawn as the deity because there is a total integration of appearances and emptiness. All sounds actually dawn as mantra and the stream of blissful primordial awareness is felt to be stable. See Bla ma dam pa Bsod nams rgyal mtshan, *Lam,* 379.

140 Cha rgan, *Lam,* 72a, notes that in the area of 'Khar chung, which was Se ston's home, there were many lepers, deaf mutes, cripples, blind persons, people with goiters, and so forth. It was thought to be a very dangerous place, and Se ston purposely chose to practice meditation retreat there for seven years because of the fact that staying in such a place would intensify the intrinsic awareness and provide opportunity to accomplish virtue. During that time he tamed the evil demoness there. After reaching attainment he meditated in other dangerous places for six years before beginning to teach.

141 According to Mang thos klu sgrub, *Bstan,* 89, Se ston Kun rig lived to the age of ninety-eight, which would place his death in the year 1122.

142 The younger brother was named Gzi bjid 'bar and the elder was Chos 'bar. According to Mang thos klu sgrub, *Bstan,* 110–11, Zhang ston Chos 'bar was born on the *chu mo sbrul* year of 1053, and died at the age of eighty-two, which would correspond to the year 1135.

143 According to Mkhan po A pad Rin po che, the term *rtsi 'gras* refers to making the texts straight, trimming the pages evenly, varnishing them, and so forth.

144 Cha rgan, *Lam,* 79b, mentions that Se ston explained to the brothers that his master 'Brog mi Lo tsā ba insisted on an auspicious dependently arisen connection *(rten 'brel)* before bestowing the teachings. 'Brog mi felt that because of the greatness of the instructions, and in order to examine the worthiness of the individual who was requesting them, a great deal of material wealth was necessary as an offering. As mentioned in note 258 in part one, both Vīravajra and Gayadhara had told 'Brog mi to require this of his disciples.

145 For interesting details, see Cha rgan, *Lam,* 79b–80a, and part one, chapter two.

146 Pha drug is a region to the north of Jo mo Glang ma ri (Mt. Everest).

147 The family name is found with the spellings Zhwa and Zha. I have standardized it to Zha everywhere in this book. Gyatso (1985), 329, 34n, first pointed out that Roerich confused Ma gcig Zha ma for Ma gcig Lab sgron in his translation of *The Blue Annals*. The section in *The Blue Annals* must have been based on historical sources from the Zha ma tradition that are no longer available. Roerich (1976), 220 and 221, gives the *chu pho stag* year of 1062 for the birth of Ma gcig Zha ma and the *sa mo bya* year of 1069 for the birth of her younger brother Chos rgyal 'Khon phu ba (=Khum bu ba Chos rgyal), who died in 1144.

148 Bla ma dam pa, *Bla,* 43, says that Ma gcig was seventeen years old when she first married. Roerich (1976), 220, gives the *shing pho spre'u* year of 1044 for the birth of Rma Lo tsā ba Chos 'bar. Rma Lo tsā ba studied with the Indian master Abhayākaragupta, who prophesied that on his return to Tibet he should seek out Ma gcig Zha ma to be his tantric consort. See both Roerich (1976), 219, and Cha rgan, *Lam,* 73a–b. Cha rgan further states that Ma gcig received all the esoteric instructions related to the Mahāmudrā teachings of Saraha's *Dohā* from Rma Lo tsā ba, but that he died after they had been together for five years. Roerich (1976), 222, says that Rma was forty-six years old (1089) when he died of poisoning. The same source provides exhaustive detail about Ma gcig's subsequent illness, and the cures prescribed by Pha dam pa Sangs rgyas.

149 Dam pa rgya gar, or "The Holy Indian," is another name for Pha dam pa Sangs rgyas, the originator of the Zhi byed system of meditation. His residence in Tibet was at Ding ri Glang 'khor near the border with Nepal. The oldest available sources from the Zhi byed tradition verify that Lady Zha chung ma was one of the twenty-four female disciples of Pha dam pa. Pha dam pa's chief disciple Kun dga' (1062–1124) wrote a very brief contemporary account of Ma gcig's life. This is the earliest information about her in any Tibetan source. It is apparent in Roerich (1976), 919–20, that Gzhon nu dpal, the author of the *Deb ther sngon po,* later had access to Kun dga's text, but for some reason chose not to reproduce the account of Ma gcig's life. Dmar ston's *Zhib mo rdo rje* is the earliest mention of her in the Sa skya tradition of the Lam 'bras. Kun dga', *Jo,* 322, has the following account.

> The twenty-second [female disciple] was Lady Zha chung ma. She was a woman from Dman chu rgyab pa, a region to the east of Ding ri. She had seven brothers, beginning with Zha ma Ston pa. Because of her natural physical beauty she served the translator Sma ban Chos 'bar. She requested the entire initiations of the Lam 'bras from paṇḍita 'Gha yan dha ra and meditated. Then, after her faults

> in meditation were cleared away by Dam pa she reached attainment. When Dam pa died and his body was being cremated, she disguised herself as a woodcutter woman and left a bundle of firewood and an ounce of gold at the crematorium. On the road back she transformed into a pigeon and flew away. So it is said.

As will become obvious below, there are several points in this story that differ from that of the Lam 'bras tradition. The most significant differences are that she received the Lam 'bras from Gayadhara and that Pha dam pa removed her illnesses. Actually, she received the Lam 'bras from Se ston and, according to the Lam 'bras histories, it was Se ston who cured her chronic ailments.

150 Kun dga', *Gnad,* 325, records the following conversation he had with Pha dam pa.

> "Dam pa, sir, this Lady Zha chung ma is said to have first been unable to produce meditation, and then even though it did arise there were many problems. Why was that?"
>
> Dam pa replied, "Her inability to produce meditation at first was a result of little devotion to a master. Then those problems in meditation were the result of having few oral instructions but great perseverance."

In Kun dga', *Jo,* 312–13, Kun dga' records this instruction from Pha dam pa to Ma gcig.

> When Lady Zha chung ma asked, Dam pa said, "Clear away obstacles! Offer initiation gifts! Take austerities to the limit! Practice the oral instructions correctly! If you act like that, you will mount the thunder and travel through space."

151 Bla ma dam pa, *Bla,* 44, states that she went into retreat for seven years and studied all the sūtras and tantras she could find, but her illness was not cured.

152 Lha rje Rnubs pa is perhaps to be identified with Lha rje Hūṃ chung, also known as Lha rje Gnubs chung, who is in the Rong lineage of transmitted precepts in the Rnying ma tradition. He was also perhaps the teacher from whom Mi la ras pa learned Rdzogs chen as a young man. See Dudjom (1991), 1: 615, and especially Martin (1982), 54–58, who has closely examined the identity of the Lha rje Gnubs chung who taught Mi la ras pa.

153 According to Grags pa rgyal mtshan, *Slob dpon klu,* 404, this verse is from the *Samāyoga (Mnyam sbyor).* The *Buddhasamāyoga (Sang rgyas mnyam sbyor)* is especially important in the Rnying ma tradition, where it is counted as one of the five inner tantric scriptures within the eighteen great

tantric scriptures of the Mahāyoga tradition. But the verse could not be located in any of the three versions of this scripture preserved in the Peking Tripitaka, vol. 1, and the *Rnying ma rgyud 'bum,* Gting skyes edition, vol. 16. However, it is apparently found in the *Guhyagarba (Gsang ba snying po),* 8, in the *Rnying ma rgyud 'bum,* Dil mgo Mkhyen brtse, Bhutan, 1973–74. This edition has not yet been consulted. The information in the annotation to the *Zhib mo rdo rje* has been incorporated into the main text of Bla ma dam pa, *Bla,* 45.

154 The meaning of this sentence appears to have been lost early in the tradition. Mkhan po A pad Rin po che could also not make sense of it. Bla ma dam pa, *Bla,* 46, has *the'u rang* instead of *pe kar.* Cha rgan, *Lam,* 74b, has *rgyal ltogs pe the'u zhang tsha.* Pe kar is the same as the Pe har demon/deity. See the multiple entries in Nebesky-Wojkowitz (1956), especially 94–133. The term *kha la* in the *Zhib mo rdo rje* annotation is an obscure term. Mkhan po A pad Rin po che was also uncertain of the meaning. Roerich (1976), 225, mistakenly interpreted this conversation to be between Pha dam pa Sangs rgyas and Se ston Kun rig.

155 Cha rgan, *Lam,* 80a, states that Rje Khum bu ba and his sister came to study with Se ston the year after the Zhang ston brothers began to receive the Lam 'bras. Roerich (1976), 229, says Khum bu ba was thirty-three years old at that time, which would correspond to the year 1101. The same source, 226–29, gives the most information about Khum bu ba, who died in the *shing pho byi* year of 1144.

156 See Bla ma dam pa, *Lam,* 379: "Having become accustomed to the stream of that meditative concentration, on some occasions, or continually, one may think that this is the great taintless bliss, or that one has seen the truth, or reached the culmination of attainment. This is also known as 'the māra of contentment.'"

157 This annotation is in the main text of Bla ma dam pa, *Bla,* 46.

158 I am grateful to Mkhan po A pad Rin po che for explaining this sentence, although the meaning of *jag dmar* remains obscure. Ma gcig and her brother had to sleep against the bellies of yaks on the path to keep warm at night.

159 Yang dgon pa Rgyal mtshan dpal, *Bar,* 548, names three texts concerning the intermediate state between lifetimes *(bar do)* that were written by Lha rje ma, as Ma gcig Zha ma was often called. This epithet may indicate that she was skilled in medical practice. Yang dgon pa states that her *Bar do snyan brgyud, Bar do mkha' spyod,* and *Bar do mngon sum* contained profound instructions on the intermediate state explained according to the

Lam 'bras of Virūpa. These texts do not seem to have survived. Yang dgon pa received the Lam 'bras of Ma gcig Zha ma from Rgyal ba Ko brag pa and the Sa skya lineage from Sa skya Paṇḍita. Although Ma gcig Zha ma wrote a number of texts, only a few lines of her teachings have survived. One couplet is recorded with some variations in two of Sa chen Kun dga' snying po's commentaries to the *Rdo rje tshig rkang*. See Sa chen Kun dga' snying po, *Lam,* 70, and *Gzhung rdo,* 195. Sa chen, *Gzhung rdo,* 195, has *jo mo lha rje ma*/ *bsgoms kyang zhen pa mi ldog pa*/ *thad ka'i chos nyid ma go'am*/.

> Lady Lha rje ma stated, "You meditate, but attachment is not repelled. Don't you recognize the true nature right in front of you?"

160 This entire annotation has been absorbed into the main text of Bla ma dam pa, *Bla,* 47. One of the four transmission lines of the Hevajra initiation is from Virūpa's disciple Kahna (Nag po pa), and another is from the scholar Kṛṣṇa (Nag po pa). Since both of these Indian names were translated into Tibetan as Nag po pa it is difficult to know which is intended here. However, the transmission of Kṛṣṇa seems to be a preferable choice because it was not passed down from Virūpa. The lineage termed the *man ngag lugs* comes from Virūpa and is synonymous with the Lam 'bras. See Davidson (1992), 109ff, for a short discussion of the four Hevajra transmission lines. The Hevajra practice of Saroruha is the *Śrī Hevajra sādhana* (*Dpal dgyes pa rdo rje'i sgrub thabs,* To. 1218).

161 Zhu byas Dngos grub was a disciple of Sa chen Kun dga' snying po. One of Sa chen's eleven commentaries on the *Rdo rje tshig rkang* was for his benefit. Other sources mention a number of other miracles performed by Lady Zha ma. For example, see 'Jam dbyangs mkhyen brtse'i dbang phyug, *Gdams,* 107.

162 Lord Dgon pa ba is Zhang ston Chos 'bar. Lady Lakṣmīṅkarā was the sister of the tantric master Indrabhūti, who was the king of Uḍḍiyana. She was a great adept and would seem to have been known as Bhikṣuṇī Lakṣmī in later life. Shaw (1994), 110–13, and 126–30, regards Lakṣmīṅkarā and Lakṣmī as two different women. Cha rgan, *Lam,* 77/78a, states that Ma gcig Zha ma lived to the age of eighty-eight, as does Roerich (1976), 226. This would correspond to the year 1149. All the chronicles of the Lam 'bras are unanimous in stating that she had an enormous number of disciples and that her system of the Lam 'bras spread widely. According to 'Jam dbyangs mkhyen brtse'i dbang phyug, *Gdams,* 107, the lineages from both Ma gcig and her brother were transmitted separately for about eight generations and are known as the female and male lines. Lord Dgon pa ba's comment about Ma gcig's excessive fondness for songs of experience is

baffling. But according to Mkhan po A pad Rin po che, it simply means that she liked songs too much.

163 Cha rgan, *Lam,* 70a, 72b, gives the name Gze sgom Byang rgyal. Bla ma dam pa, *Bla,* 48a, gives his name as Byang chub ye shes instead of Byang (chub) seng (ge). Ze sgom first came to 'Brog mi Lo tsā ba with great offerings, but 'Brog mi would not even see him. According to Cha rgan, *Lam,* 70a, 'Brog mi was sixty-three years old and in retreat. When 'Brog mi's circle urged him not to reject a faithful person who had come from far away with great offerings, 'Brog mi replied that when he was teaching, he taught, and when he was practicing meditation, he practiced, and so didn't have time to meet anyone. When someone mentioned that 'Brog mi was said to like wealth and that the man had brought great wealth, 'Brog mi immediately pointed out that he had only required large offerings before in order to emphasize the value of the teachings and to examine the sincerity of the disciple. Now he had already passed the various teachings on to those who would further transmit them, and he didn't want any more wealth. Ze sgom went away in tears. Later he succeeded in receiving the Lam 'bras from Se ston Kun rig, but he didn't have great intelligence, diligence, or ability to meditate. He is also considered the inferior recipient because he didn't receive all the esoteric instructions and didn't have great experience or realization.

164 Yar lung Jo bo, *Yar,* 146, says Lady Zhang mo was Zhang zhung Gu ru ba's sister *(sring mo).* Bla ma dam pa, *Bla,* 48, says she was his *bu sring mo* (daughter or sister?). According to 'Jam dbyangs mkhyen brtse'i dbang phyug, *Gdams,* 109, she was his daughter *(bu mo)* and lived in Mkhar sgo lung. In any case, she was the second of Dkon mchog rgyal po's two wives. According to the late Sde gzhung Rin po che, "After Ma gcig Zhang mo's death her body was interred with the body of her husband in the 'Khon Sku 'bum at Sa skya. During the troubles of the 1960's the stūpa was destroyed, but her body was recovered. Her body is tiny, and although just a corpse, it is very beautiful, and just at the sight of it a special joy arises in the mind. It is unlike any other corpse. She was a real ḍākinī." Personal communication from the late Sde gzhung Rin po che, Seattle, August 9, 1985.

165 Bra'o, or Bra bo, was where Dkon mchog rgyal po first built a small hermitage and began to teach the tantras of the Hevajra cycle that he had received from 'Brog mi Lo tsā ba. See Cha rgan, *Lam,* 36a–b. According to Yar lung Jo bo, *Yar,* 145, he lived there for several years. After his move to Sa skya the old hermitage became known as the "Sa skya ruin" *(sa skya'i gog po).*

166 According to Cha rgan, *Lam,* 36b–37a, the general region of Sa skya was

controlled by four men, who were Zhang zhung (Gu ru ba), Bsreg sgom G.yung 'bar, and two others. Yar lung Jo bo, *Yar,* 145, and 'Jam mgon A mes zhabs, *'Dzam,* 19, agree in giving a somewhat different list. Zhang zhung Gu ru ba, who was in control of the specific area of Sa skya, was either the brother or father of Sa chen's mother, Lady Zhang mo. Dkon mchog rgyal po founded the monastery of Sa skya in the *chu mo glang* year of 1073. Rdo phyug ma is Rdo rje dbang phyug ma, Dkon mchog rgyal po's first wife. Sa chen was born in 1092. For more information on the fascinating story of the events preceding Sa chen's birth, see part one, chapter two.

167 Dkon mchog rgyal po died in 1102. From the age of six Sa chen had been receiving Dharma from his father, such as the Hevajra initiation and many related teachings. See Grags pa rgyal mtshan, *Dpal,* 22; Cha rgan, *Lam,* 37a; and Bla ma dam pa, *Bla,* 49.

168 According to all the Sa skya sources the funeral ceremony and the enthronement of Ba ri Lo tsā ba were also accomplished on the same day the foundation was laid for Dkon mchog rgyal po's reliquary. The meaning of the term *ser chags* remains obscure. Other sources have *chos 'khor,* "Dharma council," and I have translated by understanding *ser chags* was a synonym.

169 Dkon mchog rgyal po's main teacher was the translator *(lo tsā ba)* 'Brog mi Lo tsā ba, and he had also studied with 'Gos Lo tsā ba and Rma Lo tsā ba.

170 G.yu 'khar mo is another name for the Sgrol ma lha khang that Ba ri Lo tsā ba Rin chen grags (1040–1111) built in Sa skya. I thank Jeffrey Schoening for this information. Instead of this sentence, manuscript B1,14b–15a, has the following paragraph:

> The disciples [of Dkon mchog rgyal po] deliberated, and [decided] that now a translator and paṇḍita were needed for the Dharma council of the master, and moreover, agreed to invite Ba ri ba. When Ba ri ba was invited, he agreed to come. Preparations were twice made in vain, and then it was said that he wasn't coming. When both Rdo rje ra dza and Gdol ban ra tshe, capable mantra practitioners who were disciples of Dkon [mchog] rgyal [po], performed sorcery from Sa skya toward Ba ri ba who was staying in La stod, the enchanted objects fell on the robe of Ba ri and he came. Then, after receiving the command of Mañjuśrī, he practiced with success. The great master [Sa chen] came there to study. Ba ri also constructed the Rnam rgyal mchod rten. He maintained the monastic seat for eight years.

The most detailed information on Ba ri Lo tsā ba is found in 'Jam mgon A mes zhabs, *Dpal rdo,* 1: 222–34. He is an important lineage holder for many tantric transmissions in the Sa skya tradition. Also see Roerich (1976), 1021–23.

171 The *A ra pa tsa na* is the mantra of Mañjuśrī.

172 Acala (Mi g.yo ba) is the specific protector associated with Mañjuśrī. When Mañjuśrī appeared to Sa chen he spoke what have come to be known as the *Zhen pa bzhi bral (Parting from the Four Attachments).* These four phrases summarize the entire Mahāyāna path and have continued to be the basis for the extensive teachings on Blo sbyong (Mind Training) in the Sa skya tradition up to the present day. For a translation of Sa skya texts concerning this teaching, see Sakya Trizin and Ngawang Samten (1982).

173 This is Brang ti Dar ma snying po who was one of the foremost figures in the transmission of the Abhidharma in Tibet. See Roerich (1976), 345–46. The Abhidharma that Sa chen received at this point was probably the *Abhidharmasamuccaya* of Ārya Asaṅga.

174 Most of this annotation is found in Bla ma dam pa, *Bla,* 50.

175 A co Phag ston was one of the elders at Sa skya. Cha rgan, *Lam,* 38/39a, identifies the figure on horseback as Sa chen's father Bla chen Dkon mchog rgyal po, but other Sa skya sources usually identify him as Bdud rgyal thod phreng can, one of the two special protectors of Vajrakīlaya. See 'Jam mgon A mes zhabs, *'Dzam,* 27. This annotation in the *Zhib mo rdo rje* is found in the text of Bla ma dam pa, *Bla,* 50.

176 Brang ti is another name for Ngur dmig pa. See note 297 in part one for a list of the five Divisions of the *Yogacaryābhūmi (Sa sde)* of Ārya Asaṅga. The translation of the term *skyed ma* is uncertain.

177 Sa chen received the Seven Treatises on Epistemology by the Indian master Dharmakīrti, except for the *Pramāṇavārtikka,* which is the first of the set. The remaining six are the *Pramāṇaviniścaya,* the *Nyāyabindu,* the *Hetubindu,* the *Vādanyāya,* the *Saṃbandhaparīkṣa,* and the *Saṃtānāntarasiddhi.* Khyung Rin chen grags was one of the four most important disciples of Rngog Lo tsā ba Blo ldan shes rab (1059–1109). See Roerich (1976), 326.

178 In addition to these Mahāyāna sūtras, Sa chen also received a large number of tantric transmissions from Ba ri Lo tsā ba, such as many kriyā and caryātantras. He also received different lineages of the Guhyasamāja, Yamāntaka, the *Kye rdor rgyud gsum (The Tantra Trilogy of Hevajra),* the

Bde mchog rgyud gsum (The Tantra Trilogy of Cakrasaṃvara), and so forth. See also Grags pa rgyal mtshan, *Dpal,* 22–23, who places Sa chen's studies with Ba ri before those with Brang ti and the others. Ba ri Lo tsā ba passed away in 1111.

179 The enormous number of teachings Sa chen received from master Kha'u pa are listed in Grags pa rgyal mtshan, *Dpal,* 26–28.

180 Garlic is often considered a forbidden food for yogins and would certainly have been considered extremely eccentric as an offering to the Triple Gem. The meaning of *'o bya 'phrang pa* is obscure.

181 The information in this annotation is found with even more detail in Bla ma dam pa, *Bla,* 51–52.

182 Gsal snying is Gsal ba'i snying po, the disciple of 'Brog mi Lo tsā ba who was described earlier in the *Zhib mo rdo rje.* One of the main lines of 'Brog mi's explication of the *Kye rdor rgyud gsum* was transmitted through him. The information in this annotation is also found in Bla ma dam pa, *Bla,* 52.

183 Cha rgan, *Lam,* 38&39b, gives Sgyi chu ba's name as Shes rab 'bar. Grags pa rgyal mtshan, *Dpal,* 23–24, lists the many transmissions which Sa chen received from master Sgyi chu ba. In particular he received a number of Hevajra transmissions, as well as other important tantras and esoteric instructions from a variety of lineages, such as those of 'Gos Lo tsā ba and Mar pa Lo tsā ba.

184 The usual spelling for the valley in which Sa skya is located is Grom.

185 The master was Sa chen's father Dkon mchog rgyal po, with whom Se ston had studied the *Kye rdor rgyud gsum.*

186 Cha rgan, *Lam,* 40, says that Sa chen's companion Ston pa Rdor 'od, who is also mentioned below in our text, explained to Se ston the circumstances of Sa chen's birth. Se ston then felt that he was once again meeting his own teacher, Sa chen's father Dkon mchog rgyal po, who had died years before.

187 Cha rgan, *Lam,* 40b, says that Se ston bestowed on Sa chen the *Rdo rje tshig rkang, Lung skor lnga,* and the blessing of the Virūpa protection practice. See note 26 in part one about the problematic identification of the *Lung skor lnga.*

188 'Khar chung was Se ston's principal residence.

189 Master Mnga' ris pa was 'Brog mi's disciple Gsal ba'i snying po, from whom Sgyi chu ba had received the *Kye rdor rgyud gsum* and many other transmissions.

190 Se ston Kun rig passed away in 1122 at the age of ninety-eight. See Mang thos klu sgrub, *Bstan,* 89.

191 This is master Gnang (or Gnam) Kha'u pa, with whom Sa chen had studied before.

192 Mal Lo tsā ba Blo 'gros grags pa received the Cakrasaṃvara transmissions from the Newar Pham 'thing brothers and the Tibetan master Klog skya Shes rab brtsegs. He was also an important figure in the Mahākāla tradition. See 'Jam mgon A mes zhabs, *Dpal rdo,* vol. 1, 216 ff. According to Cha rgan, *Lam,* 41b, master Sgyi chu ba had left instructions in his last testament for Sa chen to request other teachings such as Cakrasaṃvara from Mal Lo tsā ba. In the biography of his father Sa chen, Grags pa rgyal mtshan mentions the Gnas gsar temple in Gung thang as the residence of Mal Lo tsā ba, and as the place visited by Sa chen to receive teachings from him. See Grags pa rgyal mtshan, *Dpal,* 24. The vast number of tantric transmissions that Sa chen received from Mal Lo tsā ba are listed in Grags pa rgyal mtshan, *Dpal,* 24–26. Perhaps the most important in terms of practice were the teachings of Nā ro Mkha' spyod ma and Gur gyi mgon po, which continue to be crucial meditation practices in the Sa skya tradition.

193 Bu ston, *Bde,* 107–8, states that Mal Lo tsā ba was testing Sa chen to see whether he was just an arrogant aristocrat or a sincere practitioner.

194 The *Bhairava sapta kalpa ('Jigs byed kyi rtog pa bdun pa)* is the main *Vajrabhairava mūla tantra.* I am grateful to Hubert Decleer for pointing this out to me. The text has been translated in Siklos (1996), 27–49. 'Jam mgon A mes zhabs, *'Dzam,* 35, makes it clear that it was the syllables of a mantra which were causing difficulties for Mal's disciples.

195 This obscure idiom was apparently common at the time. In both Grags pa rgyal mtshan, *Bde,* 298, and Bar ston, *Bar,* 7b, the idiom is clearly used to illustrate corrupt tantric practices, such as drawing a maṇḍala in a goat pen, wrapping wool around a pitcher and using it as a substitute for a ritual vase, and then claiming to give intitiations. Bar ston quotes Grags pa rgyal mtshan using the example when warning Sa skya Paṇḍita of the corrupt tantric practices that would appear in his lifetime. This episode is repeated with various details in the different historical sources about Sa chen's life.

196 According to Grags pa rgyal mtshan, *Dpal,* 25, the *Yan lag brgyad pa (The Eight Branches)* is the teaching on the eight fundamental branches of medical diagnosis in the Tibetan tradition. The *Ratnakuṭa* is actually a huge collection of forty-nine Mahāyāna sūtras. See vols. 22–24 in the Peking

edition of the Tibetan Tripitaka. The form of Mahākāla known as Pañjaranātha (Gur gyi mgon po) is one of the special Dharma protectors of the Sa skya tradition. The canonical source for Pañjaranātha is the Hevajra explanatory tantra known as the *Vajrapañjara*, which is one of the *Kye rdor rgyud gsum (The Tantra Trilogy of Hevajra).*

197 The original source for this entire annotation is Grags pa rgyal mtshan's history of the Cakrasaṃvara lineage. See Grags pa rgyal mtshan, *Bde,* 298.3–4.

198 The meaning of an annotation at this point in the *Zhib mo rdo rje* is obscure, and has not been translated: *dang po slob mar mi chod skog chod nas de las yod ri ba skad zer.*

199 Grags pa rgyal mtshan, *Dpal,* 27, lists the *Bstan pa'i nor rdzas (Wealth of the Doctrine)* as a Guhyasamāja sādhana that Sa chen received from master Gnang Kha'u pa. But he also mentions the *Tha ga na* as a commentary on the Guhyasamāja, unless this is another text being referred to by its author's name.

200 Dgon pa ba, or "The Recluse," is an epithet of Zhang ston Chos 'bar.

201 Cha rgan, *Lam,* 77/78b, states that the Zhang ston brothers learned the Rdzogs chen teachings of the *Bram ze'i skor (The Cycle of the Brahmin)* and the *Rtsa mun ti* from their grandfather, and were experts in their practice. The *Bram ze'i skor* is a group of Rnying ma tantras of the Atiyoga class that were introduced into Tibet by Padmasambhava and Vimalamitra. The "brahmin" *(bram ze)* is apparently Bram ze Bde mchog snying po, who received the lineage from Dga' rab rdo rje and passed it to Śrīsiṃha. The *Bram ze'i skor* are comprised of nos. 112–28 in Kaneko (1982), 127–49. The *Rdzogs chen rtsa mun ti (The Great Perfection of Rtsa mun ti)* is unidentified.

202 Cha rgan, *Lam,* 81b, gives the father's name as Zhang Skyabs se. 'Jam dbyangs mkhyen brtse'i dbang phyug, *Gdams,* 120, says that Jo sras 'Od mchog's father was named Ston pa Rdo rje 'od and was later known as Zhang Skyabs pa. Thus it seems that he was Sa chen's old acquaintance Ston pa Rdo rje 'od zer, from the earlier years of study under Bla ma Sgyi chu ba. Lord 'Khar chung ba, the "Lord from 'Khar chung," is an eptithet of Se ston Kun rig.

203 This would be the case if Lord Zhang had lied to the son of Dkon mchog rgyal po, who had been one of the teachers of Lord Zhang's own master Se ston Kun rig.

204 Usually spelled 'O lung.

205 Mar lo Rin chen bzang po is unidentified. Cha rgan, *Lam,* 82b, says this was a memorial Dharma council for Se ston Rdo rje 'byung.

206 This statement matches an annotation found in manuscript N, 16b.

207 The offering of maṇḍalas and the recitation of the hundred-syllable mantra are the normal preliminary practices for the accumulation of merit and the purification of obstacles and misdeeds. The hundred-syllable mantra is the mantra of Vajrasattva. Manuscript B1, 17b, specifies "swollen" *(skrangs),* although the text reproduced here, and Manuscript N, 16b, just say "sick" *(snyung).*

208 Manuscript N, 17a, also says Sa chen wrote with a *rdo ba,* "stone," while manuscript B1, 18a, has *rdo rje,* "vajra." Cha rgan, *Lam,* 83b–84a, merely states that Sa chen wrote some notes to assist his memory *(rjed tho)* on the back of his hand. Zhang ston forbade him to do so, telling him to be energetic in meditation and not to write it down. If he couldn't remember by thinking about it he should make intense supplications. Sa chen did as he was told and it had great mental benefits.

209 As pointed out in Bla ma dam pa, *Bla,* 61, Zhang ston gave Sa chen the complete teachings in consideration of the fact that Sa chen's father Dkon mchog rgyal po had been the teacher of Zhang ston's own master Se ston Kun rig. Sa chen's son Grags pa rgyal mtshan stated that Sa chen received the entire Lam skor dgu (Nine Cycles of the Path) from Zhang ston, as well as many other teachings. Among these, he received an explanation of the *Hevajra tantra* according to Virūpa's own system, and the transmission of exceptional explications of the *mūla tantras* of the *Guhyasamāja, Buddhasamāyoga, Hevajra, Cakrasaṃvara, Caturpiṭha, Mahāmāya,* and *Mañjuśrīnāmasaṃgīti.* See Grags pa rgyal mtshan, *Dpal,* 28–29. See note 136 in part two for an explanation of "the summation of the path and the prediction of practice" *(lam bsdus te bsgrub pa'i lung sbyin pa)* that is traditionally given at the completion of the Lam 'bras. Manuscript B1, 181, has "fifteen years," but all other sources agree with eighteen years. Cha rgan, *Lam,* 84a–b, provides Zhang ston's final advise to Sa chen in much more detail, with some very important points. See part one, chapter two, for a translation of this passage. See Stearns (1997), for a translation of the description of these events as they are recorded in 'Jam dbyangs mkhyen brtse'i dbang phyug, *Gdams,* 123, which is based on Cha rgan's passage.

210 These future disciples will be discussed below. See note 227 in part two for an explanation of "Forbearance."

211 Cha rgan, *Lam,* 85a, mentions that Sa chen's motive in requesting Zhang ston to teach the Lam 'bras to others was a fear that it might be lost. The

information in the *Zhib mo rdo rje* annotation is not found anywhere except in Cha rgan, with some significant differences. Zhang po ston pa is probably to be identified with Zhang Dkon mchog dpal, whom Mang thos klu sgrub, *Bstan,* 111, says received the Lam 'bras from Zhang ston Chos 'bar.

212 Cha rgan, *Lam,* 85a, quotes Nag ston Lo tsā ba as saying to Sa chen, "You were famous at Sgyi chu and should be ashamed to request Dharma from a lay monk." Sa chen replied, "When a master has experience and realization of the oral instructions, there is no shame."

213 According to Mkhan po A pad Rin po che, the term *spangs dug* is a synonym for *la dug,* which means altitude sickness. Bla ma dam pa, *Bla,* 61, has *la spangs dug.* According to Mang thos klu sgrub, *Bstan,* 111, Zhang ston died at the age of eighty-three, which would correspond to the year 1135.

214 Bla ma dam pa, *Bla,* 62, has much the same information as this note. He also says that since there were only a few diagrams of yogic postures, and so forth, the Lam 'bras was only an oral transmission until the latter part of Sa chen's life.

215 In place of this phrase, *only* manuscript B1, 18b, has the following paragraph, which contains much of the same information as the annotation in the text reproduced here:

> Lord Dgon pa ba's female companion, Lady 'Od zer brgyan, showed a leather bag to master Sa skya pa and said, "The master's manuscripts are in here, so if you need them you must take them." The master peeked through the mouth [of the bag] and there was a description of the channels *(rtsa'i lo rgyus).* Sa skya pa thought, "The lord said there were no written texts for the Lam 'bras. If there are some texts a lack of faith in the master would arise," and [put] the manuscripts in that bag....

216 Acording to Dung dkar Blo bzang 'phrin las, in his notes to Kun dga' rdo rje, *Deb,* 168 n. 46, Mt. Malaya (Ri Ma la ya) is the name of a mountain on the southern tip of the Indian subcontinent. He quotes the *Thang sen dzang gi lam yig,* which can be identified as the travelogue of the Chinese pilgrim Hsüan-tsang. This source mentions a mountain named Ma la ya located in Ma ru ku ṭha, or Ra me shwa ri, on which many types of sandalwood and camphor trees grew. There was a fine temple of Avalokiteśvara on the summit of the mountain. A spring gushed from one side and the stream from it flowed down circling the mountain twenty times before emptying into the ocean to the south. See Tucci (1971), 494, 499–500, etc., for a similar description from Hsüan-tsang and the Potala guidebook.

217 Mkhan po A pad Rin po che glossed the term *'khos ka* as *nus pa'i tshad*, or *las ka byed thub ma thub*, and noted that it is Central Tibetan dialect *(bod skad).*

218 According to Newman (1985), 85 n. 16, the *sen dha pa* (*sen tha ba* in our text) were Ceylonese Theravadin monks who were active in Magadha during the Pāla and Sena dynasties. There is also some information in Templeman (1983), 59–60, about the troublesome activities of these monks. It is interesting to note that the Tibetan translator and Kālacakra master Tsa mi Sangs rgyas grags pa, who was abbot of Nālandā in the twelfth century, sometimes signed his works as *sen dha pa* Sangs rgyas grags pa. *A tsa ra* is the Tibetan transliteration of the Sanskrit *ācārya*, but the term is also used to designate wandering Indian tantric yogins in general. See Cha rgan, *Lam,* 86a–b, and Bla ma dam pa, *Bla,* 66, for the sections on the Ceylonese mendicant *(a tsa ra).* Sa skya Paṇḍita, *Lam,* 310, also mentions this story, but says the monk was from Sindhu in India (Rgya gar Sindhu).

219 The great master is Sa chen Kun dga' snying po. Rgwa Lo tsā ba Rnam rgyal rdo rje also met Sa chen at Na la tse gnas po che and received teachings from him. See Bar ston, *Bar,* 29a–30a. Na la tse gnas po che is also the temple in Gung thang where Dmar ston later wrote the *Zhib mo rdo rje.*

220 At least one later source states that the Ceylonese śrāvaka paṇḍita also received the explanation of the *Rdo rje tshig rkang* from Sa chen at Na la rtse. Sa chen's disciple named Jo gdan Ldan bu also received the instructions at the same time. These instructions were recorded as one of Sa chen's famous eleven commentaries on the *Rdo rje tshig rkang,* and are known as the *Jo gdan ldan bu ma.* For the benefit of the Ceylonese monk, Sa chen is said to have spoken the instructions in Sanskrit on that occasion and later translated them into Tibetan. See Rdo rje rgyal mtshan, *Man,* 237. The commentary for Jo gdan Ldan bu is the only one of the eleven that opens with a Sanskrit title followed by a Tibetan translation. There are also numerous transliterated Sanskrit terms throughout the text. The *Lam sbas bshad* is one of the special teachings of the Lam 'bras imparted by Virūpa directly to Sa chen during a retreat that will be mentioned below in our text. Sa skya Paṇḍita later wrote an instruction manual for its practice as he had received it from his uncle Grags pa rgyal mtshan. See Sa skya Paṇḍita, *Lam.* The location of Śrīparvata in Uḍḍiyana (U rgyan) is curious. It is usually said to be in southern India. See note 51 in part two for different information about the location of Śrīparvata.

221 Bla ma dam pa, *Bla,* 66–67, basically follows our text, but also wonders whether Kyi 'bar is to be identified with the yogin from Mtshar kha who is mentioned below, as does Cha rgan, *Lam,* 86b. Kyi 'bar's special success

was achieved through the practice of the vocal enunciations which form part of the practice of the Fourth Initiation *(dbang bzhi pa)* in the Lam 'bras. See 'Jam dbyangs mkhyen brtse'i dbang phyug, *Gdams,* 129.

222 Gnyan Phul byung ba Gtsug tor rgyal po, also known as Bsod nams rdo rje, was an important disciple of Sa chen Kun dga' snying po. He edited the many miscellaneous explanations of difficult points in the Lam 'bras that Sa chen had recorded for his sons Bsod nams rtse mo and Grags pa rgyal mtshan into the most extensive and cherished of Sa chen's eleven commentaries on Virūpa's *Rdo rje tshig rkang,* which is known as the *Sras don ma.* See 'Jam dbyangs mkhyen brtse'i dbang phyug, *Gdams,* 128. Some also say that he held the monastic seat at Sa skya for three years during the minority of Sa chen's sons. See Sa chen Kun dga' snying po, *Lam,* 445. Gnyan Phul byung ba also received the Cakrasaṃvara teachings from Mal Lo tsā ba and the *Cakrasaṃvara tantra* from the master Sumatikīrti. He then composed a commentary on the tantra based on the instructions of all three of his teachers, entitled *Mu tig phreng ba.* See Go rams Bsod nams seng ge, *Bde,* 56.2. Gnyan Phul byung ba's commentary is the *Dpal 'khor lo bde mchog gi rtsa ba'i rgyud kyi ṭī ka mu tig phreng ba,* found in the *Sa skya bka' 'bum* (Tokyo: Toyo Bunko, 1968), 1: 288.3–380.3.

223 Mtsho snying Ma hā dhe'u is a small island in Lake Kokonor in the eastern Tibetan region of Mdo smad. It is an ancient holy site. According to Bar ston, *Bar,* 21b, another of Sa chen's disciples named Dbus chung Ser po also went to the island to meditate. See the many references to Tsonying (Mtsho snying) in Ricard et al. (1994). Cha rgan, *Lam,* 86b, says that Stag went to the pure land of Khecara. Bla ma dam pa, *Bla,* 66, simply copied the information in the *Zhib mo rdo rje.* Cha rgan, *Lam,* 86b, says of Stag only that he abandoned the body for seven days, then his mind returned to it and he departed to the pure land of Khecara.

224 Gnyags, whose name was Dbang phyug rgyal mtshan, was a disciple of Sa chen for whom one of the eleven commentaries on the *Rdo rje tshig rkang* was written. According to Cha rgan, *Lam,* 86b, Gnyags was traveling among the nomads to gather offerings for the memorial services to be held after Sa chen's death. As mentioned in note 221 in part two, both Cha rgan and Bla ma dam pa seem to think that this nomad from Tshar kha might be the same as Sgom pa Kyi 'bar. But our text seems to question whether he is the same as Stag. Later, 'Jam dbyangs mkhyen brtse'i dbang phyug, *Gdams,* 132–33, lists the Tshar kha nomad as one of the seven disciples who reached the spiritual level of Forbearance, and does not question his identity nor mention any confusion with any other disciples.

225 The translation of the phase *'chi mo thug ma tshor* is uncertain. According

to Bla ma dam pa, *Bla,* 65, Sa chen's elder disciples avowed that he had never traveled to Tshar ka. But after his death they conferred and realized that he had simultaneously manifested bodies at six different locations. Sa skya Paṇḍita, *Grub,* 245, is the earliest source for this story, which he states came from Bla chen, probably to be understood here as his teacher and uncle Grags pa rgyal mtshan. Also see Cha rgan, *Lam,* 86b, and especially Bla ma dam pa, *Bla,* 64–65, for details on the story. According to Sa skya Paṇḍita the signs that were evident on the Tshar ka nomad were of having stabilized the bindu from the throat center down. This and other related signs are described in detail in the Lam 'bras. The translation of *tshe gzhug* is also uncertain.

226 The teacher's name is spelled Bho ta Ru hu la in the text, which has been corrected to Bho ta Rā hu la in the translation. Bho ta Rā hu la was an Indian yogin from whom Sa chen received many esoteric instructions. See Grags pa rgyal mtshan, *Dpal,* 30. The Lord of Yogins is Virūpa. The translation of *zangs rga rdo 'dra ba* is uncertain.

227 The stage of Forbearance *(bzod pa thob)* refers to the attainment of a specific stage on the Path of Application *(sbyor lam),* during a bodhisattva's progression toward total enlightenment. It is a point when forbearance has been achieved and there is no fear of emptiness because the truth of reality has been perceived. A large degree of certainty in the nonsubstantiality of apprehended objects, and a lesser certainty in the nonsubstantiality of the apprehending mind, has been achieved.

228 Rje btsun is Sa chen's son Rje btsun Grags pa rgyal mtshan. Master Zhu yas, usually spelled Zhu byas, was named Dngos grub, and was a disciple for whom Sa chen composed one of the eleven surviving commentaries on the *Rdo rje tshig rkang.* Bla ma dam pa, *Bla,* 67–68, provides several stories about Zhu byas, as does Bar ston, *Bar,* 21a.

229 An interesting tale of 'Od grags's experience in meditation after receiving initiation and teachings from Sa chen is found in Bla ma dam pa, *Bla,* 69. Also see Bar ston, *Bar,* 31a. Sgom Jo lcags is Jo sras Lcags kyi rdo rje. He is known for requesting Rje btsun Grags pa rgyal mtshan to compose the first instruction manual focusing on the "three appearances" *(snang gsum)* and the "three continuums" *(rgyud gsum),* which are two main sections of the Lam 'bras. This text, usually referred to as the *Jo lcags ma,* was the model for a new genre in the Lam 'bras literature. The *Snang gsum* and *Rgyud gsum* treatises have become the basic format for teaching and practicing the Lam 'bras. See Grags pa rgyal mtshan, *Gzhung.* One of Sa chen's eleven commentaries was composed for Lady Mang chung ma, but it is not among the eleven that have survived. One of her experiences

in meditation is related in Bla ma dam pa, *Bla,* 69. Also see Bar ston, *Bar,* 31b. Stories about Gnas brtan Bsod shes are given in Bar ston, *Bar,* 23a and 31a. Bla ma dam pa, *Bla,* 70, only mentions that Bsod shes is sometimes listed among the seven. Sa chen wrote one of the eleven commentaries on the *Rdo rje tshig rkang* for the benefit of Zla ba rgyal mtshan. According to Bla ma dam pa, *Bla,* 68, Rga ston (whose name is also spelled Sga and Dga') was a disciple of both Sa chen and Grags pa rgyal mtshan. He spent most of his life in meditation. Grags pa rgyal mtshan wrote a very important epistle concerning the practice of the four initiations at the request of Rga ston Rdo rje grags. See Grags pa rgyal mtshan, *Rje,* 41–49. In place of the last five disciples in this list manuscript B1, 19a, has "Khri bzang, Dar ra, Grub ston, and so forth." Manuscript N, 18b, has "Zangs ri phub pa, Khams pa Dga' ston, Byangs sems Zla rgyal, Se Ye shes snying po, and Rtod Rgyal ba 'byung gnas." See Bla ma dam pa, *Bla,* 67–70, for a different list of seven and much information on them. On page 70 he discusses different opinions about the seven. Cha rgan, *Lam,* 86b–871, lists not seven, but eleven disciples who reached the stage of Forbearance.

230 The main text of manuscript N, 18b, adds, "Also, the many people taken across the first bridge were the immeasurable disciples in general."

231 Before this sentence, manuscript B1, 19a–b, has an extra sentence: "On one occasion in La stod he became gravely ill and thereafter forgot all the Oral Instructions [of the Lam 'bras]. It was cured by offering and making prayers to master Zhang." This point will be elaborated just below in the *Zhib mo rdo rje.*

232 The original source for the following story, which is the most important visionary event in Sa skya history, is Grags pa rgyal mtshan, *Rje btsun gyis ldan,* 13–15. Grags pa rgyal mtshan first heard it from his father's disciple Gnyan Phul byung ba, the editor of the *Sras don ma,* the most important of Sa chen's eleven commentaries on the *Rdo rje tshig rkang.* Grags pa rgyal mtshan then recorded it for the benefit of Sga theng, who was the recipient of another of the eleven commentaries. Sa chen had been poisoned in Gung thang, and was in a coma for about a month. Then he was still affected by the poisoning for about three years, after which he forgot all the teachings he had received. Sa skya Paṇḍita's account of the same story, which he heard from Grags pa rgyal mtshan, is found in Sa skya Paṇḍita, *Grub,* 244–45.

233 Sa chen went into retreat in the cave at Sa skya where he had received the teachings of the *Zhen pa bzhi bral* directly from Mañjuśrī when he was a young boy. Cha rgan, *Lam,* 87a, says that Sa chen was forty-one years old

when he now went into retreat again, which would correspond to the year 1132.

234 When Sa chen was blessed by Zhang ston he wrote a eulogy to his master in which he says that he was cured of the illness by Zhang ston's compassion. See Sa chen, *Zhang.* From the experience of receiving the prolonged teachings from Virūpa, a stunning eulogy to him arose in Sa chen's mind. See Sa chen, *Dpal.* The identification of the seventy-two tantric teachings has created much confusion in the tradition. Glo bo mkhan chen Bsod nams lhun grub finally wrote a short text to clarify the issue. He enumerates fifty anuttarayoga, four yoga, three caryā, and fifteen kriyātantras. See Glo bo mkhan chen, *Rgyud.* Mang thos klu sgrub, *Bstan,* 130, dates the meeting with Virūpa to the year 1138 *(sa rta),* when Sa chen was forty-six years old.

235 This paragraph in the reproduced text of the *Zhib mo rdo rje,* but not the annotations, is found in an annotation in manuscript N, 18b, but not in manuscript B1! The teachings of the *Sbas bshad,* the *Rnal 'byor dbang phyug gi bsrung 'khor,* and the *'Bir 'joms,* are all found in the *Pod dmar* collection in vol. 13 of the *Sa skya Lam 'bras Literature Series* (Dehra Dun: Sa skya Centre, 1983).

236 A seng Rdo rje brtan pa was the nephew of Sa chen's teacher Skyu ra A skyabs. Early in his life Sa chen had invited Skyu ra A skyabs to Sa skya and requested many tantric transmissions from him, chiefly the different Guhyasamāja systems. See 'Jam mgon A mes zhabs, *'Dzam,* 36–37. A respectful letter from Sa chen to his teacher Skyu ra A skyabs is preserved in the *Sa skya bka' 'bum* (Tokyo: Toyo Bunko, 1968), 1: 284.

237 The *Lam 'bras mdor bsdus ma (The Condensed Path with the Result),* more often known as the *A seng ma (The Explication for A seng),* was the first of Sa chen's famous eleven commentaries on the *Rdo rje tshig rkang.* According to Mang thos klu sgrub, *Bstan,* 130, and 'Jam mgon A mes zhabs, *Gsung ngag rin po che Lam,* 567, Sa chen first taught the Lam 'bras to A seng in the *lcags mo bya* year of 1041.

238 The number nine refers to Hevajra with his consort Vajra Nairātmyā and the eight other goddesses in the Hevajra maṇḍala. According to the Lam 'bras tradition, the Hevajra initiation must not be given to a group larger than twenty-five.

239 From among the teachings of the "three continuums" *(rgyud gsum)* as explained in the *Rdo rje tshig rkang,* the renewal of damaged sacred commitments is usually counted as the fourth of the five sections of the "method continuum" *(thabs rgyud).* See Dmar ston Chos kyi rgyal po, *Gzhung,* 129–33.

240 Dga' theng is usually spelled Sga theng. According to 'Jam mgon A mes zhabs, *Yongs,* 187, the commentary for Sga theng was the first of the major works on the *Rdo rje tshig rkang,* preceded only by the short verse *A seng ma.* The order of the composition of the other nine is unknown, except for the *Gnyags ma* that was written last.

241 Most of this annotation is also in N, 19a. See Bla ma dam pa, *Bla,* 63, for the same information. These are two of the eleven available commentaries of Sa chen. This statement may indicate that the *Zhu byas ma (The Explication for Zhu byas)* was also one of the earliest of the eleven.

242 This statement indicates that Grags pa rgyal mtshan and Sa skya Paṇḍita used the *Gnyags ma (The Explication for Gnyags)* when teaching the Lam 'bras. Also see Dmar ston, *Gzhung,* 4. The *Gnyags ma* was the only one of the extensive commentaries included by Grags pa rgyal mtshan in the *Pod ser* collection. The *Gnyags ma* is still the commentary most commonly used for explanation of the *Rdo rje tshig rkang.*

243 This is a very interesting statement. Could it be that the other commentaries such as the *Yum don ma (The Explication for the Wife)* and the *Sras don ma (The Explication for the Benefit of the Sons)* were quite scarce, and had actually not been seen by the author of these notes or by his teacher Tshogs sgom Rin po che? A comment at the end of the *Sras don ma* itself says that no one else (except the editor Rje Phul byung ba) had the text of the *Sras don ma.* Then the names of the next three teachers who received the text are given. See Sa chen Kun dga' snying po, *Lam,* 445–46. The four commentaries referred to in the *Zhib mo rdo rje* annotation are apparently the *A seng ma, Sga theng ma, Zhu byas ma,* and *Gnyags ma.*

244 This event is mentioned in Bla ma dam pa, *Bla,* 65, as one of the six instances when Sa chen emanated to different places simultaneously. Bla ma dam pa refers to the place as Mgron la byams temple in 'Bring mtshams, and to the maṇḍala as Nam mkha' dri med.

245 This event is also mentioned by Bla ma dam pa, *Bla,* 65, as one of the times when Sa chen manifested a body in different places. Sgo lnga was in the region of Shab.

246 See Rje btsun Grags pa rgyal mtshan, *Dpal.*

247 It is generally accepted that Sa chen was sixty-six years old at his death. The temple of Skya bo kha gdangs was near Ngam ring, the capital of the Byang district.

248 The form of Vairocana alluded to here is Vairocana Sarvavid, who has

four faces, one looking in each of the four directions. One of Sa chen's eleven commentaries was written for Bzang ri phug pa, although it is not among the eleven now available.

249 Ma gcig Btsad tsha was the first of Sa chen's two wives. She was also known as Jo lcam Phur mo. See 'Jam mgon A mes zhabs, *'Dzam,* 50 and 62. According to 'Jam dbyangs mkhyen brtse'i dbang phyug, *Gdams,* 127, from among the eleven commentaries to the *Rdo rje tshig rkang,* the *Yum don ma* was written for Ma gcig Btsad tsha. 'Jam mgon A mes zhabs, *Yongs,* 185, agrees with Mkhyen brtse, and explains that after Kun dga' 'bar's death in India, his mother turned to serious Dharma practice, and Sa chen wrote this commentary for her. Kun dga' 'bar is known to have died at the age of twenty-two in Magadha, but no other source mentions that he was poisoned. Sa skya Paṇḍita, *Bla,* 661, specifies that Kun dga' 'bar went to India to learn the art of translation *(lo tsā slob pa).* Also see 'Jam mgon A mes zhabs, *'Dzam,* 62–63.

250 Ma gcig 'Bro tsha was Sa chen's second wife. According to 'Jam mgon A mes zhabs, *'Dzam,* 63, she was also known as Ma gcig 'Od sgron. Bsod nams rtse mo studied epistemology and other subjects with Phya pa Chos kyi seng ge (b. 1109), the greatest Tibetan logician of his time. *Durgacandra (Mi thub zla ba) was the teacher of Vīravajra, who was in turn the teacher of 'Brog mi Lo tsā ba. Also see note 33 in part two. Rje btsun pa is Grags pa rgyal mtshan. Sa skya Paṇḍita's father, Dpal chen 'od po (1150–1203), was the younger brother of Grags pa rgyal mtshan.

251 Rje btsun Grags pa rgyal mtshan was born in 1147. The great master is his father Sa chen, and Slob dpon Rin po che is his elder brother Slob dpon Bsod nams rtse mo.

252 Grags pa rgyal mtshan himself told this to Sa skya Paṇḍita. See Sa skya Paṇḍita, *Bla,* 665. The same event is also mentioned in Bla ma dam pa, *Bla,* 75.

253 Perhaps the most significant of these events was when Grags pa rgyal mtshan was fifty-six years old, which was forty-four years after the death of his father Sa chen. Sa chen appeared again and again in Grags pa rgyal mtshan's dreams, and finally actually appeared to him, in much the same way that Virūpa had first appeared to Sa chen in dreams, and then actually came. Sa chen then gave Grags pa rgyal mtshan a succinct and profound teaching which summarized all the essential points for the practice of the Lam 'bras. This teaching has come to be known as the *Brda don gsal ba.* See Sa skya Paṇḍita, *Brda.*

254 In particular, Grags pa rgyal mtshan wrote a large number of indispensable

texts on the practice of the Lam 'bras. These are mostly found in the collection referred to as the *Pod ser,* although several important works are also in the *Pod dmar.* These collections are respectively found in the *Sa skya Lam 'bras Literature Series* (Dehra Dun: Sa skya Centre, 1983), vols. 11 and 13.

255 The honorable Bzang po (Bzang po'i zhabs) is Sa skya Paṇḍita Kun dga' rgyal mtshan dpal bzang po. For his biography of Grags pa rgyal mtshan, see Sa skya Paṇḍita, *Bla.*

256 In the early sources Sa skya Paṇḍita is frequently referred to as the Master Translator (Bla ma Lo tsā ba), the Translator of Sa skya (Sa skya Lo tsā ba), or the Great Translator (Lo tsā ba chen po). His important translations of Sanskrit epistemological works have been noted in Jackson (1987), 1: 112–13. But no attention has been drawn to the fact that he also translated a number of tantric works, most of which were done in collaboration with his Indian teacher Sugataśrī. In particular, they translated several yogatantras that had never been translated into Tibetan. Sa skya Paṇḍita himself mentions their new translations of the *Guhyamaṇitilaka* (*Gsang ba nor bu'i thig le,* To. 493), the *Vajrapātāla* (*Rdo rje sa 'og,* To. 744), the *Guhyālaṃkāra* (*Gsang ba rgyan,* To. 492), and the *Vajramaṇḍālaṃkāra* (*Rdo rje snying po rgyan gyi rgyud,* To. 490). See Sa skya Paṇḍita, *Chag,* 556. For a discussion of these works and their place in the tantric tradition, see Tāranātha, *Dge,* 551–53. According to Sa skya Paṇḍita's disciple and biographer Lho pa Rin chen dpal, Sa skya Paṇḍita and Sugataśrī also translated many other works related to these tantras. See Lho pa, *Dpal,* 98. These translations would have been made between 1205 and 1207, which was the period of Sugataśrī's residence in Sa skya. See Jackson (1987), vol. 1, 26. Sometime later Sa skya Paṇḍita recovered and translated alone the Sanskrit manuscript of a fragment of the *Vajrakīlaya mūla tantra* (To. 439), which is certainly his most significant tantric translation.

257 As mentioned in part one, the following sketch of Sa skya Paṇḍita's life is perhaps the earliest of all sources, and can now be identified as the missing biography known to have been written by Dmar ston. See Jackson (1987), 1: esp. 15–38, for information on the life of Sa skya Paṇḍita, and the various Tibetan sources.

258 As discussed in part one, Rin po che is Sa skya Paṇḍita's disciple Tshogs sgom Rin po che Kun dga' dpal. The quoted verse is found in Mātṛceṭa, *Sangs,* 42.1.

259 Sa skya Paṇḍita was born in 1182.

260 The lord is the child's uncle, Rje btsun Grags pa rgyal mtshan.

261 These are two of the different scripts in which Sanskrit was written.

262 The Dharma Lord is Grags pa rgyal mtshan.

263 The Hevajra *sādhana* by Saroruha, also known as Padmavajra, is the *Śrī Hevajra sādhana* (*Dpal dgyes pa rdo rje'i sgrub thabs*, To. 1218).

264 Manuscript N, 20b, has "As soon as he awoke all the words and meaning unmistakably arose in his mind."

265 The *Pramāṇasamuccaya (Kun las btsus)* of the Indian master Dignāga was the main work on epistemology that Sa skya Paṇḍita transmitted to later generations. See Jackson (1987), 1: 137, etc. The final statement in the *Zhib mo rdo rje* annotation is very curious, considering that Sa skya Paṇḍita had obviously mastered the *Pramāṇasamuccaya* long before his trip to China. Perhaps it is a reference to another unknown dream in which he later looked through the text.

266 According to Jackson (1987), 1: 25–26, 106, Zhu ston Rdo rje skyabs was a disciple of Grags pa rgyal mtshan, as well as of Phya pa Chos kyi seng ge. In addition to the *Byams chos (The Dharmas of Maitreya)*, Sa skya Paṇḍita also studied four of Nāgārjuna's *Rigs tshogs (The Yukti Collection)*, the *Satyadvayavibhaṅga* of Jñānagarbha, and the *Madhyamakālaṃkāra* of Śāntarakṣita.

267 The *Pramāṇaviniścaya* is one of the Indian master Dharmakīrti's Seven Sets on Epistemology. Mtshur ston was the disciple of both the great logician Phya pa Chos kyi seng ge and his famous student Gtsang nag pa Brtson 'grus seng ge. In addition to epistemology, Sa skya Paṇḍita also first studied Prāsaṅgika Madhyamaka with Mtshur ston on the basis of the *Prasannapadā* of Candrakīrti. See Jackson (1987), 1: 26, 105–7, for a detailed discussion of the various events in connection with Sa skya Paṇḍita's studies with Mtshur ston. Dpal chen 'od po, the younger brother of Grags pa rgyal mtshan, passed away in 1203. See 'Jam mgon A mes zhabs, *'Dzam*, 84–85.

268 The information in this annotation has all been included in Bla ma dam pa, *Bla*, 83–84.

269 Cf. Jackson (1987), 1: 107, and note 14.

270 He received Nāgārjuna's *Dbu ma rigs tshogs (The Madhyamaka Yukti Collection)*. See Jackson (1987), 2: 179, for references.

271 See Jackson (1987), 1: 107–10, for details on Sa skya Paṇḍita's studies with the Indian master Śākyaśrībhadra, who was immensely influential in Tibet. See Jackson (1990) and van der Kuijp (1994b) for information on the life

of Śākyaśrī. The commentary is the Indian master Dharmottara's *Pramāṇaviniścayaṭīka* (To. 4229), explaining Dharmakīrti's *Pramāṇaviniścaya.*

272 An annotation in manuscript N, 21b, states that Śākyaśrī gave him the name "Sa skya Paṇḍita" on this occasion.

273 Jackson (1987), 1: 27, mentions that he also studied part of the commentary on the *Amarakoṣa* with Dānaśīla.

274 This entire annotation is found in the main text of Bla ma dam pa, *Bla,* 84.

275 All the previous material in this paragraph is missing in Manuscript N.

276 Manuscript N, 21b, says that it was Saṃghaśrī who was invited to Sa skya, which is not attested to in other accounts, and states that Sa skya Paṇḍita studied with him for two years.

277 Manuscript N, 21b, has Rong.

278 Rje btsun Grags pa rgyal mtshan.

279 This account is also found in Bla ma dam pa, *Bla,* 85.

280 The *Ālaṃkāra* is Prajñākaragupta's *Pramāṇavārtikkālaṃkāra* (To. 4221), a commentary on the *Pramāṇavārtikka* of Dharmakīrti. As mentioned above, Dharmottara's text is a commentary on the *Pramāṇaviniścaya.* Dharmakīrti's seven treatises on epistemology were identified in note 177 in part two. The Set of Three is probably to be understood as the first three of the seven, which are the *Pramāṇavārtikka,* the *Pramāṇaviniścaya,* and the *Nyāyabindu.* These three are often thought of as the basic body, and the remaining four as the connected limbs.

281 Manuscript N, 22a, does not have this sentence. The other paṇḍita referred to in our text may have been either Saṃghaśrī or Dānaśīla, both of whom also instructed Sa skya Paṇḍita in epistemology. See Jackson (1987), 1: 110–11.

282 An annotation in manuscript N, 22a, specifies that Sa skya Paṇḍita also received the commentary to the *Kālacakra tantra* entitled *'Grel chung Pad dkar,* (probably to be identified as the *Padmani nāma pañjikā,* Peking Tripitaka, vol. 47, no. 2067) and the explanation of the maṇḍala rite, the practice of the ṣaḍaṅgayoga, and the sādhana. See Newman (1987) for information on the Kālacakra system, and a translation of the first section of the *Vimalaprabhā* (Peking no. 2064), an immense commentary on the *Kālacakra tantra* by the Śambhala emperor Kalkī Puṇḍarīka.

283 An annotation in manuscript N, 22a, mentions that he received most of the teachings of Saṃvara, such as the *Phyag rdor bstod 'grel,* which is the

Lakṣābhidhanād uddhṛta laghutantra piṇḍārthavivaraṇa (Peking no. 2317), a commentary on the *Cakrasaṃvara tantra* by Bodhisattva Vajrapāṇi.

284 This is clearly a reference to Sa skya Paṇḍita's summons to the court of the Mongol prince Ködän in 1244.

285 This presumably refers to the five greater fields of knowledge *(rig gnas che ba lnga),* which are art, medicine, grammar, reasoning, and Buddhist Doctrine. The five lesser fields of knowledge, of which Sa skya Paṇḍita was also a master, are poetics, synonymy, metrics, drama, and astrology.

286 Manuscript B1, 23a, adds: "...because [his] obviously brilliant radiance among the glacial ranges, like the excellent glow of the waxing [moon], has ignited the excellent splendor of the moon lilies of living beings."

287 Liang-chou (Byang ngos) was Ködän Khan's capital.

288 The honorable Bzang po *(Bzang po'i zhabs)* is Sa skya Paṇḍita, the last element of whose name is Bzang po.

289 As mentioned above in the text, Na la tse gnas po che in Gung thang is where Sa chen had also earlier studied with Mal Lo tsā ba, and later spent time teaching.

290 This paragraph is basically the same in manuscript B1, 23a–23b, but has been reduced to an annotation in manuscript N, 23a.

291 This sentence is found only in the manuscript reproduced here.

Bibliography

Tibetan Sources

Authors and works are listed in Tibetan alphabetical order.

Anonymous. *Kha rag gnyos kyi gdung rabs khyad par 'phags pa.* In *Kha-rag-gnyos kyi gdung-rabs and Rlangs-kyi po-ti bse-ru bsdus-pa.* Dolanji: Khedup Gyatso, 1978.

Anonymous (Gnyags Snying po rgyal mtshan?). *Chos kyi rje sa skya paṇḍi ta'i dngos kyi thugs kyi sras bla ma tshogs sgom rin po che'i rnam thar.* (Title taken from opening line.) In *Sa skya Lam 'bras Literature Series,* vol. 1, pp. 338–41. Dehra Dun: Sakya Centre, 1983.

Anonymous. *Bhir ba pa'i lo rgyus.* In *Gzhung bshad klog skya ma and Other Related Esoteric Sa-skya-pa Texts,* vol. 1, pp. 347–404. New Delhi: Tibetan Bonpo Monastic Centre, 1975.

Anonymous. *Gsung ngag slob bshad thun mong ma yin pa'i khrid kyi khyad chos yongs 'dzin dam pa'i gsung gi bdud rtsi zin bris su bkod pa khrid yig zla ba'i thig phreng gi gsal byed slob bshad bstan pa rgyas pa'i nyi 'od.* In *Sa skya Lam 'bras Literature Series,* vol. 18, pp. 187–226. Dehra Dun: Sakya Centre, 1983.

Karma chags med. *Ri chos mtshams kyi zhal gdams.* n.d. n.p. Rtsib ri edition.

Kun dga'. *Jo mo nyi shu rtsa bzhi'i zhu lan lo rgyus dang bcas pa.* In *Zhi byed snga phyi bar gsum gyi skor,* vol. 4, pp. 302–23. Thimphu: Druk Sherik Parkhang, 1979.

_____. *Gnad kyi zhus lan me long rnam par gsal ba.* In *Zhi byed snga phyi bar gsum gyi skor,* vol. 2, pp. 315–36. Thimphu: Druk Sherik Parkhang, 1979.

Kun dga' grol mchog, Jo nang Rje btsun. *Khrid brgya'i brgyud pa'i lo rgyus.* In *Gdams ngag mdzod,* vol. 12, pp. 309–40. Delhi: N. Lungtok and N. Gyaltsan, 1972.

_____. *Khrid brgya'i spyi chings rnam par spel ba ngo mtshar chos kyi sgo mang.* In *Gdams ngag mdzod,* vol. 12, pp. 289–308. Delhi: N. Lungtok and N. Gyaltsan, 1972.

_____. *Zab khrid brgya dang brgyad kyi yi ge.* In *Gdams ngag mdzod,* vol. 12, pp. 369–595. Delhi: N. Lungtok and N. Gyaltsan, 1972.

———. *Zhen pa rang grol gyi lhug par brjod pa'i gtam skal bzang dad pa'i shing rta 'dren byed.* In *The Autobiographies of Jo nang Kun dga' grol mchog and His Previous Embodiments,* vol. 2, pp. 285–534. New Delhi: Tibet House, 1982.

———. *Untitled.* In *Gsung thor bu ba'i bskor,* fol. 63a–65a (no folio numbered 64, but seems complete). Beijing: Cultural Palace of Nationalities, *dbu med* ms.

Kun dga' rdo rje, Tshal pa. *Deb ther dmar po rnams kyi dang po hu lan deb ther 'di.* Beijing: Mi rigs dpe skrun khang, 1981.

Kun dga' dbang phyug, Rgyal tshab. *Zab mo'i gnad rnams lhan cig tu bsgrigs pa mtshan pusti dmar chung zhes bya ba' dkar chag rin chen phreng ba.* (Title taken from the colophon.) In *Sa skya Lam 'bras Literature Series,* vol. 13, pp. 2–5. Dehra Dun: Sakya Centre, 1983.

Kun dga' bzang po, Ngor chen (Completed by Gung ru ba Shes rab bzang po). *Lam 'bras bu dang bcas pa'i man ngag gi byung tshul gsung ngag rin po che bstan pa rgyas pa'i nyi 'od.* In *The Complete Works of the Great Masters of the Sa skya Sect of Tibetan Buddhism (Sa skya pa'i bka' 'bum),* vol. 9, pp. 108–26. Tokyo: The Toyo Bunko, 1968.

Ko brag pa Bsod nams rgyal mtshan. *Lam 'bras snyan brgyud/ lam 'bras bu dang bcas pa'i gdams ngag.* In *Gzhung bshad klog skya ma and Other Related Esoteric Sa-skya-pa Texts,* vol. 1, pp. 405–590. New Delhi: Tibetan Bonpo Monastic Centre, 1975.

Krang dbyi sun, ed. *Bod rgya tshig mdzod chen mo.* 2 vols. Beijing: Mi rigs dpe skrun khang, 1993.

Dkon mchog bstan pa rab rgyas, Brag dgon pa. *Yul mdo smad kyi ljongs su thub bstan rin po che ji ltar dar ba'i tshul gsal bar brjod pa deb ther rgya mtsho.* Kansu: Mi rigs dpe skrun khang, 1987.

Mkhan po A pad. *Dkar chag mthong bas yid 'phrog chos mdzod bye ba'i lde mig.* New Delhi: Ngawang Tobgyal, 1987.

Gung ru ba Shes rab bzang po, (Completing the work of Ngor chen Kun dga' bzang po). *Lam 'bras bu dang bcas pa'i man ngag gi byung tshul gsung ngag rin po che bstan pa rgyas pa'i nyi 'od.* In *The Complete Works of the Great Masters of the Sa skya Sect of Tibetan Buddhism (Sa skya pa'i bka' 'bum),* vol. 9, pp. 108–26. Tokyo: The Toyo Bunko, 1968.

Go rams Bsod nams seng ge. *Bde mchog chos 'byung brgyud pa'i rnam thar dang bcas pa.* In *The Complete Works of the Great Masters of the Sa skya Sect of Tibetan Buddhism (Sa skya pa'i bka' 'bum),* vol. 15, pp. 52.1.–66.1. Tokyo: The Toyo Bunko, 1968.

_____. *Gsung ngag lam 'bras don bsdus ma'i rnam bshad zab don gnad kyi sgron me.* In *The Complete Works of the Great Masters of the Sa skya Sect of Tibetan Buddhism (Sa skya pa'i bka' 'bum),* vol. 15, pp. 145.1.–152.1. Tokyo: The Toyo Bunko, 1968.

Grags pa rgyal mtshan, Rje btsun. *Kun gzhi rgyu rgyud las 'phros nas 'khor 'das dbyer med kyi lta ba'i rtsa ba.* In *Sa skya Lam 'bras Literature Series,* vol. 11, pp. 191–94. Dehra Dun: Sakya Centre, 1983.

_____. *'Khor 'das dbyer med kyi lta ba'i 'grel pa.* In *Sa skya Lam 'bras Literature Series,* vol. 11, pp. 194–243. Dehra Dun: Sakya Centre, 1983.

_____. *Rgyud kyi mngon par rtogs pa rin po che'i ljon shing.* In *Sa skya Lam 'bras Literature Series,* vol. 22, pp. 1–277. Dehra Dun: Sakya Centre, 1983.

_____. *Rje btsun gyis dga' ston rdo rje grags la gdams pa.* In *Sa skya Lam 'bras Literature Series,* vol. 13, pp. 41–49. Dehra Dun: Sakya Centre, 1983.

_____. *Rje btsun gyis ldan ma sga 'theng la gdams pa.* In *Sa skya Lam 'bras Literature Series,* vol. 13, pp. 13–15. Dehra Dun: Sakya Centre, 1983.

_____. *Ḍombi he ru kas mdzad pa'i lhan cig skyes grub.* In *Sa skya Lam 'bras Literature Series,* vol. 11, pp. 387–95. Dehra Dun: Sakya Centre, 1983.

_____. *Bde mchog lū hi pa'i lugs kyi bla ma brgyud pa'i lo rgyus dang/ bla ma sa chen gyi lo rgyus nyung ngu.* In *The Complete Works of the Great Masters of the Sa skya Sect of Tibetan Buddhism (Sa skya pa'i bka' 'bum),* vol. 3, pp. 293.2–298.4. Tokyo: The Toyo Bunko, 1968.

_____. *Dpal sa skya pa chen po kun dga' snying po'i rnam thar.* In *Sa skya Lam 'bras Literature Series,* vol. 1, pp. 18–32. Dehra Dun: Sakya Centre, 1983.

_____. *Bla ma brgyud pa rgya gar ba'i lo rgyus.* In *Sa skya Lam 'bras Literature Series,* vol. 11, pp. 581–93. Dehra Dun: Sakya Centre, 1983.

_____. *Bla ma brgyud pa bod kyi lo rgyus.* In *Sa skya Lam 'bras Literature Series,* vol. 11, pp. 594–99. Dehra Dun: Sakya Centre, 1983.

_____. *Nag po u tsi ṭa 'chi ba med pas mdzad pa yon po bsrang ba'i gdams pa.* In *Sa skya Lam 'bras Literature Series,* vol. 11, pp. 457–61. Dehra Dun: Sakya Centre, 1983.

_____. *Phrin las sum cu rtsa gnyis kyi 'khrul 'khor.* In *Sa skya Lam 'bras Literature Series,* vol. 11, pp. 288–92. Dehra Dun: Sakya Centre, 1983.

_____. *Gzhung ji lta ba bzhin du dkri ba'i gzhung shing.* (Title taken from colophon.) In *Sa skya Lam 'bras Literature Series,* vol. 11, pp. 300–314. Dehra Dun: Sakya Centre, 1983.

———. *Lam 'bring du bstan pa dang bsdus pa'ang yod.* In *Sa skya Lam 'bras Literature Series,* vol. 11, pp. 292–300. Dehra Dun: Sakya Centre, 1983.

———. *Slob dpon klu sgrub kyis mdzad pa'i mchod rten drung thob.* In *Sa skya Lam 'bras Literature Series,* vol. 11, pp. 400–405. Dehra Dun: Sakya Centre, 1983.

———. *Slob dpon ngag dbang grags pas mdzad pa'i phyag rgya chen po yi ge med pa.* In *Sa skya Lam 'bras Literature Series,* vol. 11, pp. 406–19. Dehra Dun: Sakya Centre, 1983.

———. *Slob dpon nag po spyod pas mdzad pa'i gtum mo lam rdzogs.* In *Sa skya Lam 'bras Literature Series,* vol. 11, pp. 445–57. Dehra Dun: Sakya Centre, 1983.

———. *Slob dpon indra bhu tis mdzad pa'i phyag rgya'i lam skor.* In *Sa skya Lam 'bras Literature Series,* vol. 1, pp. 461–79. Dehra Dun: Sakya Centre, 1983.

———. *Gsung ngag rin po che lam 'bras bu dang bcas pa'i don gsal bar byed pa glegs bam gyi dkar chags.* In *Sa skya Lam 'bras Literature Series,* vol. 11, pp. 1–8. Dehra Dun: Sakya Centre, 1983.

———. *Untitled.* In *Sa skya Lam 'bras Literature Series,* vol. 11, pp. 298–300. Dehra Dun: Sakya Centre, 1983.

Glo bo mkhan chen Bsod nams lhun grub. *Grub chen yon tan dpal dang/ la ru ba bsod nams seng ge'i rnam par thar pa. Dbu med* ms., 3 fols. Kathmandu: Nepal-German Manuscript Preservation Project, Reel no. L-102/15.

———. *Rgyud sde bdun cu rtsa gnyis kyi dkar chag gsal ba'i sgron me. Dbu med* ms., 1 fol. Kathmandu: Nepal-German Manuscript Preservation Project, Reel no. L-102/28, running no. L-1256.

———. *Bla ma dmar chos kyi rgyal po'i rnam par thar pa. Dbu med* ms., 4 fols. Kathmandu: Nepal-German Manuscript Preservation Project, Reel no. L-102/15.

'Gos Lo tsa ba Khug pa lhas btsas. *'Gos khug pa lhas btsas kyi sngags log sun 'byin.* In *Chag lo tsā bas mdzad pa'i sngags log sun 'byin dang 'gos khug pa lhas btsas kyi sngags log sun 'byin,* pp. 18–25. Thimphu: Kunsang Topgyel and Mani Dorji, 1979.

'Gos Lo tsa ba Gzhon nu dpal. *Deb ther sngon po.* 2 vols. Chengdu: Mi rigs dpe skrun khang, 1984.

Ngag dbang chos grags, Paṇ chen. *Gsung ngag rin po che lam 'bras bu dang bcas pa'i lo rgyus dang dmigs pa'i zab gnad cung zad bshad pa'i yi ge kha'u brag rdzong pa'i bzhed pa ma nor ba paṇ chen ngag dbang chos grags kyis mdzad pa.* In *Sa skya Lam 'bras Literature Series,* vol. 18, pp. 58–65. Dehra Dun: Sakya Centre, 1983.

Ngag dbang rnam rgyal, Stag lung. *Brgyud pa yid bzhin nor bu'i rtogs pa brjod pa ngo mtshar rgya mtsho (=Stag lung chos 'byung).* Lhasa: Bod ljongs bod yig dpe rnying dpe skrun khang, 1992.

Ngag dbang blo gros grags pa. *Dpal ldan jo nang pa'i chos 'byung rgyal ba'i chos tshul gsal byed zla ba'i sgron me.* Kokonor: Krung go'i bod kyi shes rig dpe skrun khang, 1992.

Ngag dbang blo bzang rgya mtsho, Ta la'i bla ma V. *Za hor gyi ban de ngag dbang blo bzang rgya mtsho'i 'di snang 'khrul ba'i rol rtsed rtogs brjod kyi tshul du bkod pa du kū la'i gos bzang.* 3 vols. Lhasa: Bod ljongs mi dmangs dpe skrun khang, 1989.

_____. *Zab pa dang rgya che ba'i dam pa'i chos kyi thob yig gangā'i chu rgyun,* vol.1. Delhi: Nechung and Lhakhar, 1970.

_____. *Rigs dang dkyil 'khor kun gyi khyab bdag rdo rje 'chang blo gsal rgya mtsho grags pa rgyal mtshan dpal bzang po'i rnam par thar pa slob bshad bstan pa'i nyi'od.* In *Sa skya Lam 'bras Literature Series,* vol. 2, pp. 399–637. Dehra Dun: Sakya Centre, 1983.

_____. *Gsung ngag rin po che lam 'bras bu dang bcas pa'i khrid kyi zin bris gsang chen bstan pa rgyas byed ces bya ba las/ bum dbang gi rmi lam man gyi zin bris kha'u brag rdzong pa'i bzhed pa ma nor ba.* In *Sa skya Lam 'bras Literature Series,* vol. 14, pp. 519–53. Dehra Dun: Sakya Centre, 1983.

Bcom ldan Rig pa'i ral gri. *Bstan pa sang rgyas pa rgyan gyi me tog.* Beijing: Library of the Cultural Palace of Nationalities. *Dbu med* ms., 37 fols.

Cha rgan Dbang phyug rgyal mtshan. *Cha rgan gyi mdzad pa'i rnal 'byor dbang phyug gi lo rgyus.* Beijing: Library of the Cultural Palace of Nationalities. *Dbu med* ms., 12 fols.

_____. *Lam 'bras kyi bla ma bod kyi lo rgyus rgyas pa bod dang bstan pa'i byung 'dems ma.* Beijing: Library of the Cultural Palace of Nationalities. *Dbu med* ms., 92 fols.

'Jam mgon Kong sprul Blo gros mtha' yas. *Sgrub brgyud shing rta chen po brgyad kyi smin grol snying po phyogs gcig bsdus pa gdams ngag rin po che'i mdzod kyi dkar chag bkra shis grags pa'i rgya mtsho.* In *Gdams ngag mdzod,* vol. 12, pp. 621–787. Delhi: N.Lungtok and N. Gyaltsan, 1972.

_____. *Theg pa'i sgo kun las btus pa gsung rab rin po che'i mdzod bslab pa gsum legs par ston pa'i bstan bcos shes bya kun khyab.* 3 vols. Beijing: Mi rigs dpe skrun khang, 1982.

'Jam mgon A mes zhabs Ngag dbang kun dga' bsod nams. *Dpal rdo rje nag po chen po'i zab mo'i chos skor rnams byung ba'i tshul legs par bshad pa bstan srung chos kun gsal ba'i nyin byed.* 2 vols. New Delhi: T. G. Dhongthog Rinpoche, 1979.

_____. *Dpal sa skya pa'i yab chos kyi nying khu 'khor lo sdom pa'i dam pa'i chos byung ba'i tshul legs par bshad pa bde mchog chos kun gsal ba'i nyin byed.* Dehra Dun: Sakya Centre, 1985.

_____. *Dpal gsang ba 'dus pa'i dam pa'i chos byung ba'i tshul legs par bshad pa gsang 'dus chos kun gsal ba'i nyin byed.* Dehra Dun: Sakya Centre, 1985.

_____. *'Dzam gling byang phyogs kyi thub pa'i rgyal tshab chen po dpal ldan sa skya pa'i gdung rabs rin po che ji ltar byon pa'i tshul gyi rnam par thar pa ngo mtshar rin po che'i bang mdzod dgos 'dod kun 'byung.* Beijing: Mi rigs dpe skrun khang, 1986.

_____. *Yongs rdzogs bstan pa rin po che'i nyams len gyi man ngag gsung ngag rin po che'i byon tshul khog phub dang bcas pa rgyas par bshad pa legs bshad 'dus pa'i rgya mtsho.* In *Sa skya Lam 'bras Literature Series,* vol. 22, pp.1–314. Dehra Dun: Sakya Centre, 1983.

_____. *Lam 'bras bu dang bcas pa'i gdams ngag zab mo 'chad cing nyams su len pa la nye bar 'kho ba'i bla ma gong ma'i gsung bgros zab mo rnams bsgrigs pa'i bar ston zin bris su grags pa'i gsung rab nas shin tu zab pa'i gsung bgros kyi gnad rnams logs su bkol ba bsgrub pa po rnams kyi yid kyi 'dod 'jo. Dbu med* ms., 36 fols.

_____. *Gsung ngag rin po che lam 'bras bu dang bcas pa'i gdams ngag zab mo byung tshul gyi yi ge don gnyer dga' ba bskyed byed.* In *Sa skya Lam 'bras Literature Series,* vol. 24, pp. 555–89. Dehra Dun: Sakya Centre, 1983.

_____. *Gsung ngag rin po che slob bshad dang tshogs bshad kyi dbye ba rje klu sgrub rgya mtsho'i gsung gi zin bris la slar yang rje nyid kyi zhus dag mdzad pa'i yid ches can gyi dpe la bar skabs su yi ge pas ma dag pa'i skyon rnams sa skya pa sngags 'chang ngag dbang kun dga'i ming can gyi zhus dag bgyis pa'i legs bshad blo gsal kun dga'. Dbu med* ms., 13 fols.

'Jam dbyangs mkhyen brtse'i dbang phyug. *Gdams ngag byung tshul gyi zin bris gsang chen bstan pa rgyas byed ces bya ba kha'u brag rdzong pa'i bzhed pa ma nor ba ban rgan mkhyen brtse'i nyams len.* In *Sa skya Lam 'bras Literature Series,* vol. 14, pp. 1–154. Dehra Dun: Sakya Centre, 1983.

_____. *Snang ba gsum du bstan pa'i lam gyi zin bris kha'u brag rdzong pa'i bzhad pa ma nor ba.* In *Sa skya Lam 'bras Literature Series,* vol. 14, pp. 253–343. Dehra Dun: Sakya Centre, 1983.

_____. *Byung ba'i chos la bshad sgrub bya tshul gyi zin bris kha'u brag rdzong pa'i bzhed pa ma nor ba ban rgan mkhyen brtse'i nyams len.* In *Sa skya Lam 'bras Literature Series,* vol. 14, pp. 195–225. Dehra Dun: Sakya Centre, 1983.

_____. *Bla ma rin po che mkhan chen pa'i rnam thar ngo mtshar snye ma zhes bya ba sgro bkur dang bral zhing yid ches la dgod bro ba zhig.* In *Sa skya Lam 'bras Literature Series,* vol. 3, pp. 1–250. Dehra Dun: Sakya Centre, 1983.

'Jam dbyangs chos kyi blo gros, Rdzong gsar Mkhyen brtse. *Khyab bdag bla ma 'khor lo'i mgon po padma ye shes rdo rje'i gsang ba'i rnam thar gyi cha shas dad gsum pad dkar bzhad pa'i nyin byed.* In *The Complete Works of Rdzong-gsar mkhyen-brtse rin-po-che 'Jam-dbyangs chos-kyi blo-gros,* vol. 8. Gangtok: Sherab Gyaltsen, 1985.

'Jam dbyangs blo gter dbang po. *Dpal phyag na rdo rje 'khor lo chen po'i sgrub dkyil dbang chog bdud sde'i dpung 'joms.* In *Rgyud-sde kun-btus,* vol. 8, pp. 32–118, Delhi: N. Lungtok and N. Gyaltsan, 1972.

______. *Phyag na rdo rje 'khor lo chen po'i sgrub thabs rnam dag 'od.* In *Rgyud-sde kun-btus,* vol. 8, pp. 1–31, Delhi: N. Lungtok and N. Gyaltsan, 1972.

Nyang ral Nyi ma 'od zer. *Chos 'byung me tog snying po sbrang rtsi'i bcud.* Lhasa: Bod ljongs mi dmangs dpe skrun khang, 1988.

Tāranātha, Jo nang rje btsun. *Dge bshes dpal ldan shākya bstan 'dzin gyis dri lan gnad kyi gsal byed.* In *The Collected Works of Jo-nang rje-btsun Tāranātha,* vol. 13, pp. 511–65. Leh: Smanrtsis Shesrig Spendzod, 1983.

_____. *Rgyal khams pa ta ra na thas bdag nyid kyi rnam thar nges par brjod pa'i deb ther/ shin tu zhib mo ma bcos lhug pa'i rtogs brjod.* Paro: Ngodrup and Sherab Drimay, 1978.

_____. *Rgyud rgyal gshin rje gshed skor gyi chos 'byung rgyas pa yid ches ngo mtshar.* In *The Collected Works of Jo-nang rje-btsun Tāranātha,* vol. 10, pp. 1–147. Leh: Smanrtsis Shesrig Spendzod, 1983.

_____. *Jo nang gi gnas bshad.* In *Bod kyi gnas yig bdams bsgrigs,* vol. 27 of *Gangs can rig mdzod,* pp. 237–55. Lhasa: Bod ljongs bod yig dpe rnying dpe skrun khang, 1995.

_____. *Stag lung zhabs drung gi gsung lan.* In *The Collected Works of Jo-nang rje-btsun Tāranātha,* vol. 13, pp. 567–76. Leh: Smanrtsis Shesrig Spendzod, 1983.

_____. *Rdo rje rnal 'byor gyi 'khrid yig mthong ba don ldan gyi lhan thabs 'od brgya 'bar ba.* In *The Collected Works of Jo-nang rje-btsun Tāranātha,* vol. 3, pp. 447–805. Leh: Smanrtsis Shesrig Spendzod, 1983.

Tog tse pa (Kuddālapāda). *Dpal tog tse pa'i bsam mi khyab kyi gdams ngag.* In

Sa skya Lam 'bras Literature Series, vol. 11, 347–62. Dehra Dun: Sakya Centre, 1983.

Stag tshang Lo tsā ba Shes rab rin chen. *Dpal ldan sa skya pa'i gdung rabs 'dod dgu'i rgya mtsho.* Beijing: Library of the Cultural Palace of Nationalities. *Dbu med* ms., 34 fols.

Thu'u bkwan Blo bzang chos kyi nyi ma. *Rje btsun rdo rje rnal 'byor ma nā ro mkha' spyod ma'i lam gyi rim pa'i spyi don gsang chen sgo brgya 'byed pa'i lde mig.* In *The Collected Works of Thu'u bkwan Blo bzang chos kyi nyi ma,* vol. 8, pp. 7–169. New Delhi: Gandan Sungrab Minyam Gyunphel Series, 1971.

Bde chen rdo rje, Rgyal thang pa. *'Gro ba'i mgon po phag mo gru pa'i rnam thar.* In *Dkar brgyud gser 'phreng,* pp. 387–435. Tashijong: Sungrab Nyamso Gyunphel Parkhang, 1973.

Rdo rje rgyal mtshan, Gtsang byams pa (=Mus srad pa). *Gnas chen muk gu lung gi khyad par bshad pa.* In *Bod kyi gnas yig bdams bgrigs,* vol. 27 of *Gangs can rig mdzod,* pp. 293–99. Lhasa: Bod ljongs bod yig dpe rnying dpe skrun khang, 1995.

______. *Man ngag gsal byed las/ rnam 'grel bcu gcig gi ngos 'dzin.* In *Sa skya Lam 'bras Literature Series,* vol. 18, pp. 237–41. Dehra Dun: Sakya Centre, 1983.

______. *Lam 'bras lam skor lhag ma rnams dang bcas pa'i tho yig.* (Title taken from colophon.) In 'Jam mgon A mes zhabs Ngag dbang kun dga' bsod nams, *Yongs rdzogs bstan pa rin po che'i nyams len gyi man ngag gsung ngag rin po che'i byon tshul khog phub dang bcas pa rgyas par bshad pa legs bshad 'dus pa'i rgya mtsho,* pp. 301–9. In *Sa skya Lam 'bras Literature Series,* vol. 22, pp. 1–314. Dehra Dun: Sakya Centre, 1983.

Sde gzhung sprul sku Kun dga' bstan pa'i nyi ma. *Rje btsun bla ma dam pa 'jam dbyangs rgyal mtshan gyi rnam thar mdor bsdus skal bzang rna rgyan.* New Delhi: T. G. Dhongthog Rinpoche, 1983.

Nam mkha' dpal bzang, Nyi lde ba. *Untitled.* In 'Jam mgon A mes zhabs Ngag dbang kun dga' bsod nams, *Yongs rdzogs bstan pa rin po che'i nyams len gyi man ngag gsung ngag rin po che'i byon tshul khog phub dang bcas pa rgyas par bshad pa legs bshad 'dus pa'i rgya mtsho,* pp. 295–301. In *Sa skya Lam 'bras Literature Series,* vol. 22, pp. 1–314. Dehra Dun: Sakya Centre, 1983.

Nub pa Rig 'dzin grags. *Nub pa rigs 'dzin grags kyis mdzad pa'i zhen pa bzhi bral gyi zin bris.* In *Gdams ngag mdzod,* vol. 4, pp. 804–6. Delhi: N. Lungtok and N. Gyaltsan, 1972.

Padma dkar po, 'Brug chen. *Bka' brgyud kyi bka' 'bum gsil bu rnams kyi gsan yig.*

In *Collected Works (Gsung-'bum) of Kun-mkhyen Padma-dkar-po,* vol. 4, pp. 309–496. Darjeeling: Kargyud Sungrab Nyamso Khang.

_____. *Chos 'byung bstan pa'i padma rgyas pa'i nyin byed.* Lhasa: Bod ljongs bod yig dpe rnying dpe skrun khang, 1992.

Padmavajra. *Slob dpon padma badzras mdzad pa'i rdzogs rim mar me'i rtse mo lta bu'i gdams ngag.* In *Sa skya Lam 'bras Literature Series,* vol. 11, pp. 419–41. Dehra Dun: Sakya Centre, 1983.

Dpa' bo Gtsug lag phreng ba. *Chos byung mkhas pa'i dga' ston.* 2 vols. Beijing: Mi rigs dpe skrun khang, 1986.

Phag mo gru pa Rdo rje rgyal po. *Lam 'bras kyi 'phrin las sum bcu.* In vol. 4 of *Dpal phag mo gru pa'i bka' 'bum,* ms., fols. 171a–173a.

_____. *Lam 'bras kyi yan lag lnga sbyong.* In vol. 4 of *Dpal phag mo gru pa'i bka' 'bum,* ms., fols. 180a–181a.

_____. *Lam 'bras bu dang bcas pa'i zhal gyi gdams pa.* In vol. 4 of *Dpal phag mo gru pa'i bka' 'bum,* ms., fols. 186a–194a.

_____. *Lam 'bras gzhung bshad dpe mdzod ma.* In vol. 4 of *Dpal phag mo gru pa'i bka' 'bum,* ms., fols. 13b–155b.

Bar ston Rdo rje rgyal mtshan. *Bar ston zin bris.* In 'Jam mgon A mes zhabs, *Lam 'bras bu dang bcas pa'i gdams ngag zab mo 'chad cing nyams su len pa la nye bar 'kho ba'i bla ma gong ma'i gsung bgros zab mo rnams bsgrigs pa'i bar ston zin bris su grags pa'i gsung rab nas shin tu zab pa'i gsung bgros kyi gnad rnams logs su bkol ba bsgrub pa po rnams kyi yid kyi 'dod 'jo. Dbu med* ms., fols. 2a–35b.

Bu ston Rin chen grub. *Bde mchog rtsa ba'i rgyud kyi bsdus don gsang ba 'byed pa.* In *The Collected Works of Bu ston,* pt. 6, pp. 1–118. New Delhi: International Academy of Indian Culture, 1966.

_____. *Bla ma dam pa rnams kyis rjes su bzung ba'i tshul bka' drin rjes su dran par byed pa.* In *The Collected Works of Bu ston,* pt. 26, pp. 1–142. New Delhi: International Academy of Indian Culture, 1971.

Byang chub rtse mo, Lo chen. *Chos rje bla ma dam pa'i rnams thar thog mtha bar gsum du dge ba.* Beijing: Cultural Palace of Nationalities, *dbu can* ms., 75 fols.

Bla ma dam pa Bsod nams rgyal mtshan. *Bla ma brgyud pa'i rnam par thar pa ngo mtshar snang ba.* In *Sa skya Lam 'bras Literature Series,* vol. 16, pp. 2–121. Dehra Dun: Sakya Centre, 1983.

———. *Lam 'bras bu dang bcas pa'i gdams ngag gi rnam par bshad pa man ngag gter mdzod.* In *Sa skya Lam 'bras Literature Series,* vol. 16, pp. 123–432. Dehra Dun: Sakya Centre, 1983.

———. *Lam 'bras bu dang bcas pa'i gzhung ji lta ba bzhin dkri ba'i khrid yig sbas don kun gsal.* In *Sa skya Lam 'bras Literature Series,* vol. 16, pp. 451–543. Dehra Dun: Sakya Centre, 1983.

Mātṛceṭa, Ācārya. *Sangs rgyas bcom ldan 'das la bstod pa bsngags par 'os pa bsngags pa las bstod par mi nus par bstod pa.* In *The Tibetan Tripitaka: Peking Edition,* vol. 46, pp. 41.2.–49.3. Tokyo: Tibetan Tripitaka Research Institute, 1956.

Mang thos klu sgrub rgya mtsho. *(Gsung ngag slob bshad khrid rim nyi gzhon gsar pa'i thig phreng skal bzang utpal gzhon nu'i kha 'byed las) Skyon med gnyug ma ye shes la brtan pa khams 'dus pa tha ma'i khrid.* In *Sa skya Lam 'bras Literature Series,* vol. 15, pp. 379–403. Dehra Dun: Sakya Centre, 1983.

———. *(Gsung ngag slob bshad sngags lam gyi khrid yig nyi gzhon gsar pa'i thig phreng skal bzang utpal gzhon nu'i kha 'byed las) 'Khor 'das dbyer med lta ba'i skabs.* In *Sa skya Lam 'bras Literature Series,* vol. 15, pp. 153–240. Dehra Dun: Sakya Centre, 1983.

———. *Bstan rtsis gsal ba'i nyin byed lhag bsam rab dkar.* Lhasa: Bod ljongs mi dmangs dpe skrun khang, 1987.

———. *(Gsung ngag slob bshad khrid rim nyi gzhon gsar pa'i thig phreng skal bzang utpal gzhon nu'i kha 'byed las) Bum dbang gi 'da' ka ma/ bar do/ rmi lam/ sgyu lus dang bcas pa'i khrid rim.* In *Sa skya Lam 'bras Literature Series,* vol. 15, pp. 275–315. Dehra Dun: Sakya Centre, 1983.

———. *Rang gi rnam par thar pa yul sna tshogs kyi bdud rtsi myong ba'i gtam du byas pa zol zog rdzun gyis ma bslad pa sgeg mo'i me long.* In *Sa skya Lam 'bras Literature Series,* vol. 3, pp. 395–625. Dehra Dun: Sakya Centre, 1983.

———. *Gsung ngag slob bshad khog phub gnad kyi be'u bum.* In *Sa skya Lam 'bras Literature Series,* vol. 18, pp. 161–83. Dehra Dun: Sakya Centre, 1983.

———. *Gsung ngag slob bshad snang gsum gyi khrid yig zla ba bdud rtsi'i thigs phreng skal bzang ku mud gsar pa'i kha 'byed.* In *Sa skya Lam 'bras Literature Series,* vol. 15, pp. 31–151. Dehra Dun: Sakya Centre, 1983.

Mus chen Dkon mchog rgyal mtshan. *Lam 'bras bu dang bcas pa'i gnad kyi gsung sgros zin bris.* In *Sa skya Lam 'bras Literature Series,* vol. 13, pp. 447–69. Dehra Dun: Sakya Centre, 1983.

Dmar ston Chos kyi rgyal po. *Gegs sel bka' rgya ma.* In *Sa skya Lam 'bras Literature Series,* vol. 13, pp. 149–58. Dehra Dun: Sakya Centre, 1983.

_____. *Gegs sel glengs gzhi ma.* In *Sa skya Lam 'bras Literature Series,* vol. 13, pp. 128–29. Dehra Dun: Sakya Centre, 1983.

_____. *Rgyas pa'i las sgrub pa'i bla ma'i rnal 'byor.* In *Sa skya Lam 'bras Literature Series,* vol. 13, pp. 295–300. Dehra Dun: Sakya Centre, 1983.

_____. *Pod ser du bzhugs pa'i lung 'di nyid dang zhib tu sbyar ba'i kha skong.* In *Sa skya Lam 'bras Literature Series,* vol. 31, pp. 254–78. Dehra Dun: Sakya Centre, 1983.

_____. *Bla ma dam pa bod kyi lo rgyus.* Beijing: Library of the Cultural Palace of Minorities. Catalogue no. 002864(3). *Dbu med* ms., 21 fols.

_____. *Gzhung rdo rje'i tshig rkang gi 'grel pa 'jam dbyangs bla ma'i gsung sgros ma zhes dmar chos rgyal gyi gsung.* In *Sa skya Lam 'bras Literature Series,* vol. 30, 1–295. Dehra Dun: Sakya Centre, 1983.

_____. *Lam bsdus pa 'dod pa'i lcags kyu.* In *Sa skya Lam 'bras Literature Series,* vol. 13, pp. 227–28. Dehra Dun: Sakya Centre, 1983.

_____. *Lam 'bras kyi bla ma brgyud pa'i lo rgyus* (=Ms. B1). Beijing: Library of the Cultural Palace of Minorities. Catalogue no. 004345. *Dbu med* ms., 23 fols.

_____. *Lam 'bras sa lugs bod kyi lo rgyus* (=Ms. N). Kathmandu: Nepal-German Manuscript Preservation Project. Running no. E-34356, Reel no. E-1784/8. *Dbu med* ms., 23 fols.

_____. *Lus gnad kyi gdams ngag.* In *Sa skya Lam 'bras Literature Series,* vol. 13, pp. 57–59. Dehra Dun: Sakya Centre, 1983.

_____. *Legs par bshad pa rin po che'i gter dang de'i grel pa.* Gangtok: Sherab Gyaltsen, 1983. Reproduction of 1982 Lhasa Tibetan People's Publishing House edition.

Tshar chen Blo gsal rgya mtsho. *Khams gsum chos kyi rgyal po bdag chen rdo rje 'chang blo gros rgyal mtshan dpal bzang po'i rnam par thar pa yid 'phrog utpa la'i do shal.* In *Sa skya Lam 'bras Literature Series,* vol. 2, pp. 35–151. Dehra Dun: Sakya Centre, 1983.

_____. *Dpal kye rdo rje'i phyi bskyed rim gyi rnam par bshad pa legs bshad nyi ma'i 'od zer.* In *Sa skya Lam 'bras Literature Series,* vol. 10, pp. 327–513. Dehra Dun: Sakya Centre, 1983.

_____. *Dpal ldan bla ma dam pa kun spangs chos kyi rgyal po'i rnam par thar pa ngo mtshar dad pa'i spu long g'yo ba.* In *Sa skya Lam 'bras Literature Series,* vol. 2, pp. 153–247. Dehra Dun: Sakya Centre, 1983.

_____. *Gsung ngag rin po che brgyud pa gsum 'dus kyi bla ma la gsol ba 'debs pa lam rim smon lam dang bcas pa.* In *Sa skya Lam 'bras Literature Series,* vol. 14, pp. 235–48. Dehra Dun: Sakya Centre, 1983.

Tshul khrims rin chen, Zhu chen. *Kun mkhyen nyi ma'i gnyen gyi bka' lung gi dgongs don rnam par 'grel ba'i bstan bcos gangs can pa'i skad du 'gyur ro 'tshal gyi chos sbyin rgyun mi 'chad pa'i ngo mtshar 'phrul gyi phyi mo rdzogs ldan bskal pa'i bsod nams kyi sprin phyung rgyas par dkrigs pa'i tshul las brtsams pa'i gtam ngo mtshar chu gter 'phel ba'i zla ba gsar pa.* Lhasa: Bod ljongs mi dmangs dpe skrun khang, 1985.

Tshe dbang nor bu, Kaḥ thog Rig 'dzin. *Mar mi dwags po jo bo rje yab sras sogs dam pa 'ga' zhig gi rnam thar sa bon dus kyi nges pa brjod pa dag ldan nyung gsal.* In *Selected Writings of Kaḥ thog rig 'dzin Tshe dbang nor bu,* vol. 1, pp. 669–705. Darjeeling: Kargyud Sungrab Nyamso Khang, 1973.

Tshe dbang lhun grub rab brtan. *Gsung ngag rin po che lam 'bas bu dang bcas pa ngor rdzong rdo rje gdan pa'i gsung rab rin po che'i sgo brgya 'byed pa'i lde'i mig kha'u brag rdzong pa'i khyad chos thun mong ma yin pa.* In *Sa skya Lam 'bras Literature Series,* vol. 18, pp. 134–61. Dehra Dun: Sakya Centre, 1983.

Vajrāsanapāda. *Grub thob brgyad cu rtsa bzhi'i gsol 'debs.* In *The Tibetan Tripitaka: Peking Edition,* vol. 81, pp. 238.4.5–240.2.3. Tokyo: Tibetan Tripitaka Research Institute, 1956.

Virūpa. *Lam 'bras bu dang bcas pa'i gdams ngag dang man ngag tu bcas pa.* In *Sa skya Lam 'bras Literature Series,* vol. 11, pp. 10–19. Dehra Dun: Sakya Centre, 1983.

Zhang G.yu grags pa Brtson 'grus grags pa. *Dpal gyi rnam thar.* In *Writings (Bka' 'Thor-bu) of Zhang G.yu-brag-pa Brtson-'grus grags-pa,* pp. 360–93. Tashijong: Sungrab Nyamso Gyunpel Parkang, 1972.

Yang dgon pa Rgyal mtshan dpal. *Bar do 'phrang sgrol gyi lo rgyus tshe rings ma'i zhus len.* In *The Collected Works (Gsung 'bum) of Yang dgon pa Rgyal mtshan dpal,* vol. 2, pp. 531–49. Thimphu: Kunzang Topgey, 1976.

Yar lung Jo bo Shākya rin chen sde. *Yar lung jo bo'i chos 'byung.* Chengdu: Szechuan People's Publishing House, 1987.

Ratnavajra. *Ting nge 'dzin sems kyi bar chad bsrung ba'i man ngag.* In *Sa skya Lam 'bras Literature Series,* vol. 13, 400–401. Dehra Dun: Sakya Centre, 1983.

Rig 'dzin Padma phrin las. *Bka' ma mdo dbang gi bla ma brgyud pa'i rnam thar.* Leh: Smanrtsis Shesrig Spendzod, 1972.

Rin chen ldan, Spyan snga. *Rin po che lha gdong pa'i rnam thar bstod pa ma.* In *The Collected Works (Gsung 'bum) of Yang dgon pa Rgyal mtshan dpal,* vol. 1, pp. 21–103. Thimphu: Kunzang Topgey, 1976.

Shākya mchog ldan, Paṇ chen. *Rdo rje'i tshig rkang gi rnam bshad sngon med nyi ma.* In *The Complete Works (Gsung 'bum) of Gser mdog Paṇ chen Shākya mchog ldan,* vol. 13, pp. 604–30. Thimphu: Kunzang Topgey, 1975.

_____. *Dpal ldan bla ma ku ma ra ma ti'i rnam par thar pa ngo mtshar bkod pa'i sprin gyi rnga sgra.* In *The Complete Works (Gsung 'bum) of Gser mdog Paṇ chen Shākya mchog ldan,* vol. 16, pp. 379–400. Thimphu: Kunzang Topgey, 1975.

_____. *Lam skor brgyad kyi gsal byed bdud rtsi'i thig pa.* In *The Complete Works (Gsung 'bum) of Gser mdog Paṇ chen Shākya mchog ldan,* vol. 13, pp. 630–40. Thimphu: Kunzang Topgey, 1975.

Śraddhākaravarman. *Rnal 'byor bla na med pa'i rgyud kyi don la 'jug pa bsdus pa.* In *The Tibetan Tripitaka: Peking Edition,* vol. 81, pp. 154.3.–159.3. Tokyo: Tibetan Tripitaka Research Institute, 1956.

Sa skya Paṇḍi ta Kun dga' rgyal mtshan. *Grub chen bcu.* In *Sa paṇ Kun dga' rgyal mtshan gyi gsung 'bum,* vol. 3, pp. 243–58. Lhasa: Bod ljongs bod yig dpe rnying dpe skrun khang, 1992.

_____. *Sgrub pa lung 'bogs pa.* In *Sa paṇ Kun dga' rgyal mtshan gyi gsung 'bum,* vol. 3, pp. 222–23. Lhasa: Bod ljongs bod yig dpe rnying dpe skrun khang, 1992.

_____. *Sgrub pa'i lung sbyin.* In *Sa paṇ Kun dga' rgyal mtshan gyi gsung 'bum,* vol. 3, pp. 224–30. Lhasa: Bod ljongs bod yig dpe rnying dpe skrun khang, 1992.

_____. *Chag lo tsā ba'i zhus lan.* In *Sa paṇ Kun dga' rgyal mtshan gyi gsung 'bum,* vol. 3, pp. 535–57. Lhasa: Bod ljongs bod yig dpe rnying dpe skrun khang, 1992.

_____. *Rten 'brel lnga rdzogs.* In *Sa paṇ Kun dga' rgyal mtshan gyi gsung 'bum,* vol. 3, pp. 231–39. Lhasa: Bod ljongs bod yig dpe rnying dpe skrun khang, 1992.

_____. *Rtogs ldan gyan po'i dris lan.* In *Sa paṇ Kun dga' rgyal mtshan gyi gsung 'bum,* vol. 3, pp. 167–73. Lhasa: Bod ljongs bod yig dpe rnying dpe skrun khang, 1992.

_____. *Rdo rje theg pa'i rtsa ba dang yan lag gi dam tshig bshad pa.* In *Sa paṇ Kun dga' rgyal mtshan gyi gsung 'bum,* vol. 3, pp. 378–85. Lhasa: Bod ljongs bod yig dpe rnying dpe skrun khang, 1992.

_____. *Sdom pa gsum gyi rab tu dbye ba'i bstan bcos.* In *Sa paṇ Kun dga' rgyal mtshan gyi gsung 'bum,* vol. 3, pp. 1–101. Lhasa: Bod ljongs bod yig dpe rnying dpe skrun khang, 1992.

_____. *Sdom pa gsum gyi rab tu dbye ba'i bstan bcos (=Sdom gsum rang mchan).* Bod ljongs mi dmangs dpe skrun khang, 1986.

_____. *Brda don gsal ba.* In *Sa skya Lam 'bras Literature Series,* vol. 13, 205–12. Dehra Dun: Sakya Centre, 1983.

_____. *Bla ma rje btsun chen po'i rnam thar.* In *Sa paṇ Kun dga' rgyal mtshan gyi gsung 'bum,* vol. 1, pp. 653–79. Lhasa: Bod ljongs bod yig dpe rnying dpe skrun khang, 1992.

_____. *Lam sbas bshad.* In *Sa skya Lam 'bras Literature Series,* vol. 13, 300–311. Dehra Dun: Sakya Centre, 1983.

Sa chen Kun dga' snying po. *Rten 'brel lnga.* In *Sa skya Lam 'bras Literature Series,* vol. 11, pp. 163–66. Dehra Dun: Sakya Centre, 1983.

_____. *Thams cad kyi don bsdus pa'i tshigs su bcad pa.* In *Sa skya Lam 'bras Literature Series,* vol. 11, pp. 188–191. Dehra Dun: Sakya Centre, 1983.

_____. *Dpal ldan bi rū pa la bstod pa.* In *The Complete Works of the Great Masters of the Sa skya Sect of Tibetan Buddhism (Sa skya pa'i bka' 'bum),* vol. 1, pp. 1.1–2.2. Tokyo: The Toyo Bunko, 1968.

_____. *Byung rgyal du mi gtong ba'i gnad rnam pa bzhi.* (Title taken from catalogue and end of text.) In *Sa skya Lam 'bras Literature Series,* vol. 11, pp. 267–87. Dehra Dun: Sakya Centre, 1983.

_____. *Zhang ston la bstod pa.* In *The Complete Works of the Great Masters of the Sa skya Sect of Tibetan Buddhism (Sa skya pa'i bka' 'bum),* vol. 1, pp. 2.2.–2.3. Tokyo: The Toyo Bunko, 1968.

_____. *Gzhung rdo rje'i tshig rkang gi 'grel pa rnal 'byor gyi dbang phyug dpal sa skya pa chen po la khams pa sga theng gis zhus pa.* In *Sa skya Lam 'bras Literature Series,* vol. 28, pp. 149–491. Dehra Dun: Sakya Centre, 1983.

_____. *Gzhung bshad gnyags ma.* In *Sa skya Lam 'bras Literature Series,* vol. 11, pp. 21–128. Dehra Dun: Sakya Centre, 1983.

_____. *Lam'bras gzhung bshad sras don ma.* In *Sa skya Lam 'bras Literature Series,* vol. 12, 1–446. Dehra Dun: Sakya Centre, 1983.

Sangs rgyas phun tshogs, Ngor chen. *Dam pa'i chos kyi byung tshul legs par bshad pa bstan pa rgya mtshor 'jug pa'i gru chen zhes bya ba rtsom 'phro kha skong bcas.* New Delhi: Ngawang Topgay, 1973.

Sog bzlog pa Blo gros rgyal mtshan. *Gsang sngags snga 'gyur la bod du rtsod pa snga phyir byung ba rnams kyi lan du brjod pa nges pa don gyi 'brug sgra.* In *The Collected Works of Sog-bzlog-pa Blo-gros rgyal-mtshan,* vol. 1, 261–601. New Delhi: Sanje Dorji, 1975.

Bsod nams rgyal mtshan, Dgon gsar ba. *Dpal ldan bla ma dam pa rdo rje 'chang chen po ngag dbang chos kyi grags pa'i rnam thar byin rlabs kyi char rgyun dad pa'i dbyar mtsho rgyas byed.* In *Sa skya Lam 'bras Literature Series,* vol. 4, 337–87. Dehra Dun: Sakya Centre, 1983.

Bsod nams chos 'phel, Sngags 'chang. *Bhu su ku'i rnal 'byor pa 'bru'i sngags 'chang bsod nams chos 'phel gyis rgyal khams bskor ba'i rtogs brjod kyi phreng ba bzhad gad chen mo.* (Edited and supplemented by Dkon mchog rdo rje.) In *Sa skya Lam 'bras Literature Series,* vol. 4, pp. 153–335. Dehra Dun: Sakya Centre, 1983.

Bsod nams dpal, Chos sgo ba. *Bde gshegs phag mo gru pa'i rnam par thar pa.* In *Bka' brgyud gser 'phreng rgyas pa,* vol. II, 143–83. Darjeeling: Kargyud Sungrab Nyamso Khang, 1982.

Bsod nams dbang po. (Edited by 'Jam mgon A mes zhabs.) *Dpal sa skya'i gnas bshad rje btsun gong ma rnams kyi rnam thar snyan brgyud dang bcas pa phun tshogs rgya mtsho'i gter zhes bya ba grub pa'i dbang phyug chen po 'jam dbyangs bsod nams dbang po'i gsung rtsoms gnang 'phro thor bur bzhugs pa rnams sa skya pa sngags 'chang ngag dbang kun dga' bsod nams kyi bla ma'i [...] gyi rnam thar rnams dran pa'i rkyen gyis dad pa'i dbang gi phyogs gcig tu bsgrigs pa bzhugs/ 'di'i tshig [ ] phal skad lta bur mdzad pa ni kun gyi go bla ba la dgongs par snang bas dregs ldan nga rgyal can rnams kyi log lta ma byed cig. Dbu med* ms., 65 fols.

Lho pa Rin chen dpal. *Dpal ldan sa skya paṇḍi ta'i rnam thar kun mkhyen rin chen dpal gyis mdzad pa.* In *Sa skya Lam 'bras Literature Series,* vol. 1, 76–113. Dehra Dun: Sakya Centre, 1983.

Secondary Sources

Aris, Michael (1980). *Bhutan: The Early History of a Himalayan Kingdom.* New Delhi: Vikas Publishing House.

Broido, Michael (1987). "Sa-skya Paṇḍita, the White Panacea and the Hva-shang Doctrine." In *The Journal of the International Association of Buddhist Studies,* vol. 10: pp. 27–68.

Chang, Garma C. C., trans. (1962). *The Hundred Thousand Songs of Milarepa.* Secaucus: University Books.

Chimpa, Lama, and Chattopadhyaya, Alaka, trans. (1990). *Tāranātha's History of Buddhism in India.* Delhi: Motilal Banarsidass.

Davidson, Ronald (1991). "Reflections on the Maheśvara Subjugation Myth: Indic Materials, Sa-skya-pa Apologetics, and the Birth of Heruka." In *The Journal of the International Association of Buddhist Studies,* vol. 14, no. 2, pp. 197–235.

_____ (1992). "Preliminary Studies on Hevajra's *Abhisamaya* and the *Lam-'bras Tshogs-bshad.*" In *Tibetan Buddhism: Reason and Revelation,* pp. 107–32. Edited by Steven Goodman and Ronald Davidson. Albany: State University of New York Press.

Decleer, Hubert (1992). "The Melodious Drumsound All-Pervading: Sacred Biography of Rwa Lotsāwa: About early Lotsāwa *rnam thar* and *chos 'byung.*" In *Tibetan Studies,* vol. 1, pp. 13–28. Edited by Ihara Shōren and Yamaguchi Zuihō. Narita: Naritasan Shinshoji.

Deshung Rinpoche (1995). *The Three Levels of Spiritual Perception.* Translated by Jared Rhoton. Boston: Wisdom Publications.

Dudjom Rinpoche, Jikdrel Yeshe Dorje (1991). *The Nyingma School of Tibetan Buddhism: Its Fundamentals and History.* 2 vols. Translated by Gyurme Dorje and Matthew Kapstein. Boston: Wisdom Publications.

Edou, Jérôme (1996). *Machig Labdrön and the Foundations of Chöd.* Ithaca: Snow Lion Publications.

Eimer, Helmut (1978). "Life and Activities of Atiśa (Dīpaṃkaraśrījñāna). A Survey of Investigations Undertaken." In *Tibetan Studies,* pp. 125–35. Edited by Martin Brauen and Per Kvaerne. Zurich: Völkerkundemuseum der Universität Zürich.

Gómez, Luis (1995). "Unspoken Paradigms: Meanderings through the Metaphors of a Field." In *The Journal of the International Association of Buddhist Studies,* vol. 18, no. 1: 183–230.

Guenther, Herbert (1963). *The Life and Teachings of Nāropa.* Oxford: Clarendon Press.

Gyatso, Janet (1985). "The Development of the *Gcod* Tradition." In *Soundings in Tibetan Civilization,* pp. 320–41. New Delhi: Manohar Publications.

Hirakawa, Akira (1990). *A History of Indian Buddhism From Śākyamuni to Early Mahāyāna.* Translated and edited by Paul Groner. Honolulu: University of Hawaii Press.

Jackson, David P. (1987). *The Entrance Gate for the Wise (Section III)*. 2 vols. Vienna: Arbeitskreis für Tibetische und Buddhistische Studien Universität Wien.

_____ (1989). *The Early Abbots of 'Phan-po Na-lendra: The Vicissitudes of a Great Tibetan Monastery in the 15th Century.* Vienna: Arbeitskreis für Tibetische und Buddhistische Studien Universität Wien.

_____ (1990). *Two Biographies of Śākyaśrībhadra: The Eulogy of Khro phu Lo tsā ba and its "Commentary" by bSod nams dpal bzang po.* Tibetan and Indo-Tibetan Studies 4. Stuttgart: Franz Steiner Verlag.

_____ (1990a). "Sa-skya Paṇḍita the 'Polemicist': Ancient Debates and Modern Interpretations." In *The Journal of the International Association of Buddhist Studies,* vol. 13–2: pp. 17–116.

_____ (1994). *Enlightenment by a Single Means.* Vienna: Der Österreichischen Akademie der Wissenschaften.

Kaneko, Eiichi (1982). *Ko-Tantora Zenshū Kaidai Mokuroku.* (Catalogue to the Gting skyes Edition of the *Rnying ma rgyud 'bum*). Tokyo: Kokusho Kankōkai.

Kapstein, Matthew (1996). "*gDams ngag:* Tibetan Technologies of the Self." In *Tibetan Literature,* eds. José Cabezón and Roger Jackson, pp. 275–89. Ithaca: Snow Lion Publications.

Karmay, Samten Gyaltsen (1988). *The Great Perfection (Rdzogs chen): A Philosophical and Meditative Teaching in Tibetan Buddhism.* Leiden: E. J. Brill.

van der Kuijp, Leonard W. J. (1994). "Apropos of Some Recently Recovered Texts Belonging to the *Lam 'bras* Teachings of the Sa skya pa and Ko brag pa." *Journal of the International Association of Buddhist Studies,* vol. 17, no. 2: pp. 175–202.

_____ (1994a). "Fourteenth-Century Tibetan Cultural History I: Ta'i-si-tu Byang-chub rgyal-mtshan as a Man of Religion." *Indo-Iranian Journal* 37: 139–49.

_____ (1994b). "On the *Lives* of Śākyaśrībhadra (?–?1225)." *Journal of the American Oriental Society* 114.4: 599–616.

Kvaerne, Per (1986). *An Anthology of Buddhist Tantric Songs.* Bangkok: White Orchid Press.

Lamotte, Etienne (1988). *History of Indian Buddhism: from the Origins to the Śaka Era.* Translated by Sara Webb Boin. Louvain: Institut Orientaliste.

Lhalungpa, Lobsang P., trans. (1977). *The Life of Milarepa.* New York: E. P. Dutton.

Lhundrub, Ngorchen Konchog (1991). *The Beautiful Ornament of the Three Visions.* Translated by Lobsang Dagpa, Ngawang Samten Chophel (Jay Goldberg), and Jared Rhoton. Ithaca: Snow Lion Publications.

Martin, Dan (1982). "The Early Education of Milarepa." In *The Journal of the Tibetan Society,* vol. 2, pp. 53–76.

_____ (1991). "The Emergence of Bon and the Tibetan Polemical Tradition." Ph.D. Dissertation, Indiana University.

_____ (1996). "The Star King and the Four Children of Pehar: Popular Religious Movements of 11th-to 12th-Century Tibet." In *Acta Orientalia Hungarica* XLIX, pp. 171–95.

Nālandā Translation Committee (1982). *The Life of Marpa the Translator.* Boulder: Prajñā Press.

de Nebesky-Wojkowitz, René (1956). *Oracles and Demons of Tibet.* London: Oxford University Press.

Newman, John (1985). "A Brief History of the Kalachakra." In *The Wheel of Time: The Kalachakra in Context,* eds. Geshe Lhundub Sopa, Roger Jackson, and John Newman, pp. 51–90. Madison: Deer Park Books.

_____ (1987). "The Outer Wheel of Time: Vajrayāna Buddhist Cosmology in the Kālacakra Tantra." Ph.D. Dissertation, University of Wisconsin.

Obermiller, E., trans. (1932). *History of Buddhism.* 2 vols. Heidelberg: O. Harrassowitz.

Ricard, Matthieu, et al. (1994). *The Life of Shabkar: The Autobiography of a Tibetan Yogin.* Albany: State University of New York.

Roerich, George N., trans. (1959). *Biography of Dharmasvamin.* Patna, K. Jayaswal Research Institute.

_____ trans. (1976). *The Blue Annals.* Delhi: Motilal Banarsidas.

Ruegg, David Seyfort (1984). "Problems in the Transmission of Vajrayāna Buddhism in the Western Himalaya about the Year 1000." In *Acta Indologica* VI, pp. 369–81.

_____ (1981). *The Literature of the Madhyamaka School of Philosophy in India.* Wiesbaden: Otto Harrassowitz.

Sakya Trizin, H.H., and Ngawang Samten Chophel (1982). *A Collection of*

Instructions on Parting from the Four Attachments. Singapore: The Singapore Buddha Sasana Society.

Śāntideva (1981). *Śikṣa-samuccaya: A Compendium of Buddhist Doctrine, Compiled by Śāntideva Chiefly from Earlier Mahāyāna Sūtras.* Translated from the Sanskrit by Cecil Bendall and W.H.D. Rouse. Delhi: Motilal Banarsidass. Reprint of 1922 London edition.

Schwabland, Peter (1996). *Lcom ldan ral gri's Catalogue of Canonical Texts: an edition and translation of the Bstan pa sangs rgyas pa rgyan gyi me tog.* Unpublished.

Shastri, Raghuvara Mitthulal (1931). "A Comprehensive Study into the Origin and Status of the Kayasthas." *Man in India* XI/2, pp. 116–59.

Shaw, Miranda (1994). *Passionate Enlightenment: Women in Tantric Buddhism.* Princeton: Princeton University Press.

Siklos, Bulcsu (1996). *The Vajrabhairava Tantras.* Tring: The Institute of Buddhist Studies.

Smith, E. Gene (1970). Introduction to *Kongtrul's Encyclopedia of Indo-Tibetan Culture.* Śatapiṭaka Series 90. New Delhi: International Academy of Indian Culture.

Snellgrove, David (1987). *Indo-Tibetan Buddhism.* 2 vols. Boston: Shambhala Publications.

_____ and Skorupski, Tadeusz (1980). *The Cultural Heritage of Ladakh.* 2 vols. Boulder: Prajñā Press.

Sørenson, Per K. (1994). *Tibetan Buddhist Historiography: The Mirror Illuminating the Royal Geneaologies: An Annotated Translation of the XIVth Century Tibetan Chronicle rGyal rabs gsal ba'i me-long.* Wiesbaden: Harrassowitz Verlag.

_____ (1999). "The Prolific Ascetic lCe-sgom Śes-rab rdo-rje *alias* lCe-sgom zhig-po: Allusive, but Elusive." In *Journal of the Nepal Research Centre* XI, pp. 175–200.

Sperling, Elliot (1994). "Rtsa mi lo tsa ba Sangs rgyas Grags pa and the Tangut background to early Mongol Tibetan relations." In *Tibetan Studies,* vol. 2: pp. 801–24. Oslo: The Institute for Comparative Research in Human Culture.

Stearns, Cyrus (1980). "The Life and Teachings of the Tibetan Saint Thang-stong rgyal-po, 'King of the Empty Plain.'" M.A. Thesis, University of Washington.

_____ (1996). "The Life and Tibetan Legacy of the Indian *Mahāpaṇḍita* Vibhūticandra." *Journal of the International Association of Buddhist Studies,* vol. 19.1, pp. 127–71.

_____ (1997). "Sachen Kunga Nyingpo's Quest for *The Path and Result.*" In *Religions of Tibet in Practice.* Princeton: Princeton University Press, pp. 188–99.

_____ (1999). *The Buddha from Dolpo: A Study of the Life and Thought of the Tibetan Master Dolpopa Sherab Gyaltsen.* Albany: State University of New York Press.

_____ (2000). *Hermit of Go Cliffs: Timeless Instructions from a Tibetan Mystic.* Boston: Wisdom Publications.

Tatz, Mark (1987). "The Life of the Siddha Philosopher Maitrīgupta." *The Journal of the American Oriental Society,* vol. 107.4, pp. 695–711.

Templeman, David (1983). *The Seven Instruction Lineages.* Dharamsala: Library of Tibetan Works & Archives.

Translation Bureau of the Library of Tibetan Works and Archives (1976). *Fifty Verses of Guru Devotion.* Dharamsala: Library of Tibetan Works and Archives.

Tucci, Giuseppe (1971). "Buddhist Notes." In *Opera Minora,* vol. 1, pp. 489–527. Rome.

_____(1988). *Rin-chen bzang-po and the Renaissance of Buddhism in Tibet Around the Millenium (Indo-Tibetica II).* Translated by Nancy Kipp Smith. New Delhi: Śata-Piṭaka Series, vol. 348. English version of *Indo-Tibetica II,* Roma: Real Accademia d'italia, 1932.

Vitali, Roberto (1996). *The Kingdoms of Gu.ge Pu.hrang.* Dharamsala: Tho ling gtsug lag khang lo gcig stong 'khor ba'i rjes dran mdzad sgo'i go sgrig tshogs chung.

Yuthok, Lama Choedak (1997). *The Triple Tantra by Panchen Ngawang Choedak.* Canberra: Gorum publications.

Index

H

I

J

N

O

About Wisdom

Wisdom Publications, a not-for-profit publisher, is dedicated to making available authentic Buddhist works. We publish translations of the sutras and tantras, commentaries and teachings of past and contemporary Buddhist masters, and original works by the world's leading Buddhist scholars. We publish our titles with the appreciation of Buddhism as a living philosophy and with the special commitment to preserve and transmit important works from all the major Buddhist traditions.

If you would like more information or a copy of our mail-order catalog, please contact us at:

Wisdom Publications
199 Elm Street
Somerville, Massachusetts 02144 USA
Telephone: (617) 776-7416 • Fax: (617) 776-7841
Email: info@wisdompubs.org • www.wisdompubs.org

Wisdom Publications is a non-profit, charitable 501(c)(3) organization affilated with the Foundation for the Preservation of the Mahayana Tradition (FPMT).

Studies in Indian and Tibetan Buddhism

This series was conceived to provide a forum for publishing outstanding new contributions to scholarship on Indian and Tibetan Buddhism and also to make accessible seminal research not widely known outside a narrow specialist audience, including translations of appropriate monographs and collections of articles from other languages. The series strives to shed light on the Indic Buddhist traditions by exposing them to historical-critical inquiry, illuminating through contextualization and analysis these traditions' unique heritage and the significance of their contribution to the world's religious and philosophical achievements. We are pleased to make available to scholars and the intellectually curious some of the best contemporary research in the Indian and Tibetan traditions.